THE
IBM
COBOL
ENVIRONMENT

ROBERT T. GRAUER, Ph.D.

University of Miami, Florida

PRENTICE-HALL, INC., Englewood Cliffs, New Jersey 07632

Library of Congress Cataloging in Publication Data

Grauer, Robert T., (date)
   The IBM COBOL Environment.

   Includes index.
   1. IBM computers—Programming. 2. COBOL (Computer
program language) I. Title. II. Title: I.B.M.
C.O.B.O.L. environment.
QA76.8.I1015G7 1984   001.64'2   83-13868
ISBN 0-13-448654-4

Editorial/production supervision
  and interior design: *Lynn Frankel*
Manufacturing buyer: *Gordon Osbourne*

Printed in the United States of America

10 9 8 7 6 5 4 3 2 1

ISBN 0-13-448654-4

Prentice-Hall International, Inc., *London*
Prentice-Hall of Australia Pty. Limited, *Sydney*
Editora Prentice-Hall do Brasil, Ltda., *Rio de Janeiro*
Prentice-Hall Canada Inc., *Toronto*
Prentice-Hall of India Private Limited, *New Delhi*
Prentice-Hall of Japan, Inc., *Tokyo*
Prentice-Hall of Southeast Asia Pte. Ltd., *Singapore*
Whitehall Books Limited, *Wellington, New Zealand*

TO KARL KARLSTROM

In Appreciation

Contents

Preface

The professional COBOL programmer must be able to interact with the operating system, debug his or her programs, and leave well written programs for those who follow. In short, there is need for several skills in conjunction with COBOL. The author's *original* work, *The COBOL Environment*, was developed with these goals in mind. It focused on structured programming, advanced elements of the COBOL language, and information required by the commercial programmer in an IBM environment. The original 12 chapters in *The COBOL Environment* have been significantly expanded and spread over *two* books, this work and *Structured Methods Through COBOL* (R. Grauer, Prentice Hall, 1983).

The IBM COBOL Environment is intended for the COBOL programmer working in an OS environment, and is dedicated to the premise that knowledge of COBOL alone does not yield a competent COBOL programmer. Accordingly, it contains material on JCL, procedures, utilities, VSAM, ABEND debugging, and Assembler Language Programming. All subjects are presented from the viewpoint of the COBOL programmer.

The IBM COBOL Environment offers many improvements over its predecessor. In particular:

- More rigorous, and substantially more complete, coverage of OS JCL.
- An entirely new chapter on procedures, with emphasis on the rules associated with overrides and symbolic parameters.
- Two new chapters on Assembler, providing an overview of the language, and promoting the link between COBOL and BAL.
- A new chapter on VSAM organization, containing several IDCAMS examples, including the establishment of alternate indexes.
- Expanded coverage of OS utilities to include SORT/MERGE, the linkage-editor, IEBCOPY, and IEBUPDTE, among others.
- Enhanced treatment of system messages to facilitate the solution of Data Management ABENDs.
- A substantial increase in the number of exercises and solutions.

Chapter 1 presents an extensive introduction to OS JCL. It begins simply by *viewing JCL as a means of communication* between the programmer and the operating system. The chapter removes the mystique surrounding the subject by viewing the many available options as providing flexibility rather than complexity. The syntax of OS JCL is presented and the most common parameters of the JOB, EXEC, and DD statements are covered.

Chapter 2 addresses the special JCL requirements of the COBOL programmer. It presents typical DD statements as well as special DDnames (SYSUDUMP, STEPLIB, and SYSLIB, etc.). The chapter introduces the procedure concept via the COBOL compile, link, and go sequence, and the utility of the associated system messages. It includes several typical jobstreams, including: use of a subprogram, SORT and COPY; access of a VSAM file, and JCL for a sequential update.

Chapter 3 is devoted entirely to procedures. The reader is taught how to override parameters on an existing DD statement, and how to add new DD statements in their entirety. The proper sequence of statements in the submitted jobstream is stressed, and common errors are explained. The chapter discusses symbolic parameters, and concludes with the PROC and PEND statements for instream testing.

Chapter 4 motivates the need for utility programs, and covers several in detail. These include: IEBGENER, IEBUPDTE, IEBPTPCH, IEBISAM, IEHPROGM, and IEBCOPY. In addition, the sort/merge and linkage-editor programs are discussed as they relate to COBOL. Tables from the vendor's reference manual are also included to aid in choosing the correct utility.

Chapter 5 covers VSAM. It begins with a conceptual discussion of key sequenced data sets, control intervals and control areas, allocation of free space, addition and/or deletion of records, and the catalog structure. The chapter discusses the Access Methods Services utility (IDCAMS), and its applicability to both VSAM and non-VSAM data sets. It contains examples to establish a primary and/or a secondary index, and includes the associated COBOL program to access a file on an ALTERNATE RECORD KEY.

Chapter 6 develops the necessary background for ABEND debugging. It includes material on number systems, instruction formats, base/displacement addressing, and internal data representation. This information is tied directly to COBOL in a program which produces erroneous results due to an incorrect COBOL "group move" and associated USAGE clauses.

Chapter 7 presents a sound introduction to ABEND debugging, in both a called and calling program. It contains information on PMAPs, DMAPs, BL and BLL cells, the SAVE AREA TRACE, STATE and FLOW options, and the linkage-editor map. The chapter ends with a 40 part exercise to reinforce the material. (Appendix C contains a parallel exercise for additional practice.)

Chapter 8 focuses on debugging data management ABENDs. These errors are particularly irksome to the COBOL programmer in that they are often attributable to data rather than a program. Nevertheless, the competent individual must be able to resolve these problems. The chapter shows that analysis of the submitted JCL and/or the associated system messages is often sufficient. A list of 19 common completion codes, with suggestions for corrective action, is also included.

Chapter 9 highlights the relationship between COBOL and Assembler. Although the applications programmer can and does exist without knowledge of Assembler, even a superficial understanding promotes a superior capability in writing efficient COBOL, and is invaluable in debugging. This is best appreciated when one realizes that the computer does not execute COBOL instructions per se, but rather the compiler generated machine language.

Chapter 10 addresses the strong internal need of most programmers for continued self-improvement. It aims at achieving an overall appreciation for Assembler, rather than detailed proficiency in individual instructions. Nevertheless, it covers rudiments of over 50 instructions, and concludes with a list of techniques employed by the Assembler programmer.

Chapter 11 continues the discussion of Assembler language programming. The chapter focuses on linkage conventions, save areas, the special uses of registers 0, 1, 13, 14, and 15, and the applicability of this information to *any* programming language.

Every chapter contains numerous exercises, with selected solutions included in an appendix. A particular strength is the large number of actual listings including: four dumps (in Chapter 7 and Appendix C), four additional ABENDs with appropriate system messages (Chapter 8), five examples of procedures and overrides (Chapter 3), six utility listings (Chapter 4), four IDCAMS examples (Chapter 5), a complete Assembler program with multiple versions illustrating a dump and syntactical errors (Chapter 11), and four COBOL programs scattered in various chapters.

The IBM COBOL Environment is dedicated to Karl Karlstrom, a senior editor and Assistant Vice-President of Prentice-Hall. The author is very grateful to Karl for the inspiration and guidance he has provided through the years.

A note of special thanks goes to Lynn Frankel, production editor at Prentice-Hall. The quality of any book is directly related to those individuals who labor unannounced, and often unappreciated, behind the scenes. The author warmly acknowledges the significant contribution Lynn has made in bringing this work to press.

Once again, the author thanks Sheila Grossman for typing and retyping the manuscript. He compliments Herb Daehnke for his artwork, and Jackie Clark, Barbara Morck, and Steve Ballenger for their eagle eyes as proofreaders. Last and certainly not least, the author appreciates the contributions of his principal reviewers, Stu Meisel, Don Sordillo, and Rick Weiland.

ROBERT T. GRAUER

Introduction to OS JCL

Overview

Although COBOL is a higher-level language, and as such is theoretically machine independent, the COBOL programmer cannot function in a vacuum. He or she is required to surround a program with *control statements* that are unique to the particular operating system. In other words, like it or not, he or she is forced to interact with the operating system. Accordingly, this section is directed at the individual who continually uses these facilities, but whose knowledge of JCL is typically below his or her COBOL capability. "Just give me the control cards" is a phrase heard far too often.

Unfortunately, OS JCL retains a mystique which makes both student and practitioner shy away. Admittedly, the multipage collection of /'s, X's, and so on, is somewhat foreboding, but given half a chance, it becomes thoroughly understandable. Our objective is to remove the apprehension associated with OS JCL. We begin *by viewing JCL simply as a means of communicating with the operating system.* We describe the *limited* number

1

of JCL statements, cover their fundamental syntax, and distinguish between *keyword* and *positional* parameters.

The remainder of the chapter focuses on specifics of the JOB, EXEC, and DD statements, the details of which can be overwhelming to the beginner. *Do not be concerned if you fail to remember everything on a first reading; don't even try.* Concentrate instead on obtaining an overview of the material. *View the many available parameters as providing flexibility rather than complexity.* The next chapter focuses on specific needs of the COBOL programmer and contains typical jobstreams that illustrate the statements discussed therein. At that point, much of this material will crystallize, increasing your productivity as you begin to effectively utilize OS JCL.

JCL AS A MEANS OF COMMUNICATION

The intent of any language is *communication.* In that sense, the purpose of IBM's Job Control Language, or JCL for short, is like that of any other language, namely, *to enable communication between a programmer and the operating system.* Consider, for example, the *hypothetical* dialog of Figure 1.1, in which one John Smith describes his problem to the operating system.

At present, Figure 1.1 merely represents wishful thinking. We do not communicate with OS in the user-friendly and interactive fashion implied by that conversation. Instead, we state all our requirements in precise syntax at one time, and submit them to the Operating System. Our request is called a jobstream and takes the form of Figure 1.2.

It suffices to say that the reader who has not previously confronted OS JCL is in no way, shape, or form expected to grasp the syntax and/or coding requirements of Figure 1.2. Nevertheless, he or she will recognize many of the specifications of the hypothetical dialog embedded in the jobstream. The JOB statement, for example, contains a jobname, EXAMPLE, a programmer name, JOHN SMITH, accounting information, PROGRAMMING, and a TIME requirement. The EXEC statement calls for execution of a program named UPDATE, and the three DD statements define each of the required files. One may recognize various keyword parameters which were extracted from the dialog; e.g., TAPE, DISK, volume serial numbers, expiration dates, and so on.

In conclusion, a JCL jobstream is merely a precise means of communicating with the operating system. Hence, in order to use the operating system effectively, one must learn JCL, its rules, and its capabilities. We begin with a brief syntactical overview of JCL statements.

Programmer:	I have a job for you.
OS:	Tell me about it. In particular, I need to know the job's name, your name, how long the job will take, and whom to bill my services to.
Programmer:	The job's name is Example. My name is John Smith, it should take no more than one minute and 30 seconds, and bill it to Programming.
OS:	Very well. What is the name of the program you will run?
Programmer:	Update.
OS:	How many files do you require, and what kind are they?
Programmer:	I have three files altogether, two input and one output. The input files are both on tape, and the output file is on disk.
OS:	You have to be more specific about your input files. Tell me on which tape volumes they are located, and the exact name of each file as it appears on the tape.
Programmer:	The first file is called OLD.MASTER.FILE and is the third file on the tape whose serial number is 111111. The second input file is called TRANSACT and is the first file on volume number 222222. Both have standard labels. Incidentally, my program knows these files simply as INPUT1 and INPUT2, respectively.
OS:	Tell me about your output file.
Programmer:	Call it NEW.MASTER.FILE and put it on any disk you want. I estimate that it will require 10 tracks. Keep it until the last day in 1985. My program knows this file simply as OUTPUT.
OS:	That should do it. Have a nice day.

FIGURE 1.1 Hypothetical Dialog Between Programmer and OS

```
//EXAMPLE JOB (PROGRAMMING),'JOHN SMITH',TIME=(1,30)

//    EXEC PGM=UPDATE

//INPUT1 DD UNIT=TAPE,VOL=SER=111111,
//    DSNAME=OLD.MASTER.FILE,LABEL=(3,SL),
//    DISP=(OLD,KEEP)

//INPUT2 DD UNIT=TAPE,VOL=SER=222222,
//    DSNAME=TRANSACT,LABEL=(1,SL),
//    DISP=(OLD,KEEP)

//OUTPUT DD UNIT=DISK,DSNAME=NEW.MASTER.FILE,
//    LABEL=EXPDT=85365,DISP=(NEW,KEEP),
//    SPACE=(TRK,10)

//
```

FIGURE 1.2 JCL Statements Corresponding to Dialog of Figure 1.1

THE RULES OF JCL

JCL is made simpler when one realizes that the entire language consists of *only* eight types of statements. These are: JOB, EXEC, DD, /*, //*, //, PROC, and PEND. Of these, we focus on the first three, with special emphasis on the DD statement.

All JCL statements are divided into five fields which appear in specified order, as shown in Figure 1.3. JCL statements, with the exception of the /* (delimiter) statement, begin with // in columns 1 and 2. The statement name, *if present*, begins in column 3. A JOB statement *must* have a *jobname*, an EXEC statement *may* have a *stepname*, and most DD statements have a *DDname*. The same rules apply to the formation of all three types of simple names, namely:

♦ Statement names must be eight or fewer characters.
♦ Statement names must begin with a letter or $, @, or #.
♦ Statement names may include letters, numbers, or the special characters $, @, or # (hyphens and/or blanks are not allowed).

Figure 1.4 contains examples of JOB, EXEC, and DD statements. Four of the five statements shown are named; only the first EXEC state-

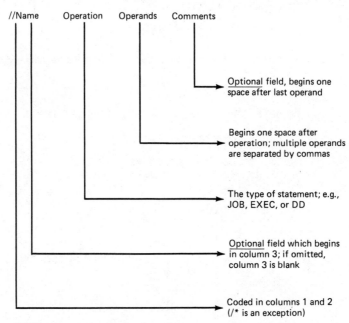

//Name   Operation   Operands   Comments

Optional field, begins one space after last operand

Begins one space after operation; multiple operands are separated by commas

The type of statement; e.g., JOB, EXEC, or DD

Optional field which begins in column 3; if omitted, column 3 is blank

Coded in columns 1 and 2 (/* is an exception)

NOTE: One or more spaces are required to separate the name, operation, operand, and comment fields.

FIGURE 1.3 Components of a JCL Statement

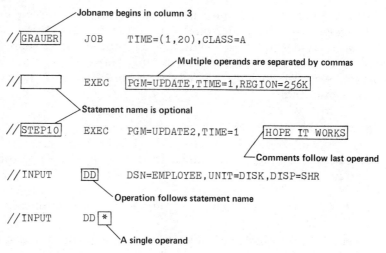

FIGURE 1.4 Examples of JOB, EXEC, and DD Statements

ment is unnamed. The statement name (if present) is followed by the *operation*—e.g., JOB, EXEC, or DD. One or more spaces separate the name and operation fields, but the operation is required to begin in column 16 or before. Operands follow the operation, with multiple operands separated by commas. (See, for example, the unnamed EXEC statement, which contains three operands, PGM, TIME, and REGION.) Comments are permitted on any statement, after the last operand. (They are included only on the second EXEC statement of Figure 1.4.)

Although the rules associated with Figures 1.3 and 1.4 are straightforward, they are frequently violated, resulting in the frustrating message "JOB NOT RUN DUE TO JCL ERROR." Consider, for example, Figure 1.5, which depicts *invalid* JCL statements. The figure is clearly labeled to

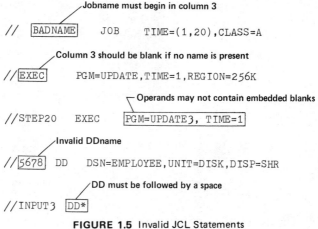

FIGURE 1.5 Invalid JCL Statements

indicate the nature of the various JCL errors. Compare Figures 1.4 and 1.5, make sure you understand the reason for the various errors, and try to understand the overall syntax. We proceed with rules for continuing JCL statements and for distinguishing between keyword and positional parameters. We include a brief discussion of the null, delimiter, and comment statements.

Continuation

JCL statements may be continued from one card image to the next, according to the following rules:

♦ The card to be continued must end with a comma in column 71 or before.
♦ The continued card must have // in columns 1 and 2, a blank in column 3, and may begin anywhere in columns 4 through 16.
♦ A nonblank character is required in column 72 of the first card in order to continue a comments field. The nonblank character need not be present otherwise, although many people code it anyway.

Keyword versus Positional Parameters

Parameters are of two types, *keyword* and *positional*. Keyword parameters may appear in any order within a statement; it is the keyword itself which conveys meaning to the system. Positional parameters, as the name implies, are recognized by the order in which they appear. If a positional parameter is omitted, its absence must be denoted by a comma, unless no additional positional parameters follow in the statement.

Figure 1.6 contains additional JCL statements to illustrate these concepts. Both JOB statements contain the same keyword parameters, which may appear in any order; i.e., either TIME or CLASS may come first. The TIME parameter, however, contains two *positional subparameters* for

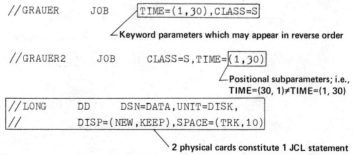

FIGURE 1.6 Rules for Continuation and Keyword versus Positional Parameters

minutes and seconds respectively. Thus, TIME=(1,30) denotes one minute and 30 seconds, and is *not* the same as TIME=(30,1).

Figure 1.6 also contains a *single* DD statement which is continued on a second card image. The first card ends on a comma after UNIT=DISK; the second (i.e., continued) card has // coded in columns 1 and 2, leaves column 3 blank, and begins somewhere between columns 4 and 16.

Null, Delimiter, and Comment Statements

The *delimiter* statement, denoted by a /*, denotes the end of data in an input jobstream; i.e., it signifies the end of a "card" file. Its use is optional in most instances because OS will assume that the end of a data set has been reached when it encounters another control statement. The delimiter statement is required, however, if JCL statements are part of the input jobstream. It is further discussed in the section on the * and DATA parameters of the DD statement.

The *null* statement contains a // in columns 1 and 2, with the remainder of the statement blank. It is the *last* statement in a jobstream and signals that the end of job has been reached.

The null statement is *optional*, as OS automatically concludes that a job has ended when it encounters the next JOB statement. However, if there is an error in a subsequent JOB statement, OS will include the second job (i.e., the one with the invalid JOB statement) with the preceding job and flush the combined jobstream with a JCL error. To prevent this from happening, it is suggested that every job be terminated with a null statement.

The *comment* statement consists of a //* in columns 1, 2, and 3 with the remainder of the statement available for comments. (Comments may also appear on other statements as explained in the preceding section.)

We now proceed with the JOB, EXEC, and DD statements.

JOB STATEMENT

Format:

```
//jobname JOB (Accounting Information),'Programmer Name',
//    Keyword parameters
```

Useful Keywords:

```
CLASS
REGION
MSGLEVEL
TIME
COND
MSGCLASS
```

Example:

```
//RTG010 JOB (MAS424,10),'R GRAUER X345',
//    CLASS=X,TIME=(1,30)
```

The JOB statement is the first statement in a jobstream and contains some or all of the following information: jobname, accounting information, programmer's name, time and/or region requirements, class, priority, and an indication of whether or not control statement and allocation messages are to be printed.

If accounting information is supplied, it must be coded prior to any other parameters. Accounting information varies from installation to installation according to the particular accounting system in effect. If more than one accounting parameter is required, then all accounting information must be enclosed in parentheses. If, however, only a single accounting parameter is used, parentheses are optional.

The programmer name is an *optional positional parameter.* It is limited to 20 characters and follows the accounting information. If the programmer name contains any special characters (e.g., a space or a period), then it must be enclosed in apostrophes. Figure 1.7 contains several examples which combine the accounting and programmer-name parameters. (In Figure 1.7, the accounting information is assumed to consist of four positional subparameters, but the actual number will vary from installation to installation.)

Valid Statements

```
//GOOD1 JOB (MAS424,XXX,YY,Z),'R. GRAUER'

//GOOD2 JOB (MAS424,XXX,YY,Z)

//GOOD3 JOB ,'R. GRAUER'

//GOOD4 JOB (MAS424,,YY),GRAUER

//GOOD5 JOB MAS424,GRAUER
```

Invalid Statements

```
//BAD1 JOB (MAS424,XXX,YY,Z),R. GRAUER

//BAD2 JOB MAS424,XXX,YY,Z

//BAD3 JOB 'R. GRAUER'

//BAD4 JOB (MAS424,YY), GRAUER

//BAD5 JOB GRAUER,MAS424
```

FIGURE 1.7 Accounting and Programmer-name Information

The GOOD1 JOB statement encloses the four accounting subparameters in parentheses. The programmer name is in apostrophes to accommodate the period and space, and follows the accounting information. GOOD2 and GOOD3 omit programmer name and accounting information, respectively. Note well that a comma is required in GOOD3 to indicate that a positional parameter has been omitted and another positional parameter follows. The comma is *not* present in GOOD2, because no positional parameters were coded after the accounting information.

The accounting information in GOOD4 omits the second and fourth positional subparameters, XXX and Z respectively. An extra comma is present between the first and third subparameters to indicate that XXX has been left out, but a comma is not used after YY. GOOD5 contains only a single accounting parameter, which need not be in parentheses. The lone accounting parameter is followed by a programmer name not in apostrophes, as it does not contain any special characters.

The BAD1 JOB statement lacks apostrophes around the programmer name. BAD2 requires parentheses for the accounting information. BAD3 is missing a comma to indicate the omitted positional parameter; hence, 'R. GRAUER' will falsely be construed as accounting information. BAD4 needs an extra comma before YY in the accounting information and should not have a space before GRAUER. Finally, BAD5 reversed the order of the accounting and programmer name fields.

In addition to the positional parameters just discussed, the JOB statement has several optional keyword parameters. The more common ones are discussed as follows:

TIME=(MM,SS):   MM = CPU time in minutes
                SS = CPU time in seconds
                These parameters need not be in parentheses if only minutes are specified; they are both positional subparameters.

MSGLEVEL=(S,M): Controls the type of output produced by the system; specifically:
                S = 0 if only the job statement is to be printed
                    1 if all input job control and all catalogued procedure statements are to be printed
                    2 if only input JCL is to be printed.
                M = 0 if no allocation messages are to be printed
                    1 if all allocation messages are to be printed.
                The meaning of this parameter will become clearer after the system output is discussed in Chapter 2. Most installations have default values of MSGLEVEL=(1,1), which results in the maximum amount of information.

REGION=NNNNK: NNNN specifies the amount of main storage (in units of 1024 bytes (1K=1024 bytes)) that is to be allocated to the entire job.

MSGCLASS=class: Class is a single character, A to Z, or 0 to 9, denoting the output class for job scheduler messages. The latter consists of all messages not printed as a result of the actual job being executed—e.g., JCL statements and error messages, device allocations, data set dispositions, etc.

CLASS=class: Class may be any value from A to Z, or 0 to 9, with the significance determined by the individual installation according to a job's requirements. CLASS=A, for example, may indicate a job requiring less than 30 seconds of CPU time, that prints less than 20,000 lines, and does not require magnetic tape.

COND: The CONDition parameter indicates any special circumstances to preclude the execution of individual job steps. It is explained fully under the EXEC statement.

EXEC STATEMENT

Format:

```
//stepname EXEC operands
```

Useful Keywords:

```
COND
REGION
TIME
```

Example:

```
//STEP1 EXEC PGM=UPDATE,TIME=2,COND=EVEN
```

A typical jobstream contains several EXEC statements, each of which denotes a job *step*. The EXEC statement executes a *program* or invokes a *procedure*. (A procedure is defined as a set of catalogued JCL—i.e., a series of JCL statements which have been stored in a library. The procedure concept is explained fully in Chapter 3 in conjunction with the COBOL pro-

cedure, COBVCLG, to compile, link, and execute a COBOL program.)
Variations in the EXEC statement are conveniently explained through
"COBOL-like" notation. Consider:

$$//[\text{stepname}] \quad \text{EXEC} \quad \left\{ \begin{array}{l} \text{PGM=program name} \\ [\text{PROC=}]\text{procedure name} \end{array} \right\}$$

If a program is to be executed, the keyword PGM must be specified
(e.g., // EXEC PGM=UPDATE). If a procedure is to be invoked, the keyword PROC is optional. Both statements below are valid:

```
// EXEC PROC=COBVCLG
// EXEC COBVCLG
```

The step name is optional in the EXEC statement. If used, it must
begin in column 3 immediately following the //; if omitted, a space is
required in column 3. Accordingly, both statements below are valid:

```
//STEP1 EXEC COBVCLG        (the step name is STEP1)
// EXEC COBVCLG             (the step name is not supplied)
```

REGION and TIME Parameters

The REGION and TIME parameters are permitted on either the JOB or
EXEC statement. It is generally preferable, however, to supply this information at the step rather than job level. Consider Figure 1.8, as follows.

```
//POORER JOB TIME=6,REGION=512K
//STEP1 EXEC PGM=FIRST
        .
        .
        .
//STEP2 EXEC PGM=SECOND
        .
        .
        .
//STEP3 EXEC PGM=THIRD
```
          (a) Specification at the job level

```
//BETTER JOB
//STEP1 EXEC PGM=FIRST,REGION=256K,TIME=2
        .
        .
        .
//STEP2 EXEC PGM=SECOND,REGION=512K,TIME=1
        .
        .
        .
//STEP3 EXEC PGM=THIRD,REGION=256K,TIME=3
```
          (b) Specification at the step level

FIGURE 1.8 TIME and REGION Parameters

In Figure 1.8*a*, the TIME parameter is specified at the job level, and an ABEND occurs as soon as six minutes of CPU time have been used. The ABEND may occur during *any* of the three steps, depending on when the time limit was exceeded.

Tighter control is obtained by providing information at the step level, as was done in Figure 1.8*b*. An overall limit of six minutes is still imposed, but the job ABENDs if step one exceeds two minutes, or step two exceeds one minute, or step three exceeds three minutes.

In similar fashion, the CPU resource is better allocated at the step level. Thus, 256K is requested for steps one and three, and 512K for step two. Specification of 512K at the job level allocates this amount of storage for the entire job, even though several steps may not require the full amount.

COND Parameter

The CONDitional parameter avoids unnecessary use of CPU time by suppressing execution of specified job steps. Essentially, it ties execution of the present step to the results of a previous step. To understand this important parameter, realize that when a program completes execution, it produces a *return* code to indicate its degree of success. The COBOL compiler, for example, yields one of four return codes:

0	if there were no diagnostics
4	if a W-level diagnostic was the most severe error
8	if a C-level diagnostic was the most severe error
12	if an E-level diagnostic was the most severe error

Realize further that three distinct steps are required for a COBOL program to run: it must be compiled, link-edited, and, finally, executed. However, one would probably not bother with the link-edit step if the compilation phase was not successful. In similar fashion, one would not try execution if either the compilation or the link-edit step was unsuccessful. Accordingly, the COBOL programmer will encounter the statement

```
//LKED EXEC PGM=LKED,COND=(5,LT,COB)
```

in a *procedure* which compiles, links, and executes a COBOL program. (The procedure concept is fully explained in Chapter 2. For the present, however, we are concerned only with the COND parameter itself.) *The COND parameter permits execution of the link-edit* step (stepname LKED) only if the compile step (stepname COB) *returns a condition code of 5 or less.* This makes considerable sense if we recall that a condition code of 4 indicates a warning, while higher condition codes indicate C- or E-level diagnostics. Subsequent execution would most likely be incorrect if either of the latter two were present. A warning diagnostic, however, need not necessarily cause incorrect execution, and therefore it is allowed.

The precise format of the COND parameter is:

```
COND=(code,operator,stepname)
```

The code in the COND parameter is compared to the return code from the indicated step. *If the relationship is true, the step is bypassed; if it is false, the step is executed.* (This may appear backward, but that is the way IBM established its JCL; "ours is not to reason why. . . .") Assume, for example, a return code of 8 after the compile step (i.e., a C-level diagnostic). The comparison in the previous LKED EXEC statement would be (5,LT,8), which is true, and hence the step would be bypassed.

Permissible operators in the COND parameter are:

LT: Less than
LE: Less than or equal
EQ: Equal
NE: Not equal
GT: Greater than
GE: Greater than or equal

In addition to the six relational operators, the COND parameter may also be coded as COND=EVEN or COND=ONLY. Specification of COND=EVEN will execute a step *even* if a previous step ABENDed; COND=ONLY will cause execution *only* if the indicated step ABENDed.

COND may also specify *multiple* conditions, for example:

```
//GO EXEC PGM=UPDATE,COND=((5,LT,COB),(5,LT,LKED))
```

Note the nested parentheses which specify that the GO step is executed only if *both* steps were successful—i.e., if both comparisons are false.

DD STATEMENT

Format:

```
//DDname DD operands
```

Useful Keywords:

```
DSN
DISP
```

```
LABEL
SPACE
UNIT
DCB
VOL
```

Positional Parameters:

```
*
DATA
DUMMY
SYSOUT
```

Example:

```
//DATASET DD DSN=ABC,DISP=(NEW,KEEP),
//          UNIT=DISK,SPACE=(TRK,(1,1)),
//          DCB=(LRECL=50,BLKSIZE=500,RECFM=FB)
```

The DD (Data Definition) statement appears more often than any other JCL statement. Every file in every program requires a DD statement to specify the *physical* location and characteristics for the logical files referenced by a programmer.

The COBOL SELECT statement ties a programmer-chosen filename to a DDname; the DD statement provides information on the location and disposition of the file. Consider:

COBOL:

```
SELECT TRANSACTION-FILE ASSIGN TO UT-S-TRANS.
SELECT PRINT-FILE ASSIGN TO UT-S-REPORT.
```

JCL: ➤Matching entries

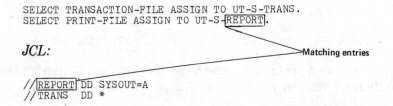

```
//REPORT DD SYSOUT=A
//TRANS  DD *
```

The last entry in the COBOL SELECT statement matches the DDname in the JCL statement; hence, REPORT and TRANS appear in both SELECT and DD statements. In the COBOL program, PRINT-FILE is assigned to the DDname REPORT; the corresponding DD statement assigns REPORT to a printer via the JCL parameter SYSOUT=A. In similar fashion TRANSACTION-FILE is assigned to the DDname TRANS, which in turn is tied to a card file via the * JCL parameter.

More than one printer and/or card reader can be conceptually specified via multiple pairs of DD and SELECT statements. Suppose that one is processing a series of transactions, several of which are in error. The erroneous transactions are randomly scattered throughout the input file, but the requirements of the problem call for separate reports for the valid and invalid transactions. This is easily accomplished by creating two print files.

COBOL:

```
SELECT VALID-FILE ASSIGN TO UT-S-PRINT.
SELECT ERROR-FILE ASSIGN TO UT-S-ERROR.
```

JCL:

```
//PRINT DD SYSOUT=A
//ERROR DD SYSOUT=A
```

In the COBOL program, valid transactions are output to the file VALID-FILE. Invalid transactions are written to ERROR-FILE. The system saves up the print lines separately, usually on a disk, and then prints them one at a time after job termination. This process is called *spooling*. The two DD statements specify that both PRINT and ERROR are assigned to a printer, and the reports will list individually.

We continue now with a discussion of the individual parameters which appear on the DD statement.

SYSOUT

Specification of the SYSOUT parameter indicates a unit record output device; i.e., a printer or card punch. For example:

```
//FIRST  DD SYSOUT=A
//SECOND DD SYSOUT=B
//THIRD  DD SYSOUT=T
```

The SYSOUT parameter is followed by a letter indicating the class of output device. The meaning of the output class varies from installation to installation, but SYSOUT=A is almost universally accepted as printed output on stock paper. SYSOUT=B generally indicates punched card output (which is becoming increasingly rare, if not disappearing entirely). Other letters are installation dependent and imply special forms, a printer on a particular floor, etc.

* and DATA

An asterisk indicates that the file in question follows immediately; e.g., the statement:

```
//TRANS DD *
```

specifies that the file with DDname TRANS follows immediately in the jobstream and is in effect a "card" file. The file is terminated when the next JCL statement is recognized. Consider:

```
//TRANS DD *
AAAA
BBBB
CCCC
//OLDMAST DD ...
```

A COBOL program which reads the TRANS file will hit the "end of file" condition when the OLDMAST DD statement is read. (A /* delimiter statement could optionally be included to indicate the end of file.) Suppose, however, that JCL statements are to be considered as input data. This is accomplished by coding DATA in lieu of *; i.e., *DATA specifies that the file follows immediately in the jobstream, and further that it will be terminated only by a /* delimiter statement.* Thus:

The file associated with the EXAMPLE DD statement consists of four JCL statements, and is terminated when /* is encountered.

It is also possible to have a /* included in the file *by defining an alternate delimiter via the DLM* subparameter; for example:

```
//EXAMPLE2    DD    DATA,DLM=XX
//FILE1       DD    *
AA
BB
/*
//FILE2       DD    *
CC
DD
/*
XX
```

Delimiter associated with the EXAMPLE2 DD statement

As can be seen by the associated caption, eight card images, including two /* statements, are associated with the EXAMPLE2 DD statement.

The *, DATA, and SYSOUT parameters are mutually exclusive and immediately follow the DD operation. The remaining DD parameters are keyword in nature.

DSNAME (DSN) Parameter

The Data Set Name, DSNAME or DSN, parameter specifies the name of a file (or data set) as it exists on a physical device—e.g., a tape or disk. *Note well the data set name is not the same as the DDname.* For example, the statement:

```
//TRANS DD DSN=TRANSACT,DISP=SHR
```

has a *DDname* of TRANS, and a *dataset name* of TRANSACT.

The data set name must begin with a letter, and is restricted to letters and numbers. Periods may be used for clarification. The maximum length of a name is 44 characters, with a second restriction that no more than eight characters may appear between periods. Some examples are:

DSNAME=A	(Shortest possible name)
DSN=A	(Alternate coding; DSN in lieu of DSNAME)
DSN=UM.MAS524.OLD	(Use of periods)
DSN=&&TEMP	(Temporary Data Set—see Chapter 4)
DSN=&PARAM	(Symbolic Parameter—see Chapter 3)
DSN=MASTER.FILE(0)	(Generation Data Group—see Chapter 2)

DISP (DISPosition) Parameter

The DISP parameter indicates the status of the data set at the start and conclusion of processing. It has three positional subparameters with possible values as follows:

$$
DISP = \left(\begin{bmatrix} NEW \\ OLD \\ SHR \\ MOD \end{bmatrix}, \begin{bmatrix} DELETE \\ KEEP \\ PASS \\ CATLG \\ UNCATLG \end{bmatrix}, \begin{bmatrix} DELETE \\ KEEP \\ CATLG \\ UNCATLG \end{bmatrix} \right)
$$

The first parameter indicates the status of a data set at the start of the job step. NEW specifies the data set is to be created, whereas OLD and SHR mean it already exists. In addition, a shared data set may be used simultaneously by other jobs. MOD implies that the data set is to be extended (i.e., *mod*ified), and causes the read/write mechanism to be positioned after the last record in an existing data set. (If, however, the data set does not yet exist, MOD has the same meaning as NEW.)

The second positional parameter specifies the disposition at the normal conclusion of the job step. KEEP causes the data set to be retained permanently. PASS allows the data set to be used by a subsequent job step, but not kept after the job has ended. DELETE implies that a data set is no longer needed, and deletes it. CATLG causes the data set to be retained and establishes an entry in the system catalog pointing to the data set. UNCATLG also causes the data set to be retained, but removes the entry from the catalog.

It is common practice not to code all three subparameters, and to rely instead on system defaults. Omission of the second positional parameter causes new data sets to be deleted and existing (old) data sets to be retained. (Data sets created in a previous step with disposition of (NEW,PASS) will not be retained unless a disposition of KEEP is specified later in the jobstream.)

The third subparameter specifies disposition should the job terminate abnormally. If this parameter is omitted, disposition defaults to that specified for normal processing. Some examples are:

DISP=(NEW,KEEP, DELETE)   (Creates a new data set, keeps it if job step successfully executes, deletes it if the step ABENDs)

DISP=SHR   (Allows an existing data set to be used simultaneously by other jobs and retains it under all circumstances—i.e., KEEP is implied for both normal and abnormal termination)

DISP=OLD   (Specifies an existing data set, and keeps it under both normal and abnormal termination; note that parentheses are not required, since only the first positional parameter was specified)

DISP=(NEW,CATLG)   (Creates a new data set and catalogs it if job step executes successfully)

DISP=(,KEEP)   (The comma indicates that the first positional subparameter has been omitted; the default is (NEW,KEEP))

LABEL Parameter   LABEL=([seg-no][,label-type][,PASSWORD/,NOPWREAD][,IN/,OUT][,RETPD=/,EXPDT=

The LABEL parameter uses two positional subparameters to specify the type of label processing and the location of a data set on a tape volume. The first entry provides the relative position of the file on a reel of tape. The second indicates whether labels are used, and the type of label processing (e.g., SL—standard labels, NL—no labels, etc.). For example, the entry LABEL=(2,SL) implies the second file on a standard label tape. The entries (1,SL) and (,SL) are equivalent and indicate the first file on the volume. The latter omitted the positional parameter as indicated by the leading comma, and the system defaults to the first file.

Retention period is specified by a keyword subparameter in one of two ways. An explicit number of days may be indicated by the keyword RETPD, or an explicit expiration date may be specified via EXPDT. RETPD=1000 retains a file for 1000 days. EXPDT=99365 retains a file until the last day of 1999.

SPACE Parameter

The SPACE parameter is required when creating a data set on a direct-access device. Its symbolic format is

$$\text{SPACE=}\left(\left\{\begin{array}{l}\text{TRK}\\\text{CYL}\\\text{block}\end{array}\right\},\text{(primary-amount,secondary-amount),RLSE,CONTIG}\right)$$

Additional subparameters are available but are beyond the scope of this discussion. The SPACE parameter indicates how much space is required for an output data set. It is not used for an input data set since the file already exists and such information would be superfluous.

The SPACE parameter requests space on a direct-access device in terms of *tracks*, *cylinders*, or *blocks*. SPACE=(TRK,400) requests 400 tracks, SPACE=(CYL,100) requests 100 cylinders, and SPACE=(1000,3000) requests space for 3000 blocks, each 1000 bytes long. The number of tracks or cylinders required for a given data set varies with the device. The number of blocks is a function of the file itself and is device-independent.

The SPACE parameter also provides for a secondary allocation if the primary allocation is insufficient. SPACE=(TRK,(100,20)) specifies a *primary* allocation of 100 tracks, and a *secondary* amount of 20 tracks. In this example, OS will assign an additional 20 tracks to the data set if the primary allocation is insufficient. It will try the secondary allocation a maximum of 15 times (total = 300 tracks in this example), at which time the job step terminates if space is still inadequate.

Two additional subparameters, RLSE and CONTIG, are frequently specified. RLSE returns any unused portion of the primary allocation, a highly desirable practice. The CONTIG subparameter requires that the primary allocation be contiguous, which speeds up subsequent I/O since the access delay (seek time) is reduced. However, one must be sure that sufficient contiguous space is available, or else execution will be delayed and perhaps terminated. Some examples are:

SPACE=(TRK,2)   (Primary allocation only)

SPACE=(TRK,(2,1))   (Secondary allocation requires extra parentheses)

SPACE=(CYL,5)   (Space is requested in cylinders)

SPACE=(500,1000)   (Space is requested for 1000 blocks, each 500 bytes long)

SPACE=(CYL,(5,1),, CONTIG)   (Extra comma indicates omission of a positional subparameter, prior to the contiguous specification)

UNIT Parameter $UNIT = \left(\left\{ \begin{array}{l} address \\ device\text{-}type \\ group\text{-}name \end{array} \right\} \left[\begin{array}{l} , unit\text{-}count \\ , P \end{array} \right] \left[, DEFFER \right] \left[, SEP = ddname \right] \right)$

The UNIT parameter indicates the physical device on which a data set is to be processed, and is specified in one of three ways: unit address, device type, or group name. Specification of the *unit address* (e.g., UNIT=185) calls for a particular device (e.g., tape drive 185). It is not a good technique, since the system must wait for the particular tape drive, even if others are available. The *device type* indicates the class of tape drive (e.g., UNIT=3400), which calls for a series 3400 tape drive to be used. The system determines which 3400 units are available, selects one, and issues the appropriate message to the operator, who will mount the tape, in conjunction with the VOL parameter.

UNIT=TAPE illustrates how a *group name* is specified. This instructs the system to use any available tape device. Often this corresponds exactly to specification of a device type, as in the case in which only 3400 series drives are present. However, the group name can provide greater flexibility if all sequential devices (tape and disk) are combined under SYSSQ and the request is for UNIT=SYSSQ. Of course, such specification is not always feasible.

The UNIT parameter is specified in similar fashion for direct access devices. The most common specification is to use a group name (e.g., UNIT=SYSDA) in lieu of the device type (e.g., UNIT=3330). This permits an installation to upgrade its hardware (e.g., to use 3350's instead of 3330's without having to modify its production JCL).

DCB Parameter

OS must have information on the physical characteristics of a program's files before execution can be successfully completed. In COBOL, this information is obtained from a combination of three sources in the specific sequence: the COBOL FD, the DCB parameter on the DD statement, and the data set header label. The information in the COBOL FD is taken first. The latter sources are used only if an earlier source does not contain the necessary information. Consider the following:

COBOL:

```
SELECT OLD-MASTER-FILE ASSIGN TO UT-S-OLD.
      .
      .
      .
FD  OLD-MASTER-FILE
    LABEL RECORDS ARE STANDARD
    BLOCK CONTAINS 0 RECORDS
    RECORD CONTAINS 100 CHARACTERS
    DATA RECORD IS OLD-MASTER.
```

JCL:

```
//OLD DD DCB=(BLKSIZE=500,RECFM=FB)...
```

The COBOL FD implies that OLD-MASTER-FILE has standard labels and fixed-length records of 100 bytes. It specifies BLOCK CONTAINS 0 RECORDS, which is *not* a typographical error. Rather, it is COBOL's way of informing the system that block size will be entered through the JCL. (A similar capability is also possible with the RECORD CONTAINS clause. However, it is the author's preference to code record size explicitly within the FD so that the compiler will verify that individual picture clauses sum to the proper record size.)

What is gained by using the DCB over the COBOL FD? The answer, in a word, is flexibility, as the same COBOL program may be used to process files with different blocking factors. If block size is not specified in the COBOL FD, the only necessary modification is in the execution time JCL, but the program itself need not be recompiled. The DCB parameter can be specified for any file type (i.e., tape, disk, etc.).

Most shops have adopted BLOCK CONTAINS 0 RECORDS as a standard. *Realize also that if this clause is omitted, the OS compiler adopts a blocksize of 1 as a default.* This may cause an 001 ABEND due to a wrong length record, when the incoming records are blocked, and the BLOCK CONTAINS clause was omitted. Another common error is to specify BLOCK CONTAINS 0 RECORDS for an output file, and then forget to code the necessary JCL parameter, producing a 013-34 ABEND.

VOLUME (VOL) Parameter $VOL = \left([PRIVATE]\ [RETAIN]\ [,vol\text{-}seq\text{-}no]\ [,vol\text{-}count] \begin{bmatrix} SER = (ser\text{-}no,\ldots) \\ REF = reference \end{bmatrix} \right)$

The VOLUME parameter indicates the specific volume on which an input data set may be found, or where an output data set is to be created. For example, specification of the VOL=SER *subparameter*—e.g., VOL=SER= USR001—writes an output data set on the volume whose serial number is USR001. (A mount message will be issued to the operator if this volume is not currently available.)

The VOLUME parameter is *not* required for output data sets. Its omission implies that one does not care where a data set is placed, and OS will make an arbitrary choice. The VOLUME parameter is required for uncatalogued input data sets—i.e., one must supply the system with VOLUME information indicating where the data set may be found. If, however, the data set was catalogued on creation, the system will remember this information, and VOLUME need not be specified.

Summary

The most important portion of the chapter is the initial discussion of *JCL as a means of communication*, and the basic syntax of JCL statements. The material on specific JOB, EXEC, and DD parameters is dry reading, only until one needs to apply the information. The next chapter addresses specific needs of the COBOL programmer and clarifies the subject.

In the interim, we list, as a review, the keyword and positional parameters which were discussed:

JOB Statement:

Accounting information:	First positional parameter; installation dependent
Programmer name:	Second and last positional parameter; limited to 20 characters; requires apostrophes for special characters
CLASS:	Assigns a class to a job; the meaning of a specific class is installation dependent
REGION:	Assigns an amount of memory for the job
MSGLEVEL:	Controls printing of system output and messages
TIME:	Assigns a maximum CPU time allocation to a job
MSGCLASS:	Assigns a class for job scheduler messages

EXEC Statement:

COND:	Prevents execution of unnecessary job steps
REGION:	Assigns an amount of memory for a job step
TIME:	Assigns a maximum CPU time for a job step

DD Statement:

*:	Indicates the file follows immediately in the jobstream
DATA:	Indicates the file follows immediately in the jobstream and that JCL statements, except for /*, may appear in the file
SYSOUT:	Directs an output data set to a printer or punch
DSN:	Specifies the data set name
UNIT:	Specifies the physical device—e.g., tape or disk—to process the data set
DCB:	Supplements the COBOL FD with physical characteristics of the file—e.g., record length, block size, etc.
DISP:	Specifies status and disposition of data sets
SPACE:	Assigns space for an output data set on a direct access device
VOLUME:	Directs the operator to mount a specified volume; also used in label checking
LABEL:	Specifies type of label processing, location of a data set on a volume (tape only), and retention period

TRUE/FALSE EXERCISES

1. A given JCL statement may contain either positional or keyword parameters, but not both.
2. A jobstream contains only one /* statement.
3. A procedure is invoked by the EXEC statement.
4. The DD and EXEC statements must have a blank in column 3.
5. Comments are not permitted on JCL statements.
6. The /* statement is the last statement in a jobstream.
7. Omission of a positional parameter *always* requires a comma.
8. The EXEC statement does not require a step name.
9. DD * indicates the data set follows immediately in the jobstream.
10. BLOCK CONTAINS 0 RECORDS is a valid entry within an IBM COBOL FD.

11. The SPACE parameter is required for input data sets.

12. The DISP parameter has three positional subparameters.

13. The SPACE parameter must specify required space in terms of tracks.

14. VOL=SER= is required if UNIT is specified.

15. The secondary space allocation in the SPACE parameter is attempted only once.

16. DD DATA implies the file follows immediately in the jobstream.

17. DD statements precede the associated EXEC statement.

18. Certain parameters may appear on either the JOB or EXEC statement.

19. The DCB parameter overrides information in the COBOL FD.

20. If the normal disposition of an existing data set is not specified, the data set is deleted at the end of the job step.

21. A data set name may consist of more than eight characters.

22. REGION and TIME are better specified on the JOB rather than the EXEC statement.

PROBLEMS

1. Given the jobstream of Figure 1.9:

```
//SMITH   JOB     (123,456),'J. SMITH',CLASS=A
//STEP10  EXEC    PGM=EDIT
//TRANS   DD      DSN=UM.TRANS.DATA,DISP=SHR
//EDITED  DD      DSN=UM.EDIT.DATA,DISP=(NEW,CATLG),
//   UNIT=SYSDA,SPACE=(TRK,(5,1)),
//   DCB=(LRECL=50,BLKSIZE=500,RECFM=FB)
//REPORT  DD      SYSOUT=A
//STEP20  EXEC    PGM=UPDATE,COND=(0,LT,STEP10)
//TRANS   DD      DSN=UM.EDIT.DATA,DISP=(OLD,KEEP)
//OLD     DD      DSN=OLDMAST,DISP=(OLD,KEEP)
//NEW     DD      DSN=NEWMAST,DISP=(NEW,CATLG),
//   UNIT=TAPE,DCB=(LRECL=60,BLKSIZE=900,RECFM=FB),
//   LABEL=(,SL),VOL=SER=USR001
//ERRORS  DD      SYSOUT=A
```

FIGURE 1.9 Jobstream for Problem 1

Answer the following questions:

(a) What is the job name? The programmer name?

(b) How many accounting parameters were supplied?

(c) How many steps are there in the job? What are the step names?

(d) What is the name of the program that is executed in the second step? Will this step always be executed?

(e) What is the name of a data set that is output from the first step and input to the second step?

(f) What is the blocking factor for the data set UM.EDIT.DATA? for the data set NEWMAST?

(g) What is the name of a data set stored on tape? on disk?

(h) What is the maximum amount of space that will be allocated for the data set UM.EDIT.DATA before the job ABENDs?

(i) Where is the data set NEWMAST stored?

2. Analyze the JOB statements below for syntactical errors. Some statements may be correct as written, whereas others may contain more than one mistake.

(a) `// FIRST JOB (ACCTNO,PROJNO),SMITH, CLASS=A, MSGCLASS=A`

(b) `//SECOND JOB (ACCTNO,PROJNO),SMITH,MSGLEVEL=1,1`

(c) `//THIRD JOB ,SMITH,MSGLEVEL=(1,1)`
`//     TIME=(1,30),CLASS=A`

(d) `//FOURTH$ JOB (ACCTNO,PROJNO),'SMITH - X0345',`
`//     TIME=30,CLASS=A,REGION=120`

(e) `//FIFTH$$$$ JOB ACCTNO,SMITH,CLASS=A,`
`//REGION=120K,MSGLEVEL=(1,1)`

(f) `//SIXTH JOB`

(g) `//SEVENTH JOB SMITH,(ACCTNO,PROJNO),MSGCLASS=FIRST`

(h) `//EIGHTH ACCTNO,SMITH,TIME=2 CLASS=F`

(i) `//NINTH JOB (ACCTNO,PROJNO)`

(j) `//   JOB (ACCTNO,PROJNO),SMITH - X0345,`
`//CLASS=F,TIME=3,MSGLEVEL=1`

3. Analyze the EXEC statements for syntactical and/or logical errors. Some statements may be correct as written, whereas others may contain more than one mistake. (Assume IEBGENER is a program name and COBUCLG a procedure name.)

(a) `// EXEC PGM=IEBGENER`

(b) `//EXEC PGM=IEBGENER`

(c) `//STEPONE EXEC PGM=IEBGENER TIME=3`

(d) `//STEPSEVEN EXEC PGM=IEBGENER`

(e) `//STEP7 EXEC IEBGENER`

(f) `// EXEC PGM=IEBGENER  CREATE MASTER FILE`

(g) `// STEP1 EXEC PGM=COBUCLG`

(h) `//STEP1 EXEC PROC=COBUCLG,PARM.COB='PMAP,DMAP'`

(i) `//STEP1 EXEC COBUCLG PARM.COB='PMAP,DMAP',REGION=120K`

(j) `//STEP1 EXEC IEBGENER,TIME(30),REGION=120`
`            COND=(4,LT,STEP2)`

(k) `// EXECUTE PGM=IEBGENER,`
`//   TIME=(1,30),`
`//   REGION=64K,`

(l) `//LAST EXEC COBUCLG,PARM.COB=(PMAP,DMAP)`
`//   TIME=(3,30)`
`//   REGION=256K`

4. Analyze the DD statements for syntactical and/or logical errors. Some statements may be correct as written, whereas others may contain more than one mistake.

    (a)
    ```
    //FILE 1 DD DSN=FIRST,DISP=NEW,KEEP,VOL=SER=USR001,
    //     SPACE=(TRK,(1,1),UNIT=SYSDA
    ```

    (b)
    ```
    //STEP1FILE1 DD DSN=FIRST.FILE,DISP=(NEW,PASS)
    //     SPACE=(CYL,(10,1)),UNIT=TAPE
    ```

    (c)
    ```
    //FILE2 DD* A CARD FILE
    ```

    (d)
    ```
    //   FILE2 DD SYSOUT=A ** A PRINT FILE
    ```

    (e)
    ```
    //STEP3.FILE2 DD DSN=ABCDE,DISP=(NEW,KEEP),UNIT=DISK,
    //     DCB=BLKSIZE=80,LRECL=40,RECFM=FB
    ```

    (f)
    ```
    //FILE4 DSN=A.B.C.D,DISP=OLD,KEEP,DELETE,LABEL=(,SL),
    //     VOL=SER=USR003,UNIT=TAPE
    ```

    (g)
    ```
    //GO.SYSIN DD DSN=NEWERFILE,DISP=(NEW,KEEP),
    //UNIT=TAPE,DCB=(BLKSIZE=1000,LRECL=100)
    ```

    (h)
    ```
    //OUTPUT DD DCB=(BLOCKSIZE=1000,LREC=100),UNIT=3330,
    //     SPACE=(1000,(100,10)),DISP=OLD
    ```

    (i)
    ```
    //MARION DD DSN=A.B.C.D.E.F.G.H.I.J.K,
    //     DISP=SHR
    //     SPACE=(CYL,(10,2),,CONTIG),
    //     UNIT=DISK,
    ```

    (j)
    ```
    //SYSOUT DD SYSOUT=A
    ```

    (k)
    ```
    //PRINTER DD *
    ```

    (l)
    ```
    //FILEEIGHT DD DSN=&&TEMP,DISP=(NEW,KEEP),
    //     UNIT=DISK,SPACE=(CYL,(3,1),CONTIG),
    //     DCB=(LRECL=50,RECFM=FB,BLKSIZE=540)
    ```

    (m)
    ```
    //FILE9 DD DSN=MYTEMP.FILE,DISP=(OLD),
    //     SPACE=(CYL,3),  VOL=SER=123456,UNIT=SYSDA
    ```

5. Given the DD specification

    ```
    //TAPEFILE DD DISP=(OLD,KEEP),LABEL=(,SL),
    // DSN=TESTFILE,VOL=SER=USR456,UNIT=3400
    ```

    answer true or false:

    (a) TAPEFILE is the entry on the COBOL SELECT statement.
    (b) TESTFILE is the first file on the tape.
    (c) The operator will be directed to mount the tape with an external label TESTFILE.
    (d) The tape will be scratched if the job ABENDs.
    (e) The tape will be mounted on any available 3400 tape drive.

6. Given the DD specifications

    ```
    //NEWFILE DD DISP=(NEW,KEEP),SPACE=(CYL,20),
    // DSN=OUTPUT,UNIT=SYSDA,LABEL=EXPDT=84365,
    // VOL=SER=USR456
    ```

answer true or false:

(a) OUTPUT is the entry in the COBOL SELECT statement.
(b) The file will be retained indefinitely if the job executes successfully.
(c) The file will be deleted if the job ABENDs.
(d) The job will terminate if more than 20 cylinders are required.
(e) The file will be stored in contiguous cylinders.
(f) Any available disk pack may be used.
(g) A message to mount volume number USR456 will definitely be issued.

7. Complete the following table; indicate whether the job step is executed or bypassed:

Code in COND Parameter	Operation	System Return Code from Last Step	Executed or Bypassed
5	LT	4	
9	GT	8	
5	LT	(C-level diagnostic)	
5	LT	(W-level diagnostic)	
12	EQ	(E-level diagnostic)	
12	NE	12	

8. Does your shop have any JCL standards? If so, locate the standards manual and find those pertaining to the JOB, EXEC, and DD statements as discussed in the chapter. If not, do you think JCL standards are necessary? Can you suggest a limited set?

JOB STMT

// Jobname JOB (ACT, INF), "name"

2

Needs of the COBOL Programmer

Overview

It is not necessary that the reader retain every facet of every JCL parameter. Instead, he or she should develop a general appreciation for the language, especially its syntax and intent. Details of seldom-used features can always be obtained from the ubiquitous vendor manual. (IBM is the largest publisher in the world with respect to the number of printed pages, exceeding even the United States government.)

This chapter moves from JCL in isolation to the specific needs of the COBOL programmer. We begin with a brief discussion of typical DD statements, and continue with special DDnames encountered by the COBOL programmer. We introduce the procedure concept, in conjunction with the COBOL "proc" COBVCLG to compile, link, and execute a COBOL program. We present the advanced JCL concepts of concatenated data sets, generation data groups, and partitioned data sets. We highlight typical jobstreams used by the COBOL programmer, including: SORT, COPY, subprograms, sequential updates on tape and/or disk, and indexed files.

TYPICAL DD STATEMENTS

Figure 2.1 illustrates typical DD statements, and thereby serves as an effective review of much of Chapter 1. It is also a suitable prelude to the forthcoming section on COBOL requirements. Realize, however, that although Figure 2.1 shows acceptable ways of coding, it does *not* represent the only way of accomplishing these tasks. JCL is a *flexible* language, and possesses many alternatives which are adopted to varying degrees by different individuals and/or installations. Nevertheless, Figure 2.1 contains common techniques, and the beginner is urged to review it carefully.

Figure 2.1a creates a permanent data set on a direct access device. The DSN and UNIT parameters are straightforward. The DISP parameter specifies that the data set is to be catalogued and facilitates subsequent retrieval (see Figure 2.1c). The SPACE parameter is *required* for output data sets on disk, and indicates primary and secondary allocations of five and two tracks, respectively. Inclusion of the DCB parameter implies use of the COBOL clause, BLOCK CONTAINS 0 RECORDS, which mandates that the blocksize be entered in the JCL.

Figure 2.1b stores an output data set on a 3400 series tape drive. DISPosition is coded as (,KEEP), which is equivalent to (NEW,KEEP)—i.e.,

```
//DISKDS DD DSN=NEWMAST,UNIT=SYSDA,
//     DISP=(NEW,CATLG),SPACE=(TRK,(5,2)),
//     DCB=(RECFM=FB,BLKSIZE=400,LRECL=40)
```
(a) Creating a Permanent Data Set on Disk

```
//TAPEDS DD DSN=UM.OLD.MAST,UNIT=3400,
//     DISP=(,KEEP),LABEL=(1,SL),VOL=SER=USR001,
//     DCB=(RECFM=FB,BLKSIZE=8000,LRECL=80,DEN=3)
```
(b) Creating a Permanent Data Set on Tape

```
//OLDDS DD DSN=NEWMAST,DISP=SHR
```
(c) Retrieving a Catalogued Data Set

```
//OLDDS2 DD DSN=UM.OLD.MAST,UNIT=3400,
//     DISP=OLD,LABEL=(,SL),VOL=SER=USR001
```
(d) Retrieving an Uncatalogued Data Set

```
//UNCAT DD DSN=NEWMAST,DISP=(OLD,UNCATLG)
```
(e) Uncataloguing a Data Set

```
//TEMP DD DSN=&&TEMPDATA,UNIT=SYSDA,
//     DISP=(,PASS),SPACE=(CYL,6)
```
(f) Creating a Temporary Data Set

FIGURE 2.1 Typical DD Statements

NEW is the default status. Keeping a data set rather than cataloguing it, as was done in Figure 2.1a, requires that subsequent retrieval include UNIT and VOLUME information. Inclusion of the VOL parameter causes the data set to be written to the specific volume. (This is in contrast to Figure 2.1a, where VOL was omitted, and the system in turn selected any available pack.) The LABEL parameter causes the output data set to be written as the first file on the volume whose serial number is USR001. The DCB parameter contains the familiar subparameters for record length and blocksize, and in addition specifies DEN=3, which writes the file at 1600 bpi rather than 6250.

Figure 2.1c retrieves a catalogued data set, and requires only the DSN and DISP parameters. Disposition of SHR (share) allows other jobs to access the NEWMAST file concurrently, whereas a disposition of OLD would deny access to other jobs. Figure 2.1d references a kept data set and requires the additional UNIT and VOLUME information. The LABEL parameter (,SL) is equivalent to (1,SL)—i.e., the first file is the default value.

Figure 2.1e uncatalogs a data set, and uses only the DSN and DISP parameters. Note well, however, that the file is still available to anyone with the proper UNIT, VOLUME, and LABEL information.

Figure 2.1f creates a *temporary* data set, as indicated by the two ampersands in the DSN parameter. The new data set (the default status is new, as in Figure 2.1b) is *passed* to a subsequent step, at which point it may be passed further. (A temporary data set is automatically deleted when a job ends, unless a subsequent disposition keeps or catalogs the file.) Observe also that the space allocation is in terms of cylinders, and that no secondary allocation is specified.

SPECIAL DDNAMES

The COBOL SELECT statement ties a programmer-chosen file name to a DDname, which the programmer is free to choose within syntactical limits. There are, however, a limited number of DDnames with predetermined significance to the operating system. Examples are shown in Figure 2.2.

```
//SYSUDUMP DD SYSOUT=A

//SYSLIB   DD DSN=COBOL.COPY.LIB,DISP=SHR

//STEPLIB  DD DSN=UM.LOAD.LIB,DISP=SHR

//JOBLIB   DD DSN=UM.LOAD.LIB,DISP=SHR

//STEPCAT  DD DSN=UM.VSAM.CATALOG,DISP=SHR

//JOBCAT   DD DSN=UM.VSAM.CATALOG,DISP=SHR
```

FIGURE 2.2 Special DDnames

The SYSUDUMP DD statement specifies where a dump is written if the program ABENDs. It is usually assigned to a printer, typically SYSOUT=A. The SYSLIB DD statement is required, if the COBOL program contains a COPY statement, to reference the library in which the copied members are located. The STEPLIB DD statement defines a private library containing executable programs for a particular step; JOBLIB is similar in concept except that it applies to the entire job. In similar fashion, STEPCAT and JOBCAT define the location of the VSAM catalog for the step and job, respectively.

In addition to the preceding DDnames, the COBOL programmer may encounter: SYSLIN and SYSLMOD (associated with the linkage-editor and discussed in Chapter 4), SYSIN, SYSPRINT, SYSUT1, and SYSUT2 (associated with utilities and discussed in Chapter 4), and SORTLIB, SORTWK01, SORTWK02, etc. (associated with the SORT verb and discussed later in this chapter).

THE PROCEDURE CONCEPT

A *procedure* is a set of catalogued JCL statements that are *invoked* as the result of a single EXEC statement. Procedures are essential to OS in that they allow a programmer to achieve the effects of multiple JCL statements with a single EXEC. Figure 2.3 depicts a system flowchart used to compile, link, and execute a COBOL program, and illustrates the procedure concept.

The COBOL compiler accepts COBOL source statements and translates them to machine language, producing an *object* module. The linkage-editor (an IBM supplied program) accepts the object module produced by the compiler, combines it with other object modules (e.g., COBOL subroutines, IBM I/O modules, etc.) and produced a *load* module. Finally, the load module is executed. *Three* distinct programs—the COBOL compiler, the linkage-editor, and the resulting load module—are involved, and each of these requires one or more DD statements to describe its associated files.

Consider now the unfortunate COBOL programmer who merely wishes to test a simple "card to print" program. As implied by Figure 2.3, *three* EXEC statements are needed, plus *multiple* DD statements for the object module, load module, work files, etc. Moreover, this abundant JCL will be duplicated repeatedly by every programmer in the shop. The operation is greatly simplified by the technique of Figure 2.4, which invokes a preestablished *procedure*, COBVCLG.

Figure 2.4 contains a *single* EXEC statement to invoke the procedure COBVCLG, which in turn takes the necessary JCL from a *procedure library*. This is made clearer by examining Figure 2.5.

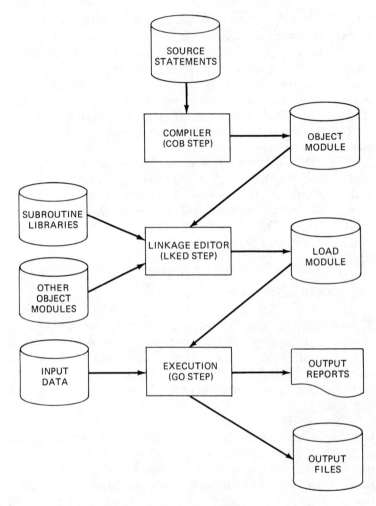

FIGURE 2.3 Compile, Link, and Execute Sequence

EXEC statement invokes the procedure

```
//JCS$3924    JOB (MAS526),JACKIE,MSGLEVEL=(1,1)
//STEP1       EXEC COBVCLG
//COB.SYSLIB  DD DSN=MEN.PGM.JSC.RTG,DISP=SHR
//COB.SYSIN   DD DSN=MEN.PGM.JSC.RTG(FILEDUMP),DISP=SHR
//GO.FILEOUT  DD SYSOUT=R
//GO.FILEIN   DD DSN=MEN.PGM.JSC.RTG(DUMPDATA),DISP=SHR
//GO.SYSUDUMP DD SYSOUT=R
```

FIGURE 2.4 Jobstream to Compile, Link, and Execute a COBOL Program

System Messages

A COBOL program which merely goes "card to print" typically results in the series of messages shown in Figure 2.5. The reaction of most beginners is to bypass Figure 2.5 as quickly as possible and turn immediately to the COBOL listing. This is indeed unfortunate as Figure 2.5 contains a wealth of useful information. We avoid however, line-by-line detailed explanations and aim instead at an overall level of conceptual understanding.

The first part of Figure 2.5 consists of *numbered* JCL statements. (Figure 2.5 was produced under MVS. Earlier versions of OS—e.g., OS/MVT —contained essentially the same information as Figure 2.5, but arranged it differently. See, for example, Grauer and Crawford, *Structured COBOL: A Pragmatic Approach*, Prentice-Hall, 1981, pages 333–334.) The statement numbers in Figure 2.5 are logical, rather than physical (i.e., a JCL statement may be continued over several card images, but only a single statement number is assigned).

The JCL statements in Figure 2.5 begin with either // or XX. State-

```
 1    //JSC$3924 JOB (MAS526),JACKIE,MSGLEVEL=(1,1)
 2    //STEP1        EXEC COBVCLG ──── // indicates submitted JCL statement
 3    XXCOBVCLG PROC OUT=R
 4    XXCOB EXEC PGM=IKFCBL00,PARM=(LOAD,SUPMAP,LIB,'LINECNT=60',
      XX           'SXREF','PMAP','DMAP','STATE','FLOW=10','NOSEQ',
      XX           'BUF=63922','SIZE=217088')
 5    XXSTEPLIB DD DSN=SYS2.LINKLIB,DISP=SHR
 6    XX         DD DSN=SYS1.COBLIB,DISP=SHR
 7    XXSYSPRINT DD SYSOUT=&OUT            ── 3 lines constitute 1 JCL statement
 8    XXSYSPUNCH DD DUMMY
 9    //COB.SYSLIB  DD DSN=MEN.PGM.JSC.RTG,DISP=SHR
      X/SYSLIB    DD DUMMY
10    XXSYSUT1     DD UNIT=3350,SPACE=(1024,(120,120)),DSN=&&SYSUT1
11    XXSYSUT2     DD UNIT=3350,SPACE=(1024,(120,120)),DSN=&&SYSUT2
12    XXSYSUT3     DD UNIT=3350,SPACE=(1024,(120,120)),DSN=&&SYSUT3
13    XXSYSUT4     DD UNIT=3350,SPACE=(1024,(120,120)),DSN=&&SYSUT4
14    XXSYSUT5     DD UNIT=3350,SPACE=(1024,(120,120)),DSN=&&SYSUT5
15    XXSYSLIN     DD DSN=&&OBJ,DISP=(MOD,PASS),UNIT=3350,
      XX              SPACE=(3040,(40,40)),
      XX              DCB=(BLKSIZE=3040,LRECL=80,RECFM=FBS,BUFNO=1)
16    //COB.SYSIN   DD DSN=MEN.PGM.JSC.RTG(FILEDUMP),DISP=SHR
17    XXLKED EXEC PGM=HEWL,PARM='LIST,XREF,LET,MAP',COND=(5,LT,COB)
18    XXSYSLIN     DD DSN=&&OBJ,DISP=(OLD,DELETE)
19    XXSYSLMOD    DD DSN=&&LOD(X),DISP=(,PASS),UNIT=3350,DCB=BUFNO=1,
      XX              SPACE=(CYL,(1,1,1))
20    XXSYSLIB     DD DSN=SYS1.COBLIB,DISP=SHR
21    XXSYSUT1     DD UNIT=3350,SPACE=(1024,(120,120)),DCB=BUFNO=1,
      XX              DSN=&&SYSUT1
22    XXSYSPRINT DD SYSOUT=&OUT
23    XXGO EXEC PGM=*.LKED.SYSLMOD,COND=((5,LT,COB),(5,LT,LKED))
24    XXSTEPLIB   DD DSN=SYS1.COBLIB,DISP=SHR
25    XXSYSOUT    DD SYSOUT=&OUT
26    XXSYSOUC    DD SYSOUT=&OUT   ── XX indicates procedure JCL statement
27    XXSYSCOUNT  DD SYSOUT=&OUT
28    XXSYSDBOUT  DD SYSOUT=&OUT
29    //GO.FILEOUT  DD SYSOUT=R
30    //GO.FILEIN   DD DSN=MEN.PGM.JSC.RTG(DUMPDATA),DISP=SHR
31    //GO.SYSUDUMP DD SYSOUT=R
```

FIGURE 2.5 System Messages for COBVCLG Procedure

```
STMT NO. MESSAGE

    7      IEF653I SUBSTITUTION JCL - SYSOUT=R
   22      IEF653I SUBSTITUTION JCL - SYSOUT=R
   25      IEF653I SUBSTITUTION JCL - SYSOUT=R
   26      IEF653I SUBSTITUTION JCL - SYSOUT=R
   27      IEF653I SUBSTITUTION JCL - SYSOUT=R
   28      IEF653I SUBSTITUTION JCL - SYSOUT=R
IEF236I ALLOC. FOR JSC$3924 COB STEP1
IEF237I 133  ALLOCATED TO STEPLIB
IEF237I 133  ALLOCATED TO
IEF237I JES2 ALLOCATED TO SYSPRINT
IEF237I DMY  ALLOCATED TO SYSPUNCH
IEF237I 113  ALLOCATED TO SYSLIB
IEF237I 113  ALLOCATED TO SYS00263
IEF237I 135  ALLOCATED TO SYSUT1
IEF237I 111  ALLOCATED TO SYSUT2
IEF237I 131  ALLOCATED TO SYSUT3
IEF237I 131  ALLOCATED TO SYSUT4
IEF237I 135  ALLOCATED TO SYSUT5
IEF237I 133  ALLOCATED TO SYSLIN          ┌Compile step executed cleanly
IEF237I 113  ALLOCATED TO SYSIN
IEF142I JSC$3924 │COB STEP1 - STEP WAS EXECUTED - COND CODE 0000│
IEF285I      SYS2.LINKLIB                             KEPT
IEF285I      VOL SER NOS= UMF133.
IEF285I      SYS1.COBLIB                              KEPT
IEF285I      VOL SER NOS= UMF133.
IEF285I      JES2.JOB01770.S00101                     SYSOUT
IEF285I      MEN.PGM.JSC.RTG                          KEPT
IEF285I      VOL SER NOS= UMF113.
IEF285I      SYSCTLG.VUMF113                          KEPT
IEF285I      VOL SER NOS= UMF113.
IEF285I      SYS83015.T134236.RA000.JSC$3924.SYSUT1   DELETED
IEF285I      VOL SER NOS= UMF135.
IEF285I      SYS83015.T134236.RA000.JSC$3924.SYSUT2   DELETED
IEF285I      VOL SER NOS= UMF111.
IEF285I      SYS83015.T134236.RA000.JSC$3924.SYSUT3   DELETED
IEF285I      VOL SER NOS= UMF131.
IEF285I      SYS83015.T134236.RA000.JSC$3924.SYSUT4   DELETED
IEF285I      VOL SER NOS= UMF131.
IEF285I      SYS83015.T134236.RA000.JSC$3924.SYSUT5   DELETED
IEF285I      VOL SER NOS= UMF135.
IEF285I      SYS83015.T134236.RA000.JSC$3924.OBJ      PASSED
IEF285I      VOL SER NOS= UMF133.
IEF285I      MEN.PGM.JSC.RTG                          KEPT
IEF285I      VOL SER NOS= UMF113.
IEF373I STEP /COB     / START 83015.1342
IEF374I STEP /COB     / STOP  83015.1342 CPU    0MIN 01.66SEC SRB
IEF236I ALLOC. FOR JSC$3924 LKED STEP1
IEF237I 133  ALLOCATED TO SYSLIN
IEF237I 135  ALLOCATED TO SYSLMOD
IEF237I 133  ALLOCATED TO SYSLIB
IEF237I 111  ALLOCATED TO SYSUT1          ┌Link-edit step executed cleanly
IEF237I JES2 ALLOCATED TO SYSPRINT
IEF142I JSC$3924 │LKED STEP1 - STEP WAS EXECUTED - COND CODE 0000│
IEF285I      SYS83015.T134236.RA000.JSC$3924.OBJ      DELETED
IEF285I      VOL SER NOS= UMF133.
IEF285I      SYS83015.T134236.RA000.JSC$3924.LOD      PASSED
IEF285I      VOL SER NOS= UMF135.
IEF285I      SYS1.COBLIB                              KEPT
IEF285I      VOL SER NOS= UMF133.
IEF285I      SYS83015.T134236.RA000.JSC$3924.SYSUT1   DELETED
IEF285I      VOL SER NOS= UMF111.
IEF285I      JES2.JOB01770.S00102                     SYSOUT
```

FIGURE 2.5 (Continued)

```
IEF373I STEP /LKED     / START 83015.1342
IEF374I STEP /LKED     / STOP  83015.1342 CPU     0MIN 00.55SEC SRB
IEF236I ALLOC. FOR JSC$3924 GO STEP1
IEF237I 135  ALLOCATED TO PGM=*.DD
IEF237I 133  ALLOCATED TO STEPLIB
IEF237I JES2 ALLOCATED TO SYSOUT
IEF237I JES2 ALLOCATED TO SYSOUC
IEF237I JES2 ALLOCATED TO SYSCOUNT
IEF237I JES2 ALLOCATED TO SYSDBOUT
IEF237I JES2 ALLOCATED TO FILEOUT
IEF237I 113  ALLOCATED TO FILEIN
IEF237I 113  ALLOCATED TO SYS00265           ╭─ GO step executed cleanly
IEF237I JES2 ALLOCATED TO SYSUDUMP
IEF142I JSC$3924 │GO STEP1 - STEP WAS EXECUTED - COND CODE 0000│
IEF285I    SYS83015.T134236.RA000.JSC$3924.LOD        KEPT
IEF285I    VOL SER NOS= UMF135.
IEF285I    SYS1.COBLIB                                 KEPT
IEF285I    VOL SER NOS= UMF133.
IEF285I    JES2.JOB01770.S00103                        SYSOUT
IEF285I    JES2.JOB01770.S00104                        SYSOUT
IEF285I    JES2.JOB01770.S00105                        SYSOUT
IEF285I    JES2.JOB01770.S00106                        SYSOUT
IEF285I    JES2.JOB01770.S00107                        SYSOUT
IEF285I    MEN.PGM.JSC.RTG                             KEPT
IEF285I    VOL SER NOS= UMF113.
IEF285I    SYSCTLG.VUMF113                             KEPT
IEF285I    VOL SER NOS= UMF113.
IEF285I    JES2.JOB01770.S00108                        SYSOUT
IEF373I STEP /GO       / START 83015.1342
IEF374I STEP /GO       / STOP  83015.1342 CPU     0MIN 00.14SEC SRB
IEF237I 135  ALLOCATED TO SYS00001
IEF285I    SYS83015.T134255.RA000.JSC$3924.R0000001   KEPT
IEF285I    VOL SER NOS= UMF135.
IEF285I    SYS83015.T134236.RA000.JSC$3924.LOD        DELETED
IEF285I    VOL SER NOS= UMF135.
IEF375I JOB /JSC$3924/ START 83015.1342
IEF376I JOB /JSC$3924/ STOP  83015.1342 CPU     0MIN 02.35SEC SRB
```

FIGURE 2.5 (Continued)

ments beginning with // indicate that the line originated in the programmer-supplied JCL, whereas statements beginning with XX imply a JCL statement pulled from the procedure. (Statements may also begin with an X/ to indicate that a procedure statement was overridden by an incoming JCL statement. Procedures and overrides are discussed in Chapter 3.)

The programmer-supplied EXEC statement of Figure 2.4 specified execution of the procedure COBVCLG, which in turn consists of three steps: compile (step name COB), link-edit (step name LKED), and execute (step name GO). Subsequent JCL statements may reference these step names; for example, GO.FILEIN refers to the DDname FILEIN in the GO step. Each procedure step begins with an XX EXEC (really // EXEC) statement, requesting execution of a program (e.g., IKFCBL00 for the compile (COB) step).

The programmer-supplied DD statements of Figure 2.4 are made clearer by a conceptual understanding of Figure 2.5. Consider the components of the statement //GO.FILEOUT DD SYSOUT=R. GO is the step name and FILEOUT is the DDname. The latter is linked to the COBOL SELECT statement. DD indicates the JCL operation, and SYSOUT=R indicates the file is to go to a class R output device—e.g., a specific printer.

The JCL statements of Figure 2.5 are followed by a set of messages which describe the results of each job step—e.g., STEP WAS EXECUTED-COND CODE 0000. The value of the condition code indicates the success encountered during that step. In the compile step, for example, a condition code of 0000 indicates no diagnostics, a code of 0004 indicates that a warning was the most severe level of error, 0008 means a C-level diagnostic, and 0012 an E-level diagnostic. If a step is abnormally terminated (i.e., ABENDs), the condition code is replaced by a *completion code* stating the reason for the termination (e.g., COMPLETION CODE S0C7). In Figure 2.5, the three steps all executed with condition codes of 0000. Thus, by examining the system output, one can tell the highest severity error encountered during the execution of each job step. One can also determine how far the COBOL program went in the compile, link-edit, and execute sequence.

The concept of a procedure (or proc) is fundamental to OS. The subject is so important that it merits its own chapter (see Chapter 3). For the time being, however, simply realize that it is perfectly permissible, albeit impractical, for the COBOL programmer to submit the entire jobstream (i.e., procedure) with his or her program. Common practice, however, is to catalog the necessary JCL into a procedure, and then invoke the procedure. In this way, the job of the individual is simplified, and every programmer has convenient access to identical jobstreams. Installations establish one or more procedure libraries, with many of the actual procs supplied by IBM (e.g., COBVCLG).

ADVANCED CONCEPTS

We will soon discuss specific needs of the COBOL programmer via a set of typical jobstreams. However, we must first present the concepts of a concatenated data set, a partitioned data set, and a generation data group.

Concatenated Data Set

A concatenated data set is defined as a logical file composed of two or more physical files. Consider the following combination of COBOL and JCL statements.

COBOL:

```
SELECT CUMULATIVE-YEARLY-SALES-FILE
    ASSIGN TO UT-S-YEAREND.
```

JCL:

```
//YEAREND DD DSN=JAN.SALES,DISP=SHR
//         DD DSN=FEB.SALES,DISP=SHR
//         DD DSN=MAR.SALES,DISP=SHR
   .
     .
       .
//         DD DSN=DEC.SALES,DISP=SHR
```

The COBOL SELECT statement ties a logical file (CUMULATIVE-YEARLY-SALES-FILE) to a DDname; the DD statement links the DDname to the physical data set(s). The yearly file is composed of twelve monthly files, and the application program is to read the January file, February file, and so on, until the entire year's transactions have been processed. The program considers the year's records as coming from a single file, when in reality they originate from 12 separate sources.

These requirements are easily met in JCL through a concatenated DD statement. The preceding example had 12 DD statements, *but only the first had a DDname. Note well these are distinct JCL statements as opposed to a single continued statement; i.e., the individual statements do not end with a comma, which would imply continuation.* In other words, the logical file associated with the DDname YEAREND is comprised of 12 physical data sets: JAN.SALES, FEB.SALES, etc. The system processes the records in all 12 files as a *single* file—i.e., when the end of the January data is reached, it reads from February, March, and so on. Only a *single end of file* condition will be returned to the program when the end of the December file is reached.

Partitioned Data Set

OS requires that a sequential data set stored on a direct access device be allocated at least one track, resulting in wasted space for smaller data sets. Consider, for example, an FD stored as a member of a COBOL COPY library, and consisting of 100 card images (8000 bytes). If the FD is stored on a single track of a 3350 pack with a capacity of some 19,000 bytes, then approximately 11,000 bytes are wasted. The proportion of wasted space increases further with even smaller data sets (e.g., a jobstream of 20 card images).

The solution is to use a *partitioned data set* (PDS), which is defined as a file consisting of one or more sequential data sets, known as *members.* The PDS itself must begin on a new track, but the individual members do not. A good analogy is a drawer in a file cabinet containing several manila folders. The drawer corresponds to the partitioned data set, and each folder corresponds to a member.

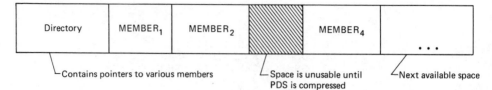

FIGURE 2.6 A Partitioned Data Set

A partitioned data set has a *directory* listing its members, and pointers to the respective locations. If a member is deleted from a PDS, the space originally used by that member *cannot be reallocated* until the entire file has been compressed. (This may be accomplished by the IEBCOPY utility, and is discussed in Chapter 4.) In similar fashion, if a member is replaced by a newer version of the same member, the space taken by the old version is unusable until the PDS has been compressed. This in turn produces several "holes" in the PDS, as indicated by Figure 2.6, with the pointers in the directory continually updated *to reflect* any changes. If, for example, MEMBER$_1$ were substituted with a newer version, the original space taken by MEMBER$_1$ becomes unusable, and the new version is physically placed after MEMBER$_4$.

A partitioned data set is indicated in JCL via parentheses in the DSN parameter, for example:

```
//SYSLIB DD DSN=COBOL.COPY.LIB(UPDATES),DISP=SHR
```

The member name, UPDATES, is enclosed in parentheses; the DSN parameter refers to the PDS itself—i.e., to COBOL.COPY.LIB.

Generation Data Groups

The system flowchart of Figure 2.7 depicts a periodic update (arbitrarily shown on a monthly cycle for illustrative purposes). The run made on February 1st uses a January 1st file as input, to produce a new master as of February 1st. On March 1st, the February 1st file is used as the *old* master to produce a new master as of March 1st, and so on. This technique requires the production jobstreams be changed every month to reflect the new data set name parameters, and is error prone and administratively complex. For example:

February 1 JCL:

```
//OLDMAST DD DSN=MASTER.JAN01,DISP=OLD
//NEWMAST DD DSN=MASTER.FEB01,DISP=(NEW,CATLG),...
```

March 1 JCL:

```
//OLDMAST DD DSN=MASTER.FEB01,DISP=OLD
//NEWMAST DD DSN=MASTER.MAR01,DISP=(NEW,CATLG),...
```

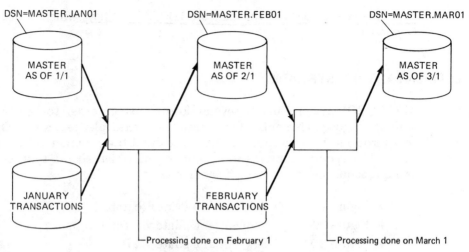

DSN=MASTER.JAN01 DSN=MASTER.FEB01 DSN=MASTER.MAR01

MASTER AS OF 1/1 MASTER AS OF 2/1 MASTER AS OF 3/1

JANUARY TRANSACTIONS FEBRUARY TRANSACTIONS

└Processing done on February 1 └Processing done on March 1

FIGURE 2.7 Periodic Update (Illustrates GDGs)

The need to change production jobstreams is eliminated through use of a *generation data group* (GDG) which permits several versions (i.e., generations) of a file to have the *same* name. A GDG is a collection of chronologically related data sets (appropriately known as generation data sets), all of which have *the same name*. The distinction between group members is made through a generation number. The current file has a relative generation number of zero—e.g., MASTER.FILE(0). Its immediate predecessor is referenced as MASTER.FILE(-1), its immediate successor as MASTER.FILE(+1). This allows the production jobstream to remain *unchanged* from month to month; for example:

```
//OLDMAST DD DSN=MASTER.FILE(0),DISP=OLD
//NEWMAST DD DSN=MASTER.FILE(+1),DISP=(NEW,CATLG),...
```

Generation (0) is always the current generation, generation (+1) the next generation, and so on. *The generation numbers are automatically updated at the conclusion of a job.* Returning to Figure 2.7, the February 1 file is referenced by a generation number of plus 1 prior to the Feb. 1 update, by a generation number of 0 after the February run (i.e., prior to the March 1 update), and by a generation number of -1 *after* the March 1 update. However, a given file is referenced by the *same* generation number throughout a job, as generations are not updated until *after* the job is completed. Hence, if a new master is created in one step, and printed in a subsequent step, it would be referenced as the plus 1 generation in both.

Generation data groups may reference sequential, direct, and partitioned data sets, and may reside on either tape or direct access volumes. A GDG must be catalogued. It is used like any other data set except for the generation number in the DSN parameter. A GDG must be established

<u>prior to its use</u>, usually through the <u>IDCAMS utility</u>, which is discussed in Chapter 5.

ELEMENTARY JOBSTREAMS

The COBOL trainee needs several jobstreams in order to be able to use various language elements. One cannot, for example, test a COBOL SORT or subroutine in isolation, but must surround the program with supporting JCL. This section contains seven jobstreams which span a typical one-year training sequence in COBOL. These include:

- Figure 2.8   A "Card" to Print Program
- Figure 2.9   Sequential Update via Tape
- Figure 2.10   Sequential Update via Disk
- Figure 2.11   Use of a Subprogram
- Figure 2.12   Creating an ISAM File
- Figure 2.13   Accessing a VSAM File
- Figure 2.14   Use of the COBOL SORT Verb

It should be emphasized that these illustrations reflect a *testing* rather than a production environment. This is because all examples invoke the procedure to compile, link, and execute the program. Execution of all three steps is fine in testing, because the source program constantly changes and hence requires recompilation. In production, however, the compilation and linkage-editor steps would not be repeated, as such repetition would be unnecessary. (Production jobstreams are discussed in Chapter 4, in conjunction with the STEPLIB DD statement.)

A "Card" to Print Program

The COBOL programmer can specify a host of available compiler options as shown in Table 2.1. This is done on the EXEC statement. It is illustrated in Figure 2.8, much of which has already been discussed in connection with Figures 2.4 and 2.5.

Observe the specification of compiler options in the EXEC statement via the JCL PARM parameter—e.g., PARM.COB=(PMAP,DMAP,STATE, 'FLOW=5'). As can be seen from Table 2.1, PMAP and DMAP produce Procedure and Data Division maps, respectively. The STATE and FLOW options are useful in debugging, and are discussed in Chapter 7. Realize also that one need not specify all the options of Table 2.1 in every run, as various defaults are assumed by the compiler; instead, one specifies

TABLE 2.1 COBOL Compilation Parameters

SOURCE:	Prints the source listing (suppressed by NOSOURCE)
CLIST:	Produces a condensed listing of the Procedure Division map in which only the address of the first machine instruction of every COBOL statement is shown (suppressed by NOCLIST—cannot be used simultaneously with PMAP)
DMAP:	Produces a Data Division map (suppressed by NODMAP)
PMAP:	Produces a Procedure Division map (suppressed by NOPMAP—cannot be used simultaneously with CLIST)
LIB:	Indicates that a COPY statement appears in the COBOL program (NOLIB indicates that COPY statements are not present and also provides more efficient compilation)
VERB:	Prints procedure and verb names on the Procedure Division map (suppressed by NOVERB)
LOAD:	Stores object program on direct-access device for input to the linkage editor or loader programs (suppressed by NOLOAD)
DECK:	Punches object deck (suppressed by NODECK)
SEQ:	Checks incoming COBOL statements for proper sequence in columns 1–6 (suppressed by NOSEQ)
LINECNT=nn:	Specifies the numbers of lines to be printed on each page of output listing (60 is default)
FLAGW:	Prints all diagnostic messages
FLAGE:	Prints C-, E-, and D-level diagnostics; suppresses W-level diagnostics
SUPMAP:	Suppresses the PMAP option if an E-level diagnostic was present (suppressed by NOSUPMAP)
QUOTE:	Specifies that quotation marks (") will enclose nonnumeric literals
APOST:	Specifies that the apostrophe (') will enclose nonnumeric literals
XREF:	Generates a cross-reference listing (suppressed by NOXREF)
SXREF:	Generates a sorted reference listing (suppressed by NOSXREF)
STATE:	Prints the statement number being executed at the time of an ABEND (see example in Chapter 7)
FLOW=N:	Lists the last *n* procedures that were executed prior to an ABEND (see example in Chapter 7)
SYMDMP:	Requests a formatted dump in the event of an ABEND and allows symbolic debugging statements to be used
COUNT:	Produces a table showing the number of times each paragraph was executed. The program must ABEND for this option to take effect.

```
//GRAUER       JOB   (Acct Information)
//             EXEC  COBVCLG,PARM.COB=(PMAP,DMAP,STATE,'FLOW=5')
//COB.SYSIN    DD    *
 .
   .
     .
      ENVIRONMENT DIVISION.
          SELECT INPUT-FILE
              ASSIGN TO UT-S-CARDS.
          SELECT PRINT-FILE
              ASSIGN TO UT-S-REPORT.
 .
   .
     .
/*
//GO.REPORT    DD    SYSOUT=A
//GO.CARDS     DD    *
     Data cards go here
/*
//GO.SYSUDUMP DD SYSOUT=A
//
```

FIGURE 2.8 A "Card" to Print Program

only those options which are different from the default values. A separate page of compiler output appears after the COBOL compilation, indicating the options in effect for the particular run.

Sequential Update Via Tape

Figure 2.9 contains JCL for a traditional sequential update, in which a new master and a printed error report are created from old master and transaction files. Both the old master and transaction files are catalogued as implied by specification of only the DSN and DISP parameters.

The new master will be stored as the *first* file on the output tape, as per the LABEL parameter (,SL). The comma indicates an omitted positional parameter, and the default position is the first file; i.e., (,SL) is equivalent to (1,SL). VOL=SER is not specified; hence, a scratch tape will be used. The RETAIN subparameter prevents the tape from being dismounted at the end of this step, implying that a subsequent step (not shown in Figure 2.9) may reference the particular file. (This courtesy is greatly appreciated by operations personnel.)

Sequential Update Via Disk

Figure 2.10 denotes a sequential update, similar in concept to Figure 2.9, except that the master files are stored on disk rather than tape. *The COBOL SELECT statements are identical in both figures*—i.e., the SELECT statements are *device independent*. Hence, a COBOL program written to process

```
//GRAUER       JOB   (Acct Information),CLASS=A
//             EXEC  COBVCLG,PARM.COB=(PMAP,DMAP)
//COB.SYSIN    DD    *
 .
   .
     .
           ENVIRONMENT DIVISION.
                SELECT OLD-MASTER-FILE
                    ASSIGN TO UT-S-OLD.
                SELECT NEW-MASTER-FILE
                    ASSIGN TO UT-S-NEW.
                SELECT TRANSACTION-FILE
                    ASSIGN TO UT-S-TRANS.
                SELECT ERROR-FILE
                    ASSIGN TO UT-S-ERRORS.


   .
     .
//GO.SYSUDUMP DD    SYSOUT=A
//GO.ERRORS   DD    SYSOUT=A
//GO.OLD      DD    DSN=OLDMAST,DISP=SHR
//GO.NEW      DD    DSN=NEWMAST,DISP=(NEW,CATLG,DELETE),
//    UNIT=3400,VOL=(,RETAIN),LABEL=(,SL),
//    DCB=(BLKSIZE=800,LRECL=40,RECFM=FB)
//GO.TRANS    DD    DSN=TRANSACT,DISP=SHR
//
```

FIGURE 2.9 Sequential Update Via Tape

```
//GRAUER       JOB   (Acct Information),'JONES X345',CLASS=B
//             EXEC COBVCLG,PARM.COB=(DMAP,PMAP,STATE,'FLOW=10')
//COB.SYSIN    DD    *
 .
   .
     .
           ENVIRONMENT DIVISION.
                SELECT OLD-MASTER-FILE
                    ASSIGN TO UT-S-OLD.
                SELECT NEW-MASTER-FILE
                    ASSIGN TO UT-S-NEW.
                SELECT TRANSACTION-FILE
                    ASSIGN TO UT-S-TRANS.
                SELECT ERROR-FILE
                    ASSIGN TO UT-S-ERRORS.

   .
     .
//GO.SYSUDUMP DD    SYSOUT=A
//GO.ERRORS   DD    SYSOUT=A
//GO.OLD      DD    DSN=MASTER(0),DISP=OLD
//GO.NEW      DD    DSN=MASTER(+1),DISP=(,CATLG),
//    SPACE=(TRK,(15,2)),UNIT=3350,VOL=SER=USR123,
//    DCB=(BLKSIZE=800,LRECL=40,RECFM=FB)
//GO.TRANS    DD    DSN=MAS526.DATA(TRANSACT),DISP=SHR
//
```

FIGURE 2.10 Sequential Update Via Disk

sequential files can access tape, disk, or unit record devices with no COBOL modification whatsoever. Any necessary changes are entered in the JCL rather than the COBOL program.

The DD statement for the new master contains a SPACE parameter which is required for new data sets on a direct access device. It also contains a DCB parameter to specify the physical characteristics of the file, implying specification of BLOCK CONTAINS 0 RECORDS in the source program. (This enables the block size to be entered at execution time in the JCL, rather than during compile time in the program. Hence, a program need not be recompiled if the blocking factor changes.) The new master will be written to a particular pack, with VOL=SER=USR123. Disposition is (,CATLG), which is equivalent to (NEW,CATLG)—i.e., NEW is the default status.

The old and new master are both specified as *generation data sets*, with generations of 0 and +1, respectively. This desirable practice allows production jobstreams to remain unchanged from cycle to cycle. The transaction file is specified as a *member*, TRANSACT, of the *partitioned data set*, MAS526.DATA.

Use of a Subprogram

Figure 2.11 illustrates one way of compiling and testing a COBOL subprogram. (An alternative technique that uses the linkage-editor explicitly is discussed in Chapter 4.) Figure 2.11 contains two EXEC statements, and invokes two different procedures. *The main program is compiled prior to the subprogram.*

STEP1 compiles the main program and does not attempt to link or execute; i.e., the procedure COBVC contains a single EXEC statement. STEP2, on the other hand, invokes the procedure COBVCLG, which compiles the subprogram, then links and executes the resulting load module consisting of *both* programs. DD statements for the files associated with either program *follow* the last EXEC statement. The SYSLIB DD statement implies use of the COBOL COPY feature. Specification of PARM.COB='LIB' is required to support the COPY clause. (COBOL compilation parameters may be enclosed in either apostrophes or parentheses.) Problem 7, at the end of the chapter, further illustrates this jobstream.

Creating an ISAM File

IBM has two distinct implementations for indexed files, ISAM and VSAM. The latter is the newer, and *far more important* method (Chapter 5 is devoted entirely to VSAM). ISAM is no longer even supported by IBM.

```
//GRAUER      JOB  (Acct information)
//STEP1       EXEC COBVC,PARM.COB='LIB'
//COB.SYSLIB  DD   DSN=UM.COBOL.COPY.LIB,DISP=SHR
//COB.SYSIN   DD   *
    .
        .
            .
            ENVIRONMENT DIVISION.
                SELECT EMPLOYEE-FILE
                    ASSIGN TO UT-S-INPUT.
                SELECT REPORT-FILE
                    ASSIGN TO UT-S-PRINT.
    .
        .
            .
//STEP2       EXEC COBVCLG,PARM.COB='LIB'
//COB.SYSLIB  DD   DSN=UM.COBOL.COPY.LIB,DISP=SHR
//COB.SYSIN   DD   DSN=UM.COBOL.SOURCE(SUBRTN),DISP=SHR
//GO.INPUT    DD   DSN=UM.EMP.FILE,DISP=SHR
//GO.PRINT    DD   SYSOUT=A
//
```

FIGURE 2.11 Use of a Subprogram

Nevertheless, Figure 2.12 is included for completeness, as some ISAM applications still exist.

Figure 2.12 creates an ISAM file from an input transaction file. The ISAM DD statement is *concatenated* and consists of three distinct DD statements for the index, prime, and overflow areas, respectively. (An ISAM file may also be specified via a *single* DD statement, in which case the index and overflow areas are embedded within the prime area. The DSN parameter of a single DD statement could specify either DSN=NEWISAM or DSN=NEWISAM(PRIME)).

The DSN parameters on the DD statements of Figure 2.12 specify NEWISAM(INDEX), NEWISAM(PRIME), and NEWISAM(OVFLOW), denoting index, prime, and independent overflow areas, respectively. The volume parameter for the index area is different from that of the other two, indicating that the three areas do not have to be stored on the same volume.

The DCB parameter is fully specified in the DD statement associated with the index area. It is specified as a *refer-back parameter* in the DD statements for the prime and overflow areas (i.e., DCB=*.GO.ISAM). The asterisk is a reference to a previous DD statement and implies that the DCB parameter is the same as on the earlier statement for GO.ISAM.

The DCB parameter for an ISAM file requires specification of the DSORG subparameter; i.e., *Data Set Org*anization is *I*ndexed *S*equential. It also requires the OPTCD subparameter, with the more common options explained:

```
//GRAUER     JOB
//           EXEC COBVCLG
//COB.SYSIN DD    *
 .
  .
   .
       ENVIRONMENT DIVISION.
           SELECT ISAM-FILE
               ASSIGN TO DA-I-ISAM.
           SELECT TRANSACTION-FILE
               ASSIGN TO UT-S-TRANS.
 .
  .
   .
//GO.TRANS  DD    DSN=UM.TRANS.FILE,DISP=SHR
//GO.ISAM   DD    DSN=NEWISAM(INDEX),DISP=(,KEEP),
//    UNIT=SYSDA,SPACE=(CYL,1),VOL=SER=USR002,
//    DCB=(DSORG=IS,OPTCD=LIMW,NTM=5,CYLOFL=2)
//          DD    DSN=NEWISAM(PRIME),DISP=(,KEEP),
//    UNIT=SYSDA,SPACE=(CYL,50,,CONTIG),VOL=SER=USR001,
//    DCB=*.GO.ISAM
//          DD    DSN=NEWISAM(OVFLOW),DISP=(,KEEP),
//    UNIT=SYSDA,SPACE=(CYL,10,,CONTIG),VOL=SER=USR001,
//    DCB=*.GO.ISAM
//
```

FIGURE 2.12 Creating an ISAM File

OPTCD=W: Requests a write validity check in which data are read back from a direct access data set immediately after being written. This ensures that the data were correctly transferred from memory. It does, however, require an extra revolution of the direct access device and is therefore time-consuming.

OPTCD=Y: Requests that a cylinder overflow area be created. Specification of this parameter requires that another DCB parameter, CYLOFL=XX, also be specified. The latter denotes the number of tracks on each cylinder devoted to overflow.

OPTCD=L: Requests that marked records (i.e., those with HIGH-VALUES in the first byte) be deleted when space is required for new records.

OPTCD=I: Requests that an independent overflow area be created. Use of this parameter requires specification of DSNAME=dsname(OVFLOW) in the DD statement for the ISAM file.

OPTCD=M: Requests that a master index be created in addition to the cylinder and track indexes. Specification of this parameter requires another DCB parameter, NTM=XX, denoting the number of tracks the cylinder index can contain prior to creating a master index. Thus, NTM=5 will cause a master index to be created when the number of tracks in the cylinder index exceeds 5.

Any combination of options may be requested. Multiple options are written together as a character string with no intervening blanks or commas. The OPTCD parameter in Figure 2.12 requests deletion of inactive records (L), independent overflow (I), creation of a master index (M), and a write validity check (W).

Accessing a VSAM File

Figure 2.13 illustrates how one accesses a VSAM file and is far simpler than its ISAM counterpart of Figure 2.12. Much of VSAM processing is accomplished through a multipurpose utility, Access Method Services (which is covered in depth in Chapter 5). This utility is used to define a VSAM data set, to catalog it, to load records into it, to convert a sequential or indexed sequential data set to VSAM, to reorganize a data set, to provide a backup copy, and to make a data set portable from one operating system to another. In other words, Access Method Services is used for virtually every operation relating to VSAM.

Owing to the multiple functions of Access Methods Services, the functions of many DD parameters are changed or no longer apply for VSAM data sets. For example, the SPACE parameter is not specified in the jobstream associated with a COBOL program to create a VSAM data set. Rather, Access Methods Services is called in a prior step to allocate space for the data set. In other words, VSAM data sets will always be regarded (by the COBOL programmer) as existing data sets, and consequently the SPACE parameter is meaningless.

The DCB parameter, as well as all its subparameters, is not used with VSAM. A special control block, the access-method control block (rather than the DCB), describes VSAM data sets, and hence the DCB parameter is not needed.

The DISP parameter has lesser meaning under VSAM, as these data sets are created, catalogued, and kept as a function of the Access Methods Services utility. If, for example, CATLG is coded, a message will be issued, but the data set will not be catalogued. Similarly, if DELETE is coded, a message will be issued, but the data set is not deleted. If DISP=NEW is specified, OS/VS will allocate space that will never be used by VSAM.

The jobstream of Figure 2.13 identifies VSAM.FILE as the name of the VSAM data set, and uses only the DISP and DSN parameters. However, a STEPCAT DD statement is necessary to indicate the user catalog which contains the data set.

```
//GRAUER        JOB  (Acct Information),CLASS=A
//              EXEC COBVCLG,PARM.COB=(PMAP,DMAP)
//COB.SYSIN     DD   *
   .
     .
       .

        ENVIRONMENT DIVISION.
           SELECT INDEXED-FILE
               ASSIGN TO DA-MASTER.
           SELECT TRANSACTION-FILE
               ASSIGN TO UT-S-TRANS.
       .
     .
   .
//GO.SYSUDUMP DD    SYSOUT=A
//GO.STEPCAT  DD    DSN=VSAM.CATALOG,DISP=SHR
//GO.MASTER   DD    DSN=VSAM.FILE,DISP=SHR
//GO.TRANS    DD    *
   .
     .
       .
/*
//
```

FIGURE 2.13 Accessing a VSAM File

Use of the COBOL SORT

At least three additional DD statements are required to define work areas for the utility sort program. These are assigned the DDnames SORTWK01, SORTWK02, and SORTWK03, as shown in Figure 2.14. (Additional work areas may also be specified as defined in a vendor reference manual.) A DD statement is *not* specified for SORT-WORK-FILE (assigned to UT-S-SORTWORK) as it is only a temporary (i.e., a work) file.

In addition to the sort work areas, a DD statement for SYSOUT is required for the messages provided by the SORT program. A SORTLIB DD statement is sometimes required to define the location of modules called by the SORT utility. Figure 2.14 also contains DD statements for the input and output files associated with the SORT statement.

```
//GRAUER        JOB  (Acct Information),CLASS=A
//              EXEC COBVCLG,PARM.COB=(PMAP,DMAP)
//COB.SYSIN     DD   *
   .
     .
       .

        ENVIRONMENT DIVISION.
            SELECT SORT-WORK-FILE
                ASSIGN TO UT-S-SORTWORK.
            SELECT INCOMING-FILE
                ASSIGN TO UT-S-INPUT.
            SELECT ORDERED-FILE
                ASSIGN TO UT-S-OUTPUT.
   .
     .
       .

        PROCEDURE DIVISION.
            SORT SORT-WORK-FILE ASCENDING KEY...
                USING INCOMING-FILE
                GIVING ORDERED-FILE.
   .
     .
       .
//GO.SYSOUT     DD   SYSOUT=A
//SORTWK01      DD   UNIT=SYSDA,SPACE=(TRK,5)
//SORTWK02      DD   UNIT=SYSDA,SPACE=(TRK,5)
//SORTWK03      DD   UNIT=SYSDA,SPACE=(TRK,5)
//SORTLIB       DD   DSN=SYS1.SORTLIB,DISP=SHR
//INPUT         DD   DSN=UM.MASTER.FILE,DISP=SHR
//OUTPUT        DD   DSN=SORTED.FILE,DISP=(,CATLG),
//       SPACE=(TRK,5),UNIT=SYSDA
//
```

FIGURE 2.14 Use of the COBOL SORT Verb

Summary

This chapter was dedicated to the needs of the COBOL programmer. The author has emphasized repeatedly that working knowledge of JCL is in the realm of the programmer's responsibility, and further, that such knowledge is not difficult to achieve.

The chapter began with a review of typical DD statements, and an introduction to special DDnames. It discussed the concepts of a partitioned data set, a generation data group, and a concatenated data set. Seven job-streams were presented to support typical COBOL situations. As a final pedagogic aid and review, we offer the following list of JCL *errors to avoid:*

1. *Improper format for EXEC statement:* The syntactical rules for this statement are simple: // in columns 1 and 2 and a blank in

column 3, if the job step is unnamed. If the step is named, the step name begins in column 3 and is followed by a blank, then the word EXEC. Valid and invalid statements are:

```
  Valid:   // EXEC COBVCLG
  Valid:   //STEP1 EXEC PGM=PROGA
Invalid:   //EXEC COBVCLG
Invalid:   // STEP1 EXEC PGM=PROGA
```

2. *Improper format for JOB statement.* The job name begins in column 3, followed by a blank and the word JOB. (Other information is installation dependent and follows JOB.) Examples are:

```
  Valid:   //JONES JOB
Invalid:   // JONES JOB
```

3. *Invalid continuation.* The line to be continued (i.e., the first line) must end on a comma in or before column 72. Continued lines begin with // in columns 1 and 2, a space in 3, then continue anywhere in columns 4 through 16.

4. *Misspelled procedure and/or program name.* These names are chosen for uniqueness, not necessarily mnemonic significance. IBM utility program names are especially difficult to remember. Copy the name correctly and completely.

5. *Misspelled keyword parameters.* Misspellings, for whatever reason, are far too common. BLKSIZE, LRECL, DSORG, LABEL, CATLG, SHR, and MSGLEVEL are *correct* spellings of frequently abused parameters.

6. *Omission of // at end of jobstream.* While not technically an error, it can have serious consequences. Omission of the null (//) statement means that subsequent statements can be taken as part of your jobstream. Thus, if the job after yours contains a JOB card JCL error, your job may "flush" through no fault of your own.

7. *Omission of a positional parameter or associated comma.* Positional parameters derive their meaning from a specified order. If omitted, their absence must be indicated by a comma.

8. *Incorrect order of DD statements.* This occurs frequently when adding or overriding statements in a proc. In COBVCLG, for example, the COB step precedes the GO step. Thus, all DD statements for the former (e.g., //COB.SYSIN DD *) must precede those of the latter (e.g., //GO.SYSIN DD *). Procedure overrides are discussed in Chapter 3.

9. *Omission of a DD statement.* Every file, in every job step, requires a DD statement. Make sure that you have them all.

10. *Incorrect or omitted DSN for an input file.* The purpose of the DSN parameter in the DD statement is to identify a data set. If this parameter is left out or misspelled, the system will not be able to locate the proper file on which to operate.

11. *Incorrect or omitted VOL=SER parameter.* This parameter causes a message to be printed informing the operator of the proper volume. Incorrect specification makes it difficult for the operator to comply with the request. The parameter is not needed for a catalogued data set.

12. *Inadvertent blank on a JCL statement.* Comments may appear on *any* JCL statement and begin one space after the last operand. If one accidentally omits a comma, subsequent fields are treated as comments. Consider the statement:

```
// EXEC COBVCLG PARM.COB='LIB'
```

The probable intent is to specify the LIB option for the compiler. However, omission of the comma following COBVCLG causes the PARM information to be treated as comments. This is not a JCL error in the sense that syntax has been violated, but an error none the less.

13. *Going past column 72.* This error can cause any of the above, as well as a host of others. JCL statements must end before column 72. This error is hard to catch because all 80 columns are listed, although not interpreted by the JCL reader.

TRUE/FALSE EXERCISES

1. DSN=MASTER.FILE(0) is an invalid data set specification.

2. DSN=MASTER.FILE(+1) refers to the current version of the data set MASTER.FILE.

3. Generation data groups can only be used for direct access files.

4. The same COBOL SELECT statement can be used for a sequential file if it is stored on tape or disk.

5. If an existing data set is catalogued, then DSN and DISP are the only required DD parameters.

6. If the COPY statement is used in a COBOL program, a SYSLIB statement is required in the JCL.

7. In a jobstream containing both a main and a subprogram, the subprogram comes first.

8. The EXEC statements for a main and subprogram will typically invoke the same procedure.

9. The DD statements for the main program will precede the EXEC statement for the subprogram.

10. JCL statements originating in a procedure begin with XX on the system message output.

11. SYSUDUMP is a DDname with preassigned meaning.

12. A partitioned data set contains one or more sequential data sets.

13. A COBOL COPY library is typically established as a partitioned data set.

14. Every DD statement must have a DDname.

15. Every EXEC statement must have a name.

16. JOBCAT and JOBLIB are equivalent DDnames.

17. A STEPLIB DD statement is required if a COBOL SORT statement is used.

18. Output from the COBOL compiler will *always* contain Procedure and Data Division maps.

19. The SYSUDUMP DD statement does not require a corresponding COBOL SELECT.

20. A COBOL sort-work file need not have a corresponding DD statement.

21. The same ISAM file may contain both cylinder and independent overflow areas.

22. The index, prime, and overflow areas of an ISAM file must all reside on the same volume.

23. Concatenated data sets omit the DD name on all DD statements after the first.

24. VSAM data sets may be optionally catalogued.

25. The SPACE and DCB parameters function identically for ISAM and VSAM.

26. DISP=(NEW,CATLG) is applicable to VSAM.

27. The DCB parameter is not used with a VSAM data set.

PROBLEMS

1. Figure 2.15 contains many typical JCL errors. Examine the error messages, and make the necessary corrections.

```
 1    //JSC$2871 JOB (MAS526),JACKIE
 2    // EXEC PGM=ERRORS
 3    //DD1    DD DSN=UNIVERSITY.OF.MIAMI.STUDENT.DATA.SECOND.SEMESTER,DISP=SHR
 4    //DD3    DD DISP=(NEW,KEEP),DCB=(LREC=80,BLKSIZE=80)
 5    // STEP2 EXEC PGM=PROBLEMS
 6    //DD4    DD DSN=ABC,DEF,DISP=SHR
 7    //DD5    DD DISP=(NEW,PASS),SPACE(TRK,(1,1),CONTIG),DISP=(NEW,CATLG)
 8    //DD6    DD*
 9    //DD7    DD SYSOUT=A
10    //EXEC    PGM=WOES
11    //DD8    DD UNIT=SYSDA,SPACE=(TRK,(6,1),CONTIG),DISP=(NEW,CATLG),
12    //DD9    DD UNIT=DISK,SPACE=(TRK,(1,1),RLSE),DISP=OLD,KEEP
13    //DD10   DD UNIT=DISK,SPACE=(CYL,(2,5))
14    //DD11   SYSOUT=A
15    //DD12   DD DSN=NEW.DISK.FILE,UNIT=SYSDA,DISP=(NEW,CATLG),
      //          SPACE=(TRK,(3,2) )
16    //DD13   DD DSN=NEW.FILE.ON.DISK1,UNIT=TAPE,LABEL=(,SL),VOL=SER=UM0100,DISP=SHR
17    //DD14   DD SPACE=(TRK,5)),UNIT=SYSDA,DCB=LRECL=80
18    //DD15   DD DSN=SDB.DATA,DCB=(LRECL=80,BLKSIZE=240),RECFM=FB
19    //DD16   DD DSN=&&SDB.MASTERFL,DISP=(NEW,PASS),SPACE=(TRK,(8))
20    //DD17   DD DCB=(LRECL=80,BLKSIZE=160),UNIT=3350,SPACE=(CYL,(3,1))
21    //DD18   DD DISP=(NEW,PASS),VOLSER=UH0050,UNIT=TAPE,LABEL=(,AL)
22    //      EXEC PGM HELP
```

STMT NO. MESSAGE

```
 3    IEF618I OPERAND FIELD DOES NOT TERMINATE IN COMMA OR BLANK
 3    IEF621I EXPECTED CONTINUATION NOT RECEIVED
 4    IEF630I UNIDENTIFIED KEYWORD IN THE DCB FIELD
 5    IEF605I UNIDENTIFIED OPERATION FIELD
 6    IEF632I FORMAT ERROR IN THE DSNAME FIELD
 7    IEF632I FORMAT ERROR IN THE DISP FIELD
 8    IEF605I UNIDENTIFIED OPERATION FIELD
 9    IEF630I UNIDENTIFIED KEYWORD ON THE DD STATEMENT
10    IEF605I UNIDENTIFIED OPERATION FIELD
11    IEF621I EXPECTED CONTINUATION NOT RECEIVED
12    IEF632I FORMAT ERROR IN THE DISP FIELD
13    IEF622I UNBALANCED PARENTHESIS ON THE DD STATEMENT
14    IEF605I UNIDENTIFIED OPERATION FIELD
15    IEF622I UNBALANCED PARENTHESIS ON THE DD STATEMENT
16    IEF632I FORMAT ERROR IN THE SER SUBPARAMETER OF THE VOLUME FIELD
16    IEF621I EXPECTED CONTINUATION NOT RECEIVED
17    IEF622I UNBALANCED PARENTHESIS IN THE SPACE FIELD
18    IEF630I UNIDENTIFIED KEYWORD IN THE BLKSIZE SUBPARAMETER OF THE DCB FIELD
19    IEF624I INCORRECT USE OF PERIOD IN THE DSNAME FIELD
20    IEF630I UNIDENTIFIED KEYWORD IN THE LRECL SUBPARAMETER OF THE DCB FIELD
21    IEF630I UNIDENTIFIED KEYWORD IN THE DISP FIELD
22    IEF612I PROCEDURE NOT FOUND
```

FIGURE 2.15 JCL Listing for Problem 1

2. Figure 2.5 and the associated discussion focused on the COBOL procedure COBVCLG, but the concepts apply equally well to Assembler programs. Accordingly, answer the following questions with respect to Figure 2.16.

(a) How many steps are there in the procedure ASMVCLG?

(b) What are the step names?

```
1    //JSC$2766 JOB (MAS499),JACKIE,MSGLEVEL=(1,1)
2    //STEP1     EXEC ASMVCLG
3    XXASMVCLG  PROC MAC='SYS1.MACLIB',MAC1='SYS1.MACLIB',OUT=R
4    XXASM      EXEC PGM=IFOX00,PARM=OBJ
5    XXSYSLIB   DD   DSN=&MAC,DISP=SHR
6    XX         DD   DSN=&MAC1,DISP=SHR
7    XXSYSUT1   DD   DSN=&&SYSUT1,UNIT=SYSDA,SPACE=(1700,(600,100))
8    XXSYSUT2   DD   DSN=&&SYSUT2,UNIT=SYSDA,SPACE=(1700,(300,50))
9    XXSYSUT3   DD   DSN=&&SYSUT3,UNIT=SYSDA,SPACE=(1700,(300,50))
10   XXSYSPRINT DD   SYSOUT=&OUT,DCB=BLKSIZE=1089
11   XXSYSPUNCH DD   DUMMY
12   XXSYSGO    DD   DSN=&&OBJSET,UNIT=SYSSQ,SPACE=(80,(200,50)),
     XX              DISP=(MOD,PASS)
13   //ASM.SYSIN DD  DSN=MEN.PGM.JSC.RTG(ASMBLER),DISP=SHR
14   XXLKED     EXEC PGM=IEWL,PARM=(XREF,LET,LIST,NCAL),
     XX              COND=(8,LT,ASM)
15   XXSYSLIN   DD   DSN=&&OBJSET,DISP=(OLD,DELETE)
16   XXSYSLMOD  DD   DSN=&&GOSET(GO),UNIT=SYSDA,SPACE=(1024,(50,20,1)),
     XX              DISP=(MOD,PASS)
17   XXSYSUT1   DD   DSN=&&SYSUT1,UNIT=SYSDA,SPACE=(1024,(50,20))
18   XXSYSPRINT DD   SYSOUT=&OUT,DCB=(RECFM=FB,LRECL=121,BLKSIZE=1210)
19   XXGO       EXEC PGM=*.LKED.SYSLMOD,COND=((8,LT,ASM),(4,LT,LKED))
20   //GO.EMPIN DD *
21   //GO.REPTOUT DD SYSOUT=R
22   //GO.SYSUDUMP DD SYSOUT=R
```

```
STMT NO. MESSAGE

    5       IEF653I SUBSTITUTION JCL - DSN=SYS1.MACLIB,DISP=SHR
    6       IEF653I SUBSTITUTION JCL - DSN=SYS1.MACLIB,DISP=SHR
   10       IEF653I SUBSTITUTION JCL - SYSOUT=R,DCB=BLKSIZE=1089
   18       IEF653I SUBSTITUTION JCL - SYSOUT=R,DCB=(RECFM=FB,LRECL=121,BLKSIZE=1210)
IEF236I ALLOC. FOR JSC$2766 ASM STEP1
IEF237I 110   ALLOCATED TO SYSLIB
IEF237I 110   ALLOCATED TO
IEF237I 135   ALLOCATED TO SYSUT1
IEF237I 111   ALLOCATED TO SYSUT2
IEF237I 131   ALLOCATED TO SYSUT3
IEF237I JES2  ALLOCATED TO SYSPRINT
IEF237I DMY   ALLOCATED TO SYSPUNCH
IEF237I 133   ALLOCATED TO SYSGO
IEF237I 113   ALLOCATED TO SYSIN
IEF237I 113   ALLOCATED TO SYS00267
IEF142I JSC$2766 ASM STEP1 - STEP WAS EXECUTED - COND CODE 0000
IEF285I   SYS1.MACLIB                                  KEPT
IEF285I   VOL SER NOS= UMF110.
IEF285I   SYS1.MACLIB                                  KEPT
IEF285I   VOL SER NOS= UMF110.
IEF285I   SYS83015.T135216.RA000.JSC$2766.SYSUT1       DELETED
IEF285I   VOL SER NOS= UMF135.
IEF285I   SYS83015.T135216.RA000.JSC$2766.SYSUT2       DELETED
IEF285I   VOL SER NOS= UMF111.
IEF285I   SYS83015.T135216.RA000.JSC$2766.SYSUT3       DELETED
IEF285I   VOL SER NOS= UMF131.
IEF285I   JES2.JOB01773.S00102                         SYSOUT
IEF285I   SYS83015.T135216.RA000.JSC$2766.OBJSET       PASSED
IEF285I   VOL SER NOS= UMF133.
IEF285I   MEN.PGM.JSC.RTG                              KEPT
IEF285I   VOL SER NOS= UMF113.
IEF285I   SYSCTLG.VUMF113                              KEPT
IEF285I   VOL SER NOS= UMF113.
IEF373I STEP /ASM    / START 83015.1352
IEF374I STEP /ASM    / STOP  83015.1352 CPU    0MIN 04.94SEC SRB
```

FIGURE 2.16 System Messages for ASMVCLG Procedure

```
IEF236I ALLOC. FOR JSC$2766 LKED STEP1
IEF237I 133   ALLOCATED TO SYSLIN
IEF237I 135   ALLOCATED TO SYSLMOD
IEF237I 111   ALLOCATED TO SYSUT1
IEF237I JES2 ALLOCATED TO SYSPRINT
IEF142I JSC$2766 LKED STEP1 - STEP WAS EXECUTED - COND CODE 0000
IEF285I    SYS83015.T135216.RA000.JSC$2766.OBJSET        DELETED
IEF285I    VOL SER NOS= UMF133.
IEF285I    SYS83015.T135216.RA000.JSC$2766.GOSET         PASSED
IEF285I    VOL SER NOS= UMF135.
IEF285I    SYS83015.T135216.RA000.JSC$2766.SYSUT1        DELETED
IEF285I    VOL SER NOS= UMF111.
IEF285I    JES2.JOB01773.S00103                          SYSOUT
IEF373I STEP /LKED    / START 83015.1352
IEF374I STEP /LKED    / STOP  83015.1352 CPU    0MIN 00.29SEC SRB
IEF236I ALLOC. FOR JSC$2766 GO STEP1
IEF237I 135   ALLOCATED TO PGM=*.DD
IEF237I JES2 ALLOCATED TO EMPIN
IEF237I JES2 ALLOCATED TO REPTOUT
IEF237I JES2 ALLOCATED TO SYSUDUMP
IEF142I JSC$2766 GO STEP1 - STEP WAS EXECUTED - COND CODE 4120
IEF285I    SYS83015.T135216.RA000.JSC$2766.GOSET         KEPT
IEF285I    VOL SER NOS= UMF135.
IEF285I    JES2.JOB01773.SI0101                          SYSIN
IEF285I    JES2.JOB01773.S00104                          SYSOUT
IEF285I    JES2.JOB01773.S00105                          SYSOUT
IEF373I STEP /GO      / START 83015.1352
IEF374I STEP /GO      / STOP  83015.1352 CPU    0MIN 00.10SEC SRB
IEF237I 135   ALLOCATED TO SYS00001
IEF285I    SYS83015.T135236.RA000.JSC$2766.R0000001      KEPT
IEF285I    VOL SER NOS= UMF135.
IEF285I    SYS83015.T135216.RA000.JSC$2766.GOSET         DELETED
IEF285I    VOL SER NOS= UMF135.
IEF375I JOB /JSC$2766/ START 83015.1352
IEF376I JOB /JSC$2766/ STOP  83015.1352 CPU    0MIN 05.33SEC SRB
```

FIGURE 2.16 (Continued)

(c) Will the LKED step be executed if the ASM step returns a condition code of 4, 8, 12?

(d) Which DD statements are included in the procedure for the ASM step?

(e) Are any of the DD statements in part (d) concatenated?

(f) What is the name of the program executed by the ASM step?

(g) Does the ASMVCLG procedure execute any programs which are likely to be executed in the COBVCLG procedure as well?

(h) What is the name of the output data set produced by the ASM step, and which is input to the LKED step?

(i) What is the name of the program executed in the GO step? Where did this program originate?

(j) What condition codes were returned by the various steps in the ASMVCLG procedure?

(k) Which JCL statements originated in the jobstream rather than the procedure?

3. The jobstream of Figure 2.11 depicted a main program and a *single* subroutine. Describe the necessary modifications to accommodate a second

called program, a third, and a fourth. What are the shortcomings of this approach when only one of the programs is modified?

4. Write the necessary JCL to compile, link, and execute a COBOL program for sequential file maintenance. Your jobstream should accommodate:

   (a) A condensed listing, the FLOW and STATE options, and a dump in the event of an ABEND.
   (b) An old master file stored as the first file on tape number USR456, with DSN=OLD.MASTER.FILE.
   (c) A transaction file coming from cards.
   (d) A new master file going to tape number USR321. Use appropriate DSN and any other parameters. Catalog this file.
   (e) Show all COBOL SELECT statements.

5. Write the necessary JCL to compile, link, and execute a COBOL program for sequential file maintenance. Your jobstream should accommodate:

   (a) The block size of the new master file is to be entered in the JCL. The blocking factor is 10 and the logical record size is 100 bytes.
   (b) Allow 15 tracks as the primary allocation for the new master and two tracks as the secondary allocation. The output device is a 3350.
   (c) Use the COBOL SELECT statements from problem 4. Part (c) also applies.
   (d) Use the data set names OLD.DISK.MASTER.FILE and NEW.DISK. MASTER.FILE for the old and new master, respectively. Both are on VOL=SER=USR001, and both data sets are not catalogued.
   (e) Use generation data groups.

6. Write the complete JCL to compile, link, and execute a COBOL program using the SORT verb. In particular:

   (a) The INPUT PROCEDURE/OUTPUT PROCEDURE is used. The COBOL program will read incoming records from tape (use appropriate parameters), and output will consist only of a printed report.
   (b) Show COBOL SELECT statements.
   (c) The COBOL program itself is stored as the member SORT. in the PDS COBOL.SOURCE.LIB.

7. Answer the following questions pertaining to compilation and execution of a subroutine, with respect to Figure 2.17:

   (a) How many *procedures* are involved?
   (b) What is the *data set name* associated with the COB.SYSLIN statement in line 15? In line 30?
   (c) What is the significance of the data sets in part (b)? Explain why the associated disposition parameters *must* be (MOD,PASS) rather than (NEW,PASS).

```
1    //JSC$3371 JOB (MAS526),JACKIE
2    //          EXEC COBVC
3    XXCOBVC PROC OUT=R
4    XXCOB EXEC PGM=IKFCBL00,PARM=(LOAD,SUPMAP,LIB,'LINECNT=60',
     XX            'SXREF','PMAP','DMAP','STATE','FLOW=10','NOSEQ',
     XX            'BUF=63922','SIZE=217088')
5    XXSTEPLIB  DD DSN=SYS2.LINKLIB,DISP=SHR
6    XX         DD DSN=SYS1.COBLIB,DISP=SHR
7    XXSYSPRINT DD SYSOUT=&OUT
8    XXSYSPUNCH DD DUMMY
9    //COB.SYSLIB  DD DSN=JESSICA.RTG.COBOL,DISP=SHR
     X/SYSLIB     DD DUMMY
10   XXSYSUT1   DD UNIT=SYSDA,SPACE=(1024,(120,120)),DSN=&&SYSUT1
11   XXSYSUT2   DD UNIT=SYSDA,SPACE=(1024,(120,120)),DSN=&&SYSUT2
12   XXSYSUT3   DD UNIT=SYSDA,SPACE=(1024,(120,120)),DSN=&&SYSUT3
13   XXSYSUT4   DD UNIT=SYSDA,SPACE=(1024,(120,120)),DSN=&&SYSUT4
14   XXSYSUT5   DD UNIT=SYSDA,SPACE=(1024,(120,120)),DSN=&&SYSUT5
15   XXSYSLIN   DD DISP=(MOD,PASS),DSN=&&OBJ,UNIT=DISK,
     XX            SPACE=(3040,(40,40)),
     XX            DCB=(BLKSIZE=3040,LRECL=80,RECFM=FBS,BUFNO=1)
16   //COB.SYSIN   DD DSN=MEN.PGM.JSC.RTG(MAIN),DISP=SHR
17   //          EXEC COBVCLG
18   XXCOBVCLG PROC OUT=R
19   XXCOB EXEC PGM=IKFCBL00,PARM=(LOAD,SUPMAP,LIB,'LINECNT=60',
     XX            'SXREF','PMAP','DMAP','STATE','FLOW=10','NOSEQ',
     XX            'BUF=63922','SIZE=217088')
20   XXSTEPLIB  DD DSN=SYS2.LINKLIB,DISP=SHR
21   XX         DD DSN=SYS1.COBLIB,DISP=SHR
22   XXSYSPRINT DD SYSOUT=&OUT
23   XXSYSPUNCH DD DUMMY
24   //COB.SYSLIB  DD DSN=JESSICA.RTG.COBOL,DISP=SHR
     X/SYSLIB     DD DUMMY
25   XXSYSUT1   DD UNIT=3350,SPACE=(1024,(120,120)),DSN=&&SYSUT1
26   XXSYSUT2   DD UNIT=3350,SPACE=(1024,(120,120)),DSN=&&SYSUT2
27   XXSYSUT3   DD UNIT=3350,SPACE=(1024,(120,120)),DSN=&&SYSUT3
28   XXSYSUT4   DD UNIT=3350,SPACE=(1024,(120,120)),DSN=&&SYSUT4
29   XXSYSUT5   DD UNIT=3350,SPACE=(1024,(120,120)),DSN=&&SYSUT5
30   XXSYSLIN   DD DSN=&&OBJ,DISP=(MOD,PASS),UNIT=3350,
     XX            SPACE=(3040,(40,40)),
     XX            DCB=(BLKSIZE=3040,LRECL=80,RECFM=FBS,BUFNO=1)
31   //COB.SYSIN   DD DSN=JESSICA.RTG.COBOL(SUBRTN1),DISP=SHR
32   XXLKED EXEC PGM=HEWL,PARM='LIST,XREF,LET,MAP',COND=(5,LT,COB)
33   XXSYSLIN   DD DSN=&&OBJ,DISP=(OLD,DELETE)
34   XXSYSLMOD  DD DSN=&&LOD(X),DISP=(,PASS),UNIT=3350,DCB=BUFNO=1,
     XX            SPACE=(CYL,(1,1,1))
35   XXSYSLIB   DD DSN=SYS1.COBLIB,DISP=SHR
36   XXSYSUT1   DD UNIT=3350,SPACE=(1024,(120,120)),DCB=BUFNO=1,
     XX            DSN=&&SYSUT1
37   XXSYSPRINT DD SYSOUT=&OUT
38   XXGO EXEC PGM=*.LKED.SYSLMOD,COND=((5,LT,COB),(5,LT,LKED))
39   XXSTEPLIB  DD DSN=SYS1.COBLIB,DISP=SHR
40   XXSYSOUT   DD SYSOUT=&OUT
41   XXSYSOUC   DD SYSOUT=&OUT
42   XXSYSCOUNT DD SYSOUT=&OUT
43   XXSYSDBOUT DD SYSOUT=&OUT
44   //GO.SORTLIB   DD DSN=SYS1.SORTLIB,DISP=SHR
45   //GO.SORTWORK  DD SPACE=(TRK,(1,1)),UNIT=DISK
46   //GO.SORTWK01  DD SPACE=(TRK,(1,1)),UNIT=DISK
47   //GO.SORTWK02  DD SPACE=(TRK,(1,1)),UNIT=DISK
48   //GO.SORTWK03  DD SPACE=(TRK,(1,1)),UNIT=DISK
49   //GO.SORTMSG   DD SYSOUT=R
50   //GO.COURSE    DD *
51   //GO.PRINT     DD SYSOUT=R
52   //GO.STUD      DD *
```

FIGURE 2.17 System Messages for Problem 7

(d) What is the name of the data set in line 33? How is it related to the data sets of part b? Explain the disposition parameters (OLD, DELETE) in line 33.

(e) What is the significance of the SYSLMOD DD statement of line 34? What is its associated DSN? DISP?

(f) Could the PGM parameter of line 38 have been coded differently? How?

Procedures

This chapter covers procedures in detail. We begin by reviewing general concepts via the commonly used COBVCLG procedure. We show how to *add* new statements and/or *override* existing ones. We stress the *order* of DD statements in the submitted jobstream and introduce *symbolic parameters* as a means of simplifying overrides. The chapter concludes with the PROC and PEND statements, and their use in testing procedures *instream*.

THE EFFECTIVE JOBSTREAM

The procedure concept combines a submitted jobstream with catalogued JCL statements to produce an effective jobstream. This approach allows many individuals to have access to the same library procedures, and simultaneously reduces the size and complexity of the submitted jobstream. The situation is shown in Figure 3.1.

```
//COBVCLG PROC OUT=R
//COB EXEC PGM=IKFCBL00,PARM=(LOAD,SUPMAP,LIB,'LINECNT=60',
//             'SXREF','PMAP','DMAP','STATE','FLOW=10','NOSEQ',
//             'BUF=63922','SIZE=217088')
//STEPLIB  DD DSN=SYS2.LINKLIB,DISP=SHR
//         DD DSN=SYS1.COBLIB,DISP=SHR
//SYSPRINT DD SYSOUT=&OUT
//SYSPUNCH DD DUMMY              ┌─── SYSLIB statement in the procedure
//SYSLIB   DD DUMMY
//SYSUT1   DD UNIT=3350,SPACE=(1024,(120,120)),DSN=&&SYSUT1
//SYSUT2   DD UNIT=3350,SPACE=(1024,(120,120)),DSN=&&SYSUT2
//SYSUT3   DD UNIT=3350,SPACE=(1024,(120,120)),DSN=&&SYSUT3
//SYSUT4   DD UNIT=3350,SPACE=(1024,(120,120)),DSN=&&SYSUT4
//SYSUT5   DD UNIT=3350,SPACE=(1024,(120,120)),DSN=&&SYSUT5
//SYSLIN   DD DSN=&&OBJ,DISP=(MOD,PASS),UNIT=3350,
//             SPACE=(3040,(40,40)),
//             DCB=(BLKSIZE=3040,LRECL=80,RECFM=FBS,BUFNO=1)
//LKED EXEC PGM=HEWL,PARM='LIST,XREF,LET,MAP',COND=(5,LT,COB)
//SYSLIN   DD DSN=&&OBJ,DISP=(OLD,DELETE)
//SYSLMOD  DD DSN=&&LOD(K),DISP=(,PASS),UNIT=3350,DCB=BUFNO=1,
//             SPACE=(CYL,(1,1,1))
//SYSLIB   DD DSN=SYS1.COBLIB,DISP=SHR
//SYSUT1   DD UNIT=3350,SPACE=(1024,(120,120)),DCB=BUFNO=1,
//             DSN=&&SYSUT1
//SYSPRINT DD SYSOUT=&OUT
//GO EXEC PGM=*.LKED.SYSLMOD,COND=((5,LT,COB),(5,LT,LKED))
//STEPLIB  DD DSN=SYS1.COBLIB,DISP=SHR
//SYSOUT   DD SYSOUT=&OUT
//SYSOUC   DD SYSOUT=&OUT
//SYSCOUNT DD SYSOUT=&OUT
//SYSDBOUT DD SYSOUT=&OUT
```

FIGURE 3.1a The COBVCLG Procedure

```
                         ┌─── SYSLIB statement in the submitted jobstream
//JSC$3603  / JOB (MAS526),JACKIE,MSGLEVEL=(1,1)
//STEP1    /   EXEC COBVCLG
//COB.SYSLIB   DD DSN=MEN.PGM.JSC.RTG,DISP=SHR
//COB.SYSIN    DD DSN=MEN.PGM.JSC.RTG(FILEDUMP),DISP=SHR
//GO.FILEOUT   DD SYSOUT=R
//GO.SYSUDUMP  DD SYSOUT=R
//GO.FILEIN    DD *
```

FIGURE 3.1b Submitted Jobstream (Does not show data)

```
 1  //JSC$3603 JOB (MAS526),JACKIE,MSGLEVEL=(1,1)
 2  //STEP1       EXEC COBVCLG
 3  XXCOBVCLG PROC OUT=R
 4  XXCOB EXEC PGM=IKFCBL00,PARM=(LOAD,SUPMAP,LIB,'LINECNT=60',
    XX            'SXREF','PMAP','DMAP','STATE','FLOW=10','NOSEQ',
    XX            'BUF=63922','SIZE=217088')
 5  XXSTEPLIB  DD DSN=SYS2.LINKLIB,DISP=SHR
 6  XX         DD DSN=SYS1.COBLIB,DISP=SHR
 7  XXSYSPRINT DD SYSOUT=&OUT              ┌─── SYSLIB statement is overridden
 8  XXSYSPUNCH DD DUMMY
 9  //COB.SYSLIB   DD DSN=MEN.PGM.JSC.RTG,DISP=SHR
    X/SYSLIB    DD DUMMY
10  XXSYSUT1   DD UNIT=3350,SPACE=(1024,(120,120)),DSN=&&SYSUT1
11  XXSYSUT2   DD UNIT=3350,SPACE=(1024,(120,120)),DSN=&&SYSUT2
12  XXSYSUT3   DD UNIT=3350,SPACE=(1024,(120,120)),DSN=&&SYSUT3
13  XXSYSUT4   DD UNIT=3350,SPACE=(1024,(120,120)),DSN=&&SYSUT4
14  XXSYSUT5   DD UNIT=3350,SPACE=(1024,(120,120)),DSN=&&SYSUT5
15  XXSYSLIN   DD DSN=&&OBJ,DISP=(MOD,PASS),UNIT=3350,
```

FIGURE 3.1c Effective Jobstream

60

```
        XX              SPACE=(3040,(40,40)),
        XX              DCB=(BLKSIZE=3040,LRECL=80,RECFM=FBS,BUFNO=1)
16      //COB.SYSIN     DD DSN=MEN.PGM.JSC.RTG(FILEDUMP),DISP=SHR
17      XXLKED EXEC PGM=HEWL,PARM='LIST,XREF,LET,MAP',COND=(5,LT,COB)
18      XXSYSLIN    DD DSN=&&OBJ,DISP=(OLD,DELETE)
19      XXSYSLMOD   DD DSN=&&LOD(X),DISP=(,PASS),UNIT=3350,DCB=BUFNO=1,
        XX              SPACE=(CYL,(1,1,1))
20      XXSYSLIB    DD DSN=SYS1.COBLIB,DISP=SHR
21      XXSYSUT1    DD UNIT=3350,SPACE=(1024,(120,120)),DCB=BUFNO=1,
        XX              DSN=&&SYSUT1
22      XXSYSPRINT DD SYSOUT=&OUT
23      XXGO EXEC PGM=*.LKED.SYSLMOD,COND=((5,LT,COB),(5,LT,LKED))
24      XXSTEPLIB   DD DSN=SYS1.COBLIB,DISP=SHR
25      XXSYSOUT    DD SYSOUT=&OUT
26      XXSYSOUC    DD SYSOUT=&OUT
27      XXSYSCOUNT DD SYSOUT=&OUT
28      XXSYSDBOUT DD SYSOUT=&OUT
29      //GO.FILEOUT    DD SYSOUT=R
30      //GO.SYSUDUMP   DD SYSOUT=R
31      //GO.FILEIN     DD *

STMT NO. MESSAGE

 7      IEF653I SUBSTITUTION JCL - SYSOUT=R
22      IEF653I SUBSTITUTION JCL - SYSOUT=R
25      IEF653I SUBSTITUTION JCL - SYSOUT=R
26      IEF653I SUBSTITUTION JCL - SYSOUT=R
27      IEF653I SUBSTITUTION JCL - SYSOUT=R
28      IEF653I SUBSTITUTION JCL - SYSOUT=R
```

FIGURE 3.1c (Continued)

Figure 3.1a contains the procedure COBVCLG as it exists in a procedure library, Figure 3.1b shows the submitted jobstream, and Figure 3.1c depicts the effective jobstream. JCL statements in Figure 3.1c begin with //, XX, or X/. // and XX indicate that the JCL statement originated in the jobstream and procedure, respectively. X/ implies that a statement from the procedure has been overridden by a jobstream statement with the same name.

Statement 9 in Figure 3.1c originated in the submitted jobstream (Figure 3.1a), as indicated by the //. It is followed immediately by an unnumbered statement, beginning with X/, indicating that the former is overridden. In other words, since the procedure JCL and the submitted jobstream both contain a DD statement for SYSLIB, the procedure information is *replaced* by that of the jobstream. Unfortunately, the system messages do not explicitly state, "DD statement overridden". Instead, the submitted statement is followed in the system messages by the overridden statement, and the programmer is left to his or her own devices to realize what happened.

ADDING DD STATEMENTS

DD statements, not appearing in a catalogued procedure, can be *added* to the effective jobstream; e.g., //COB.SYSIN DD * is often included in the submitted JCL to invoke COBVCLG. (DD * may *never* appear in a procedure as the asterisk implies that the file follows immediately in the jobstream. Inclusion of DD * would mean that the procedure contained data, an impossible situation.)

Figure 3.1*b* contains four DD statements which do not appear in the procedure JCL of Figure 3.1*a*. These are COB.SYSIN, GO.FILEIN, GO.FILEOUT, and GO.SYSUDUMP. These two figures are combined to produce an effective jobstream in Figure 3.1*c*.

New DD statements appear *after* the overriding statements for that step. For example, COB.SYSIN DD * is a new DD statement for the COB step of Figure 3.1*a*. It appears after any overriding DD statements for the COB step but *before* any overriding DD statements for the subsequent LKED and/or GO steps. *New DD statements are added in their entirety*, whereas existing DD statements are modified parameter by parameter. (All changes are *temporary* and apply only to the particular run and not to the procedure in general.)

Existing DD statements can also have individual parameters overridden, as explained in the next section.

PARAMETER OVERRIDES

DD statement parameters in an existing procedure are overridden when the name of a submitted DD statement matches the name on an existing procedure statement. *Changes are made on a parameter by parameter basis. The order of parameters on the submitted statement is immaterial.* (This does *not* imply that the order of the DD statements themselves is unimportant.)

Parameters are *overridden* if they match; e.g., if UNIT appears on *both* the submitted and procedure statements, the UNIT parameter on the submitted statement *supersedes* the value on the procedure statement. Parameters are *added* to the procedure DD statement if they appear in the submitted jobstream, but not in the procedure. Parameters in existing statements are *nullified* if they appear in the submitted jobstream followed by an equal sign, and a comma (e.g., UNIT=,).

Figure 3.2 should clarify these concepts. The submitted jobstream invokes the procedure EXAMPLE. The effective jobstream for the job SHOWOFF is obtained by combining the catalogued procedure with submitted JCL. Statements in the effective jobstream begin with either //, XX, or X/. (The author has taken some liberty in depicting the overridden statement for DEF. The OS messages would show the submitted statement followed directly by the overridden statement with no modification in either, leaving the reader to determine what happened. Figure 3.2, on the other hand, combines the two into a single statement to reflect the combination.)

```
              Catalogued Procedure
//EXAMPLE PROC
//STEP1 EXEC PGM=FIRST
//ABC DD DSN=DOLPHIN,DISP=SHR
//DEF DD DSN=COLT,UNIT=DISK,
// SPACE=(CYL,5),DISP=(NEW,KEEP)
//STEP2 EXEC PGM=SECOND
//GHI DD SYSOUT=A
```

```
                 Effective Jobstream
//SHOWOFF JOB
// EXEC EXAMPLE
XXEXAMPLE PROC
XXSTEP1 EXEC PGM=FIRST
XXABC DD DSN=DOLPHIN,DISP=SHR
X/DEF DD DSN=COLT,UNIT=TAPE,
X/ DISP=(NEW,KEEP),LABEL=(,SL)
//STEP1.SYSIN DD *
XXSTEP2 EXEC PGM=SECOND
X/GHI DD SYSOUT=B,DCB=BLKSIZE=80
```

```
               Submitted Jobstream
//SHOWOFF JOB
// EXEC EXAMPLE
//STEP1.DEF DD UNIT=TAPE,SPACE=,
// LABEL=(,SL)
//STEP1.SYSIN DD *
//STEP2.GHI DD SYSOUT=B,DCB=BLKSIZE=80
```

FIGURE 3.2 Overriding DD Statements in a Catalogued Procedure

In the effective jobstream of Figure 3.2, the DD statement for ABC is unchanged and begins with XX, indicating that it was pulled directly from the procedure. The DD statement for SYSIN, however, does not appear in the procedure, and is shown with //. The DD statement for DEF illustrates the addition, nullification, and substitution of individual DD parameters. UNIT was changed from DISK (in the original procedure) to TAPE, SPACE was nullified, and LABEL was added.

ORDER OF DD STATEMENTS WITHIN A JOBSTREAM

Figure 3.3a closely resembles the submitted jobstream of Figure 3.1b, the only difference being that the SYSLIB and SYSIN DD statements are reversed. Figure 3.1 ran to a successful end of job (the associated condition codes are not shown), whereas Figure 3.3 ABENDed in the compile step. The latter is due entirely to the fact that the submitted jobstream had its DD statements in *incorrect* sequence.

To explain what happened, consider the rules associated with the order of DD statements within a submitted jobstream:

√ 1. Statements to be overridden must appear in the *same* order in the submitted jobstream as they appear in the procedure.

√ 2. New DD statements; i.e., statements whose DDnames do not appear in the procedure, appear *after* the overriding statements for that step and before the statements for the next step.

√ 3. If the system is somehow confronted with duplicate DDnames for the same step, all occurrences but the first are ignored.

```
            //JSC$3605    JOB (MAS526),JACKIE,MSGLEVEL=(1,1)
            //STEP1       EXEC COBVCLG
            //COB.SYSIN   DD DSN=MEN.PGM.JSC.RTG(FILEDUMP),DISP=SHR
            //COB.SYSLIB  DD DSN=MEN.PGM.JSC.RTG,DISP=SHR
            //GO.FILEOUT  DD SYSOUT=R
            //GO.SYSUDUMP DD SYSOUT=R                     DD statements are out of of order
            //GO.FILEIN   DD *
```

FIGURE 3.3a Submitted Jobstream

```
  1    //JSC$3605 JOB (MAS526),JACKIE,MSGLEVEL=(1,1)
  2    //STEP1         EXEC COBVCLG
  3    XXCOBVCLG PROC OUT=R
  4    XXCOB EXEC PGM=IKFCBL00,PARM=(LOAD,SUPMAP,LIB,'LINECNT=60',
       XX           'SXREF','PMAP','DMAP','STATE','FLOW=10','NOSEQ',
       XX           'BUF=63922','SIZE=217088')
  5    XXSTEPLIB   DD DSN=SYS2.LINKLIB,DISP=SHR
  6    XX          DD DSN=SYS1.COBLIB,DISP=SHR
  7    XXSYSPRINT  DD SYSOUT=&OUT
  8    XXSYSPUNCH  DD DUMMY                        Two occurrences of SYSLIB
  9    XXSYSLIB    DD DUMMY                        DD statement
 10    XXSYSUT1    DD UNIT=3350,SPACE=(1024,(120,120)),DSN=&&SYSUT1
 11    XXSYSUT2    DD UNIT=3350,SPACE=(1024,(120,120)),DSN=&&SYSUT2
 12    XXSYSUT3    DD UNIT=3350,SPACE=(1024,(120,120)),DSN=&&SYSUT3
 13    XXSYSUT4    DD UNIT=3350,SPACE=(1024,(120,120)),DSN=&&SYSUT4
 14    XXSYSUT5    DD UNIT=3350,SPACE=(1024,(120,120)),DSN=&&SYSUT5
 15    XXSYSLIN    DD DSN=&&OBJ,DISP=(MOD,PASS),UNIT=3350,
       XX             SPACE=(3040,(40,40)),
       XX             DCB=(BLKSIZE=3040,LRECL=80,RECFM=FBS,BUFNO=1)
 16    //COB.SYSIN    DD DSN=MEN.PGM.JSC.RTG(FILEDUMP),DISP=SHR
 17    //COB.SYSLIB   DD DSN=MEN.PGM.JSC.RTG,DISP=SHR
 18    XXLKED EXEC PGM=HEWL,PARM='LIST,XREF,LET,MAP',COND=(5,LT,COB)
 19    XXSYSLIN    DD DSN=&&OBJ,DISP=(OLD,DELETE)
 20    XXSYSLMOD   DD DSN=&&LOD(X),DISP=(,PASS),UNIT=3350,DCB=BUFNO=1,
       XX             SPACE=(CYL,(1,1,1))
 21    XXSYSLIB    DD DSN=SYS1.COBLIB,DISP=SHR
 22    XXSYSUT1    DD UNIT=3350,SPACE=(1024,(120,120)),DCB=BUFNO=1,
       XX             DSN=&&SYSUT1
 23    XXSYSPRINT  DD SYSOUT=&OUT
 24    XXGO EXEC PGM=*.LKED.SYSLMOD,COND=((5,LT,COB),(5,LT,LKED))
 25    XXSTEPLIB   DD DSN=SYS1.COBLIB,DISP=SHR
 26    XXSYSOUT    DD SYSOUT=&OUT
 27    XXSYSOUC    DD SYSOUT=&OUT
 28    XXSYSCOUNT  DD SYSOUT=&OUT
 29    XXSYSDBOUT  DD SYSOUT=&OUT
 30    //GO.FILEOUT  DD SYSOUT=R
 31    //GO.SYSUDUMP DD SYSOUT=R
 32    //GO.FILEIN   DD *
```

```
STMT NO. MESSAGE

  7    IEF653I SUBSTITUTION JCL - SYSOUT=R
 23    IEF653I SUBSTITUTION JCL - SYSOUT=R
 26    IEF653I SUBSTITUTION JCL - SYSOUT=R
 27    IEF653I SUBSTITUTION JCL - SYSOUT=R
 28    IEF653I SUBSTITUTION JCL - SYSOUT=R
 29    IEF653I SUBSTITUTION JCL - SYSOUT=R
```

FIGURE 3.3b Effective Jobstream

```
14.01.14 JOB 1776  $HASP373 JSC$3605 STARTED - INIT  1 - CLASS A - SYS IPO1
14.01.17 JOB 1776  IEC141I 013-64,IFG0196J,JSC$3605,COB,SYSLIB,,,NULLFILE
14.01.18 JOB 1776  IEF450I JSC$3605 COB STEP1 - ABEND S013 U0000 - TIME=14.01.18
14.01.20 JOB 1776  $HASP395 JSC$3605 ENDED
                                          SYSLIB could not be opened as it was "dummied out"
```

FIGURE 3.3c JES2 Job Log

The first DD statement in the jobstream of Figure 3.3*a* is for COB. SYSIN. Since this DDname does not appear in the procedure, SYSIN is correctly treated as a *new* DD statement and added to the effective jobstream of Figure 3.3*b*. The system next encounters COB.SYSLIB in the submitted JCL and assumes that it, too, is a *new* DD statement. This is because overriding DD statements are assumed to precede new DD statements. Consequently when one new DD statement is reached, any subsequent DD statements for that step are also considered new. In other words, *once a new DD statement for a given step is read from the submitted jobstream, it is no longer possible to override DD statements in that step.*

In effect, the system now has *two* DD statements for COB.SYSLIB, one from the procedure and one from the submitted JCL. *In any case of duplicate DDnames in the same step, all occurrences after the first are ignored. The DD statement in the submitted jobstream of Figure 3.3a has no effect*, and the procedure statement for SYSLIB (i.e., DD DUMMY) becomes the operative statement.

Figure 3.4 contains a second example that illustrates the importance of correctly sequencing an incoming jobstream. The first submitted DD statement, //GO.SYSUDUMP, refers to the third (GO) step in the invoked procedure. Thus, all subsequent submitted DD statements must refer to this step as well. The next two statements *erroneously* refer to the COB step, which has already been passed in the effective jobstream. The system responds with the message "OVERRIDDEN STEP NOT FOUND IN PROCEDURE"; i.e., it cannot find the COB step after the GO step, and terminates the job in a JCL error.

The confusion associated with Figures 3.3 and 3.4 suggests a need for restating the rules for the order of submitted DD statements.

> ♦ Overriding DD statements for a given step precede new DD statements for that step in the same order as the DDnames appeared in the procedure.
>
> ♦ The new DD statements for a particular step may appear together in any order, but precede the overriding statements of the next step.

SYMBOLIC PARAMETERS

The method of overriding existing DD statements is easily prone to error due to the rigid sequencing requirements imposed by OS. An alternative approach is to anticipate which JCL parameters may change, and to define these as *symbolic parameters* in the procedure itself.

A symbolic parameter is preceded by a *single* ampersand. It may be from one to seven characters in length, the first of which must be alphabetic. All symbolic parameters within a procedure are listed in the initial PROC statement together with their associated *default* values. Figure 3.5*b*, for

```
//JSC$3607      JOB (MAS526),JACKIE,MSGLEVEL=(1,1)
//STEP1         EXEC COBVCLG
//GO.SYSUDUMP DD SYSOUT=R              —— DD statement out of order
//COB.SYSLIB    DD DSN=MEN.PGM.JSC.RTG,DISP=SHR
//COB.SYSIN     DD DSN=MEN.PGM.JSC.RTG(FILEDUMP),DISP=SHR
//GO.FILEOUT    DD SYSOUT=R
//GO.FILEIN     DD *
```

FIGURE 3.4a Submitted Jobstream

```
 1   //JSC$3607 JOB (MAS526),JACKIE,MSGLEVEL=(1,1)
 2   //STEP1         EXEC COBVCLG
 3   XXCOBVCLG PROC OUT=R
 4   XXCOB EXEC PGM=IKFCBL00,PARM=(LOAD,SUPMAP,LIB,'LINECNT=60',
     XX          'SXREF','PMAP','DMAP','STATE','FLOW=10','NOSEQ',
     XX          'BUF=63922','SIZE=217088')
 5   XXSTEPLIB   DD DSN=SYS2.LINKLIB,DISP=SHR
 6   XX          DD DSN=SYS1.COBLIB,DISP=SHR
 7   XXSYSPRINT DD SYSOUT=&OUT
 8   XXSYSPUNCH DD DUMMY
 9   XXSYSLIB    DD DUMMY
10   XXSYSUT1    DD UNIT=3350,SPACE=(1024,(120,120)),DSN=&&SYSUT1
11   XXSYSUT2    DD UNIT=3350,SPACE=(1024,(120,120)),DSN=&&SYSUT2
12   XXSYSUT3    DD UNIT=3350,SPACE=(1024,(120,120)),DSN=&&SYSUT3
13   XXSYSUT4    DD UNIT=3350,SPACE=(1024,(120,120)),DSN=&&SYSUT4
14   XXSYSUT5    DD UNIT=3350,SPACE=(1024,(120,120)),DSN=&&SYSUT5
15   XXSYSLIN    DD DSN=&&OBJ,DISP=(MOD,PASS),UNIT=3350,
     XX             SPACE=(3040,(40,40)),
     XX             DCB=(BLKSIZE=3040,LRECL=80,RECFM=FBS,BUFNO=1)
16   XXLKED EXEC PGM=HEWL,PARM='LIST,XREF,LET,MAP',COND=(5,LT,COB)
17   XXSYSLIN    DD DSN=&&OBJ,DISP=(OLD,DELETE)
18   XXSYSLMOD  DD DSN=&&LOD(X),DISP=(,PASS),UNIT=3350,DCB=BUFNO=1,
     XX             SPACE=(CYL,(1,1,1))
19   XXSYSLIB    DD DSN=SYS1.COBLIB,DISP=SHR
20   XXSYSUT1    DD UNIT=3350,SPACE=(1024,(120,120)),DCB=BUFNO=1,
     XX             DSN=&&SYSUT1
21   XXSYSPRINT DD SYSOUT=&OUT
22   XXGO EXEC PGM=*.LKED.SYSLMOD,COND=((5,LT,COB),(5,LT,LKED))
23   XXSTEPLIB   DD DSN=SYS1.COBLIB,DISP=SHR
24   XXSYSOUT    DD SYSOUT=&OUT
25   XXSYSOUC    DD SYSOUT=&OUT
26   XXSYSCOUNT  DD SYSOUT=&OUT
27   XXSYSDBOUT  DD SYSOUT=&OUT
28   //GO.SYSUDUMP DD SYSOUT=R
29   //COB.SYSLIB    DD DSN=MEN.PGM.JSC.RTG,DISP=SHR
30   //COB.SYSIN     DD DSN=MEN.PGM.JSC.RTG(FILEDUMP),DISP=SHR
31   //GO.FILEOUT    DD SYSOUT=R
32   //GO.FILEIN     DD *
```

Statements for the COB step must precede those in the GO step

```
STMT NO. MESSAGE

  7   IEF653I SUBSTITUTION JCL - SYSOUT=R
 21   IEF653I SUBSTITUTION JCL - SYSOUT=R
 24   IEF653I SUBSTITUTION JCL - SYSOUT=R
 25   IEF653I SUBSTITUTION JCL - SYSOUT=R
 26   IEF653I SUBSTITUTION JCL - SYSOUT=R
 27   IEF653I SUBSTITUTION JCL - SYSOUT=R          —— JCL error
 29   IEF611I OVERRIDDEN STEP NOT FOUND IN PROCEDURE
 30   IEF611I OVERRIDDEN STEP NOT FOUND IN PROCEDURE
```

FIGURE 3.4b Effective Jobstream

```
//JSC$3609    JOB (MAS526),JACKIE,MSGLEVEL=(1,1)
//STEP1       EXEC COBVCLG,OUT=A
//COB.SYSLIB  DD DSN=MEN.PGM.JSC.RTG,DISP=SHR
//COB.SYSIN   DD DSN=MEN.PGM.JSC.RTG(FILEDUMP),DISP=SHR
//GO.FILEOUT  DD SYSOUT=R
//GO.SYSUDUMP DD SYSOUT=R
//GO.FILEIN   DD *
```

FIGURE 3.5*a* Submitted Jobstream

```
1    //JSC$3609 JOB (MAS526),JACKIE,MSGLEVEL=(1,1)
2    //STEP1       EXEC COBVCLG,OUT=A ──Default value of OUT parameter
3    XXCOBVCLG PROC OUT=R
4    XXCOB EXEC PGM=IKFCBL00,PARM=(LOAD,SUPMAP,LIB,'LINECNT=60',
     XX            'SXREF','PMAP','DMAP','STATE','FLOW=10','NOSEQ',
     XX            'BUF=63922','SIZE=217088')
5    XXSTEPLIB  DD DSN=SYS2.LINKLIB,DISP=SHR
6    XX         DD DSN=SYS1.COBLIB,DISP=SHR
7    XXSYSPRINT DD SYSOUT=&OUT
8    XXSYSPUNCH DD DUMMY
9    //COB.SYSLIB DD DSN=MEN.PGM.JSC.RTG,DISP=SHR
     X/SYSLIB    DD DUMMY
10   XXSYSUT1    DD UNIT=3350,SPACE=(1024,(120,120)),DSN=&&SYSUT1
11   XXSYSUT2    DD UNIT=3350,SPACE=(1024,(120,120)),DSN=&&SYSUT2
12   XXSYSUT3    DD UNIT=3350,SPACE=(1024,(120,120)),DSN=&&SYSUT3
13   XXSYSUT4    DD UNIT=3350,SPACE=(1024,(120,120)),DSN=&&SYSUT4
14   XXSYSUT5    DD UNIT=3350,SPACE=(1024,(120,120)),DSN=&&SYSUT5
15   XXSYSLIN    DD DSN=&&OBJ,DISP=(MOD,PASS),UNIT=3350,
     XX             SPACE=(3040,(40,40)),
     XX             DCB=(BLKSIZE=3040,LRECL=80,RECFM=FBS,BUFNO=1)
16   //COB.SYSIN  DD DSN=MEN.PGM.JSC.RTG(FILEDUMP),DISP=SHR
17   XXLKED EXEC PGM=HEWL,PARM='LIST,XREF,LET,MAP',COND=(5,LT,COB)
18   XXSYSLIN    DD DSN=&&OBJ,DISP=(OLD,DELETE)
19   XXSYSLMOD   DD DSN=&&LOD(X),DISP=(,PASS),UNIT=3350,DCB=BUFNO=1,
     XX             SPACE=(CYL,(1,1,1))
20   XXSYSLIB    DD DSN=SYS1.COBLIB,DISP=SHR
21   XXSYSUT1    DD UNIT=3350,SPACE=(1024,(120,120)),DCB=BUFNO=1,
     XX             DSN=&&SYSUT1 ──Symbolic parameter
22   XXSYSPRINT DD SYSOUT=&OUT
23   XXGO EXEC PGM=*.LKED.SYSLMOD,COND=((5,LT,COB),(5,LT,LKED))
24   XXSTEPLIB  DD DSN=SYS1.COBLIB,DISP=SHR
25   XXSYSOUT    DD SYSOUT=&OUT
26   XXSYSOUC    DD SYSOUT=&OUT
27   XXSYSCOUNT DD SYSOUT=&OUT
28   XXSYSDBOUT DD SYSOUT=&OUT
29   //GO.FILEOUT  DD SYSOUT=R
30   //GO.SYSUDUMP DD SYSOUT=R
31   //GO.FILEIN   DD *
```

```
STMT NO. MESSAGE

   7     IEF653I SUBSTITUTION JCL - SYSOUT=A
  22     IEF653I SUBSTITUTION JCL - SYSOUT=A
  25     IEF653I SUBSTITUTION JCL - SYSOUT=A
  26     IEF653I SUBSTITUTION JCL - SYSOUT=A
  27     IEF653I SUBSTITUTION JCL - SYSOUT=A
  28     IEF653I SUBSTITUTION JCL - SYSOUT=A
```

FIGURE 3.5*b* Effective Jobstream

example, contains a single symbolic parameter, OUT, whose *default* value is R.

The "execution time" JCL statement of Figure 3.5a specifies OUT=A; hence, every occurrence of the symbolic parameter &OUT within the procedure will be replaced by A. The substitution JCL messages for lines 7, 22, 25, 26, 27, and 28 confirm the substitution. (The initial execution of COBVCLG in Figure 3.1 did *not* include an execution time value for &OUT. Hence, the substitution JCL messages in Figure 3.1c reflect the default value of R.)

Earlier versions of OS allowed a temporary data set to be indicated by *either* one or two ampersands, causing confusion with symbolic parameters. Accordingly, if an entry preceded by a single ampersand also appears in a PROC statement with a default value, the entry is treated as a symbolic parameter. Only if a single ampersand entry does not appear in a PROC statement is it considered a temporary data set. Good technique, however, mandates exclusive use of two ampersands to denote a temporary data set.

DEVELOPING NEW PROCEDURES

Where do procedures come from? Many are provided by the vendor as part of the operating system; e.g., COBUCLG. Others are modified versions of vendor-supplied procs (e.g., the COBVCLG procedure used throughout this chapter). More frequently, however, the applications programmer is required to develop his or her own procedures in support of a particular project.

A newly developed procedure is apt to contain JCL errors, in much the same way as a COBOL program is prone to compilation or logic errors. Hence, procedures must be tested, just as ordinary programs are debugged. Unfortunately, procedures cannot normally be invoked unless they are in a procedure library (typically SYS1.PROCLIB). A given installation may also develop additional procedure libraries. A new procedure should not, however, be placed into a "proc lib" unless it has already been tested. One is left, therefore, with a catch-22: i.e., procedures cannot be tested unless they are in a library, yet they should not be placed in a library until they have been tested. The solution is to test a procedure *instream* via the PROC and PEND JCL statements, as shown in Figure 3.6.

Figure 3.6a shows a six-statement procedure, SAVEMEM, as it was initially developed. Note well that PROC is the first JCL statement of this, and every, procedure. (OS does not require the PROC statement to have a name in column 3, although such naming is highly recommended. The actual name of the procedure is established when it is added to a proc lib.) Figure 3.6b contains a jobstream to invoke the procedure SAVEMEM, given that it is in a procedure library. Figure 3.6c *tests the procedure*

```
                                          ┌─ PROC is the first statement
┌──────────────────┐
│//SAVEMEM   PROC  │
└──────────────────┘
//SAVE      EXEC PGM=IEBUPDTE
//SYSUT1    DD  DSN=MEN.PGM.JSC.TEST,DISP=(OLD,KEEP,KEEP)
//SYSPRINT DD SYSOUT=A
//SYSUT2    DD  DSN=MEN.PGM.JSC.TEST,DISP=(OLD,KEEP,KEEP)
//SYSIN     DD  DUMMY
```

FIGURE 3.6a The Procedure Itself

```
//JSC$3437 JOB (MAS526),JACKIE
//         EXEC SAVEMEM
//SAVE.SYSPRINT DD SYSOUT=R
//SAVE.SYSIN    DD  *
```

FIGURE 3.6b Invoking the Procedure

```
//JSC$3437 JOB (MAS526),JACKIE
//SAVEMEM   PROC
//SAVE      EXEC PGM=IEBUPDTE
//SYSUT1    DD  DSN=MEN.PGM.JSC.TEST,DISP=(OLD,KEEP,KEEP)
//SYSPRINT DD SYSOUT=A
//SYSUT2    DD  DSN=MEN.PGM.JSC.TEST,DISP=(OLD,KEEP,KEEP)
//SYSIN     DD  DUMMY     ┌─ PEND indicates the end of instream procedure
┌─────────────┐
│//      PEND │
└─────────────┘
//         EXEC SAVEMEM
//SAVE.SYSPRINT DD SYSOUT=R
//SAVE.SYSIN    DD  *
```

FIGURE 3.6c Testing Instream

```
                                                   ┌─ Instream procedure and
                                                   │  PEND statement are not
1                                                  │  numbered
   //JSC$3437 JOB (MAS526),JACKIE
   ┌──────────────────────────────────────────────────────────────┐
   │//SAVEMEM   PROC                                                │
   │//SAVE      EXEC PGM=IEBUPDTE                                    │
   │//SYSUT1    DD  DSN=MEN.PGM.JSC.TEST,DISP=(OLD,KEEP,KEEP)        │
   │//SYSPRINT DD SYSOUT=A                                          │
   │//SYSUT2    DD  DSN=MEN.PGM.JSC.TEST,DISP=(OLD,KEEP,KEEP)        │
   │//SYSIN     DD  DUMMY                                           │
   │//      PEND                                                    │
   └──────────────────────────────────────────────────────────────┘
2    //         EXEC SAVEMEM          ┌─ Instream procedure statements
3   ┌─────────────────────┐          │  denoted by ++
4   │++SAVEMEM   PROC      │
    │++SAVE      EXEC PGM=IEBUPDTE│
5   ++SYSUT1    DD  DSN=MEN.PGM.JSC.TEST,DISP=(OLD,KEEP,KEEP)
6   //SAVE.SYSPRINT DD SYSOUT=R
    +/SYSPRINT DD SYSOUT=A
7   ++SYSUT2    DD  DSN=MEN.PGM.JSC.TEST,DISP=(OLD,KEEP,KEEP)
8   ┌──────────────────────────┐
    │//SAVE.SYSIN    DD  *     │
    │+/SYSIN     DD  DUMMY     │─ Instream statement is overridden
    └──────────────────────────┘
```

FIGURE 3.6d System Messages

FIGURE 3.6 Testing a Procedure Instream

instream. The JOB statement is followed immediately by the procedure, followed by a PEND statement to indicate the end of the proc. Figure 3.6*d* contains the system messages produced by the execution of Figure 3.6*c*. It resembles the output of some earlier illustrations, with two significant differences. First, the entire instream procedure is listed consecutively immediately after the JOB statement. However, neither the procedure statements themselves nor the ending PEND are numbered. Second, all statements "pulled" from the instream procedure are denoted by ++ rather than XX. In similar fashion, procedure statements which are overridden are denoted by +/ rather than X/.

Once the programmer is satisfied that a procedure is correct, it can be entered in the appropriate library via the IEBUPDTE utility (see Chapter 4). However, many installations restrict access to the procedure library to a specially authorized person.

Summary

This short but vitally important chapter covered all major aspects associated with procedures. The system messages in Figures 3.1, 3.3, 3.4, and 3.5 are especially important in clarifying these concepts. The *order* of overriding DD statements in a submitted jobstream was stressed, and *symbolic parameters* were introduced as a means of simplifying overrides. The chapter concluded with the PROC and PEND statements which allow procedures to be tested instream.

TRUE/FALSE EXERCISES

1. A procedure cannot be tested unless it is in a procedure library.
2. Symbolic parameters are denoted by two ampersands.
3. The order of DD statements in a submitted jobstream is not important when overriding a catalogued procedure.
4. The order of individual DD parameters on an overriding DD statement is not important.
5. Once a DD parameter is entered in a catalogued procedure, it can never be nullified.
6. When invoking COBVCLG, the DD statements for the COB step precede those of the GO step.
7. An overridden procedure statement is indicated by X/ in the system messages.

8. Substitution JCL messages indicate the supplied values of symbolic parameters.

9. DD * may not appear in a procedure.

10. The system messages clearly indicate duplicate DD statements.

11. The system messages clearly indicate the individual parameters which are overridden.

12. DD DATA may appear in a procedure.

13. Default values for symbolic parameters are established in the PROC statement.

14. PROC and PEND statements must appear in pairs.

15. An installation may have more than one procedure library.

16. The IBM utility, IEBUPDTE, is generally used to add procedures to a procedure library.

17. The PROC statement must have a statement name, beginning in column 3.

PROBLEMS

1. Examine Figure 3.7.

```
1    //JSC$3016 JOB (MAS526),JACKIE
2    //STEP1    EXEC UTM01X00,N='TEST.DATA'
3    XXUTM01X00 PROC
4    XXUTM01X10 EXEC PGM=IEBGENER
5    XXSYSUT2   DD DSN=&N,UNIT=SYSDA,SPACE=(TRK,(5,1)),
     XX         DCB=(LRECL=80,BLKSIZE=80,RECFM=FB),DISP=(NEW,CATLG,DELETE)
6    //UTM01X10.SYSUT1 DD DSN=MEN.PGM.JSC.TEST(TRANS),DISP=SHR
     X/SYSUT1   DD DUMMY
7    XXSYSIN    DD DUMMY
8    XXSYSPRINT DD SYSOUT=B
9    XXUTM01X20 EXEC PGM=IEBGENER
10   XXSYSUT1   DD DSN=&N,DISP=(OLD,KEEP,KEEP)
11   //UTM01X20.SYSUT2 DD SYSOUT=R
     X/SYSUT2   DD SYSOUT=1,COPIES=2
12   XXSYSIN    DD DUMMY
13   //UTM01X20.SYSPRINT DD SYSOUT=R
     X/SYSPRINT DD SYSOUT=B


STMT NO. MESSAGE

    5     IEF653I SUBSTITUTION JCL - DSN=TEST.DATA,UNIT=SYSDA,SPACE=(TRK,(5,1)),
    10    IEF653I SUBSTITUTION JCL - DSN=TEST.DATA,DISP=(OLD,KEEP,KEEP)
```

FIGURE 3.7 System Messages for Problem 1

(a) What was the submitted jobstream?

(b) Show all JCL statements for the procedure UTM01X00 as they exist in the procedure library.

(c) Which JCL statements were overridden?

(d) Does the proc UTM01X00 contain any symbolic parameters? If so, what are the associated default values? The substitution JCL values?

2. Given Figure 3.8*a* and 3.8*b*, representing a submitted jobstream and catalogued procedure respectively, show the effective jobstream.

```
//JSC$3236 JOB (MAS526),JACKIE,CLASS=W
//STEP1     EXEC CSA
//OLDCOBOL DD DISP=SHR,DSN=MEN.PGM.JSC.RTG(FILEDUMP)
//NEWCOBOL DD DISP=(NEW,PASS),DSN=&&TEMP,UNIT=SYSDA,
//              SPACE=(TRK,(5,5)),DCB=(RECFM=FB,LRECL=80,BLKSIZE=80)
//COMMANDS DD DSN=MEN.PGM.JSC.TEST(COMMANDS),DISP=SHR
//
```

FIGURE 3.8a Submitted Jobstream

```
//CSA PROC
//STEP1       EXEC PGM=TEMPNAME
//STEPLIB     DD   DSN=CSA.TEST.LOADLIB,DISP=SHR
//            DD   DSN=SYS1.COBLIB,DISP=SHR
//            DD   DSN=SYS2.LINKLIB,DISP=SHR
//WORKFL1     DD   UNIT=DISK,SPACE=(CYL,(2,1))
//WORKFL2     DD   UNIT=DISK,SPACE=(CYL,(2,1))
//PRINT       DD   SYSOUT=R
//SORTLIB     DD   DSN=SYS1.SORTLIB,DISP=SHR
//SORTWK01    DD   UNIT=DISK,SPACE=(CYL,(3),,CONTIG)
//SORTWK02    DD   UNIT=DISK,SPACE=(CYL,(3),,CONTIG)
//SORTWK03    DD   UNIT=DISK,SPACE=(CYL,(3),,CONTIG)
//SYSOUT      DD   SYSOUT=R
```

FIGURE 3.8b Catalogued Procedure

3. Answer the following questions with respect to Figure 3.1:

(a) Does the submitted jobstream require a stepname for the SYSLIB DD statement? For the FILEIN DD statement?

(b) Could the DD statement for SYSUDUMP logically have been included in the procedure? Could the DD statements for FILEIN and FILEOUT be similarly included?

(c) Indicate how to change the procedure JCL so that its SYSLIB DD statement refers to the symbolic parameter, &COPYLIB. Establish a default value of MY.COBOL.LIB.

(d) How is it possible for a procedure to contain multiple DD statements with the same DDname (e.g., SYSLIN) in lines 15 and 18 of Figure 3.1*c*)?

4. Show the effective JCL produced by the catalogued procedure HOME-WORK, and the submitted jobstream TRYIT, in Figure 3.9.

```
//HOMEWORK PROC DATASET=YOURS
//STEP1    EXEC PGM=MINE
//DD1      DD DSN=FIRST,DISP=OLD,UNIT=SYSDA
//DD2      DD DSN=SECOND,DISP=(NEW,KEEP),
//         SPACE=(CYL,(10,1)),VOL=SER=USR001,
//         UNIT=SYSDA
//DD3      DD  DSN=&DATASET,SPACE=(TRK,(10,2))

//TRYIT  · JOB
//         EXEC HOMEWORK,DATASET=OUTPUT
//DD1      DD DSN=LAST,DISP=SHR,UNIT=,DCB=BLKSIZE=80
//DD3      DD DISP=(NEW,CATLG),UNIT=SYSDA,
//         SPACE=(TRK,(100,5))
//DD4      DD *
//DD2      DD *
```

FIGURE 3.9 Jobstream for Problem 4

5. Develop a jobstream to *create and test instream* a procedure to go either "card to tape" or "card to disk." The procedure should utilize IEBGENER (see Chapter 4) and contain DD statements for SYSIN, SYSPRINT, and SYSUT2. It must *not* contain the DD statement for SYSUT1, //SYSUT1 DD *, since procedures may not contain DD statements with DD *. Instead, the DD statement for SYSUT1 will be included with the JCL to test the procedure. In addition:

   (a) Use symbolic parameters in the procedure for output device and data set name.
   (b) Specify DCB characteristics for SYSUT2 in the procedure; e.g., DCB=(BLKSIZE=800,LRECL=80). Override one or more parameters when testing.
   (c) Include a SPACE parameter for SYSUT2 in the procedure. Show how to nullify this parameter if the output is tape.

6. What would be the effect of reversing the FILEIN and FILEOUT DD statements in Figure 3.1*b*? Would there be a problem if the stepname (GO) were removed from the DD statement for SYSUDUMP? From the DD statement for FILEOUT? (Assume that FILEOUT is the first DD statement associated with the GO step.) What would be the effect of reversing the DD statements for DEF and SYSIN in the submitted jobstream of Figure 3.2?

7. Answer the following with respect to the system messages in Figure 3.10.

   (a) Why are the 13 JCL statements immediately following the JOB statement unnumbered?
   (b) How many symbolic parameters are associated with the procedure DATASET? What are the default value(s)? The execution time values?
   (c) Which DD statements in the procedure were overridden?
   (d) What is the function of the PEND statement? Why are the procedure statements preceded by ++ rather than XX?

```
 1      //JSC$3434 JOB (MAS526),JACKIE
        //DATASET   PROC N='TEST.FILE'
        //STEP1     EXEC PGM=IEBGENER
        //SYSUT2    DD DSN=&N,UNIT=SYSDA,SPACE=(TRK,(5,1)),
        //          DCB=(LRECL=80,BLKSIZE=80,RECFM=FB),DISP=(NEW,CATLG,DELETE)
        //SYSUT1    DD DUMMY
        //SYSIN     DD DUMMY
        //SYSPRINT  DD SYSOUT=B
        //STEP2     EXEC PGM=IEBGENER
        //SYSUT1    DD DSN=&N,DISP=(OLD,KEEP,KEEP)
        //SYSUT2    DD SYSOUT=1,COPIES=2
        //SYSIN     DD DUMMY
        //SYSPRINT  DD SYSOUT=B
        //          PEND
 2      //          EXEC DATASET,N='FILEONE'
 3      ++DATASET   PROC N='TEST.FILE'
 4      ++STEP1     EXEC PGM=IEBGENER
 5      ++SYSUT2    DD DSN=&N,UNIT=SYSDA,SPACE=(TRK,(5,1)),
        ++          DCB=(LRECL=80,BLKSIZE=80,RECFM=FB),DISP=(NEW,CATLG,DELETE)
 6      //STEP1.SYSUT1    DD DSN=MEN.PGM.JSC.TEST(TRANS),DISP=SHR
        +/SYSUT1    DD DUMMY
 7      ++SYSIN     DD DUMMY
 8      //STEP1.SYSPRINT DD SYSOUT=R
        +/SYSPRINT  DD SYSOUT=B
 9      ++STEP2     EXEC PGM=IEBGENER
10      ++SYSUT1    DD DSN=&N,DISP=(OLD,KEEP,KEEP)
11      //STEP2.SYSUT2    DD SYSOUT=R
        +/SYSUT2    DD SYSOUT=1,COPIES=2
12      ++SYSIN     DD DUMMY
13      //STEP2.SYSPRINT DD SYSOUT=R
        +/SYSPRINT  DD SYSOUT=B


STMT NO. MESSAGE

 5      IEF653I SUBSTITUTION JCL - DSN=FILEONE,UNIT=SYSDA,SPACE=(TRK,(5,1)),
10      IEF653I SUBSTITUTION JCL - DSN=FILEONE,DISP=(OLD,KEEP,KEEP)
```

FIGURE 3.10 System Messages for Problem 7

8. Figure 3.11 resembles the various system outputs discussed in the chapter. This particular attempt, however, produced a D-level diagnostic, which caused the compilation to be abandoned. It is especially confusing given that the COBOL source program, MEN.PGM.JSC.RTG(FILEDUMP), compiled cleanly elsewhere (e.g., in Figure 3.5). Explain the rather puzzling output of Figure 3.11*c*. (Hint: What is the effect of including a *blank* card within a submitted jobstream? Are any extraneous DD statements present in Figure 3.11*a*?)

```
//JSC$3711   JOB (MAS536),JACKIE,MSGLEVEL=(1,1)
//STEP1      EXEC COBVCLG,OUT=A
//COB.SYSLIB DD DSN=MEN.PGM.JSC.RTG,DISP=SHR

//COB.SYSIN  DD DSN=MEN.PGM.JSC.RTG(FILEDUMP),DISP=SHR
//GO.FILEOUT DD SYSOUT=R
//GO.SYSUDUMP DD SYSOUT=R
//GO.FILEIN  DD *
```

FIGURE 3.11*a* Submitted Jobstream

```
 1      //JSC$3711 JOB (MAS526),JACKIE,MSGLEVEL=(1,1)
 2      //STEP1      EXEC COBVCLG,OUT=A
 3      XXCOBVCLG PROC OUT=R
 4      XXCOB EXEC PGM=IKFCBL00,PARM=(LOAD,SUPMAP,LIB,'LINECNT=60',
        XX          'SXREF','PMAP','DMAP','STATE','FLOW=10','NOSEQ',
        XX          'BUF=63922','SIZE=217088')
 5      XXSTEPLIB   DD DSN=SYS2.LINKLIB,DISP=SHR
 6      XX          DD DSN=SYS1.COBLIB,DISP=SHR
 7      XXSYSPRINT  DD SYSOUT=&OUT
 8      XXSYSPUNCH  DD DUMMY
 9      //COB.SYSLIB  DD DSN=MEN.PGM.JSC.RTG,DISP=SHR
        X/SYSLIB     DD DUMMY
10      XXSYSUT1    DD UNIT=3350,SPACE=(1024,(120,120)),DSN=&&SYSUT1
11      XXSYSUT2    DD UNIT=3350,SPACE=(1024,(120,120)),DSN=&&SYSUT2
12      XXSYSUT3    DD UNIT=3350,SPACE=(1024,(120,120)),DSN=&&SYSUT3
13      XXSYSUT4    DD UNIT=3350,SPACE=(1024,(120,120)),DSN=&&SYSUT4
14      XXSYSUT5    DD UNIT=3350,SPACE=(1024,(120,120)),DSN=&&SYSUT5
15      XXSYSLIN    DD DSN=&&OBJ,DISP=(MOD,PASS),UNIT=3350,
        XX            SPACE=(3040,(40,40)),
        XX            DCB=(BLKSIZE=3040,LRECL=80,RECFM=FBS,BUFNO=1)
16      //SYSIN     DD *              GENERATED STATEMENT
17      //COB.SYSIN   DD DSN=MEN.PGM.JSC.RTG(FILEDUMP),DISP=SHR
18      XXLKED EXEC PGM=HEWL,PARM='LIST,XREF,LET,MAP',COND=(5,LT,COB)
19      XXSYSLIN    DD DSN=&&OBJ,DISP=(OLD,DELETE)
20      XXSYSLMOD   DD DSN=&&LOD(X),DISP=(,PASS),UNIT=3350,DCB=BUFNO=1,
        XX            SPACE=(CYL,(1,1,1))
21      XXSYSLIB    DD DSN=SYS1.COBLIB,DISP=SHR
22      XXSYSUT1    DD UNIT=3350,SPACE=(1024,(120,120)),DCB=BUFNO=1,
        XX            DSN=&&SYSUT1
23      XXSYSPRINT  DD SYSOUT=&OUT
24      XXGO EXEC PGM=*.LKED.SYSLMOD,COND=((5,LT,COB),(5,LT,LKED))
25      XXSTEPLIB   DD DSN=SYS1.COBLIB,DISP=SHR
26      XXSYSOUT    DD SYSOUT=&OUT
27      XXSYSOUC    DD SYSOUT=&OUT
28      XXSYSCOUNT  DD SYSOUT=&OUT
29      XXSYSDBOUT  DD SYSOUT=&OUT
30      //GO.FILEOUT  DD SYSOUT=R
31      //GO.SYSUDUMP DD SYSOUT=R
32      //GO.FILEIN   DD *
```

FIGURE 3.11*b* Effective Jobstream

```
6       NOPRGMID        15.13.56        JAN 15,1983

CARD    ERROR MESSAGE

        IKF1010I-D    UNUSUAL END OF DATA ON SYSIN DURING PH04 PROCESSING. COMPILATION ABANDONED.
        IKF1095I-W    WORD 'SECTION' OR 'DIVISION' MISSING. ASSUMED PRESENT.
        IKF1129I-C    DIVISION HEADER EXTRANEOUS, MISSING OR MISPLACED. ONE ASSUMED PRESENT.
        IKF1097I-E    PROGRAM-ID MISSING OR MISPLACED. IF PROGRAM-ID DOES NOT IMMEDIATELY FOLLOW
                      IDENTIFICATION DIVISION, IT WILL BE IGNORED.
        IKF1128I-W    FOUND END OF PROGRAM . EXPECTING ENVIRONMENT. ALL ENV. DIV. STATEMENTS IGNORED.
        IKF1130I-E    DATA DIV. HEADER MISSING.  WORDS IN  DATA STATEMENTS ARE INVALID.
        IKF1130I-E    PROCEDURE DIV. HEADER MISSING.  WORDS IN  PROCEDURE STATEMENTS ARE INVALID.
        IKF5019I-W    NO STOP RUN, GOBACK, OR EXIT PROGRAM STATEMENTS ENCOUNTERED IN SOURCE.

        ERROR MESSAGE

        IKF6006I-E    SUPMAP SPECIFIED AND E-LEVEL DIAGNOSTIC HAS OCCURRED. PMAP CLIST LOAD DECK IGNORE
```

FIGURE 3.11*c* Compiler Output

Utilities

Chapters 1, 2, and 3 discussed fundamentals of OS JCL. Although such material goes a long way toward strengthening the capabilities of the individual, it is by no means all that one needs to know. Accordingly, this chapter emphasizes the need for utility programs and discusses the basics of six OS utilities: IEBGENER, IEBPTPCH, IEBUPDTE, IEHPROGM, IEBCOPY, and IEBISAM. (A separate chapter is devoted exclusively to IDCAMS.) The chapter also discusses how to call the "stand alone" SORT/ MERGE program and how to make explicit use of the linkage-editor.

The author does not intend this material be a substitute for the IBM manual on OS utilities. The reader is referred to the reference manual (GT35-0005-2, *OS/VS2 Utilities*) for additional features of the utilities we cover, and for complete coverage of the many utilities we omit. The author does believe, however, that this chapter is a solid introduction to the subject, and suggests that the uninitiated reader will have a far easier time with the reference manual *after* reading this chapter.

THE NEED FOR UTILITY PROGRAMS

A *utility* program performs a basic function; i.e., it does a routine job which is required repeatedly in an installation. Utilities can copy files from one storage medium to another (e.g., card to disk, tape to print). They can back up and restore disk packs, catalog, scratch, or rename files, copy and compress partitioned data sets, and so on. (Although many of these functions can be done transparently through the IBM program product SPF, the competent individual requires knowledge of utilities to understand what is actually happening. Moreover, many installations do not have SPF, and thereby require that the utilities be called explicitly.)

A programmer is not required to use utilities, but managers discourage people from reinventing the wheel. For example, why write a COBOL "disk to print" program, if one already exists in the form of an IBM-supplied utility? The need for utilities is tremendous, much greater than the student or trainee would imagine. Consider the traditional sequential update, and its simple system flowchart, shown in Figure 4.1.

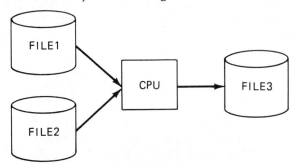

FIGURE 4.1 System Flowchart for a Sequential Update

Now consider what is actually involved in testing this program. The COBOL programmer requires two disk files as input to his or her program. In addition, one must be able to "see" the contents of those files as well as the contents of the updated file after it has been created. In essence, then, we are talking of five additional steps (two file creations and three file listings) to test adequately the update program. A more complete flowchart, showing these additional steps, is shown in Figure 4.2.

In Figure 4.2, step 1 is a "card to disk" program, which creates the first disk file. Step 2 is a "disk to print" program to print the contents of the newly created file. Steps 3 and 4 perform these tasks for the second file. Step 5 is the COBOL update. Step 6 is a "disk to print" program for the newly created file. As can be seen from Figure 4.2, the COBOL programmer needs two additional programs merely to test his or her program. A "card to disk" program to create the files is run twice in steps 1 and 3. A "disk to print" program to list the contents of the disk files is run three times, in steps 2, 4, and 6.

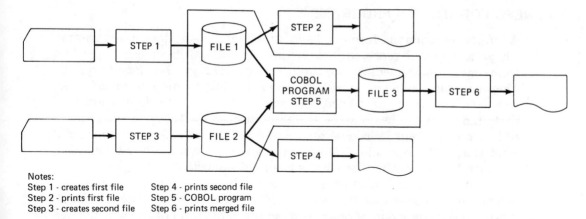

Notes:

Step 1 - creates first file   Step 4 - prints second file
Step 2 - prints first file   Step 5 - COBOL program
Step 3 - creates second file   Step 6 - prints merged file

FIGURE 4.2 System Flowchart for Testing COBOL Program

There are two approaches to obtaining the additional programs. The first is for the programmer to write *and debug* the programs in COBOL. A second and preferred approach is to use an existing program which is sufficiently general to accomplish the task; that existing program is the IBM utility IEBGENER.

IEBGENER

IEBGENER is a program that copies from one I/O device to another a sequential data set or a member of a partitioned data set. Like many IBM utilities, it requires four DD statements, as follows:

> SYSPRINT   DDname for the IEBGENER messages (usually SYSOUT=A)
>
> SYSUT1   DDname for the input file
>
> SYSUT2   DDname for the output file
>
> SYSIN   DDname for control statements; very often a "dummy" file

The JCL to go "card to disk", using IEBGENER, requires specification of four DD statements as shown in Figure 4.3:

```
//STEP1      EXEC  PGM=IEBGENER
//SYSUT1     DD    *
//SYSUT2     DD    DSN=DISK.FILE,DISP=(NEW,CATLG),
//    UNIT=SYSDA,SPACE=(TRK,(1,1)),DCB=(LRECL=80,BLKSIZE=8000,RECFM=FB)
//SYSPRINT   DD    SYSOUT=A
//SYSIN      DD    DUMMY
```

FIGURE 4.3 Use of IEBGENER ("Card to Disk")

Figure 4.3 does not contain anything new in the way of JCL. What is new are the DDnames for IEBGENER. Note in particular the use of the DUMMY parameter on the SYSIN DD statement, specifying that SYSIN is an empty file. Although IEBGENER permits the use of control statements in the SYSIN file (e.g., to copy only specified positions of the input record), that is not discussed. (The use of utility control statements is illustrated for the utilities IEBPTPCH and IEBUPDTE.)

Given the JCL to go "card to disk" in Figure 4.3, we now develop Figure 4.4 to print the newly created disk file. *Realize that the output file from Figure 4.3—i.e., DISK.FILE—is now the input file.* Thus, the DD statements, for SYSUT2 in Figure 4.3, and SYSUT1 in Figure 4.4, pertain to the *same* file. (The four DD statements associated with IEBGENER may be specified in any order. Different sequences are used in Figures 4.3 and 4.4 for illustration.)

```
//STEP2      EXEC  PGM=IEBGENER
//SYSPRINT  DD    SYSOUT=A
//SYSIN     DD    DUMMY              This file was created in Figure 4.3
//SYSUT1    DD    DSN=DISK.FILE,DISP=OLD
//SYSUT2    DD    SYSOUT=A
```

FIGURE 4.4 Use of IEBGENER ("Disk to Print")

The six-step jobstream corresponding to the system flowchart of Figure 4.2 is shown in Figure 4.5. Realize that in order to match the DD statements of the GO step, the COBOL SELECT statements in the update program must be in the form:

```
SELECT FIRST-FILE ASSIGN TO UT-S-TRANS.
SELECT SECOND-FILE ASSIGN TO UT-S-MASTER.
SELECT UPDATED-FILE ASSIGN TO UT-S-NEWMAST.
```

Note also that IEBGENER is executed a total of five times, and that comments and step names appear on the EXEC statements.

Figure 4.5 illustrates the use of *temporary data sets* (solely for the purpose of introducing the concept). A *temporary* data set exists *only* for the duration of the job. Temporary status is indicated by *two ampersands* preceding the data set name (e.g., &&TEMP1 in step 1). The name of a temporary data set is restricted to eight characters and periods are *not* permitted. The temporary data set &&TEMP1 is created in step 1 and passed to step 2; i.e., DISP=(NEW,PASS). The subsequent DD statement for SYSUT1 in step 2 specifies DISP=(OLD,PASS) for &&TEMP1. The volume of a temporary data set is not specified, as the system puts the data set wherever it chooses. The remainder of Figure 4.5 is left to the reader as an exercise.

```
                           ┌─ Step names used for clarity
                           │        ┌─ Output of STEP1 is input to STEP2
//JSC$3059 /JOB (000101),JACKIE  /
// STEP1    EXEC PGM=IEBGENER            **   CREATE FIRST DISK FILE   **
//SYSUT1    DD *
//SYSUT2    DD  DSN=&&TEMP1 ,UNIT=SYSDA,DISP=(NEW,PASS),
//              DCB=(LRECL=80,BLKSIZE=400,RECFM=FB),SPACE=(TRK,(1,1))
//SYSPRINT  DD SYSOUT=R
//SYSIN     DD DUMMY
// STEP2    EXEC PGM=IEBGENER            **   PRINT FIRST DISK FILE   **
//SYSUT1    DD  DSN=&&TEMP1 ,DISP=(OLD,PASS)
//SYSUT2    DD SYSOUT=R
//SYSPRINT  DD SYSOUT=R                     ┌─ Comments used on EXEC statements
//SYSIN     DD DUMMY
//STEP3     EXEC PGM=IEBGENER        **   CREATE SECOND DISK FILE   **
//SYSUT1    DD *
//SYSUT2    DD DSN=&&TEMP2,UNIT=SYSDA,DISP=(NEW,PASS),
//              DCB=(LRECL=80,BLKSIZE=400,RECFM=FB),SPACE=(TRK,(1,1))
//SYSPRINT  DD SYSOUT=R
//SYSIN     DD DUMMY
//STEP4     EXEC PGM=IEBGENER            **   PRINT SECOND DISK FILE   **
//SYSUT1    DD  DSN=&&TEMP2 ,DISP=(OLD,PASS)
//SYSUT2    DD SYSOUT=R
//SYSPRINT  DD SYSOUT=R         ── && indicates temporary data set
//SYSIN     DD DUMMY
//STEP5     EXEC COBVCLG
//COB.SYSLIB DD DSN=JESSICA.RTG.COBOL,DISP=SHR
//COB.SYSIN DD DSN=JESSICA.RTG.COBOL(SEQUPDT),DISP=SHR
//GO.TRANS DD DSN=&&TEMP1,DISP=(OLD,PASS)
//GO.MASTER DD DSN=&&TEMP2,DISP=(OLD,PASS)
//GO.NEWMAST DD DSN=&&NEWMAST,UNIT=SYSDA,DISP=(NEW,PASS),
//              DCB=(LRECL=80,BLKSIZE=400,RECFM=FB),SPACE=(TRK,(1,1))
//STEP6     EXEC PGM=IEBGENER          **   PRINT NEWMAST FILE   **
//SYSUT1    DD DSN=&&NEWMAST,DISP=(OLD,PASS)
//SYSUT2    DD SYSOUT=R
//SYSPRINT  DD SYSOUT=R
//SYSIN     DD DUMMY
```

FIGURE 4.5 Use of IEBGENER in Multiple Job Steps

IEBPTPCH

IEBPTPCH is a utility widely used to print or punch a data set (although the latter function is becoming increasingly rare). Despite the fact that IEBGENER can also be used to print a data set (as was done in Figures 4.4 and 4.5), IEBPTPCH offers more flexibility, and is discussed for that reason. As with IEBGENER, four DD statements are required. These are SYSPRINT, SYSUT1, SYSUT2, and SYSIN. SYSPRINT is the DDname for the utility messages. SYSUT1 and SYSUT2 denote input and output files, respectively. SYSIN is the DDname for the command file; as such it can contain a variety of control statements, only four of which are discussed. These are PRINT, PUNCH, TITLE, and RECORD.

Control statements for the SYSIN file are coded free-form in columns 2–71. The operation (e.g., PRINT) is coded first, followed by various operands, with comments permitted after the last operand. One or more spaces separate the operation from the first operand. Additional rules (i.e., for continuation and for naming the control statement) can be found in the OS Utilities manual.

```
//JSC$3229 JOB (MAS526),JACKIE
//STEP1    EXEC PGM=IEBPTPCH
//SYSUT1   DD *
//SYSPRINT DD SYSOUT=A
//SYSUT2   DD SYSOUT=A
//SYSIN    DD *
//
```

FIGURE 4.6a Submitted Jobstream

```
                                        IEBPTPCH control statements
PRINT/PUNCH DATA SET UTILITY
  PRINT  MAXFLDS=1
  TITLE  ITEM=('EXAMPLE 1 - SESAME STREET DATA SET',10)
  RECORD FIELD=(80)
EOF ON SYSIN
END OF DATA FOR SDS OR MEMBER
```

FIGURE 4.6b Utility Messages (SYSPRINT Data Set)

```
         EXAMPLE 1 - SESAME STREET DATA SET
000000000THE COUNT
111111111ERNIE
222222222BERT
333333330SCAR THE GROUCH          Printed as a result
444444444ROSEVELT FRANKLIN        of the TITLE control
555555555COOKIE MONSTER           statement
666666666BIG BIRD
777777777GROVER
888888888SHERLOCK HEMLOCK
999999999KERMIT THE FROG
```

FIGURE 4.6c Printed File (SYSUT2 Data Set)

FIGURE 4.6 Use of IEBPTPCH

Figure 4.6 uses IEBPTPCH to print an input data set via the PRINT, TITLE, and RECORD commands. Figure 4.6a shows the submitted job-stream and contains the four required DD statements. Figure 4.6b displays the utility messages which show the control statements contained in the SYSIN file. Figure 4.6c shows the printed file—i.e., the file described on the SYSUT2 DD statement. Attention is focused on the control statements of Figure 4.6b.

The MAXFLDS operand on the PRINT statement denotes the maximum number of FIELD parameters appearing on subsequent RECORD statements. The TITLE command provides an output title and beginning column for that title. The RECORD command specifies which fields of an incoming record are to be printed, and their respective output columns. FIELD=(80) means that the first 80 columns of an input record are to appear in the first 80 columns of an output record.

Figure 4.7 shows an example parallel to Figure 4.6. Attention is focused on the *FIELD operand to select and reorder fields on the output record.* It has the general form:

```
FIELD=(length(,input-location)(,conversion)(,output-location))
```

```
//JSC$3139 JOB (MAS526)
//STEP1    EXEC PGM=IFBPTPCH
//SYSUT1   DD *
//SYSPRINT DD SYSOUT=A
//SYSUT2   DD SYSOUT=A
//SYSIN    DD *
//
```

FIGURE 4.7a Submitted Jobstream

```
PRINT/PUNCH DATA SET UTILITY
  PRINT  MAXFLDS=2,SKIP=2          ─ Prints alternate records
  TITLE  ITEM=('EXAMPLE 2',18)
  TITLE  ITEM=('ALTERNATE RECORDS WITH SWITCHED FIELDS',5)
  RECORD FIELD=(9,1,,25),FIELD=(20,10,,1)
EOF ON SYSIN
END OF DATA FOR SDS OR MEMBER
```
A 20 byte field, beginning in column 10 of the input record, will appear beginning in column 1 of the output record

FIGURE 4.7b Utility Messages (SYSPRINT Data Set)

Two-line heading results from two TITLE statements

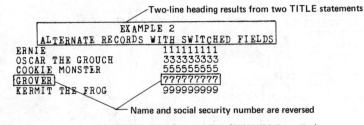

```
                    EXAMPLE 2
        ALTERNATE RECORDS WITH SWITCHED FIELDS
ERNIE                      111111111
OSCAR THE GROUCH           333333333
COOKIE MONSTER             555555555
GROVER                     777777777
KERMIT THE FROG            999999999
```
Name and social security number are reversed

FIGURE 4.7c Printed File (SYSUT2 Data Set)

FIGURE 4.7 Use of IEBPTPCH/II

where:

length = length (in bytes) of the input field

input-location = starting byte of the input field (1 is assumed if input-location is not specified)

conversion = two-byte code indicating the type of conversion (if any) to be performed before the field is printed or punched. For example, XE would cause alphanumeric data to be converted to hexadecimal data.

output-location = starting location of the output field (1 is assumed if output-location is not specified)

Specification of MAXFLDS=2 in Figure 4.7b indicates two FIELD operands on the RECORD statement. The first FIELD parameter causes the nine-byte field, beginning in column 1 of the input record, to begin in column 25 of the output record. The second FIELD parameter prints positions 10 through 29 of the input record in positions 1–20 of the output record. The SKIP=2 parameter on the PRINT statement causes every second record to appear; i.e., it prints records two, four, six, etc.

Additional operands associated with IEBPTPCH (not shown in either Figure 4.6 or 4.7) include STOPAFT (Stop After) and STRTAFT (Start After). Specification of STOPAFT=30 will cause IEBPTPCH to terminate after 30 records have been printed. In similar fashion, STRTAFT=30 will skip the first 30 records before printing begins.

IEBPTPCH can be used with partitioned data sets by coding TYP-ORG=PO on the PRINT statement. (Omission of this parameter causes IEBPTPCH to assume a sequential data set, as in the previous examples. A sequential data set may also be specified explicitly via TYPORG=PS.)

If an entire PDS is the input file, no further specification other than TYPORG=PO is necessary. If, however, a selected member (or members) is the input file, a separate MEMBER statement is required. In addition, the operand MAXNAME=n is required on the PRINT statement, where n equals the number of subsequent MEMBER statements. The control statements

```
PRINT    TYPORG=PO,STOPAFT=5,MAXFLDS=1
TITLE    ITEM=('PRINT 5 RECORDS FROM EACH MEMBER')
RECORD   FIELD=80
```

will print the first five records from *each* member of a partitioned data set. The control statements

```
PRINT    TYPORG=PO,STOPAFT=5,MAXNAME=2,MAXFLDS=1
TITLE    ITEM=('PRINT 5 RECORDS FROM TWO MEMBERS')
MEMBER   NAME=AAA
RECORD   FIELD=(80)
MEMBER   NAME=BBB
RECORD   FIELD=(40)
```

will print five records from two members, AAA and BBB, of the PDS specified in SYSUT1. Since individual RECORD statements follow the MEMBER statements to which they refer, it is possible to print different members of a PDS under different specifications.

IEBISAM

As stated previously in Chapter 2, ISAM organization is becoming less important since IBM dropped its support in favor of VSAM. Nevertheless, some information on the IEBISAM utility may prove useful with older applications.

ISAM data sets are stored in *logical rather than physical sequential order*. Hence, they require a special utility and *cannot* be referenced with the traditional programs such as IEBGENER, etc., which access sequential files. The IEBISAM utility can copy an ISAM file from one direct access volume to another. It will delete records marked for deletion (i.e., those with HIGH-VALUES in the first byte), and empty the overflow area(s) by copying records to the prime area. The utility can create a sequential (unloaded) data set on a magnetic tape as backup and can restore an ISAM file on a direct access device from an unloaded version. Figure 4.8 shows the jobstream used to reorganize an ISAM file from one direct-access device to another.

```
//GRAUER      JOB
//            EXEC  PGM=IEBISAM,PARM=COPY
//SYSPRINT    DD    SYSOUT=A
//SYSUT1      DD    DSN=OLD.ISAM.FILE,DCB=DSORG=IS,
//       UNIT=(3350,2),VOL=SER=(USR456,USR012)
//SYSUT2      DD    DSN=NEW.ISAM.FILE,DISP=(,CATLG),
//       UNIT=SYSDA,SPACE=(CYL,(50,5),,CONTIG),
//       DCB=(LRECL=75,BLKSIZE=1500,RECFM=FB,DSORG=IS,
//       KEYLEN=6,RKP=1,CYLOFL=2,NTM=4,OPTCD=LMYI)
```

FIGURE 4.8 Use of IEBISAM

As with other utilities SYSUT1 and SYSUT2 denote input and output files respectively. Conspicuous by its absence is the SYSIN DD statement to supply commands to the utility program. It is not used with IEBISAM, as the utility is controlled completely by the PARM parameter in the EXEC statement. Specification of PARM=COPY copies—i.e., reorganizes the file. Specification of PARM=(PRINTL,N) prints a file. (Other options can be found in the Utilities Manual.)

The input data set of Figure 4.8 is uncatalogued, as implied by the UNIT and VOL information. Note the rather unusual specification of the UNIT parameter which specifies that two 3350s are required, and the corresponding information in the VOL parameter.

The output data set is specified on a single DD statement with embedded index and overflow areas. (Figure 2.12 illustrated concatenated DD statements with separate overflow and index areas.) The DCB parameter is coded with a multitude of subparameters, most of which were previously explained in Chapter 2. RKP indicates the *relative key position;* e.g., RKP=1 specifies that the record key begins in the *second* byte of each record (the first byte would be indicated by RKP=0, and is generally used as the "delete" byte). The key length is six bytes, as indicated by KEYLEN=6. The combination RKP and KEYLEN parameters indicate that the record key is in bytes two through seven.

IEBUPDTE

IEBUPDTE changes (updates) information in a file. It can add, delete, or change records in a <u>sequential data set, or in a specified member of a partitioned data set.</u> It can create a new member in an existing partitioned data set, or create an entirely new partitioned data set.

IEBUPDTE requires DD statements for SYSPRINT, SYSUT1, SYSUT2, and SYSIN. SYSUT1 and SYSUT2 point to the incoming and outgoing data sets respectively, and are usually one and the same. SYSPRINT is the DDname for IEBUPDTE messages, and SYSIN references the data set for the utility control cards.

IEBUPDTE control statements begin with ./ in columns 1 and 2, followed by the operation and operands. Three control statements are discussed. These are ADD, to add a new member to an existing partitioned data set; REPL, to replace an existing member in its entirety; and ENDUP, to denote the end of input to SYSIN.

IEBUPDTE is used by the COBOL programmer to add a member to a source statement library for subsequent use in a COPY statement. Figure 4.9 shows how this is accomplished; Figure 4.9a contains the jobstream to execute the program, and Figure 4.9b the associated output.

SYSUT1 and SYSUT2 refer to MEN.PGM.JSC.TEST, a catalogued data set. The COBOL statements themselves are contained between the ./ ADD and ./ ENDUP control statements of the SYSIN file. Figure 4.9b shows that the member STUDFILE has been successfully added to the PDS MEN.PGM.JSC.TEST, and consequently may be called by a COBOL COPY statement. Use of the latter requires specification of the LIB option to the compiler—i.e., PARM.COB=LIB, and a SYSLIB DD statement to identify the PDS; e.g., MEN.PGM.JSC.TEST (see Figure 2.11). Figure 4.10 contains a COBOL segment with the COPY statement. Note well that the

```
//JSC$2990 JOB (MAS526),JACKIE
//STEP1  EXEC PGM=IEBUPDTE
//SYSPRINT DD SYSOUT=A
//SYSUT1 DD DSN=MEN.PGM.JSC.TEST,DISP=SHR
//SYSUT2 DD DSN=MEN.PGM.JSC.TEST,DISP=SHR      COBOL statements that make
//SYSIN DD *                                    up the member, STUDFILE
./ ADD LIST=ALL,NAME=STUDFILE
       FD  STUDENT-FILE
           RECORD CONTAINS 80 CHARACTERS
           LABEL RECORDS ARE STANDARD
           BLOCK CONTAINS 0 RECORDS.
           DATA RECORD IS STUDENT-RECORD.

       01  STUDENT-RECORD.
           05  STD-SOC-SEC-NUM          PIC 9(09).
           05  STD-NAME                 PIC X(36).
           05  FILLER                   PIC X(35).
./ ENDUP
//
```

FIGURE 4.9a Input to IEBUPDTE

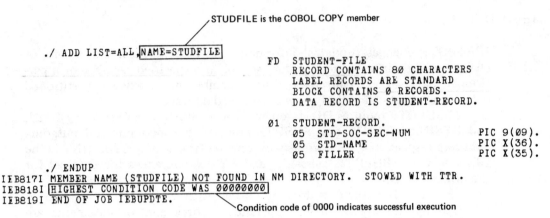

STUDFILE is the COBOL COPY member

```
./ ADD LIST=ALL,NAME=STUDFILE

              FD   STUDENT-FILE
                   RECORD CONTAINS 80 CHARACTERS
                   LABEL RECORDS ARE STANDARD
                   BLOCK CONTAINS 0 RECORDS.
                   DATA RECORD IS STUDENT-RECORD.

              01   STUDENT-RECORD.
                   05   STD-SOC-SEC-NUM        PIC 9(09).
                   05   STD-NAME               PIC X(36).
                   05   FILLER                 PIC X(35).

  ./ ENDUP
IEB817I MEMBER NAME (STUDFILE) NOT FOUND IN NM DIRECTORY.  STOWED WITH TTR.
IEB818I HIGHEST CONDITION CODE WAS 00000000
IEB819I END OF JOB IEBUPDTE.
```
Condition code of 0000 indicates successful execution

FIGURE 4.9b System Messages Produced by IEBUPDTE

COPY statement refers to the member STUDFILE which was added to the PDS in Figure 4.9.

The member STUDFILE can be altered after it has been entered in the PDS in one of two ways: either through the CHANGE and DELETE control statements, which add, alter, or delete specific card images; or by the REPL statement, which replaces the entire member. Use of CHANGE and DELETE requires sequence numbers which will be subsequently copied into the COBOL module in conjunction with columns 73-80. Since the sequence numbers referenced by IEBUPDTE may be in conflict with those in the rest of the COBOL program, it may be easier to replace the entire module. The only modification necessary to Figure 4.9a to replace the

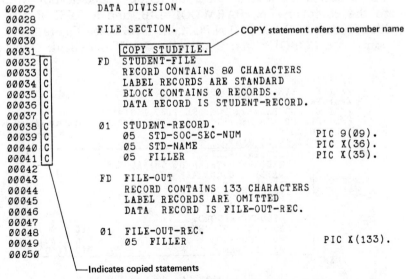

```
00027          DATA DIVISION.
00028
00029          FILE SECTION.                COPY statement refers to member name
00030
00031              COPY STUDFILE.
00032 C        FD   STUDENT-FILE
00033 C             RECORD CONTAINS 80 CHARACTERS
00034 C             LABEL RECORDS ARE STANDARD
00035 C             BLOCK CONTAINS 0 RECORDS.
00036 C             DATA RECORD IS STUDENT-RECORD.
00037 C
00038 C        01   STUDENT-RECORD.
00039 C             05   STD-SOC-SEC-NUM        PIC 9(09).
00040 C             05   STD-NAME               PIC X(36).
00041 C             05   FILLER                 PIC X(35).
00042
00043          FD   FILE-OUT
00044               RECORD CONTAINS 133 CHARACTERS
00045               LABEL RECORDS ARE OMITTED
00046               DATA  RECORD IS FILE-OUT-REC.
00047
00048          01   FILE-OUT-REC.
00049               05   FILLER                 PIC X(133).
00050
```
Indicates copied statements

FIGURE 4.10 Use of a COBOL COPY Statement

existing member, STUDFILE, is to substitute a ./ REPL statement for ./ ADD.

IEBUPDTE is also used to add (or replace) procedures in a procedure library.

IEHPROGM

IEHPROGM catalogs or uncatalogs a data set; scratches or renames a sequential data set, PDS, or member; or builds the indexes for a generation data group. It requires the SYSIN DD statement for utility commands and the SYSPRINT statement for utility messages. It uses two other DD statements (with DDnames at the user's discretion) to define the volumes containing the system catalog and the file being processed.

Figure 4.11 scratches the data set YOURFILE. DDNAME1 and DDNAME2 locate the system catalog and the individual data set, respectively. The SYSIN file contains a single control statement, with the action word SCRATCH beginning in column 2 or beyond. The parameters DSNAME and VOL indicate the location of the data set YOURFILE.

```
//SCRATCH    JOB
//           EXEC   PGM=IEHPROGM        ** USE WITH CAUTION
//DDNAME1    DD     UNIT=SYSDA,VOL=SER=USR001,DISP=OLD
//DDNAME2    DD     UNIT=SYSDA,VOL=SER=USR002,DISP=OLD
//SYSPRINT   DD     SYSOUT=A
//SYSIN      DD     *
   SCRATCH   DSNAME=YOURFILE,VOL=SYSDA=USR002
```

FIGURE 4.11 Scratching a Data Set

The MEMBER and PURGE parameters may also be specified with the SCRATCH control statement. For example, modification of Figure 4.11 to delete *only the member* GOODBYE *from the partitioned data set* YOURFILE requires the statement:

```
SCRATCH DSNAME=YOURFILE,VOL=SYSDA=USR002,MEMBER=GOODBYE
```

Inclusion of the PURGE parameter will scratch a file prior to its expiration date. (Every newly created data set is given an expiration date either by the EXPDT or RETPD parameters in associated JCL or through a system default if the parameter is omitted.) If one attempts to delete a file prior to its expiration date without including the PURGE parameter, the system responds with an error message. Inclusion of the PURGE parameter eliminates the file regardless of its expiration date. Modification of Figure 4.11 to scratch the data set YOURFILE, without concern for the expiration date, is simply:

```
SCRATCH DSNAME=YOURFILE,VOL=SYSDA=USR002,PURGE
```

IEHPROGM can also rename a data set through the RENAME command; e.g., to rename the data set OLD to NEW, use:

```
RENAME  VOL=3350=USR002,DSNAME=OLD,NEWNAME=NEW
```

An individual member of a partitioned data set can be renamed by inclusion of the MEMBER parameter. (Realize, however, that if the new name is to be catalogued and/or the old name uncatalogued, then the additional control statements CATLG and UNCATLG are required.)

IEHPROGM is also used to create the necessary indexes for generation data groups via the BLDG control statement. This particular function is not illustrated, however, as the author has chosen to build indexes through IDCAMS in Chapter 5.

IEBCOPY

IEBCOPY maintains partitioned data sets. Specifically, it can compress a PDS, merge two or more partitioned data sets into one, or simply copy a PDS from one place to another. It can operate on specific members of a PDS by selecting individual members for inclusion or excluding others from consideration. The following DDnames are necessary:

DDname1	Any DDname chosen by the user to describe the input PDS
DDname2	Any DDname chosen by the user to describe the output PDS
SYSUT3	Utility work file
SYSUT4	Utility work file
SYSIN	DDname for the utility control statements
SYSPRINT	DDname to identify the utility messages

Figure 4.12a contains a jobstream to copy five selected members from the input PDS, MAS526.DATA, to the output PDS, MEN.PGM.JSC.TEST. The COPY statement in the SYSIN command file is mandatory and specifies INDD1 and OUTDD1 as the DDnames for the input and output data sets respectively. (IBM could have made life simpler by adhering to conventions associated with other utilities: namely, that SYSUT1 and SYSUT2 refer to the input and output files, respectively. Unfortunately, such is not the case.) SYSUT3 and SYSUT4 are required, and denote temporary work

```
                                        ┌─DDname of output data set
//JSC$2987 JOB (161349),JACKIE
//STEP1    EXEC PGM=IEBCOPY
//SYSPRINT DD SYSOUT=A
//OUTDD1   DD DISP=(OLD,KEEP),DSN=MEN.PGM.JSC.TEST
//INDD1    DD DSN=MAS526.DATA,DISP=SHR
//SYSUT3   DD UNIT=SYSDA,SPACE=(TRK,(1))
//SYSUT4   DD UNIT=SYSDA,SPACE=(TRK,(1))
//SYSIN    DD *
COPYOPER   COPY OUTDD=OUTDD1
                INDD=INDD1
           SELECT MEMBER=(SEQUPEX,NONSEQUP,TRANS,PROMOTE,RWDATA)
/*
```

FIGURE 4.12a Input to IEBCOPY

```
                            IEBCOPY MESSAGES AND CONTROL STATEMENTS

           COPYOPER    COPY OUTDD=OUTDD1
                            INDD=INDD1
                       SELECT MEMBER=(SEQUPEX,NONSEQUP,TRANS,PROMOTE,RWDATA)
IEB167I  FOLLOWING MEMBER(S) COPIED FROM INPUT DATA SET REFERENCED BY INDD1   -
IEB154I  NONSEQUP HAS BEEN SUCCESSFULLY COPIED
IEB154I  PROMOTE  HAS BEEN SUCCESSFULLY COPIED    ┌─Five members were successfully copied
IEB154I  RWDATA   HAS BEEN SUCCESSFULLY COPIED  ──┤
IEB154I  SEQUPEX  HAS BEEN SUCCESSFULLY COPIED
IEB154I  TRANS    HAS BEEN SUCCESSFULLY COPIED
IEB144I  THERE ARE 0000006 UNUSED TRACKS IN OUTPUT DATA SET REFERENCED BY OUTDD1
IEB149I  THERE ARE 0000008  UNUSED DIRECTORY BLOCKS IN OUTPUT DIRECTORY
IEB147I  END OF JOB -00 WAS HIGHEST SEVERITY CODE
```

FIGURE 4.12b System Messages Produced by IEBCOPY

FIGURE 4.12 IEBCOPY Utility

files for input and output directories. One track is usually ample, and default values are adequate for DSNAME and DCB information. SYSPRINT serves the same function as with other utilities.

Figure 4.12b shows the messages produced during execution—i.e., the SYSPRINT file itself. Five members were successfully copied as per the previous SELECT statement. (What would the effect have been if EXCLUDE were substituted for SELECT in Figure 4.12a?)

SORT/MERGE

The sort/merge utility program may be called implicitly by the COBOL SORT verb, or explicitly through execution of a separate job step. The necessary DD statements include:

SORTLIB   To define the data set containing the sort/ merge load modules; typically coded with only DSN and DISP parameters

SORTWKnn   To describe intermediate work areas used by the sort/merge utility. There may be from one to six work areas, depending on the size of the file. The reader is referred to the vendor manual for additional information

SYSOUT   To describe a print file, containing the messages produced by the sort utility

SYSIN   To define input control statements to the utility

In addition, when the sort/merge is executed explicitly, SORTIN and SORTOUT DD statements must also be specified for the input and output files, respectively. (The COBOL programmer uses DDnames of his or her choosing for these files, as long as they are consistent with the SELECT statements. See, for example, Figure 2.14.)

The commands to the sort/merge program depend on how the utility is called. Figure 4.13*a* shows a COBOL SD and corresponding SORT statement. Figure 4.13*b* contains *equivalent* information but in the form of a SORT command statement which is input to the utility as part of the SYSIN file.

The SORT command has the following syntax:

$$\begin{Bmatrix} \text{SORT} \\ \text{MERGE} \end{Bmatrix} \text{FIELDS=(location,length,sequence,...),FORMAT=format}$$

where

location = starting position within a record

length = length of the field; i.e., the number of characters

```
SD   SORT-WORK-FILE
     RECORD CONTAINS 80 CHARACTERS
     DATA-RECORD IS SORT-RECORD.
01   SORT-RECORD.
     05   SRT-NAME          PIC X(12).
     05   SRT-YEAR          PIC X.
     05   FILLER            PIC X.
     05   SRT-MAJOR         PIC X(20).
     05   FILLER            PIC X(6).
  .
  .
      SORT SORT-WORK-FILE
         ASCENDING KEY SRT-MAJOR
         DESCENDING KEY SRT-YEAR
         ASCENDING KEY SRT-NAME
  .
  .
```

Primary key begins in column 15 and extends for 20 bytes

FIGURE 4.13*a* COBOL SORT Verb

Primary key begins in column 15 and extends for 20 bytes

```
SORT FIELDS (15,20,A,13,1,D,1,12,A),FORMAT=CH
```

FIGURE 4.13*b* SORT Utility Command

FIGURE 4.13 COBOL SORT Verb Versus SORT Utility

> sequence = either ascending or descending, denoted by A or D respectively
>
> format = type of data; CH for character, BI for binary, ZD for zoned decimal.

The reader should be convinced that the COBOL specification of Figure 4.13a is equivalent to the command specification of Figure 4.13b. The latter may also be specified as:

```
SORT FIELDS (15,20,CH,A,13,1,CH,D,1,12,CH,A)
```

which is useful if the sort keys have different formats—e.g., character, binary, etc.

Figure 4.14 illustrates fully the use of a stand alone sort. Figure 4.14a depicts the input jobstream, and contains the DD statements described earlier. ICEMAN is the name of the sort program. (Many OS shops have purchased an independent sort program, with the SYNCSORT utility the most common. However, the actual program is transparent to the user, as all versions adhere to a common command syntax.)

Figures 4.14b and 4.14d show the input and output files, respectively. The SORT command itself is contained in the messages of Figure 4.14c.

```
//STEP3     EXEC PGM=ICEMAN
//STEPLIB   DD DSN=SYS2.LINKLIB,DISP=SHR
//SORTLIB   DD DSN=SYS1.ICELIB,DISP=SHR
//SORTWK01  DD UNIT=DISK,SPACE=(CYL,(1),,CONTIG)
//SORTWK02  DD UNIT=DISK,SPACE=(CYL,(1),,CONTIG)
//SORTWK03  DD UNIT=DISK,SPACE=(CYL,(1),,CONTIG)
//SORTWK04  DD UNIT=DISK,SPACE=(CYL,(1),,CONTIG)
//SORTWK05  DD UNIT=DISK,SPACE=(CYL,(1),,CONTIG)
//SORTWK06  DD UNIT=DISK,SPACE=(CYL,(1),,CONTIG)
//SYSIN     DD *
//SORTIN    DD DSN=&&DATAFILE,DISP=(OLD,PASS)
//SORTOUT   DD DSN=&&SORTED,DISP=(NEW,PASS),UNIT=SYSDA,
//            DCB=(LRECL=80,BLKSIZE=80,RECFM=FB),SPACE=(TRK,(1))
//SYSOUT    DD SYSOUT=A
//SYSPRINT  DD SYSOUT=A
```

FIGURE 4.14a Jobstream to Execute SORT

```
BENJAMIN    4 BUSINESS
GRAUER      3 LIBERAL ARTS
JONES       4 ENGINEERING
EPSTEIN     2 ENGINEERING
SMITH       1 LIBERAL ARTS
ZEV         4 BUSINESS
HOWE        1 LIBERAL ARTS
FRANK       1 ENGINEERING
DEUTSCH     4 BUSINESS
ADAMS       3 BUSINESS
```

FIGURE 4.14b File Before Sorting

Contents of the SYSIN file of Figure 4.14a

```
ICE000I - --- CONTROL STATEMENTS/MESSAGES ---- 5740-SM1 REL 5.0 PTF 00
          SORT FIELDS=(15,20,A,13,1,D,1,12,A),FORMAT=CH
          RECORD TYPE=F,LENGTH=(80,,80)
ICE088I - JSC$3220.STEP3  , INPUT LRECL = 80, BLKSIZE = 80, TYPE = F
ICE093I - MAIN STORAGE = (MAX,524288,519856), NMAX = 29300, BLOCKSET
ICE080I - IN MAIN STORAGE SORT
ICE054I - RECORDS - IN: 10, OUT: 10, - END OF SORT
```

FIGURE 4.14c Sort Messages

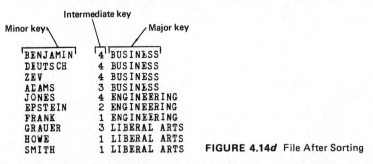

Minor key   Intermediate key   Major key

```
BENJAMIN    4 BUSINESS
DEUTSCH     4 BUSINESS
ZEV         4 BUSINESS
ADAMS       3 BUSINESS
JONES       4 ENGINEERING
EPSTEIN     2 ENGINEERING
FRANK       1 ENGINEERING
GRAUER      3 LIBERAL ARTS
HOWE        1 LIBERAL ARTS
SMITH       1 LIBERAL ARTS
```

FIGURE 4.14d File After Sorting

Figure 4.15 illustrates *a merge in which two or more input files, with identical format and already in sequence, are combined into a single output file.* Note well that the multiple input files to a merge are designated SORTIN01, SORTIN02, etc. Figure 4.15a contains the jobstream, Figures

```
//STEP5    EXEC PGM=ICEMAN
//STEPLIB  DD DSN=SYS2.LINKLIB,DISP=SHR
//SORTLIB  DD DSN=SYS1.SORTLIB,DISP=SHR
//SYSOUT   DD SYSOUT=A
//SORTWK01 DD UNIT=DISK,SPACE=(CYL,(1),,CONTIG)
//SORTWK02 DD UNIT=DISK,SPACE=(CYL,(1),,CONTIG)
//SORTWK03 DD UNIT=DISK,SPACE=(CYL,(1),,CONTIG)
//SORTWK04 DD UNIT=DISK,SPACE=(CYL,(1),,CONTIG)
//SORTWK05 DD UNIT=DISK,SPACE=(CYL,(1),,CONTIG)
//SORTWK06 DD UNIT=DISK,SPACE=(CYL,(1),,CONTIG)
//SORTIN01 DD DSN=&&FILEONE,DISP=(OLD,PASS)
//SORTIN02 DD DSN=&&FILETWO,DISP=(OLD,PASS)
//SORTOUT- DD DSN=&&MERGED,DISP=(NEW,PASS),UNIT=SYSDA,
//            DCB=(LRECL=80,BLKSIZE=80,RECFM=FB),SPACE=(TRK,(1))
//SYSIN    DD *
```

FIGURE 4.15a Input Jobstream

Multiple input files
are already in sequence

```
100000000    111111111
200000000    222222222
300000000    333333333
400000000    444444444
500000000    555555555
600000000    666666666
700000000    777777777
800000000    888888888
900000000    999999999
```

FIGURE 4.15b Input Files

```
ICE000I      ------------ CONTROL STATEMENTS/MESSAGES --------- 5740-SM1 RELEASE 5.0 PTF 00

           MERGE FIELDS=(1,9,A),FORMAT=CH

           RECORD TYPE=F,LENGTH=(80,,80)
ICE054I - RCD IN      0,OUT     18
ICE052I - END OF SORT/MERGE
```

FIGURE 4.15*c* Merge Messages

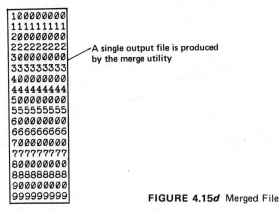

A single output file is produced
by the merge utility

FIGURE 4.15*d* Merged File

FIGURE 4.15 Use of MERGE Program

4.15*b* and 4.15*d* the input and output files, and Figure 4.15*c* the utility messages.

THE LINKAGE-EDITOR

Most COBOL programmers take the linkage-editor for granted, and know little else about its function. It is not a utility in the sense of IEBGENER, IEBUPDTE, etc. Nevertheless, it is a program whose task should be well understood. Accordingly, let us review Figure 2.5, which depicts the procedure COBVCLG.

The COBOL compiler accepts COBOL source statements and translates them into machine language. The linkage-editor takes the object module passed to it by the compiler, determines which external subprograms are necessary, and resolves all external references. The linkage-editor then combines these individual programs into a single *load module*, for subsequent execution.

The DDnames SYSLIN and SYSLMOD are found in the LKED step of Figure 2.5, and denote input and output from the linkage-editor. The data set names associated with SYSLIN and SYSLMOD are &&OBJ and &&LOD(X), respectively. Since &&OBJ is input to the linkage-editor, it must have been produced by the compiler. Accordingly, note that the data set &&OBJ was created in the COB step with disposition (MOD,PASS). In similar fashion, the output from the linkage-editor should be input to the GO step. The latter EXEC statement (// EXEC PGM=*.LKED.SYSLMOD) executes the load module on the SYSLMOD DD statement of the LKED step—i.e., &&LOD(X). (The asterisk denotes *a referback* parameter.)

One major conclusion to be drawn from Figure 2.5 is that the load module, &&LOD(X), is a temporary data set, as indicated by the two ampersands. This is acceptable in the testing phase of a *single* program, but unacceptable for production and/or for testing more than one program (e.g., a main and subprograms). The linkage-editor can be used to make the latter process more efficient, as is done in Figure 4.16.

Figure 4.16 is a jobstream to compile, link, and execute three programs: a main program and two subprograms. It makes explicit use of the linkage-editor in that the object modules produced by each of the compiles are permanently retained as members in the partitioned data set MEN.PGM.ISIS.LOD. The advantages of this technique over the more straightforward "compile, link, and go" apply when any of the programs are changed individually. For example, assume that the subprograms are completely debugged but that the main program is undergoing modification. It is inherently

```
                                              ┌SYSLIB DD statement supports COBOL COPY
//JSC$3062    JOB (MAS526),JACKIE,MSGCLASS=R ╱
//STEP1       EXEC COBVCL
//COB.SYSLIB  DD DSN=JESSICA.RTG.COBOL,DISP=SHR
//COB.SYSIN   DD DSN=JESSICA.RTG.COBOL(MAINPROG),DISP=SHR
//LKED.SYSLMOD DD DSN=MEN.PGM.ISIS.LOD(MAINPROG),DISP=(OLD,KEEP)
//STEP2       EXEC COBVCL                         └─Load module for main program
//COB.SYSLIB  DD DSN=JESSICA.RTG.COBOL,DISP=SHR
//COB.SYSIN   DD DSN=JESSICA.RTG.COBOL(SUBRTN1),DISP=SHR
//LKED.SYSLMOD DD DSN=MEN.PGM.ISIS.LOD(SUBRTN1),DISP=(OLD,KEEP)
//STEP3       EXEC COBVCL                         └─Load module for SUBRTN1
//COB.SYSLIB  DD DSN=JESSICA.RTG.COBOL,DISP=SHR
//COB.SYSIN   DD DSN=JESSICA.RTG.COBOL(SUBRTN2),DISP=SHR
//LKED.SYSLMOD DD DSN=MEN.PGM.ISIS.LOD(SUBRTN2),DISP=(OLD,KEEP)
//STEP4       EXEC PGM=IEWL,PARM='MAP'            └─Load module for SUBRTN2
//SYSUT1      DD UNIT=SYSDA,SPACE=(6144,100)
//SYSPRINT    DD SYSOUT=R
//SYSLMOD     DD DSN=MEN.PGM.ISIS.LOD(COMPLETE),DISP=(OLD,KEEP)
//ANYNAME     DD DSN=MEN.PGM.ISIS.LOD,DISP=SHR
//SYSLIN      DD *
  INCLUDE   ANYNAME(MAINPROG)
  INCLUDE   ANYNAME(SUBRTN1)  ──Linkage-editor control statements
  INCLUDE   ANYNAME(SUBRTN2)
  ENTRY MAINPROG
/*                                     ╱STEPLIB DD statement indicates where
//STEP5       EXEC PGM=COMPLETE         completed load module is located
//STEPLIB     DD DSN=MEN.PGM.ISIS.LOD,DISP=SHR
//GO.SORTLIB  DD DSN=SYS1.SORTLIB,DISP=SHR
//GO.SORTWORK DD SPACE=(TRK,(1,1)),UNIT=DISK
//GO.SORTWK01 DD SPACE=(TRK,(1,1)),UNIT=DISK
//GO.SORTWK02 DD SPACE=(TRK,(1,1)),UNIT=DISK
//GO.SORTWK03 DD SPACE=(TRK,(1,1)),UNIT=DISK
//GO.SORTMSG  DD SYSOUT=R
//GO.COURSE   DD *
//GO.PRINT    DD SYSOUT=R
//GO.STUD     DD *
```

FIGURE 4.16 Use of the Linkage-Editor

wasteful to recompile both subprograms continually when they are not changing. (This is especially true in larger systems with many independent subroutines.) Rather, *each program should be compiled separately and retained in its object form* for subsequent link-editing and eventual execution.

There are five explicit steps in Figure 4.16. Step one invokes the procedure COBVCL, consisting of two substeps COB and LKED, for the main program. The compile step produces an object module for the main program. The link-edit step produces a load module for the main program and permanently stores it as a member, MAINPROG, in the partitioned data set, MEN.PGM.ISIS.LOD. Steps two and three serve the identical function for the subroutines. Step four explicitly invokes the linkage-editor and produces a single load module, COMPLETE, from the three individual modules.

The linkage-editor program in step four requires a DD statement for SYSUT1, a scratch data set. It uses a DD statement for SYSPRINT, a print data set. It also requires DD statements for SYSLIN and SYSLMOD, the functions of which were explained earlier. This time, however, SYSLIN is in card image format (as indicated by the asterisk in its DD statement).

Control statements for the linkage-editor follow the SYSLIN DD statement and begin in column 2 or beyond. The INCLUDE statement specifies the DD statement containing the input to the linkage-editor. The format is INCLUDE DDname(member). The three INCLUDE statements in Figure 4.16 indicate that the members MAINPROG, SUBRTN1, and SUBRTN2, referenced by the DD statement ANYNAME, are input to the linkage-editor. The ENTRY statement specifies that the first executable instruction in the load module is to be the first instruction in MAINPROG.

Step five executes the program COMPLETE, the load module produced in step four. It requires a STEPLIB DD statement, to tell the system where the executable program is located. The UNIT and VOL parameters are omitted from the STEPLIB statement, implying a catalogued data set. DISP=SHR allows other jobs to access MEN.PGM.ISIS.LOD simultaneously.

Several variations are possible with Figure 4.16. For example, if changes were made in the main program only, the jobstream would consist of steps one, four, and five as the subprograms would not have to be recompiled. A second variation is the production jobstream, which would consist only of step five.

THE VENDOR'S REFERENCE MANUAL

The IBM manual on OS Utilities (GT35-0005-2) is one of its more helpful publications. Often the biggest problem confronting the programmer is identification of the proper utility. Table 4.1, reproduced from the vendor

TABLE 4.1 IBM UTILITIES, (REPRINTED WITH PERMISSION OF IBM)

Functions are listed in alphabetical order,
enabling identification of the proper utility.

Task		Utility Program
Add	a password	IEHPROGM
Analyze	tracks on direct access	IEHATLAS, IEHDASDR, IBCDASDI
Assign alternate tracks	to a direct access volume	IEHATLAS, IEHDASDR, IBCDASDI
Build	a generation-data-group index	IEHPROGM
	a generation	IEHPROGM
	an index	IEHPROGM
Catalog	a data set	IEHPROGM
	a generation data set	IEHPROGM
Change	data set organization	IEBUPDTE
	logical record length	IEBGENER
	volume serial number of direct access volume	IEHDASDR
Compare	a partitioned data set	IEBCOMPR
	sequential data sets	IEBCOMPR
Compress in place	a partitioned data set	IEBCOPY
Connect	volumes	IEHPROGM
Construct	records from MTST and MTDI input	IEBTCRIN
Convert to partitioned	a sequential data set created as a result of an unload	IEBCOPY
	sequential data sets	IEBUPDTE, IEBGENER
Convert to sequential	a partitioned data set	IEBUPDTE, IEBCOPY
	an indexed-sequential data set	IEBISAM, IEBDG
Copy	a catalog	IEHMOVE
	a direct access volume	IEHDASDR, IBCDMPRS, IEHMOVE
	a partitioned data set	IEBCOPY, IEHMOVE
	a volume of data sets	IEHMOVE
	an indexed-sequential data set	IEBISAM
	catalogued data sets	IEHMOVE
	dumped data from tape to direct access	IEHDASDR, IBCDMPRS
	job steps	IEBEDIT
	members	IEBGENER, IEBUPDTE, IEBDG
	selected members	IEBCOPY, IEHMOVE
	sequential data sets	IEBGENER, IEHMOVE, IEBUPDTE
	to tape	IBCDMPRS
Create	a library of partitioned members	IEBUPDTE
	a member	IEBDG
	a sequential output data set	IEBDG
	an index	IEHPROGM
	an output job stream	IEBEDIT
Delete	a password	IEHPROGM
	an index structure	IEHPROGM
	records in a partitioned data set	IEBUPDTE

TABLE 4.1 (Continued)

Task		Utility Program
Dump	a direct access volume	IEHDASDR, IBCDMPRS
Edit	MTDI input	IEBTCRIN
Edit and convert to partitioned	a sequential data set	IEBGENER, IEBUPDTE
Edit and copy	a job stream	IEBEDIT
	a sequential data set	IEBGENER, IEBUPDTE
Edit and list	error statistics by volume (ESV) records	IFHSTATR
Edit and print	a sequential data set	IEBPTPCH
Edit and punch	a sequential data set	IEBPTPCH
Enter	a procedure into a procedure library	IEBUPDTE
Exclude	a partitioned data set member from a copy operation	IEBCOPY, IEHMOVE
Expand	a partitioned data set	IEBCOPY
	a sequential data set	IEBGENER
Generate	test data	IEBDG
Get alternate tracks	on a direct access volume	IEHDASDR, IBCDASDI, IEHATLAS
Include	changes to members or sequential data sets	IEBUPDTE
Initialize	a direct access volume	IEHDASDR, IBCDASDI
Insert records	into a partitioned data set	IEBUPDTE
Label	magnetic tape volumes	IEHINITT
List	a password entry	IEHPROGM
	a volume table of contents	IEHLIST
	contents of direct access volume on system output device	IEHDASDR
	number of unused directory blocks and tracks	IEBCOPY
	partitioned directories	IEHLIST
	the contents of the catalog (SYSCTLG data set)	IEHLIST
Load	a previously unloaded partitioned data set	IEBCOPY
	an indexed-sequential data set	IEBISAM
	an unloaded data set	IEHMOVE
	UCS and FCB buffers of a 3211	ICAPRTBL
Merge	partitioned data sets	IEHMOVE, IEBCOPY
Modify	a partitioned or sequential data set	IEBUPDTE
Move	a catalog	IEHMOVE
	a volume of data sets	IEHMOVE
	catalogued data sets	IEHMOVE
	partitioned data sets	IEHMOVE
	sequential data sets	IEHMOVE
Number records	in a new member	IEBUPDTE
	in a partitioned data set	IEBUPDTE
Password protect	add a password	IEHPROGM
	delete a password	IEHPROGM
	list passwords	IEHPROGM
	replace a password	IEHPROGM
Print	a sequential data set	IEBGENER, IEBUPDTE, IEBPTPCH
	partitioned data sets	IEBPTPCH
	selected records	IEBPTPCH

TABLE 4.1 (Continued)

Task		Utility Program
Punch	a partitioned data set member	IEBPTPCH
	a sequential data set	IEBPTPCH
	selected records	IEBPTPCH
Read	Tape Cartridge Reader input	IEBTCRIN
Reblock	a partitioned data set	IEBCOPY
	a sequential data set	IEBGENER, IEBUPDTE
Recover	data from defective tracks on direct access volumes	IEHATLAS
Release	a connected volume	IEHPROGM
Rename	a partitioned data set member	IEBCOPY, IEHPROGM
	a sequential or partitioned data set	IEHPROGM
	moved or copied members	IEHMOVE
Renumber	logical records	IEBUPDTE
Replace	a password	IEHPROGM
	data on an alternate track	IEHATLAS
	identically named members	IEBCOPY
	logical records	IEBUPDTE
	members	IEBUPDTE
	records in a member	IEBUPDTE
	records in a partitioned data set	IEBUPDTE, IEBCOPY
	selected members	IEBCOPY
	selected members in a move or copy operation	IEBCOPY, IEHMOVE
Restore	a dumped direct access volume from tape	IBCDMPRS, IEHDASDR
Scratch	a volume table of contents	IEHPROGM
	data sets	IEHPROGM
Uncatlog	data sets	IEHPROGM
Unload	a partitioned data set	IEHMOVE, IEBCOPY
	a sequential data set	IEHMOVE
	an indexed-sequential data set	IEBISAM
Update	in place a partitioned data set	IEBUPDTE
Write	IPL records and a program on a direct access volume	IBCDASDI, IEHDASDR

manual, lists various functions in alphabetical order. Hence, to "build a generation data group index" one uses IEHPROGM; to "create a library of partitioned members" mandates use of IEBUPDTE, and so on.

Once the proper utility has been established, one locates the appropriate section in the manual. The discussion on every utility is accompanied by *well-illustrated examples* which are summarized in a separate table for every utility. Table 4.2 pertains to IEBGENER. Often there will be an example in the manual which meets the user's needs exactly. If not, one can usually adapt a similar example to the problem at hand.

TABLE 4.2 IEBGENER EXAMPLES (REPRINTED WITH PERMISSION OF IBM)

Operation	Data Set Organization	Devices	Comments	Example
COPY	Sequential	Card Reader, Tape	Blocked output.	1
COPY-with editing	Sequential	Card Reader, Tape	Blocked output.	2
COPY-with editing	Sequential	Card Reader, Tape	Blocked output. Input includes // cards.	3
COPY-with editing	Sequential	Card Reader, 2314 Disk	Blocked output. Input includes // cards.	4
PRINT	Sequential	Card Reader, Printer	Input includes // cards. System output device is a printer.	5
CONVERT	Sequential input. Partitioned output.	Tape, 2314 Disk	Blocked output. Three members are to be created.	6
COPY-with editing	Sequential	3330 Drum	Blocked output. Two members are to be merged into existing data set.	7
COPY-with editing	Sequential	Tape	Blocked output. Data set edited as one record group.	8
COPY-with editing	Sequential	2314 Disk	Blocked output. New record length specified for output data set. Two record groups specified.	9
COPY-with editing	Sequential	Tape	Blocked output. Data set edited as one record group.	10

Summary

OS utilities are a necessary tool for the applications programmer. The chapter began by motivating their use, then covered specifics of the following utilities:

IEBGENER: Copies sequential files or members of partitioned data sets from one medium to another

IEBPTPCH: Prints or punches all, or selected portions of, sequential or partitioned data sets

IEBUPDTE: Creates or modifies card image data in sequential or partitioned data sets; adds members to source statement or procedure libraries

     ✦   IEHPROGM: Catalogs or uncatalogs data sets; scratches or renames data sets and/or members; maintains data set passwords; builds an index for a generation data group

        IEBISAM: Copies an ISAM file from one direct access device to another; creates sequential backup for an ISAM file; prints an ISAM file

        IEBCOPY: Copies one or more partitioned data sets from one or more direct access volumes to a single direct access volume; compresses a partitioned data set

Since the most difficult task associated with OS utilities is often to identify the proper program, the reader was referred to the appropriate section in the vendor manual. The linkage-editor and sort/merge programs were also discussed.

TRUE/FALSE EXERCISES

1. Either IEBGENER or IEBPTPCH may be used to print a data set.
2. The statement //SYSIN DD DATA permits JCL statements to be included in the incoming jobstream.
3. SYSLIN and SYSLOUT denote input to, and output from, the linkage-editor.
4. ENTRY and INCLUDE are control statements for the linkage-editor.
5. If a job contains more than one step, step names *are required* on each EXEC statement within the jobstream.
6. The statement //SYSIN DD DUMMY is syntactically invalid.
7. SYSUT1 and SYSUT2 denote input to, and output from, the COBOL compiler.
8. A STEPLIB statement is required in the jobstream for a COBOL compile, if the COPY clause is used.
9. IEBUPDTE typically has equivalent DD statements for SYSUT1 and SYSUT2.
10. IEBUPDTE cannot reference a partitioned data set.
11. Output from the linkage-editor must go to a temporary data set.
12. Utility control statements begin in column 1.
13. IEBUPDTE is required to establish generation data groups.

14. IEHPROGM is used to scratch a data set.

15. IEBISAM can unload an ISAM file as a sequential data set on tape.

16. IEBISAM does not require a DD statement for SYSIN.

17. The SYSIN DD statement must be dummied out whenever a utility is used.

18. VSAM data sets require a special utility, IDCAMS.

19. SYSUT1, SYSUT2, SYSIN, and SYSOUT are the DD statements used with IEBGENER.

20. IEHPROGM can be used to establish indexes for a generation data group.

21. IEBCOPY is used to compress a PDS.

22. IDCAMS can be used to establish indexes for a generation data group.

23. IDCAMS can be used with non-VSAM data sets.

24. SORTIN01, SORTIN02, etc. denote work areas for the sort utility.

PROBLEMS

1. Refer to Figure 4.17.

```
//JSC$2903 JOB (MAS526),JACKIE
//CARDDISK    EXEC PGM=IEBGENER
//SYSPRINT    DD SYSOUT=A
//SYSIN       DD DUMMY
//SYSUT2      DD DSN=&&JCLFILE,DISP=(NEW,PASS),UNIT=SYSDA,
//            DCB=(LRECL=80,BLKSIZE=400,RECFM=FB),SPACE=(TRK,(1,1))
//SYSUT1      DD DATA,DLM=ZZ
//STEP1       EXEC COBVCLG
//COB.SYSIN   DD DSN=MEN.PGM.JSC.RTG(FILEDUMP),DISP=SHR
//GO.FILEIN   DD DSN=MEN.PGM.JSC.RTG(DUMPDATA),DISP=SHR
//GO.FILEOUT  DD SYSOUT=A
//GO.SYSUDUMP DD SYSOUT=A
ZZ
//DISKPRNT    EXEC PGM=IEBGENER
//SYSPRINT    DD SYSOUT=A
//SYSIN       DD DUMMY
//SYSUT2      DD SYSOUT=A
//SYSUT1      DD DSN=&&JCLFILE,DISP=(OLD,PASS)
//
```

FIGURE 4.17 Jobstream for Problem 1

(a) How many steps are there in the submitted jobstream?

(b) Show exactly what will be printed as a result of the step DISKPRNT.

2. Identify the utility (or utilities) in question which:

(a) Does not require a SYSIN DD statement.

(b) Renames a partitioned data set.

(c) Compresses a partitioned data set.

(d) Renames a member of a partitioned data set.

(e) Prints only a selected number of records from a file.

(f) Does not require DD statements for SYSUT1 and SYSUT2.

(g) Adds members to a procedure library or COBOL source statement library.

(h) Copies and/or reblocks a sequential file from tape to disk.

(i) Copies an ISAM file from one direct access volume to another.

(j) Establishes indexes for a generation data group.

(k) Prints a VSAM data set.

(l) Requires DD statements for SYSUT3 and SYSUT4.

3. Modify the jobstream of Figure 4.5 to use IEBPTPCH rather than IEBGENER in steps 2, 4, and 6. Specify appropriate control statements for IEBPTPCH to print only the first 20 columns of each record; also, print an appropriate heading before each file.

4. Write a complete jobstream, consisting of several steps as follows:

(a) Step 1: Create a disk file, with BLKSIZE=400, from cards.

(b) Step 2: Print the newly created disk file, with an appropriate heading.

(c) Step 3: Unblock the disk file created in step 1.

(d) Step 4: Print only columns 1–10 for the first five records of the unblocked file.

(e) Step 5: Rename the data set from step 1 to NEWDATA.

(f) Step 6: Scratch the data set NEWDATA.

5. Develop the necessary jobstream to put a COBOL table, COPYTAB, into the catalogued partitioned data set TEST.RTG.SYSLIB. In particular:

(a) The COBOL table is of the form

```
01   JOB-TITLE.
     05   FILLER   PIC X(20)   VALUE '010ACCOUNTANT'.
     05   FILLER   PIC X(20)   VALUE '020ADMINISTRATOR'.
     .
       .
         .
       etc.
01   JOB-TABLE REDEFINES JOB-TITLE.
     05   JOBS OCCURS 20 TIMES.
          10   JOB-CODE          PIC X(3).
          10   JOB-DESCRIPTION   PIC X(17).
```

(b) Show how the catalogued member would be called by a COBOL program; indicate both the COBOL COPY clause and any additional JCL required.

6. Develop a four step jobstream to compile, link, and execute two COBOL programs. The third step is to invoke the linkage-editor explicitly to produce an executable module. The first program is known as PROGONE, which in turn calls the second program, PROGTWO, as a subprogram. Step four should call for the execution of the load module obtained in step three. Accommodate the following:

(a) Store the load module obtained in step three as MYPROG in the partitioned data set TEST.RTG.PGMLIB.

(b) Assume that the main program uses two sequential files (one for input, and one for output). The subprogram does not have its own files. Show associated SELECT statements.

7. Develop the JCL necessary to support a COBOL MERGE statement of the form:

```
MERGE WORK-FILE
      ON ASCENDING CUSTOMER-ACCOUNT-NUMBER
         DESCENDING AMOUNT-OF-SALE
      USING
          MONDAY-SALES-FILE
          TUESDAY-SALES-FILE
          WEDNESDAY-SALES-FILE
          THURSDAY-SALES-FILE
          FRIDAY-SALES-FILE
      GIVING
          WEEKLY-SALES-FILE.
```

CUSTOMER-ACCOUNT-NUMBER and AMOUNT-OF-SALE appear in positions 10–18 and 24–30 of the input records. Use appropriate data set names for all input files, and assume that all files are catalogued.

5

VSAM Organization

Overview

IBM's Virtual Storage Access Method (VSAM) is a replacement for its earlier ISAM organization, and is far more efficient. As of this writing, most installations have converted to VSAM, and consequently this chapter focuses entirely on the newer access method. (The differences between ISAM and VSAM have been well documented. See, for example, Grauer and Crawford, Chapter Five, *The COBOL Environment*, Prentice-Hall, Englewood Cliffs, NJ, 1979.)

The chapter begins with a conceptual discussion of VSAM organization. We discuss the role of VSAM *catalogs* and show how VSAM maintains a series of indexes to permit *sequential and/or nonsequential access* to individual records. We cover the Access Methods Services utility (IDCAMS), and illustrate this program for both VSAM *and* non-VSAM data sets. We review the COBOL elements associated with indexed files, especially those statements dealing with *alternate* keys. We conclude with a complete

COBOL program to illustrate sequential and nonsequential access for both the primary and secondary key.

VSAM ORGANIZATION

The physical implementation of a VSAM file is generally of little concern to the applications programmer, as the operating system "automatically" maintains the necessary indexes. Nevertheless, a conceptual understanding is beneficial in developing more competence in the individual. This discussion focuses on *key sequenced* VSAM data sets, the most common type of VSAM organization. A key sequenced data set has its records in order according to a *unique* field in each record (e.g., employee number, part number).

A VSAM data set is divided into *control intervals*, which are continuous areas of auxiliary storage. A control interval is *independent* of the physical device on which it resides (i.e., a control interval which fits exactly on one track of a given DASD might require more or less than one track if the data set were moved to another type of device). A control interval may contain one or more records, and the records may be of either fixed or variable length. (A single record requiring more than one control interval is also permitted, and is known as a *spanned* record.)

The length of a control interval is fixed, either by VSAM or the user. VSAM will determine an optimum length based on record size, type of DASD, and the amount of space required for an I/O buffer. *Control intervals in a given data set must be the same size* and cannot be changed without creating an entirely new data set. One or more control intervals are grouped into a *control area*.

Unlike standard OS files, which may or may not be catalogued, all VSAM data sets *must* be catalogued. VSAM maintains its own catalogs(s) and does *not* use the standard system catalog.

VSAM catalogs are of two types: a *single master* catalog for the entire system, and *multiple user* catalogs. A VSAM data set is *catalogued directly* if it is referenced by the master catalog; it is *catalogued indirectly* if it is referenced by a user catalog referred to by the master catalog. Either type of catalog can reference *non-VSAM as well as VSAM data* sets, as depicted by Figure 5.1.

A key sequenced VSAM data set is defined with an index so that individual records may be located on a random basis. Entries in an index are known as index records. The lowest-level index is called the *sequence set*. Records in all higher levels are collectively called the *index set*. A VSAM data set and its associated indexes are collectively known as a *cluster*.

An entry in a sequence set contains the *highest* key in a control interval and a vertical pointer to that interval. An entry in an index set contains the

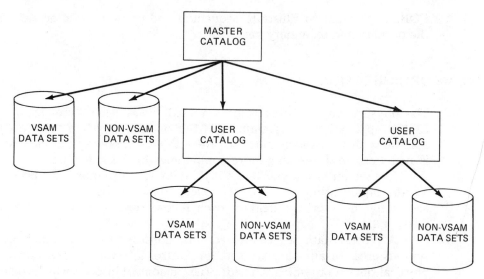

FIGURE 5.1 VSAM Catalog Structure

highest key in the index record at the next lower level and a vertical pointer to that index record. These concepts are made clearer by examination of Figure 5.2.

Figure 5.2 shows 28 records hypothetically distributed in a VSAM data set. The entire file consists of three control areas; each area in turn contains three control intervals. The shaded areas shown at the end of each control interval contain information required by VSAM. The index set has only one level of indexing. There are three entries in the index set, one for each control area. Each entry in the index set contains the highest key in the corresponding control area; thus, 377, 619, and 800 are the highest keys in the first, second, and third control areas, respectively. Each control area has its own sequence set. The entries in the first sequence set show the highest keys of the control intervals in the first control area to be 280, 327, and 377, respectively. Note that the highest entry in the third control interval, 377, corresponds to the highest entry in the first control area of the index set.

Figure 5.2 alludes to two kinds of pointers, vertical and horizontal. Vertical pointers are used for direct access to an individual record. For example, assume that the record with a key of 449 is to be retrieved. VSAM begins at the highest level of index (i.e., at the index set). It concludes that record key 449, *if it is present*, is in the second control area (377 is the highest key in the first area, whereas 619 is the highest key in the second control area). VSAM follows the vertical pointer to the sequence set for the second control area and draws its final conclusion; record key 449, if it exists, will be in the first control interval of the second control area.

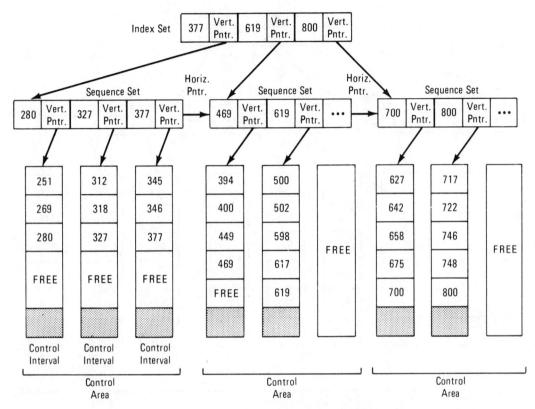

FIGURE 5.2 Initial distribution of records in a VSAM data set

Horizontal pointers are used for sequential access only. In this instance, VSAM begins at the first sequence set and uses the horizontal pointer to get from that sequence set record to the one containing the next highest key. Put another way, the vertical pointer in a sequence set record points to data; the horizontal pointer indicates the sequence set record containing the next highest record.

Figure 5.2 contains several allocations of *free space*, which is distributed in one of two ways: as free space within a control interval, or as a free control interval within a control area. In other words, as VSAM loads a file, empty space is deliberately left throughout the file. This is done to facilitate subsequent insertion of new records.

Figure 5.3 shows the changes brought about by the addition of two new records, with keys of 410 and 730, to the file of Figure 5.2. Addition of the first record, key 410, poses no problem, as free space is available in the control interval where the record belongs. Record 410 is inserted into its proper place and the other records in that control interval are moved down.

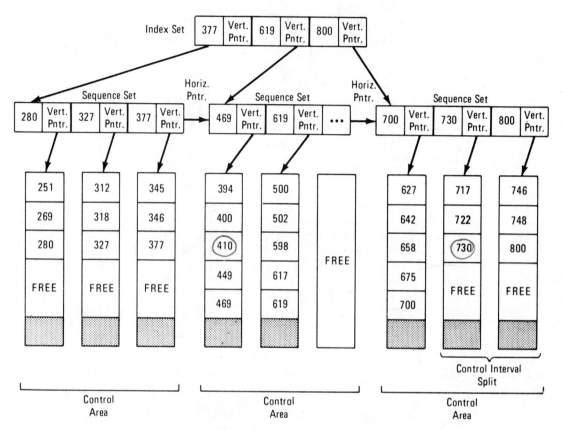

FIGURE 5.3 Illustration of control interval split

The addition of record key 730 requires different action. The control interval that should contain this record is full in Figure 5.2. Consequently, VSAM causes a *control interval split*, in which some of the records in the previously filled control interval are moved to an empty control interval in the same control area. Entries in the sequence set for the third control area will change, as shown in Figure 5.3. This makes considerable sense when we realize that each record in a sequence set contains the key of the highest record in the corresponding control interval. Thus, the records in the sequence set must reflect the control interval split. Note that after a control interval split, subsequent additions are facilitated, as free space is again readily available.

Figure 5.4 shows the results of including three additional records, with keys of 316, 618, and 680. Record 316 is inserted into free space in the second control interval of the first control area, with the other records initially in this interval shifted down. Record 618 causes a control interval split in the second control area.

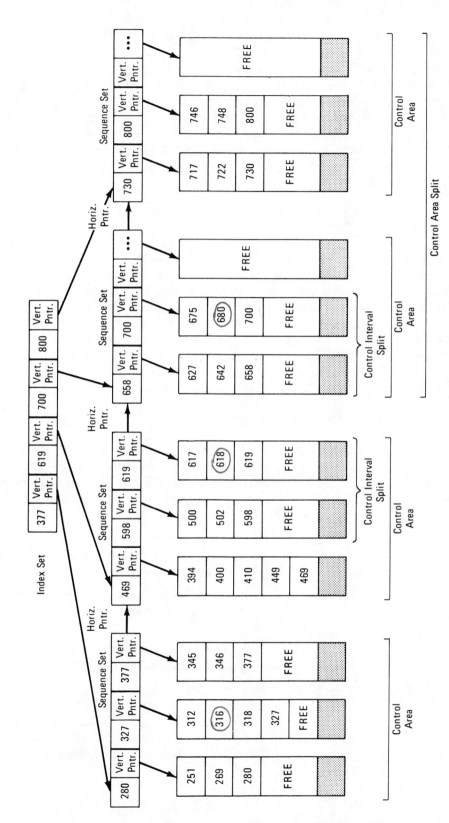

FIGURE 5.4 Illustrations of Control Area Split

109

Record 680 also requires a control interval split, except that there are no longer any free control intervals in the third control area. Accordingly, a *control area split* is initiated, in which some of the records in the old control area are moved into a new control area at the end of the data set. Both the old and the new control areas will have free control intervals as a result of the split. In addition, the index set has a fourth entry, indicating the presence of a new control area. The sequence set is also expanded to allow for the fourth control area.

ACCESS METHODS SERVICES (IDCAMS)

VSAM data sets are referenced through a special utility program known as Access Methods Services, or simply IDCAMS. Unlike other OS utilities, which are severely limited in scope, IDCAMS can perform a variety of functions on VSAM data sets. It can, for example, create or delete a file, print a data set in a variety of formats, establish primary and/or secondary indexes, and so on. The utility can also access sequential and/or ISAM files in addition to VSAM files; it cannot, however, process a partitioned data set.

Associated DD Statements

IDCAMS uses the following DD statements:

STEPCAT	An *optional* DD statement which identifies the user catalog for the particular job step; it is not needed if the VSAM file is referenced by the master catalog, or if the file is not a VSAM data set.
JOBCAT	Similar in concept to the STEPCAT DD statement except that it refers to the entire job rather than an individual step
SYSPRINT	A *required* DD statement to identify the output device for system messages; typically SYSOUT=A
ddname	Additional DDnames supplied by the user for input and/or output files
SYSIN	A *required* DD statement identifying the command file for IDCAMS; SYSIN DD * implies that the utility commands follow immediately in the jobstream. Frequently used commands, and their associated syntax, are described next.

Control Statements

Specific rules for the command statement syntax are as follows:

♦ Control statements are coded in columns 2 through 72; column 1 must be blank.

♦ Comments may be included anywhere within a command. A comment begins with /* and ends with */.

♦ Every control statement begins with a *command* (coded in column 2 or beyond) followed by one or more *parameters*. The command indicates the type of operation, and the parameters further describe the service requested.

♦ The command is separated from the first parameter by a space or comma; parameters are separated from each other by a space or comma.

♦ Commands may be continued from line to line. Each line *except the last* must end with a hyphen or a plus sign.

The vendor manual, *OS/VS2 Access Methods Services*, GC26-3841-4, documents over 20 control statements, with hundreds of associated parameters. We discuss a few of the more commonly used commands. These include: REPRO, PRINT, DELETE, and DEFINE CLUSTER.

REPRO

```
Syntax:    REPRO  INFILE(ddname) -
                  OUTFILE(ddname)

Example:   REPRO  INFILE(INPUT) -
                  OUTFILE(OUTPUT)
```

The REPRO statement is used for *all copy* operations. One can choose any combination—e.g., VSAM to VSAM, non-VSAM to non-VSAM, VSAM to non-VSAM, or non-VSAM to VSAM. Only two parameters are required, INFILE and OUTFILE, which specify DDnames (of the user's choosing) for input and output, respectively. In the preceding example, INPUT and OUTPUT are *user-chosen* DDnames which will contain the *data set names* of the input and output data sets respectively; for example:

```
//INPUT   DD  DSN=OLD.MASTER,DISP=SHR
//OUTPUT  DD  DSN=COPIED.MASTER,DISP=SHR
```

An alternative way of specifying catalogued data sets uses INDATASET and OUTDATASET parameters in lieu of a DDname reference. Hence:

```
REPRO   INDATASET(OLD.MASTER) -
        OUTDATASET(COPIED.MASTER)
```

is equivalent to the previous combination of INFILE, OUTFILE, and associated DD statements. (The hyphen in the preceding examples indicates continuation.)

PRINT

```
Syntax:    PRINT INFILE(ddname) -
           ⎰CHARACTER⎱
           ⎨HEX       ⎬
           ⎱DUMP      ⎰
```

```
Example:   PRINT INFILE(OLDMAST) -
           CHARACTER
```

The PRINT command is used for all printing operations. INFILE (or INDATASET) identifies the input file and functions identically as in the REPRO command. CHARACTER, HEX, and/or DUMP indicate the desired format of the printed data set. CHARACTER prints the output exactly as it appears in the input record, HEX converts each input character to two hexadecimal characters before printing and DUMP displays output in a format similar to a memory dump. (DUMP is the default mode.)

DELETE

```
Syntax:    DELETE (entry-name) -
               type -
               SCRATCH
```

```
Example:   DELETE (MASTER.FILE.CLUSTER) -
               CLUSTER
```

The DELETE command removes entries from a VSAM catalog. The type parameter indicates the nature of the entry to be deleted—e.g., CLUSTER, GENERATIONDATAGROUP, NONVSAM (for non-VSAM data sets). SCRATCH deletes the data set. (The PURGE parameter is required to delete a data set prior to its expiration date.)

DEFINE CLUSTER

```
Syntax:    DEFINE CLUSTER -
               (NAME(cluster-name) -
               VOLUMES(volume-serial-number) -
               UNIQUE -
               ⎰RECORDS  ⎱
               ⎨TRACKS   ⎬ -
               ⎱CYLINDERS⎰
               SHAREOPTIONS) -
```

```
DATA -
   (NAME(entry-name) -
   KEYS -
   CONTROLINTERVALSIZE -
   RECORDSIZE -
   FREESPACE) -
INDEX -
   (NAME(entry-name))
```

Example: See Figure 5.5

The DEFINE CLUSTER statement establishes a *cluster;* i.e., a VSAM data set and its associated indexes. Only a few of the many associated parameters are listed, and are best discussed in conjunction with Figure 5.5.

Establishing a VSAM Data Set

Figure 5.5 contains the jobstream to establish a cluster for a VSAM data set, copy records from an existing file into the new data set, and print the newly created VSAM file. IDCAMS is executed only once, as the SYSIN file contains *multiple* commands. (An alternative approach is to execute the utility several times, with the associated SYSIN files containing fewer commands.)

```
//JSC$3428 JOB  (000101),JACKIE
//JOBCAT    DD  DSN=CATALOG.VUMF112,DISP=SHR
//DEFINE    EXEC PGM=IDCAMS
//INDATA    DD  DSN=MFN.PGM.JSC.TEST(OLDMAST),DISP=SHR
//SYSPRINT  DD  SYSOUT=A
//SYSIN     DD  *
   DELETE (MASTER.FILE.CLUSTER) CLUSTER        ──── DELETE command removes cluster
   DEFINE CLUSTER -                                 if it already exists
      (NAME(MASTER.FILE.CLUSTER) -
      VOLUMES(UMF112) -
      UNIQUE -
      RECORDS (50 5) -                          ──── Ending hyphens indicate continuation
      SHAREOPTIONS(2)) -
      DATA -
         (NAME(MASTER.FILE.DATA) KEYS(9 0) CISZ(1024) -
         RECORDSIZE(80 80) FREESPACE(10 5)) -
      INDEX -
         (NAME(MASTER.FILE.INDEX)) -
      CATALOG (CATALOG.VUMF112)
   REPRO  INFILE(INDATA) -
          OUTDATASET(MASTER.FILE.CLUSTER)
   IF LASTCC = 0 -
      THEN -                                    ──── Output of REPRO step is input to PRINT
         PRINT  INDATASET(MASTER.FILE.CLUSTER) -
```

FIGURE 5.5 Illustration of IDCAMS.

The DEFINE CLUSTER command of Figure 5.5 extends over several card images, as denoted by the ending hyphens indicating continuation. The cluster is named MASTER.FILE.CLUSTER, and is found on volume UMF112. UNIQUE specifies that space for the components of the cluster (i.e., the data and index(es)) is allocated separately. Primary and secondary space allocations are 50 and 5 records, respectively. A SHAREOPTION of 2 indicates that any number of users can access the dataset for read processing, but only one user can do so for write processing.

The data and index portions of the cluster are known as MASTER. FILE.DATA and MASTER.FILE.INDEX, respectively. The record key is 9 bytes long and begins in the first position of each record (i.e., the displacement is *zero* bytes from the beginning of the record). The minimum and maximum record lengths are both 80; i.e., the records are of *fixed* length. Control intervals are 1024 bytes, with free space allocations of 10 and 5 percent for control intervals and areas, respectively.

The DELETE command, which appears prior to DEFINE CLUSTER, uncatalogs the cluster *if* the cluster exists previously. The REPRO statement creates the VSAM data set from an input file. It references INDATA as the DDname containing the input data set. The PRINT command is executed *conditionally* if and only if the VSAM file was created without error. (Input to the PRINT command is the output produced by the REPRO statement.)

IF–THEN–ELSE provides conditional execution of IDCAMS control statements. In the example shown, the condition code of the *last* step (LASTCC) is compared to zero. If the previous step executed without error (i.e., if its condition code is equal to zero), then the input data set MASTER.FILE.CLUSTER will be printed. Multiple commands can be stacked after THEN or ELSE, by preceding the first command with DO and following the last command with END.

Use with Non-VSAM Data Sets

IDCAMS is applicable to both VSAM and non-VSAM data sets. Figure 5.6, for example, defines a generation data group, creates the first generation from sequential input, and prints the newly created file. Access Methods Services is executed in all three steps.

Step one defines the GDG via the DEFINE GENERATIONDATA-GROUP command. The name of the GDG is JSC.MASTER.FILE and the limit is five generations. NOEMPTY uncatalogs the oldest generation when the limit is reached; i.e., the first generation is uncatalogued when the sixth is created. SCRATCH deletes the associated generation and makes the space available to other users. TO specifies an expiration date.

Step two creates the first generation via the REPRO command, with FILEIN and FILEOUT as the DDnames for input and output, respectively. Note well the specification of +1 in the DSN parameter to indicate the *next* generation. Observe also the disposition parameter to catalog the generation data set, and the presence of the requisite SPACE parameter.

Step three prints the first generation. Recall from Chapter 2 that the

```
//JSC$3130 JOB (000101),JACKIE
//STEP1     EXEC PGM=IDCAMS
//SYSPRINT DD SYSOUT=A
//SYSIN    DD *
     DEFINE GENERATIONDATAGROUP -
         (NAME(JSC.MASTER.FILE) -            Defines a GDG
         NOEMPTY -
         SCRATCH -
         LIMIT(5) -
         TO(85365))
/*
//STEP2     EXEC PGM=IDCAMS               +1 indicates the next generation
//SYSPRINT DD SYSOUT=A
//FILEOUT   DD DSN=JSC.MASTER.FILE(+1),DISP=(NEW,CATLG),UNIT=SYSDA,
//             DCB=(UIM.GDS,LRECL=80,BLKSIZE=400,RECFM=FB),
//             SPACE=(TRK,(1,1))         DDname matches entry in REPRO command
//FILEIN    DD *
100000000SUGRUE         P  12450879100E5333088022208792800010812600080
200000000CRAWFORD       MA09430678100E64440678        42000068036000078
300000000MILGROM        IR06130580200E655510814000681480000580
400000000BENJAMIN       BL10531073100E73331073        30000108128000180
600000000GRAUER         RT11450877200E590011818001180500001181145000180
/*
//SYSIN    DD *
     REPRO -
         INFILE(FILEIN) -                FILEIN and FILEOUT are DDnames for STEP2
         OUTFILE(FILEOUT)
/*
//STEP3     EXEC PGM=IDCAMS               Generations are updated at end of job
//SYSPRINT DD SYSOUT=A
//MASTER    DD DSN=JSC.MASTER.FILE(+1),DISP=SHR
//SYSIN    DD *
     PRINT -
         INFILE(MASTER)                 MASTER is the DDname for the input data set
/*
//
```

FIGURE 5.6 Use of IDCAMS with Non-VSAM Data Sets

generation numbers -1, 0, +1 denote the previous, current, and next generation, respectively. Accordingly, step two referenced the newly created generation by a generation number of +1 (as expected). However, the *existing* generation which is printed in step three is also referenced by +1. This is because *generation numbers are updated at the end of the job;* i.e., a given generation is referenced by the *same* number throughout multiple job steps. In other words, the generation data set created in step two will be referenced as JSC.MASTER.FILE(0) *only after the job terminates.*

Figure 5.7 shows the printed generation data set, and was produced by step three of Figure 5.6. Records are shown in both character and hexadecimal format; and the output closely resembles a dump. (Figure 5.7 can be shortened significantly by including the CHARACTER parameter on the PRINT command. See Figure 5.10.)

COBOL ELEMENTS

We pause in our discussion of Access Methods Services to review some of the COBOL elements associated with VSAM files. Although the reader is

```
IDCAMS  SYSTEM SERVICES                                TIME: 16:08:20      01/15/83    PAGE   2

LISTING OF DATA SET -JSC.MASTER.FILE.G0001V00

RECORD SEQUENCE NUMBER - 1
000000   F1F0F0F0 F0F0F0F0 F0E2E4C7 D9E4C540   40404040 40404040 D740F1F2 F4F5F0F8   *100000000SUGRUE          P 124508*
000020   F7F9F1F0 F0C5F5F3 F3F3F0F8 F8F0F2F2   F2F0F8F7 F9F2F8F0 F0F0F1F0 F8F1F2F6   *79100E5333088022208792800 108126*
000040   F0F0F0F0 F9F8F040 40404040 40404040                                        *0000980                       *

RECORD SEQUENCE NUMBER - 2
000000   F2F0F0F0 F0F0F0F0 F0C3D9C1 E6C6D6D9   C4404040 40404040 D4C1F0F9 F4F3F0F6   *200000000CRAWFORD        MA094306*
000020   F7F8F1F0 F0C5F6F4 F4F4F0F6 F7F84040   40404040 40F4F2F0 F0F0F0F6 F8F0F3F6   *78100E6440678           42000268036*
000040   F0F0F0F0 F6F7F840 40404040 40404040                                        *0000678                       *

RECORD SEQUENCE NUMBER - 3
000000   F3F0F0F0 F0F0F0F0 F0D4C9D3 C7D9D6D4   40404040 40404040 C9D9F0F6 F1F3F0F5   *300000000MILGROM        IR061305*
000020   F8F0F2F0 F0C5F6F5 F5F5F1F0 F8F1F4F0   F0F0F6F8 F1F4F8F0 F0F0F0F5 F8F04040   *80200E655108140006814800 00580  *
000040   40404040 40404040 40404040 40404040                                        *                               *

RECORD SEQUENCE NUMBER - 4
000000   F4F0F0F0 F0F0F0F0 F0C2C5D5 D1C1D4C9   D5404040 40404040 C2D3F1F0 F5F3F1F0   *400000000BENJAMIN       BL105310*
000020   F7F3F1F0 F0C5F7F3 F3F3F1F0 F7F34040   40404040 40F3F0F0 F0F0F1F0 F8F1F2F8   *73100E73331073          30000108128*
000040   F0F0F0F1 F0F8F040 40404040 40404040                                        *0001080                       *

RECORD SEQUENCE NUMBER - 5
000000   F6F0F0F0 F0F0F0F0 F0C7D9C1 E4C5D940   40404040 40404040 D9E3F1F1 F4F5F0F8   *600000000GRAUER         RT114508*
000020   F7F7F2F0 F0C5F5F9 F0F0F1F1 F8F1F8F0   F0F1F1F8 F0F5F0F0 F0F0F1F1 F8F1F4F5   *77200E5900118180011805000 118145*
000040   F0F0F0F1 F1F8F040 40404040 40404040                                        *0001180                       *

IDC0005I NUMBER OF RECORDS PROCESSED WAS 5

IDC0001I FUNCTION COMPLETED, HIGHEST CONDITION CODE WAS 0
```

FIGURE 5.7 Output Produced by Figure 5.6

assumed to be familiar with this material, he or she may not have had the opportunity to use all of the available options—e.g., ALTERNATE RECORD KEY and/or ACCESS IS DYNAMIC. We begin, therefore, by reviewing the necessary COBOL and subsequently incorporate the material into a complete program. We then resume coverage of IDCAMS to show support for establishing and accessing an alternate index.

The SELECT statement for ANS 74 indexed files is identical to IBM's VSAM implementation, and is shown below:

```
SELECT file-name
     ASSIGN TO implementor-name-1[,implementor-name-2]...

    ⌈                      ⌈ AREA  ⌉ ⌉
    | RESERVE integer-1    |       | |
    ⌊                      ⌊ AREAS ⌋ ⌋

    ORGANIZATION IS INDEXED

    ⌈                       ⌈ SEQUENTIAL ⌉ ⌉
    | ACCESS MODE IS        ⟨ RANDOM     ⟩ |
    ⌊                       ⌊ DYNAMIC    ⌋ ⌋

    RECORD KEY IS data-name-1

    [ALTERNATE RECORD KEY IS data-name-2[WITH DUPLICATES ]]...

    [FILE STATUS IS data-name-3].
```

Three clauses, ASSIGN, ORGANIZATION IS INDEXED, and RECORD KEY, are *required* for indexed files. The ASSIGN clause ties a programmer-chosen file-name to a DDname; the JCL links the DDname to a physical device. The RESERVE AREA clause increases processing efficiency, when the file is read sequentially, by allocating alternate I/O areas (or buffers) for the file. If the clause is omitted, the number of alternate areas defaults to the vendor's implementation. ORGANIZATION IS INDEXED is mandatory for indexed files and requires no further explanation.

The meaning of ACCESS MODE is readily apparent when either SEQUENTIAL or RANDOM is specified. ACCESS IS DYNAMIC allows a file to be read sequentially and/or nonsequentially in the *same* program. The format of the READ statement determines the access method and is discussed subsequently.

RECORD KEY references a field, *defined in the indexed record, whose value must be unique for each record in the file.* The value of the RECORD KEY is used by the operating system to establish the necessary indexes for the file.

ALTERNATE RECORD KEY provides a *second* path for random access. Unlike the RECORD KEY, which must be unique for every record, the ALTERNATE RECORD KEY may contain duplicate values. This capability is extremely powerful and gives COBOL some limited facility for data base management. A common application is to specify social security or account number as the RECORD KEY, and name as the ALTERNATE KEY. (The ALTERNATE RECORD KEY is also *expensive*, in that a second set of indexes must be maintained by the operating system. Consequently, the feature should *not* be used indiscriminately, but only when absolutely required by the application.)

FILE STATUS defines a two-byte area which can be referenced by the programmer to determine the success or failure of every I/O operation. The FILE STATUS bytes are often used in conjunction with DECLARATIVES. (Declarative procedures are fully discussed in R. Grauer, *Structured Methods Through COBOL*, Prentice-Hall, Englewood Cliffs, NJ, 1973, pages 185–193.)

Several verbs in the Procedure Division are uniquely associated with indexed files, and/or have extended formats for indexed files. These include: OPEN, READ, WRITE, REWRITE, DELETE, and START. Consider first the OPEN statement:

$$\text{OPEN} \quad \left\{ \begin{array}{l} \underline{\text{INPUT}} \\ \underline{\text{OUTPUT}} \\ \underline{\text{I-O}} \end{array} \right\} \quad \text{file-name}$$

INPUT and OUTPUT are used when an indexed file is accessed or created, respectively. OPEN I-O is required when a single master file is specified for nonsequential maintenance; i.e., the single file functions as both an input and an output file.

The READ statement has two distinct syntaxes, for sequential and nonsequential access, respectively. These are:

Format 1 (Sequential Access):

```
READ file-name [NEXT] RECORD [INTO identifier-1]
    [AT END imperative-statement-1]
```

Format 2 (Random Access):

```
READ file-name RECORD [INTO identifier-1]
    [KEY is data-name-1]
    [INVALID KEY imperative-statement-1]
```

Format 1, for sequential access, should present no difficulty. The NEXT phrase is required when a sequential read is called for, and ACCESS IS DYNAMIC was specified. Use of READ INTO is strongly suggested to simplify debugging (see Chapter 7 on ABEND debugging and the associated discussion of WS BEGINS HERE).

A *random* READ is preceded by a MOVE statement, in which the key of the desired record is moved to the data name designated as the RECORD KEY in the SELECT statement. *The INVALID KEY clause is activated if the specified key cannot be found in the indexed file.* For example:

```
MOVE 888888888 TO SOC-SEC-NUMBER.
READ INDEXED-FILE INTO WS-WORK-AREA
    INVALID KEY DISPLAY 'RECORD NOT FOUND'.
```

The indexed file is randomly accessed for the record with social security number 888888888 (assuming SOC-SEC-NUMBER was designated as the RECORD KEY in the file's SELECT statement). If record 888888888 does not exist in the indexed file, the INVALID KEY condition is raised.

If ALTERNATE RECORD KEY was specified in the SELECT statement, the KEY IS clause is used in the READ statement to indicate which field will be used to retrieve the record. For example:

```
MOVE 'SMITH' TO EMP-NAME.
READ INDEXED-FILE INTO WS-WORK-AREA
    KEY IS EMP-NAME
    INVALID KEY DISPLAY 'RECORD NOT FOUND'.
```

The indexed file is randomly accessed for the *first* record with EMP-NAME of Smith (assuming EMP-NAME was designated as the ALTERNATE RECORD KEY). If Smith cannot be found, the INVALID KEY condition is raised.

The WRITE statement includes an additional clause for indexed files. Consider

```
WRITE record-name [FROM identifier-1]
     [INVALID KEY imperative statement]
```

If ACCESS IS SEQUENTIAL is specified when an indexed file is created, then incoming records are required to be in sequential order, and, further, each record is required to have a unique key. The INVALID KEY condition is raised if either of these requirements is violated.

The REWRITE verb replaces existing records when a file has been opened as an I-O file. Its syntax is similar to that of the WRITE verb, as shown:

```
REWRITE record-name [FROM identifier-1]
       [INVALID KEY imperative statement]
```

The INVALID KEY condition is raised if the record key of the last record read does not match the key of the record to be replaced.

The DELETE statement removes a record from an indexed file. Its syntax is simply:

```
DELETE file-name RECORD
      [INVALID KEY imperative statement]
```

When a DELETE statement is successfully executed, the record that was deleted is logically removed from the file and can no longer be accessed. The DELETE statement can be used only on a file that was opened in the I-O mode.

The START statement causes the file to be positioned to the first record whose value is equal to, greater than, or not less than the value contained in the identifier. INVALID KEY is raised if no record is found that meets the specified criterion. Syntactically, the START statement has the form:

$$
\text{START file-name} \left[\text{KEY IS} \begin{Bmatrix} \text{EQUAL TO} \\ = \\ \text{GREATER THAN} \\ > \\ \text{NOT LESS THAN} \\ \text{NOT} < \end{Bmatrix} \text{identifier} \right]
$$

```
[INVALID KEY imperative statement]
```

ALTERNATE INDEXES

Figure 5.8 contains a complete COBOL program to illustrate the use of *alternate* indexes. The SELECT statement of lines 12–18 identifies RECORD KEY as INDEX-SOC-SEC-NUMBER, and ALTERNATE RECORD KEY as INDEX-NAME. Both are defined within the FD for INDEXED-FILE.

```
00001          IDENTIFICATION DIVISION.
00002          PROGRAM-ID.    ALTINDEX.
00003          AUTHOR.        JACKIE CLARK.
00004
00005          ENVIRONMENT DIVISION.
00006          CONFIGURATION SECTION.
00007          SOURCE-COMPUTER.    IBM-4341.
00008          OBJECT-COMPUTER.    IBM-4341.
00009
00010          INPUT-OUTPUT SECTION.
00011          FILE-CONTROL.
00012              SELECT INDEXED-FILE
00013                  ASSIGN TO DA-VSAMMAST
00014                  ORGANIZATION IS INDEXED ──── Permits both sequential and
00015                  ACCESS IS DYNAMIC            nonsequential access
00016                  RECORD KEY IS INDEX-SOC-SEC-NUMBER
00017                  ALTERNATE RECORD KEY IS INDEX-NAME
00018                      WITH DUPLICATES.
00019                                          ── Alternate key
00020          DATA DIVISION.                     need not be unique
00021          FILE SECTION.
00022          FD  INDEXED-FILE
00023              LABEL RECORDS ARE STANDARD
00024              RECORD CONTAINS 80 CHARACTERS
00025              DATA RECORD IS INDEXED-RECORD.
00026                                   ── RECORD KEY defined in line 16
00027          01  INDEXED-RECORD.
00028              05  INDEX-SOC-SEC-NUMBER          PIC X(9).
00029              05  INDEX-NAME                    PIC X(15).
00030              05  REST-OF-INDEXED-RECORD        PIC X(56).
00031
00032                   ── ALTERNATE KEY defined in line 17
00033          WORKING-STORAGE SECTION.
00034          01  FILLER                            PIC X(14)
00035                  VALUE 'WS BEGINS HERE'.
00036
00037          01  WS-NDX-MAST-RECORD.
00038              05  NDX-SOC-SEC-NUMBER            PIC X(9).
00039              05  NDX-NAME.
00040                  10  NDX-LAST-NAME             PIC X(15).
00041                  10  NDX-INITIALS              PIC XX.
00042              05  FILLER                        PIC X(54).
00043
00044          01  WS-ACTIVE-NAME                    PIC X(15).
00045
00046          01  WS-BALANCE-LINE-SWITCHES.
00047              05  WS-RECORD-KEY-ALLOCATED-SWITCH  PIC X(3).
00048              05  WS-END-INDEX-FILE               PIC X(3).
00049
00050          PROCEDURE DIVISION.
00051          0010-PROCESS-NAME-FILE.
00052              OPEN INPUT INDEXED-FILE.
00053
00054          ************************************************************
```

FIGURE 5.8 COBOL Program with Alternate Indexes

```
00055    *           RETRIEVE RECORDS BY SOCIAL SECURITY NUMBER            *
00056    ************************************************************************
00057
00058            MOVE '955000000' TO INDEX-SOC-SEC-NUMBER.
00059            PERFORM 0040-READ-INDEX-FILE-BY-NUMBER.
00060            IF WS-RECORD-KEY-ALLOCATED-SWITCH = 'YES'
00061                DISPLAY WS-NDX-MAST-RECORD                 ┌─Desired value is moved
00062            ELSE                                           │  to RECORD KEY
00063                DISPLAY '        '
00064                DISPLAY 'NO MATCH FOUND FOR: / 955000000'.
00065
00066            MOVE '245118095' TO  INDEX-SOC-SEC-NUMBER.
00067            PERFORM 0040-READ-INDEX-FILE-BY-NUMBER.
00068            IF WS-RECORD-KEY-ALLOCATED-SWITCH = 'YES'
00069                DISPLAY WS-NDX-MAST-RECORD
00070            ELSE
00071                DISPLAY '        '
00072                DISPLAY 'NO MATCH FOUND FOR: 245118095'.
00073
00074    ************************************************************************
00075    *      RETRIEVE RECORDS BY NAME - THE ALTERNATE RECORD KEY          *
00076    ************************************************************************
00077                                                          ┌─Desired value is moved
00078            MOVE 'GRAUER      ' TO  INDEX-NAME             │  to ALTERNATE KEY
00079                                    WS-ACTIVE-NAME.
00080            PERFORM 0020-READ-INDEX-FILE-BY-NAME.
00081            IF WS-RECORD-KEY-ALLOCATED-SWITCH = 'NO'
00082                DISPLAY '        '
00083                DISPLAY 'NO MATCH FOUND FOR:  ' WS-ACTIVE-NAME
00084            ELSE
00085                PERFORM 0030-READ-DUPLICATES
00086                    UNTIL WS-ACTIVE-NAME NOT = NDX-LAST-NAME
00087                       OR WS-END-INDEX-FILE = 'YES'.
00088
00089            MOVE 'HUMMER      ' TO  INDEX-NAME
00090                                    WS-ACTIVE-NAME.
00091            PERFORM 0020-READ-INDEX-FILE-BY-NAME.
00092            IF WS-RECORD-KEY-ALLOCATED-SWITCH = 'YES'
00093                DISPLAY WS-NDX-MAST-RECORD
00094            ELSE
00095                DISPLAY '        '
00096                DISPLAY 'NO MATCH FOUND FOR:  ' WS-ACTIVE-NAME
00097
00098            CLOSE INDEXED-FILE.
00099            STOP RUN.                         ┌─KEY clause is required if READ
00100                                              │  is on ALTERNATE KEY
00101        0020-READ-INDEX-FILE-BY-NAME.
00102            MOVE 'YES' TO WS-RECORD-KEY-ALLOCATED-SWITCH.
00103            READ INDEXED-FILE INTO WS-NDX-MAST-RECORD
00104                KEY IS INDEX-NAME
00105                INVALID KEY
00106                    MOVE 'NO' TO WS-RECORD-KEY-ALLOCATED-SWITCH.
00107
00108        0030-READ-DUPLICATES.                 ┌─NEXT clause is required
00109            DISPLAY WS-NDX-MAST-RECORD.        │  for sequential access
00110            READ INDEXED-FILE NEXT RECORD
00111                INTO WS-NDX-MAST-RECORD
00112                AT END
00113                    MOVE 'YES' TO WS-END-INDEX-FILE.
00114
00115        0040-READ-INDEX-FILE-BY-NUMBER.
00116            MOVE 'YES' TO WS-RECORD-KEY-ALLOCATED-SWITCH.
00117            READ INDEXED-FILE INTO WS-NDX-MAST-RECORD
00118                INVALID KEY
00119                    MOVE 'NO' TO WS-RECORD-KEY-ALLOCATED-SWITCH.
```

FIGURE 5.8 (Continued)

```
955000000GRAUER            B 11450877200E5900118180011805000011814500001180

NO MATCH FOUND FOR:  245118095
050555500GRAUER            RT11450877200E5900118180011805000011814500001180
638972393GRAUER            J 11450877200E5900118180011805000011814500001180
955000000GRAUER            B 11450877200E5900118180011805000011814500001180

NO MATCH FOUND FOR:  HUMMER                    Alternate key may have duplicate values
```

FIGURE 5.9 Output of Figure 5.8

The former field is unique, but the latter is not, as indicated by the WITH DUPLICATES clause of the SELECT statement.

The Procedure Division contains several forms of the READ statement. COBOL lines 58 to 72 illustrate a *random read on the primary key*. The first READ statement is successful (as seen by the output in Figure 5.9); the second is not. Both READ statements are preceded by a MOVE statement, in which the desired social security number is moved to the field defined as the RECORD KEY.

COBOL lines 78 to 87 retrieve records on the *secondary* key. The desired value, GRAUER, is moved to the field defined as the ALTERNATE RECORD KEY in line 78. The random READ statement for INDEXED-FILE contains the KEY IS clause (line 104), to indicate that retrieval is based on the *secondary* key. If retrieval is successful, the paragraph 0030-READ-DUPLICATES is executed repeatedly to retrieve all occurrences of GRAUER. The NEXT clause in the READ statement of line 110 indicates the file is read *sequentially* after the first occurrence of GRAUER was located. (This in turn requires that ACCESS IS DYNAMIC be specified in the SELECT statement, as was done in line 15.)

IDCAMS is required to establish the primary and secondary indexes associated with Figure 5.8.

Figure 5.10 defines the cluster, MASTER.FILE.CLUSTER, which contains the primary index. The essential elements of Figure 5.10 were previously described in conjunction with Figure 5.5. A slight difference is that the PRINT command of Figure 5.10 contains the CHARACTER parameter, which shortens the output considerably. (Contrast Figure 5.10*b* to Figure 5.7.)

Figure 5.11 defines the alternate index and contains much in the way of new material. This execution of IDCAMS requires two additional DD statements, IDCUT1 and IDCUT2, which define a volume containing a VSAM data space to be made available to BLDINDEX if an external sort is required. In addition, there are three new IDCAMS commands: DEFINE ALTERNATEINDEX, DEFINE PATH, and BLDINDEX.

DEFINE ALTERNATEINDEX creates an alternate index related to the cluster, MASTER.FILE.CLUSTER (established in Figure 5.10). MASTERPW and UPDATEPW specify master and update passwords for the alternate index. NONUNIQUE KEY implies that there can be multiple

```
//JSC$3647 JOB  (MAS526),JACKIE
//JOBCAT    DD  DSN=CATALOG.VUMF112,DISP=SHR
//DEFINE    EXEC PGM=IDCAMS
//INDATA    DD DSN=MEN.PGM.JSC.TEST(OLDMAST),DISP=SHR
//SYSPRINT DD SYSOUT=A
//SYSIN     DD *
  DELETE (MASTER.FILE.CLUSTER) CLUSTER
  DEFINE CLUSTER -
    (NAME(MASTER.FILE.CLUSTER) -
    VOLUMES(UMF112) -
    UNIQUE -
    RECORDS (50 5) -
    SHAREOPTIONS(2)) -
    DATA -
      (NAME(MASTER.FILE.DATA) KEYS(9 0) CISZ(1024) -
      RECORDSIZE(80 80) FREESPACE(10 5)) -
    INDEX -
      (NAME(MASTER.FILE.INDEX)) -
      CATALOG (CATALOG.VUMF112)
  REPRO  INFILE(INDATA) -
         OUTDATASET(MASTER.FILE.CLUSTER)
  IF LASTCC = 0 -
    THEN -
      PRINT  INDATASET(MASTER.FILE.CLUSTER) -
        CHARACTER
```

CHARACTER parameter shortens output

FIGURE 5.10a DEFINE CLUSTER Commands

```
LISTING OF DATA SET -MASTER.FILE.CLUSTER

KEY OF RECORD - 050555500
050555500GRAUER        RT11450877200E590011818001180500001181450001180

KEY OF RECORD - 264805298
264805298CLARK         JS06130580200E680010814000682480001580

KEY OF RECORD - 300000000
300000000MILGROM       IR06130580200E655510814000681480000580

KEY OF RECORD - 400000000
400000000BENJAMIN      BL10531073100E73331073        300001081280001080

KEY OF RECORD - 638972393
638972393GRAUER        J 11450877200E590011818001180500001181450001180

KEY OF RECORD - 800000000
800000000SMITH         BB08520681300P84440681        385000681

KEY OF RECORD - 900000000
900000000BAKER         E 06490879100G99870879        650000881550000879

KEY OF RECORD - 955000000
955000000GRAUER        B 11450877200E590011818001180500001181450001180

IDC0005I NUMBER OF RECORDS PROCESSED WAS 8

IDC0001I FUNCTION COMPLETED, HIGHEST CONDITION CODE WAS 0
```

FIGURE 5.10b Records Listed by Primary Key

FIGURE 5.10 Establishing a Primary Index

```
//JSC$3649 JOB (000104),JACKIE
//JOBCAT    DD  DSN=CATALOG.VUMF112,DISP=SHR
//VSALT     EXEC PGM=IDCAMS
//SYSPRINT  DD SYSOUT=A
//IDCUT1    DD  DSN=SORT.WORK.ONE,DISP=OLD,
//              AMP='AMORG',VOL=SER=UMF112,UNIT=DISK
//IDCUT2    DD  DSN=SORT.WORK.TWO,DISP=OLD,
//              AMP='AMORG',VOL=SER=UMF112,UNIT=DISK
//SYSIN     DD *
  DEFINE ALTERNATEINDEX -
    (NAME(MASTER.FILE.ALTNDX) -
    RELATE(MASTER.FILE.CLUSTER) -
    MASTERPW(ALTMRPW) -
    UPDATEPW(ALTUPPW) -
    KEYS(15 9) -
    RECORDSIZE(80 80) -
    VOLUMES(UMF112) -
    CYLINDERS(1 1) -
    NONUNIQUEKEY -
    UPGRADE) -
    CATALOG (CATALOG.VUMF112)
  DEFINE PATH -
    (NAME(MASTER.FILE.PATH) -
    PATHENTRY(MASTER.FILE.ALTNDX/ALTMRPW) -
    READPW(PATHRDPW)) -
    CATALOG (CATALOG.VUMF112)
  BLDINDEX INDATASET(MASTER.FILE.CLUSTER) -
    OUTDATASET(MASTER.FILE.ALTNDX/ALTUPPW) -
    CATALOG (CATALOG.VUMF112)
  PRINT INDATASET(MASTER.FILE.PATH/PATHRDPW) -
    CHARACTER
/*
//
```

Additional work areas required

FIGURE 5.11a DEFINE ALTERNATE INDEX Commands

```
LISTING OF DATA SET -MASTER.FILE.PATH

KEY OF RECORD - BAKER
900000000BAKER          E  06490879100G99870879        650000881550000879

KEY OF RECORD - BENJAMIN
400000000BENJAMIN       BL10531073100E73331073         300001081280001080

KEY OF RECORD - CLARK
264805298CLARK          JS06130580200E68001081400068248000T1580

KEY OF RECORD - GRAUER
050555500GRAUER         RT11450877200E59001181800118050000118145000T1180

KEY OF RECORD - GRAUER
638972393GRAUER         J  11450877200E59001181800118050000118145000T1180

KEY OF RECORD - GRAUER
955000000GRAUER         B  11450877200E59001181800118050000118145000T1180

KEY OF RECORD - MILGROM
300000000MILGROM        IR06130580200E65551081400068148000T0580

KEY OF RECORD - SMITH
800000000SMITH          BB08520681300P84440681         385000681

IIC00051 NUMBER OF RECORDS PROCESSED WAS 8

IDC00011 FUNCTION COMPLETED, HIGHEST CONDITION CODE WAS 0
```

FIGURE 5.11b Records Listed by Alternate Index

FIGURE 5.11 Establishing an Alternate Index

124

occurrences of the alternate key (and corresponds to the COBOL, ALTER-NATE RECORD KEY WITH DUPLICATES).   UPGRADE specifies that the alternate index is to be updated to reflect all changes associated with the primary key. DEFINE PATH establishes a path over the alternate index for records in the base cluster. Finally, the BLDINDEX command actually builds the alternate index.

The PRINT command references MASTER.FILE.PATH as the input data set, which corresponds to the NAME entry in the DEFINE PATH command. Hence, records are listed in sequence by their alternate index. (See Figure 5.11b.)

Figure 5.12 contains the jobstream to execute the COBOL program of Figure 5.8. The DSNAME parameter in the STEPCAT statement, CATA-LOG.VUMF112, corresponds to the catalog entries of Figures 5.10 and 5.11. In similar fashion, MASTER.FILE.CLUSTER and MASTER.FILE.PATH were defined in Figures 5.10 and 5.11, respectively.

```
//JSC$3520 JOB (MAS526),JACKIE
//STEP1        EXEC COBVCLG
//COB.SYSLIB  DD DSN=MEN.PGM.JSC.LIB,DISP=SHR
//COB.SYSIN   DD DSN=MEN.PGM.JSC.RTG(ALTINDX1),DISP=SHR
//GO.STEPCAT  DD DSN=CATALOG.VUMF112,DISP=SHR
//GO.VSAMMAST DD DSN=MASTER.FILE.CLUSTER,DISP=SHR
//GO.VSAMMAS1 DD DSN=MASTER.FILE.PATH,DISP=SHR
//
```

FIGURE 5.12 COBOL Jobstream to Access Alternate Index.

THE VENDOR'S REFERENCE MANUAL

The reader is referred to the IBM manual, *OS/VS2 Access Methods Services* (GC26-3841-4) for additional information on the IDCAMS utility. The author has used it extensively, and found it to be complete and informative. *He urges the reader to consult the manual* before running to "tech support" for help.

Unfortunately, a distinguishing trait of both programmer trainees and students is their steadfast refusal to "read the manual." This is indeed a pity, for the vendor publications usually have the desired information. (A case in point is Appendix D of this book, which contains solutions to many of the chapter exercises. It is a source of continual amazement to the author that students fail to check their answers before presenting them in class. Only at the end of the semester does this instructor reveal the existence of the solutions to their almost total surprise. The point is simply: *read the manual.*)

Long-time users of OS are familiar with multiple utility programs and the difficulty in selecting the proper program. Access Methods Services presents a different problem, in that a *single* program accomplishes almost all of the functions of the traditional utilities. The difficulty is in selecting the proper command. Accordingly, Table 5.1 (which is analogous to Table

TABLE 5.1 IDCAMS COMMANDS (REPRINTED WITH PERMISSION OF IBM)

Operation		Command
Alter	the information in a catalog entry	ALTER
Attach	a user catalog to the master catalog	DEFINE USERCATALOG or IMPORT CONNECT
Backup	a VSAM data set	EXPORT or REPRO
	a nonVSAM data set	REPRO
	a VSAM catalog	REPRO
Bind	data to the subsystem storage of a particular device within an IBM 3880 Storage Control Model 13	BINDDATA
Build	an alternate index	DEFINE ALTERNATEINDEX and BLDINDEX
	a generation data group	DEFINE GENERATIONDATAGROUP
Catalog	a VSAM data set	DEFINE CLUSTER and DEFINE ALTERNATE INDEX
	a nonVSAM data set	DEFINE NONVSAM
Change	a data set's description in the catalog the device type of the volume on which the catalog resides	ALTER REPRO
Connect	a user catalog to a master catalog	IMPORT CONNECT
	an OS/VS CVOL to a master catalog	DEFINE NONVSAM
Convert	a data set to VSAM format	REPRO
	a VSAM data set to sequential format	REPRO
	OS/VS CVOL entries to VSAM catalog entries	CNVTCAT
Copy	a data set or catalog	REPRO
Create	a backup copy of a data set	REPRO or EXPORT
	a catalog	DEFINE USERCATALOG
	an alias for a nonVSAM data set	DEFINE ALIAS
	an alias for a VSAM data set	DEFINE PATH
	a VSAM data set	DEFINE CLUSTER
	an alternate index	DEFINE ALTERNATEINDEX and BLDINDEX
	the relationship between an alternate index and its base cluster	DEFINE PATH
	a generation data group	DEFINE GENERATIONDATAGROUP
	a generation data set	DEFINE NONVSAM
	a page space	DEFINE PAGESPACE
	a VSAM data space	DEFINE SPACE
	a catalog entry for a nonVSAM data set	DEFINE NONVSAM

126

TABLE 5.1 (Continued)

Operation		Command
Define	(see above entries for Create)	
Delete	a user catalog	DELETE USERCATALOG
	an alias	DELETE ALIAS
	an alternate index and its paths	DELETE ALTERNATEINDEX
	a path	DELETE PATH
	any type of catalog entry	DELETE
	a VSAM data set	DELETE CLUSTER
	a VSAM data space	DELETE SPACE
	a generation data group	DELETE GENERATIONDATAGROUP
	a nonVSAM data set	DELETE NONVSAM
	a page space	DELETE PAGESPACE
Disable	use of the cache in an entire subsystem or for a particular device within the subsystem of an IBM 3880 Storage Control Model 13	SETCACHE
Disconnect	a user catalog	EXPORT DISCONNECT
Display	a catalog's contents	LISTCAT
	a catalog recovery area's contents	LISTCRA
Enable	use of cache in an entire subsystem or for a particular device within the subsystem of an IBM 3880 Storage Control Model 13	SETCACHE
Enter	a nonVSAM data set in a catalog	DEFINE NONVSAM
Export	a user catalog	EXPORT DISCONNECT
	a VSAM data set	EXPORT or EXPORTRA
Import	a user catalog	IMPORT CONNECT
	a VSAM data set	IMPORT or IMPORTRA
List	a password	LISTCAT
	a data set's contents	PRINT
	contents of a catalog or of a catalog entry	LISTCAT
	contents of a catalog recovery area	LISTCRA
	tapes mounted at a checkpoint	CHKLIST
	subsystem counters and subsystem status of an IBM 3880 Storage Control Model 11 and an IBM 3880 Storage Control Model 13	LISTDATA
Load	records into a data set	REPRO
	an alternate index	BLDINDEX
Modify	a data set's description in the catalog	ALTER

TABLE 5.1 (Continued)

Operation		Command
Move	a catalog to another system	EXPORT DISCONNECT and IMPORT CONNECT
	a VSAM data set to another system	EXPORT and IMPORT
	a nonVSAM data set to another system	REPRO
Password	establish for a VSAM data set	DEFINE CLUSTER
Protect	alternate index	DEFINE ALTERNATEINDEX
	path	DEFINE PATH
	catalog	DEFINE USERCATALOG or DEFINE MASTERCATALOG
	page space	DEFINE PAGESPACE
	modify an existing password, or add a password to an existing catalog entry	ALTER
	delete a password	ALTER
	list passwords	LISTCAT
Print	a data set	PRINT
Recover	from a processing-program failure	VERIFY
	from a catalog failure	LISTCRA and EXPORTRA and IMPORTRA RESETCAT
Release	a user catalog from the master catalog	EXPORT DISCONNECT
Rename	a data set	ALTER
Reproduce	a VSAM or nonVSAM data set	REPRO
Restore	a data set's end-of-file information	VERIFY
	a catalog entry and/or the contents of its object	EXPORTRA and IMPORTRA RESETCAT
Unbind	data from the subsystem storage of an entire subsystem or a particular device within an IBM 3880 Storage Control Model 13	BINDDATA
Uncatalog	a data set	DELETE
Unload	a data set or catalog	REPRO
Verify	a VSAM data set's end-of-file indicators	VERIFY

4.1, on OS Utilities) lists various operations in alphabetical order, and the associated IDCAMS command.

Summary

The chapter was devoted exclusively to VSAM organization. It began with a brief description of the *VSAM catalog structure*, and continued with a conceptual view of *key sequenced data sets*. A complete example was developed to illustrate a *sequence set, index set, control interval split*, and *control area split*.

The Access Methods Services (IDCAMS) utility was covered in some detail. We discussed the basic commands: REPRO, PRINT, DELETE, and DEFINE CLUSTER. We showed how IDCAMS can be applied to VSAM and/or non-VSAM data sets, in particular to generation data groups.

The chapter reviewed the COBOL elements associated with indexed files, with emphasis on ACCESS IS DYNAMIC and ALTERNATE RECORD KEY. We developed a complete COBOL program to show sequential and nonsequential access, for both the primary and secondary index. The program was accompanied by the needed IDCAMS statements to build the necessary indexes.

TRUE/FALSE EXERCISES

1. VSAM data sets must be catalogued.
2. A specific VSAM file may be catalogued in either the master catalog or a user catalog.
3. IDCAMS can manipulate non-VSAM data sets.
4. The VSAM master catalog is equivalent to the OS system catalog.
5. Generations of a GDG are updated at the end of a job step, rather than the end of a job.
6. A control interval contains one or more control areas.
7. A given control interval may contain more than one logical record.
8. A single logical record may extend over more than one control interval.
9. The sequence set is the highest level index.
10. The JOBCAT and STEPCAT statements are equivalent.
11. IDCAMS requires both a SYSPRINT and a SYSIN DD statement.

12. IDCAMS can process a sequential data set.
13. IDCAMS can process a partitioned data set.
14. The STEPCAT DD statement is required if the VSAM master catalog is referenced.
15. IDCAMS control statements begin in column 1.
16. A hyphen indicates continuation of an IDCAMS control statement.
17. A VSAM file may have more than one ALTERNATE KEY.
18. ALTERNATE RECORD KEYS need not be unique.
19. The primary RECORD KEY must be unique.
20. READ NEXT indicates sequential access.
21. A VSAM file may be read sequentially and nonsequentially in the same program.
22. The FILE STATUS clause is required for VSAM files.
23. The REPRO command may copy a non-VSAM data set to a VSAM data set.
24. The PRINT command can display the output data set in a variety of formats.
25. INFILE and OUTFILE *must* be specified with the REPRO command.
26. Multiple IDCAMS commands may be specified in a single SYSIN file.
27. IDCAMS provides for conditional execution of its commands.

PROBLEMS

1. Assume that record key 289 is to be inserted in the first control area of the VSAM data set of Figure 5.4. Logically, it could be added as either the *last* record in the first control interval or the *first* record in the second control interval. Is there a preference?

   In similar fashion, should record 620 be inserted as the *last* record in the third interval of the second area, or as the *first* record in the first interval of the third area?

   Finally, will record 900 be inserted as the *last* record in the fourth control area, or will it require *creation of a fifth control area?* Can you describe in general terms how VSAM adds records at the end of control areas and/or control intervals?

2. Describe the changes to Figure 5.4 if record keys 401, 723, 724, and 725 were added. What would happen if record keys 502 and 619 were deleted?

3. A bank uses an indexed file for its outstanding loans. The record key is CUSTOMER–LOAN–NUMBER, which consists of a unique six-digit customer number and a three-digit sequence number. Each loan a customer receives is assigned a new sequence number. Customer 111111, for example, may have two outstanding loans, with keys of 111111001 and 111111002. Develop the necessary Procedure Division statements to retrieve all outstanding loans for a given customer. (Hint: use the START verb.)

4. Modify the jobstream of Figure 5.6 to accomplish all of the following changes:

   (a) Execute IDCAMS once rather than three times; i.e., put multiple commands in the SYSIN file.
   (b) Execute the PRINT command conditionally—i.e., if and only if the REPRO command was successful.
   (c) Allow for 10 generations in lieu of 5, and an expiration date of December 31, 1986.

5. Modify the jobstream of Figure 5.5 to accommodate all of the following changes:

   (a) Each IDCAMS command is to appear in a separate job step; i.e., IDCAMS is to be executed four times. (Which technique do you prefer?)
   (b) The VSAM cluster is to be known as VSAM.CLUSTER rather than MASTER.FILE.CLUSTER; be sure you make the change in every necessary occurrence.
   (c) The key is 6 bytes long, and begins in the fourth column of every record. The data set contains an estimated 500 records, and individual records are 47 bytes long.
   (d) Allow 20% of each control interval and 10% of each control area for free space.
   (e) Eliminate all occurrences of INDATASET and OUTDATASET, substituting INFILE and OUTFILE, as appropriate.

6

Assembler Fundamentals

Overview

The next several chapters are designed to increase competence in COBOL through study of Assembler. The author is of the firm belief that even a superficial knowledge of BAL greatly enhances one's capabilities with respect to both debugging and efficiency considerations. This is readily appreciated when one realizes that the computer does not execute COBOL instructions per se, but rather the machine language statements generated by the COBOL compiler.

The chapter opens with a basic treatment of the binary and hexadecimal number systems. We discuss simple arithmetic, conversion from one base to another, and two's complement notation. We cover internal data representation—i.e., packed, binary, zoned decimal, and floating point formats—and relate this material to COBOL with an example on debugging. The chapter concludes with a discussion of base/displacement addressing and instruction formats.

NUMBER SYSTEMS

A number system is a set of symbols controlled by a well-defined set of rules for measuring quantities. The value of every digit is determined by its position; as one moves from right to left (i.e., away from the decimal point), each succeeding digit is multiplied by a higher power of the base in which one is working. For example, the number 1976 in base 10 is equal to

$$1000 + 900 + 70 + 6 = 1 \times 10^3 + 9 \times 10^2 + 7 \times 10^1 + 6 \times 10^0$$

We commonly use the decimal number system (base 10), but the choice of a base is actually quite arbitrary. Ten was picked a few thousand years ago, probably because man has ten fingers and ten toes. The advent of digital computers has forced consideration of bases other than 10, and that is what this section is all about.

Number systems are easily understood if one approaches the subject from existing knowledge, i.e., base 10. Everything about any other base can be related back to base 10. *All concepts are identical.* Thus, the decimal system has 10 digits, 0 to 9; the octal (base 8) system has 8 digits, 0 to 7; and the binary (base 2) system has 2 digits, 0 and 1; etc. Engineering considerations make it impractical to build a "base 10" computer because 10 different physical levels would be required to represent the 10 digits. On the other hand, a binary machine is very easy to build, as only two values are required. A current may be on or off, a switch up or down, a magnetic field right or left, etc. All computers are built as binary machines, and for this reason we shall begin our study of number systems with base 2. To indicate which base we are talking about, we shall surround the number by ( )'s and use a subscript to indicate the base. If the parentheses are omitted, base 10 is assumed.

BINARY NUMBERS

Base 2 has two digits, 0 and 1. The value of a digit is determined by its position, which represents some power of 2. The binary number $(10110)_2 = (22)_{10}$. The decimal value is obtained by expanding digits in the binary number by increasing powers of 2 as one moves away from the decimal point; thus,

$$(10110)_2$$

$$0 \times 2^0 = 0 \times 1 = 0$$
$$1 \times 2^1 = 1 \times 2 = 2$$
$$1 \times 2^2 = 1 \times 4 = 4$$
$$0 \times 2^3 = 0 \times 8 = 0$$
$$1 \times 2^4 = 1 \times 16 = \underline{16}$$
$$(22)_{10}$$

Easy enough? Try the following examples as practice:

$$(11011)_2 = (27)_{10} \quad \text{and} \quad (100101)_2 = (37)_{10}$$

Decimal to Binary Conversion

The reader should now be able to convert from binary to decimal; how does one go from decimal to binary? For example, what does $(18)_{10}$ equal in binary? One approach is to determine by trial and error which powers of 2 make up 18. After a few seconds or minutes, we arrive at 16 and 2 and the binary number 10010. That approach is fine for small decimal numbers but doesn't work very well for large numbers. A more systematic way to go from decimal to binary is to repeatedly divide the decimal number by 2 until a quotient of zero is reached. The remainders, read in reverse order, constitute the binary number. Returning to the example, $(18)_{10} = (?)_2$,

$2\underline{/\,18}$ Answer = $(10010)_2$

$2\underline{/\ \ 9}$ remainder of 0

$2\underline{/\ \ 4}$ remainder of 1

$2\underline{/\ \ 2}$ remainder of 0

$2\underline{/\ \ 1}$ remainder of 0

$\ \ \ \ 0$ remainder of 1

As practice, consider the examples

$$(35)_{10} = (100011)_2 \quad \text{and} \quad (71)_{10} = (1000111)_2$$

Binary Addition

Just as one adds in decimal, one can add in binary. Binary addition is much less complicated than decimal addition; it just takes a little getting used to.

However, the principles of addition in either base are identical, and if one truly understands decimal arithmetic, it should not be too difficult to work in binary, or, for that matter, in any other base. Consider first the following addition in base 10:

$$
\begin{array}{r}
38 \\
+\ 46 \\
\hline
84
\end{array}
$$

If you add like most people, your thoughts begin with "8 + 6 = 14; write down 4 and carry 1." Now analyze that statement. We are working in base 10 with valid digits 0 to 9. "14" cannot be written as a single digit; thus, we subtract 10 (i.e., the base) from 14, and the result of 4 is valid as a single digit; we subtracted once and hence have a carry of 1. Involved? Yes, but that is precisely the process we follow. Addition in base 10 has become so ingrained over the years that we do all of that automatically. Now let's translate that thought process to the binary system.

$$
\begin{array}{r}
(10)_2 \\
+\ (11)_2 \\
\hline
=\quad ?
\end{array}
$$

First, determine the result by converting each number to base 10, adding in base 10, and then converting the sum back to binary:

$$
\begin{array}{r}
(10)_2\ --\rightarrow\ (2)_{10} \\
(11)_2\ --\rightarrow\ (3)_{10} \\
\hline
(101)_2\ \leftarrow--\ (5)_{10}
\end{array}
$$

We need, however, to be able to perform the addition directly in binary without having to go through decimal, so let us add in binary, one column at a time. First, $(0)_2 + (1)_2 = (1)_2$. In the next column, we add 1 and 1 to get 2, except we can't write 2 as a single binary digit. Therefore, we subtract 2 from 2 and get zero, which is acceptable; we subtracted once and hence have a carry of 1. Returning to the initial example,

$$
\begin{array}{r}
\text{Carry} =\quad 1 \\
(10)_2 \\
(11)_2 \\
\hline
(101)_2
\end{array}
$$

TABLE 6.1 BINARY AND
DECIMAL EQUIVALENTS

Decimal	Binary
1 ←――――――→	1
	+ 1
2 ←――――――→	10
	+ 1
3 ←――――――→	11
	+ 1
4 ←――――――→	100
	+ 1
5 ←――――――→	101
	+ 1
6 ←――――――→	110
	+ 1
7 ←――――――→	111
	+ 1
8 ←――――――→	1000
	+ 1
9 ←――――――→	1001
	+ 1
10 ←――――――→	1010

It takes a little getting used to. To check your understanding and also to gain a little practice, consider Table 6.1, in which the binary equivalents of the decimal numbers 1 to 10 are obtained through repeated addition. The reader should now be able to convert from binary to decimal, from decimal to binary, and be able to do binary addition.

HEXADECIMAL NUMBERS

Although all computers function as binary machines, one never sees the internal contents displayed as binary numbers, simply because binary is too cumbersome. Nor does one see internal contents displayed as decimal numbers because binary-to-decimal conversion is time consuming and can be inexact with fractional numbers. The hexadecimal (base 16) number system solves both problems. It is much more concise than binary and provides direct and exact conversions to and from binary; i.e., four binary digits are exactly equal to one hex digit ($2^4 = 16$).

Just as base 10 has 10 digits, 0 to 9, base 16 has 16 digits, 0 to 15. The letter A represents 10, B represents 11, C is 12, D is 13, E is 14, and F is 15.

In a decimal number each digit represents a power of 10; in a hex number each digit represents a power of 16. Consider the hex number $(12AB)_{16}$ and obtain its decimal equivalent:

$(12AB)_{16}$

$$B \times 16^0 = 11 \times \quad 1 = \quad 11$$
$$A \times 16^1 = 10 \times \quad 16 = \quad 160$$
$$2 \times 16^2 = \quad 2 \times \quad 256 = \quad 512$$
$$1 \times 16^3 = \quad 1 \times 4096 = \underline{4096}$$
$$(4779)_{10}$$

Decimal to Hexadecimal Conversion

Conversion from decimal to hex is accomplished much the same as conversion from decimal to binary, except that we divide by 16 instead of 2. For example, $(1000)_{10} = (?)_{16}$:

$16 / 1000$ Answer $= (3E8)_{16}$

$16 / \quad 62$ remainder of 8

$16 / \quad\quad 3$ remainder of 14 = E

0 remainder of 3

The remainders are read from the bottom up. Note that the remainder of 14 in decimal is converted to E in hex. As a check, we can convert $(3E8)_{16}$ to a decimal number and arrive at $(1000)_{10}$:

$(3E8)_{16}$

$$8 \times 16^0 = \quad 8 \times \quad 1 = \quad\quad 8$$
$$E \times 16^1 = 14 \times \quad 16 = \quad 224$$
$$3 \times 16^2 = \quad 3 \times 256 = \underline{768}$$
$$(1000)_{10}$$

Hexadecimal Addition

Hexadecimal addition is made simple if we again use the thought processes of decimal arithmetic. Consider

$$\text{Carry} = \quad 1$$
$$(39)_{16}$$
$$+ (59)_{16}$$
$$\overline{(92)_{16}}$$

9 plus 9 equals 18; hex cannot express 18 as a single-digit number; therefore, subtract 16 and get 2. 2 is valid; we subtracted once and hence have a carry of 1. It seems complicated only because we are so used to decimal arithmetic. The concepts of addition are identical in both bases, and it should only be a matter of time and practice to be comfortable in both.

Since hexadecimal includes some "strange-looking" digits—i.e., A, B, C, D, E, and F—perhaps another example will be helpful. Consider

$$\text{Carry} = \quad 1$$
$$(AB)_{16}$$
$$+ (37)_{16}$$
$$\overline{(E2)_{16}}$$

B plus 7 equals 18 (remember, B denotes 11). Hex cannot express 18 as a single digit; thus subtract 16, get 2, and carry 1. Now A, 3 and 1 (the carry) equal 14, which is represented by E in hex.

Binary to Hexadecimal Conversion

A computer functions internally as a binary machine, but its contents are often displayed as hex numbers. How does the conversion take place? Consider

$$(10110100)_2 = (??)_{16}$$

One way is to convert the binary number to a decimal number by expanding powers of 2 and then to convert the decimal number to its hex equivalent by repeated division by 16. Thus, $(10110100)_2 = (180)_{10} = (B4)_2$.

There is, however, a shortcut. Since $2^4 = 16$, there are exactly four binary digits to one hex digit. Simply take the binary number and divide it into groups of four digits; begin at the decimal point and work right to left, i.e., 1011 0100. Then take each group of four digits and mentally convert to hex. Thus, $(0100)_2 = (4)_{10} = (4)_{16}$ and $(1011)_2 = (11)_{10} = (B)_{16}$. The answer is then B4 in hex, which was obtained earlier.

The process works in reverse as well. The hex number ABC can be immediately converted to the binary number 101010111100. As verification, convert ABC to decimal and then go from decimal to binary.

The advantages of hex notation should now be apparent. It is a more concise representation than binary of the internal workings of a machine, yet unlike decimal conversion, it is immediate and exact. It should also occur to you that octal (base 8) would also be suitable as a shorthand, and indeed several computers use octal notation in lieu of hex.

A Shortcut to Conversion

Table 6.2 is reproduced from the IBM reference card (FX20–1850–3) and is a shortcut to converting from hex to decimal, and vice versa. Consider $(95AB6)_{16} = (\ ? \ )_{10}$

TABLE 6.2 HEXADECIMAL/DECIMAL CONVERSION

Hex 5 in 4th column = $(20{,}480)_{10}$

HEXADECIMAL COLUMNS					
6	5	4	3	2	1
HEX = DEC	HEX = DEC	HEX = DEC	HEX = DEC	HEX = DEC	HEX = DEC
0 0	0 0	0 0	0 0	0 0	0 0
1 1,048,576	1 65,536	1 4,096	1 256	1 16	1 1
2 2,097,152	2 131,072	2 8,192	2 512	2 32	2 2
3 3,145,728	3 196,608	3 12,288	3 768	3 48	3 3
4 4,194,304	4 262,144	4 16,384	4 1,024	4 64	4 4
5 5,242,880	5 327,680	5 20,480	5 1,280	5 80	5 5
6 6,291,456	6 393,216	6 24,576	6 1,536	6 96	6 6
7 7,340,032	7 458,752	7 28,672	7 1,792	7 112	7 7
8 8,388,608	8 524,288	8 32,768	8 2,048	8 128	8 8
9 9,437,184	9 589,824	9 36,864	9 2,304	9 144	9 9
A 10,485,760	A 655,360	A 40,960	A 2,560	A 160	A 10
B 11,534,336	B 720,896	B 45,056	B 2,816	B 176	B 11
C 12,582,912	C 786,432	C 49,152	C 3,072	C 192	C 12
D 13,631,488	D 851,968	D 53,248	D 3,328	D 208	D 13
E 14,680,064	E 917,504	E 57,344	E 3,584	E 224	E 14
F 15,728,640	F 983,040	F 61,440	F 3,840	F 240	F 15
0 1 2 3	4 5 6 7	0 1 2 3	4 5 6 7	0 1 2 3	4 5 6 7
BYTE		BYTE		BYTE	

A hex 9 in 5th column = $(589{,}824)_{10}$

To convert from hexadecimal to decimal, one locates each hex digit in the appropriate column of Table 6.2, notes its decimal value, and sums the decimal equivalents. Hence, a hexadecimal 9 in the fifth column has a decimal value of 589,824; a hex 5 in the fourth column has a decimal value of 20,480, and so on. The decimal equivalent of $(95AB6)_{16}$ is therefore:

589,824   (from 5th column in Table 6.2)

20,480   (from 4th column in Table 6.2)

2,560   (from 3rd column in Table 6.2)

176   (from 2nd column in Table 6.2)

+   6   (from 1st column in Table 6.2)

613,046

A conversion from decimal to hexadecimal may also be accomplished by using Table 6.2. As a check on the previous example, let us obtain the hexadecimal equivalent of 613,046; i.e., $(613,046)_{10} = (\ ? \ )_{16}$.

Step 1 is to find the largest number which fits into the decimal number slated for conversion; i.e., 589,824 is the largest number in Table 6.2 which fits into the original number, 613,046.

The hex digit and corresponding column is noted—i.e., hex 9 in column 5. We compute the decimal remainder—i.e., $613,046 - 589,824 = 23,222$—and repeat the process until the remainder is zero. The necessary calculations follow:

First hex digit = 9 in column 5

613,046 = (number for conversion)

- 589,824 = (largest value from Table 6.2)

23,222 = (remainder for subsequent step)

Second hex digit = 5 in column 4

23,222 = (remainder from previous step)

- 20,480 = (largest value from Table 6.2)

2,742 = (remainder for subsequent step)

Third hex digit = A in column 3

2,742 = (remainder from previous step)

- 2,560 = (largest value from Table 6.2)

182 = (remainder for subsequent step)

Fourth hex digit = B in column 2

182 = (remainder from previous step)

- 176 = (largest value from Table 6.2)

6 = (remainder for subsequent step)

Fifth hex digit = 6 in column 1

The process terminates when a hex digit is computed for the last column. Thus $(613,046)_{10} = (95AB6)_{16}$, which checks with the original example.

INTERNAL REPRESENTATION OF DATA

The smallest addressable unit of storage is the *byte*, consisting of eight *bits* (binary digits). The amount of memory required to store individual data items is expressed in terms of bytes. The COBOL programmer indicates how data is to be stored through the USAGE clause, with three formats commonly used. These are DISPLAY, COMPUTATIONAL, and COMPUTATIONAL-3. Two additional formats, COMPUTATIONAL-1 and COMPUTATIONAL-2, are used in special instances.

DISPLAY Data (EBCDIC)

Data represented according to EBCDIC (Extended Binary Coded Decimal Interchange Code) use specific bit combinations of 0's and 1's to denote different characters. Since a byte contains 8 data bits, each of which can assume either a 0 or 1, there are $2^8 = 256$ different combinations for a given byte. Table 6.3 displays the bit combinations for letters, numbers, and some special characters, in both binary and hexadecimal.

Yes, reader, there is rhyme and reason to Table 6.3, at least where the letters and numbers are concerned. The 8 bits of a byte are divided into a zone and numeric portion, as follows:

xxxx	xxxx
zone	digit

The four leftmost bits constitute the zone portion, the four rightmost bits make up the digit portion. Notice from Table 6.3 that the letters A through I all have the same zone (1100 in binary or C in hex). Note further that the letters J through R, S through Z, and the digits 0 through 9 also have the same zones: D, E, and F, respectively.

Consider the word 'COBOL' in EBCDIC. Since COBOL contains five characters, five bytes of storage are required. Using Table 6.3, COBOL would appear internally as shown in Figure 6.1.

(Binary)	11000011	11010110	11000010	11010110	11010011
(Hex)	C3	D6	C2	D6	D3

FIGURE 6.1 EBCDIC Representation of "COBOL"

Now suppose that we wanted to represent the number 678 in EBCDIC. This time, three bytes are required and, using Table 6.3, we get Figure 6.2.

TABLE 6.3 EBCDIC CONFIGURATION FOR LETTERS, NUMBERS, AND SOME SPECIAL CHARACTERS

Letters: Character	EBCDIC Binary	EBCDIC Hex	Numbers: Character	EBCDIC Binary	EBCDIC Hex
A	1100 0001	C1	0	1111 0000	F0
B	1100 0010	C2	1	1111 0001	F1
C	1100 0011	C3	2	1111 0010	F2
D	1100 0100	C4	3	1111 0011	F3
E	1100 0101	C5	4	1111 0100	F4
F	1100 0110	C6	5	1111 0101	F5
G	1100 0111	C7	6	1111 0110	F6
H	1100 1000	C8	7	1111 0111	F7
I	1100 1001	C9	8	1111 1000	F8
J	1101 0001	D1	9	1111 1001	F9
K	1101 0010	D2			
L	1101 0011	D3	*Special Characters:*	EBCDIC Binary	EBCDIC Hex
M	1101 0100	D4	Character		
N	1101 0101	D5			
O	1101 0110	D6			
P	1101 0111	D7	Blank	0100 0000	40
Q	1101 1000	D8	.	0100 1011	4B
R	1101 1001	D9	(	0100 1101	4D
S	1110 0010	E2	+	0100 1110	4E
T	1110 0011	E3	$	0101 1011	5B
U	1110 0100	E4	*	0101 1100	5C
V	1110 0101	E5	)	0101 1101	5D
W	1110 0110	E6	—	0110 0000	60
X	1110 0111	E7	/	0110 0001	61
Y	1110 1000	E8	,	0110 1011	6B
Z	1110 1001	E9	'	0111 1101	7D
			=	0111 1110	7E

(Binary)	11110110	11110111	11111000
(Hex)	F6	F7	F8

FIGURE 6.2 EBCDIC Representation of "678"

The zone portion of each byte is the same in Figure 6.2, and does it not seem inherently wasteful to use half of each byte for the zone, when, in a numeric field, that zone is always 1111? The solution is an alternative form of data representation, known as packed format.

COMPUTATIONAL-3 Data (Packed Format)

The *packed format* is used to represent numeric data more concisely. Essentially, it stores two numeric digits in one byte by eliminating the zone. This is done throughout, except in the rightmost byte, which contains a numeric digit in the zone portion and the sign of the entire number in the digit portion. The hex digits C or F denote a postive number, and the digit D represents a negative number. Figure 6.3 shows both positive and negative packed representations of the numbers 678 and 112233. Only two bytes are required to represent the number 678 in packed format, compared to three bytes in EBCDIC (Figure 6.2). Note, however, that the packed representation of numbers with an even number of digits (e.g., 112233) always contains an extra half-byte of zeros.

Both the EBCDIC and packed formats are said to represent variable-length fields in that the number of bytes required depends on the data that are stored. "COBOL" requires five bytes for EBCDIC representation, "IBM" only three. "112233" takes four bytes in packed format, "678" only two.

```
(a)  Positive configuration (112233):
00000001     00010010     00100011     00111100     (Binary)
    01           12           23           3C       (Hex)

(b)  Negative configuration (112233):
00000001     00010010     00100011     00111101     (Binary)
    01           12           23           3D       (Hex)

(c)  Positive configuration (678):
             01100111     10001100     (Binary)
                 67           8C       (Hex)

(d)  Negative configuration (678):
             01100111     10001101     (Binary)
                 67           8D       (Hex)
```

FIGURE 6.3 Packed Representation

COMPUTATIONAL Data (Binary Format)

Numeric data can also be stored in fixed-length units as binary numbers. Two bytes (half-word), four bytes (full-word), or eight bytes (double-word) are used depending on the size of a decimal number according to the rule:

Up to 4 decimal digits:	2 bytes
5 to 9 decimal digits:	4 bytes
10 to 18 decimal digits:	8 bytes

Some explanation is in order. Consider a half-word (16 bits). The largest positive number that can be represented is a 0 and fifteen 1's (the high-order zero indicates a positive number), which equals $2^{15} - 1$, or 32,767. Any four-digit decimal number will fit in a half-word, since the largest four-digit decimal number is only 9999. However, not all five-digit numbers will fit, hence the limitation to four digits in a half-word.

The largest binary number that can be stored in a full-word is $2^{31} - 1$, or 2,147,483,647 in decimal, hence the limit of nine decimal digits in a full-word. In similar fashion, a limit of 18 decimal digits is obtained for a double-word.

Two's-Complement Notation

The sign of a binary number is indicated by its leftmost (high-order) bit. This is true regardless of whether the number occupies a half-word, full-word, or double-word. *A 0 in the sign bit indicates a positive number; a 1 means that the number is negative and stored in two's-complement notation.*

The two's-complement of a number is obtained in two steps:

1. Reverse all bits; wherever there is a 0, make it 1, and wherever a 1 occurs, make it 0.
2. Add 1 to your answer from step 1.

For example, suppose that we want the two's complement of 01101111:

$$\begin{array}{ll}
\text{Step 1: Reverse all bits} & 10010000 \\
\text{Step 2: Add 1 to answer from step 1} + & \underline{\hspace{1.5em}1} \\
& 10010001
\end{array}$$

Thus, the two's-complement of 01101111 is 10010001. As a check on the answer, simply add the original number and its calculated complement. The result should be all 0's and a high-order carry of 1:

$$\begin{array}{lr}
\text{Check:} & 01101111 \\
+ & \underline{10010001} \\
\text{high-order carry} \longrightarrow & 1\ 00000000
\end{array}$$

Now that we can determine the sign of a number in storage and calculate its two's-complement if necessary, consider the following half-words in storage:

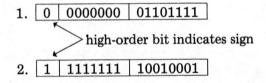

In the first example, the number is positive, as indicated by the high-order bit. Accordingly, its decimal value is simply +111. The second example, however, has a high-order bit of 1, indicating a negative number, and further that the number itself is stored in two's-complement. In order to get its decimal value, we must first get the two's-complement of the number, then put a minus sign in front of the answer. You should get -111.

Two's-complement notation facilitates addition or subtraction of signed numbers. For example, to add two binary numbers of whatever sign, just do a binary add and discard the high-order carry. In order to subtract a number, convert it to its two's complement, add the complement to the number from which you are subtracting, and ignore the high-order carry. (The absence of a high-order carry implies that the result of the subtraction is negative and stored in its two's-complement form. See problems 14 and 15.)

COMPUTATIONAL-1 and -2 Data (Floating Point)

Many excellent and most typical COBOL programmers go through entire careers without encountering floating-point data. However, this feature is useful in applications requiring either very large or very small quantities; hence, we present some introductory material. There are two kinds of floating-point numbers, denoted as COMPUTATIONAL-1 (short precision) and COMPUTATIONAL-2 (long precision). Both forms consist of a sign bit, a characteristic (exponent), and a mantissa (the digits in the number itself). Short-precision floating-point numbers (COMP-1) are assigned a full-word in storage; long-precision numbers (COMP-2) occupy a double-word. Consider the COMP-1 representation for the decimal number 133 shown below in both hex and binary.

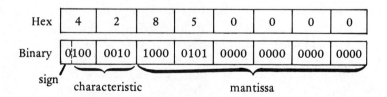

The first bit represents the sign of the entire number; a 0 indicates a positive number, and a 1 denotes a negative number. Unlike binary numbers, negative numbers are *not* stored in their two's-complement. The characteristic (or exponent) consists of the next 7 bits, and is 66 in this example. Exponents are stored with a bias of 64, so the true exponent is always obtained by subtracting 64 from the stored exponent. Thus, the true exponent in this example is 2 (66 - 64). (The sign bit is already in use and hence the bias is necessary to accommodate both positive and negative exponents.)

The remaining 24 bits are the mantissa, the actual digits of the number, expressed as a hexadecimal fraction. To obtain the value of the number, we take the mantissa (a fraction in base 16) and multiply it by the appropriate power of 16 (i.e., shift the decimal point the number of places equal to the exponent). The example above has a mantissa of .850000 and an exponent of 2; hence, the true number is $(85.0000)_{16} = (133)_{10}$.

Consider some additional examples:

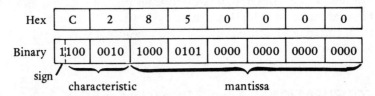

This example is exactly like the first, except that the sign bit is 1, meaning a negative number of $(-85.0000)_{16}$ or $(-133)_{10}$.

Now consider a negative exponent (i.e., a negative number results after subtraction of 64):

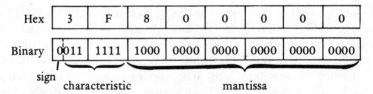

The sign bit is 0; thus, the entire number is positive. The stored characteristic is 63; hence, the true exponent is -1 (63 - 64). A negative exponent means that the decimal point is moved to the left instead of to the right. Thus, the actual number is $(.080)_{16} = (.03125)_{10}$.

Long-precision floating-point numbers (COMP-2) are stored in a double-word (64 bits). The allocation for the sign bit and characteristic is exactly as with short precision; the difference is in the mantissa. Long-precision floating-point numbers use the extra 32 bits for the mantissa, making a total of 56 bits for the mantissa. The other 8 bits are used for the sign and characteristic, as described previously.

THE COBOL USAGE CLAUSE AND DATA FORMATS

The COBOL USAGE clause explicitly specifies how data are to be stored internally. (Omission of the clause causes default to DISPLAY, which can result in inefficient object code.) Consider the following COBOL entries:

```
05  FIELD-A       PICTURE IS S9(4)
        USAGE IS DISPLAY          VALUE IS 1.
05  FIELD-B       PICTURE IS S9(4)
        USAGE IS COMPUTATIONAL-3  VALUE IS 1.
05  FIELD-C       PICTURE IS S9(4)
        USAGE IS COMPUTATIONAL    VALUE IS 1.
05  FIELD-D       PICTURE IS S9(4)
        USAGE IS COMPUTATIONAL-1  VALUE IS 1.
05  FIELD-E       PICTURE IS S9(4)
        USAGE IS COMPUTATIONAL-2  VALUE IS 1.
```

A numeric constant of 1 is defined in every instance. However, each entry has a different usage specified, hence the fields will have very different internal formats. In particular, USAGE IS DISPLAY indicates storage in zoned-decimal (EBCDIC) format, COMPUTATIONAL-3 packed format, COMPUTATIONAL binary format, COMPUTATIONAL-1 short precision floating point, and COMPUTATIONAL-2 long precision floating point.

FIELD-A occupies four bytes of storage and stores the constant 1 in zoned decimal format, with high-order zeros. The internal representation of FIELD-A, shown in hex, is as follows:

F0	F0	F0	C1

FIELD-B occupies three bytes of storage and stores the constant 1 in packed format, again with high-order zeros. Internal representation of FIELD-B, shown in hex, is as follows:

00	00	1C

FIELD-C is stored as a binary number with the number of bytes determined as in the previous discussion. Thus, FIELD-C will occupy two bytes of storage, as follows.

In binary:

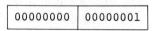

00000000	00000001

In hex:

00	01

FIELD-D and FIELD-E are both stored as floating-point numbers, requiring four and eight bytes, respectively. The sign bit and exponent are the same for both fields, but FIELD-E has an additional 32 bits allocated to the mantissa. Hex representations for each field are as follows:

FIELD-D:

41	10	00	00

FIELD-E:

41	10	00	00	00	00	00	00

COBOL IMPLICATIONS—DEBUGGING

We have identified several distinct forms of internal data representation—also that the COBOL USAGE clause determines actual storage allocation. This limited knowledge of assembler considerations is immediately applicable to COBOL debugging. Consider Figure 6.4, a COBOL listing which illustrates both *correct* and *incorrect* ways of initializing group fields. The output produced by Figure 6.4 is shown in Figure 6.5. The values of FIRST-BINARY, FIRST-DISPLAY, and FIRST-PACKED are all 1, as expected. The value of SECOND-DISPLAY is also 1, but the value of SECOND-BINARY is 3855, and attempted execution of statement 53 (to calculate SECOND-PACKED) resulted in abnormal job termination and subsequent dump. Why? Simply stated, the difficulties with SECOND-BINARY and SECOND-PACKED are caused by the group move of line 45. *All group moves are treated as alphanumeric moves.* Hence, the "wrong" kind of zeros are moved to SECOND-BINARY and SECOND-PACKED; in effect, these fields are not initialized to zero at all.

The preceding discussion provides a technically correct, albeit unsatisfying, explanation of the problem. Nevertheless, it is typical of the wording found in COBOL manuals, where discussion contains examples of valid and invalid moves, padding, truncation, and so on. This is followed by a one-sentence disclaimer stating that the rules above apply only to elementary moves and that group moves are considered as alphanumeric.

The net effect is to leave the student with a correct, but thoroughly incomplete, understanding of the COBOL language. The student goes merrily on his or her way, until one day trouble occurs and the student indubitably feels betrayed by the machine. He or she looks everywhere, usually to no avail. In reality, the explanation is apparent, if only he or she knew how to find it. All that is required are some very basic assembler concepts, which have already been covered in this chapter. Unfortunately, many programmers never obtain the total picture because they learned COBOL as a high-level language and never studied assembler at all, or because COBOL and assembler were covered in separate courses and no one ever linked the two.

```
00001          IDENTIFICATION DIVISION.
00002          PROGRAM-ID.      GROUPMV.
00003          AUTHOR.          R GRAUER.
00004
00005          ENVIRONMENT DIVISION.
00006          CONFIGURATION SECTION.
00007          SOURCE-COMPUTER.     IBM-4341.
00008          OBJECT-COMPUTER.     IBM-4341.
00009
00010          DATA DIVISION.
00011          WORKING-STORAGE SECTION.
00012          01  FILLER                          PIC X(18)
00013                  VALUE '* WS BEGINS HERE *'.
00014
00015          01  FIRST-GROUP-FIELD.
00016              05  FIRST-DISPLAY               PIC 9(04).
00017              05  FIRST-BINARY                PIC 9(04)   COMP.
00018              05  FIRST-PACKED                PIC 9(04)   COMP-3.
00019
00020          01  SECOND-GROUP-FIELD.
00021              05  SECOND-DISPLAY              PIC 9(04).
00022              05  SECOND-BINARY               PIC 9(04)   COMP.
00023              05  SECOND-PACKED               PIC 9(04)   COMP-3.
00024
00025          01  FILLER                          PIC X(18)
00026                  VALUE '** WS ENDS HERE **'.
00027
00028          PROCEDURE DIVISION.
00029      *          CORRECT INITIALIZATION          *
00030
00031          MOVE ZEROS  TO  FIRST-DISPLAY.
00032          ADD 1  TO  FIRST-DISPLAY.
00033          DISPLAY 'FIRST-DISPLAY = ' FIRST-DISPLAY.
00034
00035          MOVE ZEROS  TO  FIRST-BINARY.
00036          ADD 1  TO  FIRST-BINARY.
00037          DISPLAY 'FIRST-BINARY = ' FIRST-BINARY.
00038
00039          MOVE ZEROS  TO  FIRST-PACKED.
00040          ADD 1  TO  FIRST-PACKED.
00041          DISPLAY 'FIRST-PACKED = ' FIRST-PACKED.
00042
00043      *          INCORRECT INITIALIZATION          *
00044
00045          MOVE ZEROS  TO  SECOND-GROUP-FIELD.
00046
00047          ADD 1  TO  SECOND-DISPLAY.
00048          DISPLAY 'SECOND-DISPLAY = ' SECOND-DISPLAY.
00049
00050          ADD 1  TO  SECOND-BINARY.
00051          DISPLAY 'SECOND-BINARY = ' SECOND-BINARY.
00052
00053          ADD 1  TO  SECOND-PACKED.
00054          DISPLAY 'SECOND-PACKED = ' SECOND-PACKED.
00055
00056          STOP RUN.
```

FIGURE 6.4 Example of a Group Move

```
FIRST-DISPLAY = 0001
FIRST-BINARY = 0001
FIRST-PACKED = 0001
SECOND-DISPLAY = 0001
SECOND-BINARY = 3855
```

FIGURE 6.5 Output of Figure 6.4

149

The Binary Problem

Given the knowledge of internal data representation, we can intuitively explain the "strange" output associated with Figure 6.5. From previous discussion we expect SECOND-DISPLAY, SECOND-BINARY, and SECOND-PACKED to have lengths of four, two, and three bytes, respectively. The MOVE ZEROS statement of line 45 in Figure 6.4 is a group move; hence, alphanumeric (i.e., EBCDIC) zeros are moved to the three fields as follows:

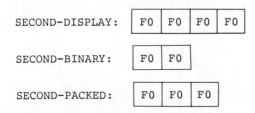

```
SECOND-DISPLAY:   | F0 | F0 | F0 | F0 |

SECOND-BINARY:    | F0 | F0 |

SECOND-PACKED:    | F0 | F0 | F0 |
```

Now consider COBOL statement 50, ADD 1 TO SECOND-BINARY. The compiler generates the instructions to do binary addition and the contents of SECOND-BINARY, before and after, are shown in binary:

SECOND-BINARY (before):   1111 0000 1111 0000
                         + 0000 0000 0000 0001
                         ─────────────────────
SECOND-BINARY (after):   1111 0000 1111 0001

Since the high-order bit in the sum is a 1, the sum is negative and stored in two's-complement form.   However, since SECOND-BINARY is defined as an unsigned field (COBOL line 22), the minus sign is dropped after the two's-complement is obtained.

SECOND-BINARY (after addition):   1111 0000 1111 0001
          Reverse 0's and 1's: 0000 1111 0000 1110
                     Add 1:   + _____1
                                   ───────────────────
          Two's-complement: 0000 1111 0000 1111

The two's-complement is converted to a hex 0F0F, then to its decimal value of 3855; the latter is the displayed value.

The Packed Problem

Packed fields *must always* have a sign as the low-order hex digit. Valid signs are a hex C or F for positive numbers, and a hex D for negative numbers.

Anything else is invalid as a sign and will cause problems in subsequent execution. *Specifically, any attempt to do arithmetic on a packed field with an invalid sign will invariably fail and produce a data exception.*

The field SECOND–PACKED has been initialized by the group move to contain F0F0F0. The low-order hex digit is 0, which is invalid as a sign. Hence, attempted execution of the COBOL ADD in statement 53 failed. Complete explanation requires knowledge of base/displacement addressing and BAL instruction formats, topics to be covered next. In addition, one must be familiar with various compiler aids, such as the memory dump, and Data and Procedure Division maps. The latter are presented in Chapter 7.

BASE/DISPLACEMENT ADDRESSING

The 360/370/303X/4300 machines were all designed to reach 24-bit memory addresses. (The maximum addressable location with these systems was 16,776,215—i.e., $2^{24} - 1$, or simply 16 megabytes.) A single instruction to reference two storage addresses would require six bytes (48 bits) for the addresses alone, and this was judged to be too costly in terms of storage requirements. The solution was a technique known as *base/displacement addressing*.

The addressing scheme uses the CPU's general-purpose registers (GPRs) to reduce storage requirements. A GPR is a hardware device capable of holding information during processing. Information is transferred to or from a register much faster than from main storage. There are 16 GPRs numbered from hex 0 to F; each contains 32 bits.

In the base/displacement method, a 24-bit base address is loaded into a register which is then designated as a base register. A 12-bit displacement is calculated for each location. (The displacement of a location is defined as the number of bytes beyond its base address.) The address of a particular location is determined by specifying a base register and displacement from that base. Since it takes only 4 bits to designate a base register (0 through F) and 12 bits for a displacement, we are effectively providing a 24-bit address in only 16 bits.

Consider the following example. GPR 9 has been designated as the base register. A program is to be stored beginning at memory address $(8800)_{16}$, which is loaded into the 24 low-order bits of register 9 as the base address. It is required to reference memory location $(8950)_{16}$. Given a base address of $(8800)_{16}$, the displacement for location $(8950)_{16}$ is calculated to be $(150)_{16}$. Now we have the 16 bits to specify the address of memory location $(8950)_{16}$, as shown in Figure 6.6. Four are used to designate GPR 9, and 12 bits are used for the hex displacement 150.

There is another major advantage to the base/displacement method, in addition to economy of space. All programs are easily relocatable, that is,

Assumptions:

1. GPR 9 is the base register.
2. $(8800)_{16}$ is the base address, which is loaded into register 9.
3. $(150)_{16}$ is the calculated displacement.

	Base	Displacement		
(Binary)	1001	0001	0101	0000
(Hex)	9	1	5	0

FIGURE 6.6 Base/Displacement Representation of Address $(8950)_{16}$

all addresses in a given program are easily changed by altering only the contents of the base register(s).

IBM's newest series, the 308X machines, use a 31-bit address in lieu of the original 24-bit scheme. Accordingly, the maximum addressable location in real storage is $2^{31} - 1$, or two *gigabytes* (approximately 2 billion bytes).

INSTRUCTION FORMATS

There are several different, but parallel, instructions for the "same" operation, depending on the type of data to be manipulated. The instruction to add two packed numbers is different from the instruction to add two binary numbers; indeed, the instruction to add binary half-words is different from that for binary full-words. The instruction set is designed in such a way that the instruction's length and format are dependent on the type and location of data on which the instruction is to operate. Specifically, there are five types of instructions:

RR: Register to Register (two bytes long)
RX: Register and Indexed Storage (four bytes long)
RS: Register to Storage (four bytes long)
SI: Storage Immediate (four bytes long)
SS: Storage to Storage (six bytes long)

Any of these instruction types provides the following information to the computer:

1. The operation to be performed (e.g., addition, subtraction, etc.)
2. The location of the operands [e.g., in registers, storage, or immediate (i.e., in the instruction)]
3. The nature of the data [i.e., fixed or variable in length, and if the latter, then the length of the data field(s)]

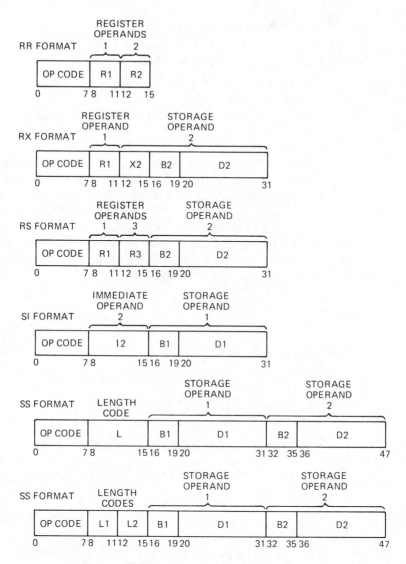

FIGURE 6.7 Instruction Formats

Machine instruction formats are displayed in Figure 6.7. Although Figure 6.7 may not make much sense now, it will assume greater importance in Chapters 7 and 8, when dump reading is studied. An explanation of the notation of Figure 6.7 follows:

OP: Operation code

B: Base register

D: Displacement

X: Register designated as an index register (RX only)

R: Register designated as an operand

I: Immediate data [i.e., the operand is contained in the instruction itself (SI only)]

L: Length used only for variable-length operands in SS format

In later chapters, we will dissect a machine instruction into its component parts—e.g., consider the instruction D208B0156250. Using Figure 6.7, we must somehow decipher this cryptic combination of characters. The key is the first byte of the instruction, which contains the op code D2. Armed with this essential piece of information, we go to Appendix A and find that D2 is the machine op code for MVC (move characters), an SS instruction. We are therefore able to separate the essential components of the instruction according to Figure 6.7.

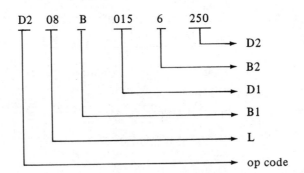

Essentially, the instruction is moving nine bytes (always one more than the length code) beginning at the address specified in the second operand to the address specified in the first operand. Both addresses are derived according to the base/displacement scheme. Thus, the address of the first operand is obtained by taking the base address contained in register 11, plus a hex displacement of 015. The address of the second operand is found by taking the base address in register 6 and adding a hex displacement of 250.

Appreciation for the different instruction formats comes from the realization that data is stored internally in varying formats, as explained further in subsequent chapters.

Summary ━━━━━━━━━━━━━━━━━━━━━━━━━━

The material developed in this chapter is essential to a deeper understanding of COBOL, especially since the computer does not execute COBOL instructions as such, but the machine instructions generated by the COBOL compiler. It is imperative that the reader become familiar with the material on base/displacement addressing and instruction formats before proceeding to the chapters on ABEND debugging. Moreover, these concepts are also helpful in writing more efficient programs (as will be shown in Chapter 9). We do not mean that the applications programmer should spend entire days scrutinizing his or her work to save a few nanoseconds or bytes of storage. We are saying that he or she should at least be aware of what the compiler is doing.

In conclusion, the COBOL programmer can and does function with no knowledge of the machine on which he or she is working. However, a little information in this area goes a long way toward genuine understanding of debugging and efficiency considerations. We hope this point has been made effectively. We firmly believe that the best COBOL programmers are those who also know, or at least have a fundamental understanding of, Assembler.

TRUE/FALSE EXERCISES

1. Every instruction must contain an op code.
2. Mathematically, there are 256 possible op codes.
3. The op code is the second byte in the instruction.
4. Instructions are 2, 4, 6, or 8 bytes in length.
5. Instructions are a half-word, full-word, or double-word in length.
6. There are 16 general-purpose registers in the 360/370/303X/4300/308X series.
7. If the COBOL USAGE clause is omitted, the default is to COMPUTATIONAL.
8. Mathematically, there are 256 possible EBCDIC characters.
9. The EBCDIC representation for the letter A is D1.
10. The displacement takes 12 bits in an instruction.
11. The base/displacement scheme provides for an effective address of 24 bits.

12. The 308X machines have a 31-bit address.

13. 123 is a valid number in base 16.

14. There are five different instruction types.

15. USAGE IS COMP-3 corresponds to the packed format.

16. Binary data are stored internally in 2, 4, or 6 bytes.

17. There are two formats for the SS instruction.

18. The high-order bit of a binary number denotes its sign.

19. The high-order 4 bits of a packed field denote its sign.

20. For packed numbers, either C or F indicates a plus sign.

21. For packed numbers, D indicates a minus sign.

22. A three-digit decimal number requires 2 bytes if USAGE is specified as COMP or COMP-3.

23. A five-digit decimal number requires 4 bytes if USAGE is specified as COMP or COMP-3.

24. The two's complement of a number is obtained just by switching 0's and 1's.

PROBLEMS

1. Can you think of any peculiar output you may have seen where a knowledge of Assembler would have been helpful?

2. Show internal representation for the following COBOL entries:

```
(a)  05   FIELD-A   PIC 9(4)    DISPLAY   VALUE 20.
(b)  05   FIELD-B   PIC 9(4)              VALUE 20.
(c)  05   FIELD-C   PIC 9(4)    COMP      VALUE 20.
(d)  05   FIELD-D   PIC 9(3)    COMP      VALUE 20.
(e)  05   FIELD-E   PIC 9(5)    COMP      VALUE 20.
(f)  05   FIELD-F   PIC 9(10)   COMP      VALUE 20.
(g)  05   FIELD-G   PIC 9(10)   COMP-3    VALUE 20.
(h)  05   FIELD-H   PIC 9(5)    COMP-3    VALUE 20.
(i)  05   FIELD-I   PIC 9(9)    COMP-3    VALUE 20.
```

3. Express the decimal equivalents of the following half-words, all of which represent binary numbers:

(a)

0000 0101	1101 0010

(b)

1111 1111	1111 1111

(c) | 0111 1111 | 1111 1111 |

(d) | 1000 0000 | 0000 0000 |

4. Express the decimal equivalents of the following, all of which represent packed numbers:

(a) | 12 | 34 | 5F |

(b) | 12 | 34 | 5C |

(c) | 54 | 32 | 1D |

5. The largest positive binary number that can be stored in a half-word is 32,767. The largest (in magnitude) negative number that can be stored in the same space is $-32,768$. Explain why there is a difference.

6. Is it efficient (or possible) to use packed fields on card input to a COBOL program? Discuss. What about binary input?

7. Show the internal representation of the largest number that can be stored as a single-precision floating-point number; show the internal representation for the smallest (in magnitude) single-precision floating-point number. What are the approximate decimal values?

8. How many places of decimal accuracy can be achieved with a single-precision floating-point number? How many places of decimal accuracy can be achieved with a double-precision number?

9. Do the indicated arithmetic operation:

(a) $(1234)_{16}$
    $+ (ABCD)_{16}$

(b) $(ABCD)_{16}$
    $+ (FACE)_{16}$

(c) $(ABCD)_{16}$
    $- (1234)_{16}$

(d) $(FACE)_{16}$
    $- (ABCD)_{16}$

10. Indicate the instruction type which:

   (a) Has an operand contained in the instruction itself.
   (b) Uses two registers to calculate a storage address.
   (c) References two storage locations.
   (d) Is six bytes long.
   (e) Does not reference a storage location.

(f) Is two bytes long.

(g) Contains one length code.

(h) Contains two length codes.

11. Assume that the contents of register 4 is $(00001234)_{16}$, and that the contents of register 11 is $(00005678)_{16}$. Given the instruction F2124123B500:

(a) What is the effective address of the second operand?

(b) What is the effective address of the first operand?

(c) What is the nature of the instruction?

12. Use the Table 6.2 to do the following conversions:

(a) $(ABCDEF)_{16} = (\ ?\ )_{10}$

(b) $(987654)_{10} = (\ ?\ )_{16}$

Check your work in parts (a) and (b) by converting the answer to the original number.

13. Why should binary data names be specified with a COBOL PICTURE of 9(4) rather than 9, 99, or 999?

14. Do the following binary additions. (In these examples, the highest possible positive number is 01111111; i.e., the leftmost bit indicates the sign, and negative numbers are stored in two's complement.)

(a)	00001111	(b)	11111111	(c)	00001111
	+ 11111111		+ 11111111		+ 00001111

Get the decimal equivalents for parts a, b, and c. Can you see how two's complement notation facilitates the addition of signed numbers?

15. Represent the decimal numbers 7 and 9 as eight-bit binary numbers. Subtract 7 from 9; then subtract 9 from 7, producing plus and minus 2, respectively. Use two's complement addition to perform the subtractions as described in the text. Can you see how a computer does not subtract per se, but accomplishes subtraction by the process of complement addition?

Introduction to
ABEND Debugging

Overview

This is the first of two chapters on ABEND debugging. It begins with a presentation of two compiler aids, the Data and Procedure Division maps. Next a working COBOL program is "ABENDed" in three distinct places, and the resulting dumps are utilized to determine the cause of each error. Substantial material is presented in conjunction with the dump analyses. We cover both BL and BLL cells, the SAVE AREA TRACE, occurrence in a COBOL subprogram, and use of the link-edit map. In addition, the STATE and FLOW options are discussed.

It should be emphasized that while a dump may yield the technical cause of an ABEND, it is up to the programmer to relate this information to the source program. Thus a dump will not, in and of itself, pinpoint an error. It is only a tool, and like all tools, it must be used properly; else it is worthless.

Unfortunately, too many COBOL programmers give up almost immediately upon encountering a dump. We attempt, therefore, in this chapter and the next, to provide some insight into dump reading. We assume elementary knowledge of some assembler concepts, specifically: internal data representation (i.e., packed versus display fields), base/displacement addressing, and instruction formats.

There is one final point before we begin: the best way to debug a program is to avoid bugs altogether. While bugs are invariably present in the initial and even revised versions of most programs, many bugs can be eliminated by sound programming design and prudent error checks. Indeed, each of the three ABENDs considered in this chapter *should* have been prevented by defensive programming. In other words, any debugging procedure suffers from the fact that it is applied *after* a bug has occurred. It is, however, inherently easier to insert defensive checks at the source level before problems arise. In spite of this rather lofty advice, dumps can, do, and probably will always happen—hence, the reason for this chapter and the next.

THE PROBLEM AT HAND

A COBOL program and subprogram have been written to calculate and print student transcripts. Specifications are as follows:

Input

Read a file of student records containing name, major code, number of courses taken in the last semester, and, for each course, number, credits, and grade.

Processing

Calculate a grade-point average for each student. A four-point system is used, in which A, B, C, D, and F are worth 4, 3, 2, 1, and 0, respectively. The quality points for each course are equal to the numerical value of the grade times the number of credits. Thus, an A in a three-credit course is worth 12 quality points; a D in a two-credit course, 2 points; and so on. The grade-point average is equal to the total number of quality points divided by the total number of credits.

Output

Print a separate transcript for each student as shown. Also, calculate and print the total number of transcripts processed.

```
┌─────────────────────────────────────────────────┐
│                  TRANSCRIPT                       │
│                                                   │
│  NAME:BENJAMIN, L              MAJOR:BIOLOGY      │
│                                                   │
│             COURSE#   CREDITS   GRADE             │
│               111        3        A               │
│               222        3        B               │
│               333        3        C               │
│               444        3        B               │
│               555        3        B               │
│                 AVERAGE:  3.00                    │
└─────────────────────────────────────────────────┘
```

The COBOL program to accomplish these specifications is shown in Figure 7.1a and b. Figure 7.1a consists of a main program which reads the student file, determines the student's major from the incoming code, and prints the transcript. Figure 7.1b consists of a COBOL subroutine to calculate the grade-point average. Note well the use of the same copy entry in both programs to obtain the incoming record layouts. This is good technique to ensure that both the main and subprograms are working on identical record descriptions. The logic in Figure 7.1a and b is straightforward and will not be discussed further.

COMPILER AIDS

A compiler translates a source program into an object program, and it is the latter which is eventually executed. The COBOL compiler can supply both Data and Procedure Division maps as debugging aids. Figure 7.2 is a truncated Data Division map for the COBOL program of Figure 7.1a. It lists the data names in a program and ties them to internal addresses by specifying a base locator (later tied to a base register) and a displacement. Reading from left to right in Figure 7.2, the seven columns denote:

1. The internal data name.
2. The COBOL level number.
3. The COBOL data name.
4. The base locator.
5. The displacement.
6. The internal name repeated.
7. The length of the data name, as in an assembler DS or DC statement.

All data names within the same file are assigned the same base locator. Thus, in Figure 7.2, BL = 1 for the entry(entries) in CARD-FILE and BL = 2 for the entry(entries) in PRINT-FILE. All entries in Working-Storage are assigned BL = 3.

```
00001          IDENTIFICATION DIVISION.
00002          PROGRAM-ID.    'MAINPROG'.
00003          AUTHOR.        GRAUER.
00004
00005
00006          ENVIRONMENT DIVISION.
00007
00008          CONFIGURATION SECTION.
00009          SOURCE-COMPUTER.   IBM-370.
00010          OBJECT-COMPUTER.   IBM-370.
00011          SPECIAL-NAMES.
00012              C01 IS TOP-OF-PAGE.
00013
00014          INPUT-OUTPUT SECTION.
00015          FILE-CONTROL.
00016              SELECT CARD-FILE ASSIGN TO UT-S-CARDS.
00017              SELECT PRINT-FILE ASSIGN TO UT-S-SYSOUT.
00018
00019
00020          DATA DIVISION.
00021          FILE SECTION.
00022          FD  CARD-FILE
00023              RECORDING MODE IS F
00024              LABEL RECORDS ARE OMITTED
00025              RECORD CONTAINS 80 CHARACTERS
00026              DATA RECORD IS STUDENT-RECORD.
00027          01  STUDENT-RECORD          PIC X(80).
00028          FD  PRINT-FILE
00029              RECORDING MODE IS F
00030              LABEL RECORDS ARE OMITTED
00031              RECORD CONTAINS 133 CHARACTERS
00032              DATA RECORD IS PRINT-LINE.
00033          01  PRINT-LINE              PIC X(133).
00034          WORKING-STORAGE SECTION.
00035          77  FILLER                  PIC X(14)
00036                       VALUE 'WS BEGINS HERE'.
00037          77  WS-SUB                  PIC S9(4)     COMP.
00038          77  WS-END-OF-FILE          PIC X(3)   VALUE 'NO '.
00039          77  WS-FOUND-MAJOR-SWITCH   PIC X(3)   VALUE 'NO '.
00040          77  WS-GRADE-AVERAGE        PIC S9V99.
00041          77  WS-TOTAL-STUDENTS       PIC 999       COMP-3.
00042          01  WS-STUDENT-RECORD    COPY STUDREC.
00043   C      01  WS-STUDENT-RECORD.
00044   C          05  ST-NAME                PIC A(15).
00045   C          05  ST-MAJOR-CODE          PIC 9(4).
00046   C          05  ST-NUMBER-OF-COURSES   PIC 99.
00047   C          05  ST-COURSE-TABLE OCCURS 8 TIMES.
00048   C              10  ST-COURSE-NUMBER   PIC X(3).
00049   C              10  ST-COURSE-GRADE    PIC A.
00050   C              10  ST-COURSE-CREDITS  PIC 9.
00051          01  HEADING-LINE-ONE.
00052              05  FILLER             PIC X(20)  VALUE SPACES.
00053              05  FILLER             PIC X(10)  VALUE 'TRANSCRIPT'.
00054              05  FILLER             PIC X(103) VALUE SPACES.
00055          01  HEADING-LINE-TWO.
00056              05  FILLER             PIC X(6)   VALUE ' NAME:'.
00057              05  HDG-NAME           PIC A(15).
00058              05  FILLER             PIC X(5)   VALUE SPACES.
00059              05  FILLER             PIC X(6)   VALUE 'MAJOR:'.
00060              05  HDG-MAJOR          PIC X(10).
```

Literal to facilitate ABEND debugging

Data name was never initialized

Copied entry

FIGURE 7.1a Main Program for Transcript Problem

162

```
00061          05   FILLER                   PIC X(91)  VALUE SPACES.
00062     01   HEADING-LINE-THREE.
00063          05   FILLER                   PIC X(10)  VALUE SPACES.
00064          05   FILLER                   PIC X(9)   VALUE 'COURSE#  '.
00065          05   FILLER                   PIC X(9)   VALUE 'CREDITS  '.
00066          05   FILLER                   PIC X(5)   VALUE 'GRADE'.
00067          05   FILLER                   PIC X(100) VALUE SPACES.
00068     01   DETAIL-LINE.
00069          05   FILLER                   PIC X(13)  VALUE SPACES.
00070          05   DET-COURSE               PIC X(3).
00071          05   FILLER                   PIC X(9)   VALUE SPACES.
00072          05   DET-CREDITS              PIC 9.
00073          05   FILLER                   PIC X(5)   VALUE SPACES.
00074          05   DET-GRADE                PIC A.
00075          05   FILLER                   PIC X(101) VALUE SPACES.
00076     01   TOTAL-LINE.
00077          05   FILLER                   PIC X(16)  VALUE SPACES.
00078          05   FILLER                   PIC X(9)   VALUE 'AVERAGE: '.
00079          05   TOT-GPA                  PIC 9.99.
00080          05   FILLER                   PIC X(104) VALUE SPACES.
00081     01   MAJOR-VALUE.
00082          05   FILLER                   PIC X(14)  VALUE '1234ACCOUNTING'.
00083          05   FILLER                   PIC X(14)  VALUE '1400BIOLOGY   '.
00084          05   FILLER                   PIC X(14)  VALUE '1976CHEMISTRY '.
00085          05   FILLER                   PIC X(14)  VALUE '2100CIVIL ENG '.
00086          05   FILLER                   PIC X(14)  VALUE '2458E. D. P.  '.
00087          05   FILLER                   PIC X(14)  VALUE '3245ECONOMICS '.
00088          05   FILLER                   PIC X(14)  VALUE '3960FINANCE   '.
00089          05   FILLER                   PIC X(14)  VALUE '4321MANAGEMENT'.
00090          05   FILLER                   PIC X(14)  VALUE '4999MARKETING '.
00091          05   FILLER                   PIC X(14)  VALUE '5400STATISTICS'.
00092     01   MAJOR-TABLE REDEFINES MAJOR-VALUE.             Table of major codes
00093          05   MAJORS      OCCURS 10 TIMES.
00094               10   MAJOR-CODE          PIC 9(4).
00095               10   MAJOR-NAME          PIC X(10).
00096     01   FILLER                        PIC X(12)
00097                    VALUE 'WS ENDS HERE'.
00098     PROCEDURE DIVISION.
00099     001-MAINLINE.
00100         OPEN INPUT CARD-FILE,
00101              OUTPUT PRINT-FILE.
00102         READ CARD-FILE INTO WS-STUDENT-RECORD,
00103              AT END MOVE 'YES' TO WS-END-OF-FILE.
00104         PERFORM 020-PROCESS-CARDS THRU 025-PROCESS-CARDS-EXIT
00105              UNTIL WS-END-OF-FILE = 'YES'.
00106         DISPLAY 'TOTAL PROCESSED = ' WS-TOTAL-STUDENTS.
00107         CLOSE CARD-FILE, PRINT-FILE.
00108         STOP RUN.
00109
00110     020-PROCESS-CARDS.
00111         ADD 1 TO WS-TOTAL-STUDENTS.
00112         CALL 'SUBRTN'
00113              USING WS-STUDENT-RECORD            Call to subprogram
00114                    WS-GRADE-AVERAGE.
```

FIGURE 7.1a (Continued)

163

```
00116          *DETERMINE MAJOR
00117               MOVE 1 TO WS-SUB.
00118               MOVE 'NO ' TO WS-FOUND-MAJOR-SWITCH.
00119               PERFORM 030-FIND-MAJOR THRU 030-FIND-MAJOR-EXIT
00120                   UNTIL WS-FOUND-MAJOR-SWITCH = 'YES'.

00122          *WRITE HEADING LINES
00123               WRITE PRINT-LINE FROM HEADING-LINE-ONE
00124                   AFTER ADVANCING TOP-OF-PAGE LINES.
00125               MOVE ST-NAME TO HDG-NAME.
00126               WRITE PRINT-LINE FROM HEADING-LINE-TWO
00127                   AFTER ADVANCING 2 LINES.
00128               WRITE PRINT-LINE FROM HEADING-LINE-THREE
00129                   AFTER ADVANCING 2 LINES.

00131          *WRITE DETAIL LINES - 1 PER COURSE
00132               PERFORM 040-WRITE-DETAIL-LINE THRU 040-WRITE-DETAIL-EXIT
00133                   VARYING WS-SUB FROM 1 BY 1
00134                   UNTIL WS-SUB > ST-NUMBER-OF-COURSES.

00136          *WRITE GRADE POINT AVERAGE
00137               MOVE WS-GRADE-AVERAGE TO TOT-GPA.
00138               WRITE PRINT-LINE FROM TOTAL-LINE
00139                   AFTER ADVANCING 2 LINES.
00140               READ CARD-FILE INTO WS-STUDENT-RECORD,
00141                   AT END MOVE 'YES' TO WS-END-OF-FILE.
00142
00143          025-PROCESS-CARDS-EXIT.
00144               EXIT.
00145
00146          030-FIND-MAJOR.
00147               IF ST-MAJOR-CODE = MAJOR-CODE (WS-SUB)
00148                   MOVE 'YES' TO WS-FOUND-MAJOR-SWITCH
00149                   MOVE MAJOR-NAME (WS-SUB) TO HDG-MAJOR
00150
00151               ELSE
00152                   ADD 1 TO WS-SUB.
00153
00154          030-FIND-MAJOR-EXIT.
00155               EXIT.
00156
00157          040-WRITE-DETAIL-LINE.
00158               MOVE ST-COURSE-NUMBER (WS-SUB) TO DET-COURSE.
00159               MOVE ST-COURSE-CREDITS (WS-SUB) TO DET-CREDITS.
00160               MOVE ST-COURSE-GRADE (WS-SUB) TO DET-GRADE.
00161               WRITE PRINT-LINE FROM DETAIL-LINE
00162                   AFTER ADVANCING 1 LINES.
00163
00164          040-WRITE-DETAIL-EXIT.
00165               EXIT.
```

FIGURE 7.1a (Continued)

```
00001              IDENTIFICATION DIVISION.
00002              PROGRAM-ID.  'SUBRTN'.
00003              AUTHOR.      GRAUER.
00004
00005
00006              ENVIRONMENT DIVISION.
00007
00008              CONFIGURATION SECTION.
00009              SOURCE-COMPUTER.  IBM-370.
00010              OBJECT-COMPUTER.  IBM-370.
00011
00012
00013              DATA DIVISION.
00014              WORKING-STORAGE SECTION.
00015              77  WS-TOTAL-CREDITS              PIC 999.
00016              77  WS-QUALITY-POINTS             PIC 999.
00017              77  WS-MULTIPLIER                 PIC 9.
00018              77  WS-SUB                        PIC S9(4)    COMP.

00020              *****************************************************
00021              LINKAGE SECTION.
00022              77  LS-CALCULATED-AVERAGE             PIC S9V99.
00023              01  DATA-PASSED-FROM-MAIN    COPY STUDREC.
```

```
00024 C   01  DATA-PASSED-FROM-MAIN.
00025 C       05   ST-NAME                PIC A(15).          ── Copied entry
00026 C       05   ST-MAJOR-CODE          PIC 9(4).
00027 C       05   ST-NUMBER-OF-COURSES   PIC 99.
00028 C       05   ST-COURSE-TABLE OCCURS 8 TIMES.
00029 C           10   ST-COURSE-NUMBER   PIC X(3).
00030 C           10   ST-COURSE-GRADE    PIC A.
00031 C           10   ST-COURSE-CREDITS  PIC 9.
```

```
00032              *****************************************************
00034              PROCEDURE DIVISION                  ── Arguments passed
00035                  USING DATA-PASSED-FROM-MAIN        from main program
00036                        LS-CALCULATED-AVERAGE.
00037              *****************************************************
00038              * ROUTINE TO COMPUTE GRADE POINT AVERAGE
00039              * WEIGHTS:   A=4, B=3, C=2, D=1, F=0
00040              * NO PLUS OR MINUS GRADES
00041              * QUALITY POINTS FOR A GIVEN COURSE = WEIGHT X CREDITS
00042              * GRADE POINT AVERAGE = TOTAL QUALITY POINTS / TOTAL CREDITS
00043              *****************************************************
00044              001-MAINLINE.
00045                  MOVE ZERO TO WS-QUALITY-POINTS.
00046                  MOVE ZERO TO WS-TOTAL-CREDITS.
00047                  PERFORM 010-COMPUTE-QUALITY-POINTS
00048                      VARYING WS-SUB FROM 1 BY 1
00049                      UNTIL WS-SUB > ST-NUMBER-OF-COURSES.
00050                  COMPUTE LS-CALCULATED-AVERAGE ROUNDED
00051                      = WS-QUALITY-POINTS / WS-TOTAL-CREDITS.
00052              005-RETURN-TO-MAIN.
00053                  EXIT PROGRAM.
00054
00055              010-COMPUTE-QUALITY-POINTS.
00056                  MOVE ZERO TO WS-MULTIPLIER.
00057              * NESTED IF COULD BE USED, BUT ISN'T IN ORDER TO OBTAIN
00058              * GREATER CLARITY.
00059                  IF ST-COURSE-GRADE (WS-SUB) = 'A', MOVE 4 TO WS-MULTIPLIER.
00060                  IF ST-COURSE-GRADE (WS-SUB) = 'B', MOVE 3 TO WS-MULTIPLIER.
00061                  IF ST-COURSE-GRADE (WS-SUB) = 'C', MOVE 2 TO WS-MULTIPLIER.
00062                  IF ST-COURSE-GRADE (WS-SUB) = 'D', MOVE 1 TO WS-MULTIPLIER.
00063                  COMPUTE WS-QUALITY-POINTS =  WS-QUALITY-POINTS
00064                      + ST-COURSE-CREDITS (WS-SUB) * WS-MULTIPLIER.
00065                  ADD ST-COURSE-CREDITS (WS-SUB) TO WS-TOTAL-CREDITS.
```

FIGURE 7.1b Subprogram for Transcript Problem

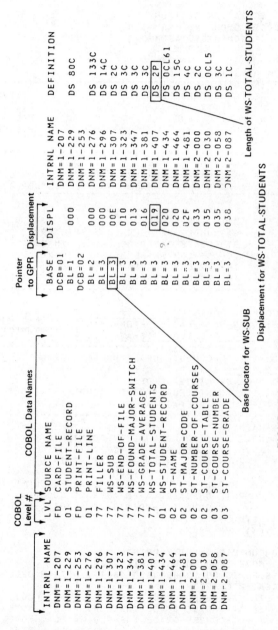

FIGURE 7.2 Truncated Data Division Map for Figure 7.1a

REGISTER ASSIGNMENT

REG 6	BL = 3	Base locator three is
REG 7	BL = 1	tied to register six
REG 8	BL = 2	

FIGURE 7.3 Table of Register Assignments

The base locators are tied to specific base registers by a table of register assignments shown in Figure 7.3. BL = 1 points to register 7, BL = 2 to register 8, and BL = 3 to register 6.

Figure 7.4 is a truncated Procedure Division map corresponding to Figure 7.1a. It contains information about the machine language instructions generated by the compiler. Reading from left to right in Figure 7.4, the five columns denote:

1. The computer-generated COBOL statement number.
2. The COBOL verb referenced in the statement number.
3. The relative location, in hex, of the machine instruction.
4. The actual machine instruction.
5. The symbolic instruction format.

Recall that the "instruction-explosion" effect causes a single COBOL instruction to generate one or more machine language statements (e.g., COBOL statement 147 (IF) generated 10 machine language statements; statement 148 (MOVE), 2 statements, etc.).

THE MEMORY DUMP

A memory dump is a picture of the computer's memory at an instant of time. Usually, dumps are taken only if an ABEND (ABnormal END of job) occurs. Realize that the contents of main storage are strictly binary, but that they are displayed in a dump in hexadecimal for conciseness. Dumps appear foreboding to the uninitiated, but, as with everything else, a little practice goes a long way.

Consider Figure 7.5, which contains a portion of a dump. The leftmost column indicates the internal location number. Subsequent digits are the contents of that location and others. Since the smallest addressable location is the byte (8 bits or two hex digits), every two hex digits indicate the contents of a particular byte.

Go down the first column in Figure 7.5 until you read "26CB20." The two hex digits immediately following are F5, indicating that the contents of byte 26CB20 are F5. The next two hex digits, F4, are the contents of the next sequential location, 26CB21. In similar fashion, F3 is the con-

COBOL Card #	COBOL Verb	Relative Location	Machine Instruction	Mnemonic	Symbolic Assembler Format	Comment	Comment
111	ADD	000B32	FA 10 6 019 C 0A8	AP	019(2,6),0A8(1,12)		LIT+0
112	CALL	000B38	96 0F 6 01A	OI	01A(6),X'0F'	DNM=1-407	
		000B3C	41 10 6 020	LA	1,020(0,6)	DNM=1-407+1	
		000B40	50 10 D 250	ST	1,250(0,13)	DNM=1-434	
		000B44	41 10 6 016	LA	1,016(0,6)	DNM=1	
		000B48	50 10 D 254	ST	1,254(0,13)	DNM=1-381	
		000B4C	96 80 D 254	OI	254(13),X'80'	PRM=2	
		000B50	41 10 D 250	LA	1,250(0,13)	PRM=2	
		000B54	58 F0 C 014	L	15,014(0,12)	PRM=1	
		000B58	05 EF	BALR	14,15	V(ILBODBG4)	
		000B5A	96 40 D 049	OI	049(13),X'40'		
		000B5E	58 F0 C 024	L	15,024(0,12)		
		000B62	05 EF	BALR	14,15	V(SUBRTN)	
		000B64	94 BF D 049	NI	049(13),X'BF'		
		000B68	40 F0 D 05C	STH	15,05C(0,13)		
		000B6C	58 F0 D 1B8	L	15,1B8(0,13)		
		000B70	50 D0 F 080	ST	13,080(0,15)		
117	MOVE	000B74	D2 01 6 00E C 0A9	MVC	00E(2,6),0A9(12)	DNM=1-307	LIT+1
118	MOVE	000B7A	D2 02 6 013 C 0C6	MVC	013(3,6),0C6(12)	DNM=1-347	LIT+30
⋮							
144	EXIT	000D0A	58 10 D 238	L	1,238(0,13)	VN=01	
		000D0E	07 F1	BCR	15,1		
146	*030-FIND-MAJOR	000D10	PN=03	EQU	*		
147	IF	000D10	58 F0 C 010	L	15,010(0,12)	V(ILBOFLW1)	
		000D14	05 1F	BALR	1,15		
		000D16	00000092	DC	X'00000092'		
		000D1A	41 40 6 308	LA	4,308(0,6)	DNM=3-366	
		000D1E	48 30 6 00E	LH	3,00E(0,6)	DNM=1-307	
		000D22	5C 20 C 0B4	M	2,0B4(0,12)	LIT+12	
		000D26	1A 43	AR	4,3		
		000D28	5B 40 C 0B4	S	4,0B4(0,12)	LIT+12	
		000D2C	F2 73 D 200 6 02F	PACK	200(8,13),02F(4,6)	TS=01	DNM=1-481
		000D32	F2 73 D 208 4 000	PACK	208(8,13),000(4,4)	TS=09	
		000D38	F9 22 D 205 D 20D	CP	205(3,13),20D(3,13)	TS=06	TS=014
		000D3E	58 F0 C 084	L	15,084(0,12)	GN=016	
		000D42	07 7F	BCR	7,15		
148	MOVE	000D44	50 40 D 220	ST	4,220(0,13)	SBS=1	
		000D48	D2 02 6 013 C 0C3	MVC	013(3,6),0C3(12)	DNM=1-347	LIT+27
149	MOVE	000D4E	41 40 6 30C	LA	4,30C(0,6)	DNM=3-389	

Location B38 → 000B38

Instruction at D3E → 58 F0 C 084

Symbolic Assembler Formats

FIGURE 7.4 Truncated Procedure Division Map for Figure 7.1a

168

```
                    0003D85C  403F2FD2

26C8A0  4126C8A0 7F00065D 02000000 7F26BF20   0026C8D0 0C000000 4026C8C8 0026C8D0   *....H.".)....H...... .HH..H.*
26C8C0  00000000 00010000 0126B1A0 2000065D   00000000 00000000 00000000 00000033   *...........".....)....CS....*
26C8E0  00818300 00000001 00004000 00000001   04000001 54000000 00A40020 0002E27C   *........................Sä.*
26C900  923FC8E8 003FC688 06000001 00C00660   28012828 4126C8A0 013FCCF8 003FCCF8   *..HY..F.......H...8..8.*
26C920  0000007D 00000001 4126C958 7F000000   00000000 7F26C92C 0026C958 7F000000   *...'........I."....I....*
26C940  4026C950 0024D8B0 00000000 00010000   0126C9F0 20000085 0026C928 7F000000   *.I&...Q......I0....I.".*
26C960  00000000 0026C95C 00000000 00000000   0026C980 0024D8B0 00000000 00010000   *........I*......I.C....*
26C980  0126CA78 20000085 0126C9B8 7F000000   00000000 7F26C98C 0026C9B8 7F000000   *....I."....I...."I.".*
26C9A0  4026C9B0 0024D7FC 00000000 00010000   0226C808 00000050 0026C988 7F000000   *.I&...P......&...I.".*
26C9C0  00000000 7F26C98C 0026C9E8 0C000000   4026C9E0 0024D7FC 00000000 00010000   *...."...IY....I.P....*
26C9E0  0226C858 00000050 00000000 00020088   F1E2E3E4 C4C5D5E3 40D5C1D4 C5404040   *.&......&..1STUDENT NAME  *
26CA00  40404040 40404082 D6C340E2 C5C340D5   E4D44040 C3D9C5C4 C9E3E240 40E3E4C9   *      SOC SEC NUM CREDITS TUI*
26CA20  E3C9D6D5 4040E4D5 C9D6D540 C6C5C540   40C1C3E3 40C6C5C5 4040E2C3 C8D6D3C1   *TION UNION FEE  ACT FEE  SCHOLA*
26CA40  D9E2C8C9 D74040E3 D6E3C1D3 40C2C9D3   D3404040 40404040 40404040 40404040   *RSHIP TOTAL BILL         *
26CA60  40404040 40404040 40404040 40404040   40404040 40000000 40606060 60606060   *         ... -------*
26CA80  60606060 60606060 60606060 60606060   60606060 60606060 60606060 60606060   *--------------------*

   LINE 26CAA0 SAME AS ABOVE

26CAC0  60606060 60606060 60606060 60606060   60606060 60606060 60404040 40E8E2C9   *--------------------      YSI*
26CAE0  40404040 40404040 40404040 40404040   40404040 40404040 40404040 F9F8F7F6   *                       9876*
26CB00  00000000 00020050 C8C5D5D9 E84001C1   D4C5E240 40404040 40404040 40404040   *.......&HENRY JAMES     *
26CB40  40404040 40404040 40404040 40404040   40404040 40404040 D1D6C8D5 40E2D4C9   *              JOHN SMI*
26CB60  E3C84040 40404040 40404040 F1F2F3F4   40404040 40404040 F9F1F5E8 F0F0C3D6   *TH          1234567891 5YO0CO*
26CB80  40404040 40404040 40404040 40404040   40404040 40404040 40404040 40404040   *                    *
```

─ Hex contents of location 26CB24

─ Hex contents of location 26CB20

─ EBCDIC equivalent for location 26CB24

─ EBCDIC equivalent for location 26CB20

FIGURE 7.5 Illustrative Memory Dump

tents of 26CB22, F2 is the contents of 26CB23, and so on. There are a total of 64 hex digits on the line beginning with 26CB20. Accordingly, the contents of 32 bytes beginning at 26CB20 and continuing to 26CB3F are shown on the same line.

Immediately following the 64 hex digits on a given line is the corresponding alphabetic interpretation of those digits. According to the EBCDIC configurations of Table 6.3, F5 is the representation for 5, F4 for 4, and so forth. Many of the interpretation columns are blank because the contents of the corresponding locations are hex 40s, which is the internal representation of a blank.

Now that we are vaguely familiar with the basic debugging tools of the memory dump and Procedure and Data Division maps, we are ready to try an actual problem.

EXAMPLE 7.1.   DUMP READING

When execution of Figure 7.1a and b was attempted, the computer vehemently objected. We received a message 'COMPLETION CODE = 0C7' followed by pages of semi-intelligible data, culminating in a dump. An 0C7 is a data exception, which occurs when one attempts to use invalid decimal (i.e., packed) data. To debug the program, one has to determine where within the COBOL program the data exception occurred. Some of the more relevant information associated with the dump has been extracted and grouped into Figure 7.6. Specifically, Figure 7.6 contains:

1. Job Identification (i.e., name, time, and date).
2. The completion code.
3. The contents of the *Program Status Word* (PSW) at the time of the ABEND.
4. The *Entry Point Address* (EPA) of the COBOL program.
5. The contents of the 16 registers at the time of the ABEND.

We now begin the analysis of a dump. The last three bytes (6 hex digits) of the PSW provide the location of the interrupt. Subtraction of the *Entry Point Address* (EPA) of the COBOL program from the three bytes in the PSW yields the relative address (i.e., the location within the COBOL program of the error). Thus, using numbers obtained from Figure 7.6:

Address from PSW	1C1830
− Entry point of COBOL Program	− 1C0CF8
Relative Address	B38

```
JOB  ARTJHM22            STEP GO                    TIME 141604   DATE 77340

COMPLETION CODE         SYSTEM = 0C7 ── Completion code

PSW AT ENTRY TO ABEND   071D1000 00 1C1830         ILC 6   INTC 0007
                                     Last three bytes of PSW


CDE                                                                           Entry point address

C4F140  ATR1 0B  NCDE 000000  ROC-RB 00C4ED10  NM GO       USE 01  EPA 1C0CF8  ATR2 20  XL/MJ C4F018
FFE500  ATR1 B9  NCDE FFE4D8  ROC-RB 00000000  NM IGG019BA  USE 08  EPA F67480  ATR2 20  XL/MJ FFE518
FFE4D8  ATR1 B8  NCDE FFA348  ROC-RB 00000000  NM IGG019BB  USE 03  EPA F67690  ATR2 20  XL/MJ FFE4F0
FF9A18  ATR1 B1  NCDE FF97F0  ROC-RB 00000000  NM IGG019CF  USE 0C  EPA D4E618  ATR2 20  XL/MJ FF9A30
FF97F0  ATR1 B0  NCDE FFE528  ROC-RB 00000000  NM IGG019CL  USE 0D  EPA F37938  ATR2 20  XL/MJ FF9808
FFE460  ATR1 B8  NCDE FFE118  ROC-RB 00000000  NM IGG019AI  USE 14  EPA F67A90  ATR2 20  XL/MJ FFE478


REGS AT ENTRY TO ABEND

FLTR 0-6   000000000000000000   0001E5E2F2F1F7F1   4040404040404040   4040404040404040

REGS 0-7   001C172E   501C1826   501C1740   5CC4EB50   001C11F8   001C171E   001C0D98   001FEA58
REGS 8-15  001C12B0   001C1B76   001C0CF8   001C0CF8   001C15B8   001C1338   001C182A   001C3D16
                                                      Contents of            Contents of
                                                      register 12            register 6
```

FIGURE 7.6 Information Associated with Memory Dump of Example 1

Since all addresses in a dump are specified in hexadecimal, the subtraction is in hex as well. Now take the relative address (B38) to the Procedure Division map of Figure 7.4 and find that B38 occurs within COBOL statement 111, indicating that program execution terminated within this COBOL statement. *The instruction at B38 is the next instruction that would have been executed had the ABEND not occurred; the instruction that caused the problem is the one immediately before, at B32.* However, both machine instructions are contained within the COBOL ADD.

In order to determine the exact cause of the error, we examine the machine language instruction at B32 which failed to execute. It has an op code of FA, and from previous knowledge, or the material in Chapter 6, we dissect the instruction as follows:

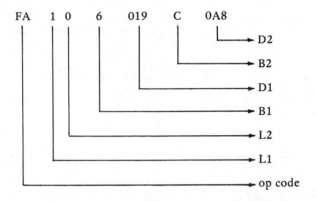

From Appendix A we learn that FA is the op code for Add Packed. The instruction at B32 will add the contents of the second operand to the contents of the first operand and store the results in the first operand. The addresses of both operands are calculated in accordance with the base/displacement addressing scheme discussed in Chapter 6.

The first operand has a displacement of 019 (in hex) from the address in register 6; the second operand has a displacement of 0A8 (also in hex) from the address in register 12. Figure 7.6 shows the addresses (i.e., the three low-order bytes) in registers 6 and 12, respectively, to be 1C0D98 and 1C15B8. Thus, the actual addresses of both operands are calculated as follows:

Contents of register 6	=	1C0D98
+ 1st displacement	= +	019
Location of 1st operand	=	1C0DB1
Contents of register C	=	1C15B8
+ 2nd displacement	= +	0A8
Location of 2nd operand	=	1C1660

The first operand begins at location 1C0DB1. Its length code in the Add Packed instruction is one, so the first operand extends one byte past 1C0DB1 (i.e., the first operand is in locations 1C0DB1 and 1C0DB2). The actual number of bytes in the operand is always one more than the corresponding length code contained in the instruction. In similar fashion, the second operand is one byte long beginning at 1C1660.

Now we can use the dump produced by the ABEND, and shown in Figure 7.7, to determine the cause of the data exception. The value of the second operand, located in location 1C1660, is 1C, a packed one, and a valid decimal number. The value of the first operand, located in location 1C0DB1 and 1C0DB2, is 0000, an invalid packed number (the sign is missing) and hence the data exception. We have determined the cause of the data exception: invalid data in the first operand. Unfortunately, it seems to have little relation to the COBOL program. Let us therefore consider COBOL statement 111, which generated the machine language instruction in the first place, to try for a more satisfying explanation. COBOL statement 111 is

```
ADD 1 TO WS-TOTAL-STUDENTS.
```

In effect, statement 111 is counting the number of records processed. WS-TOTAL-STUDENTS is defined as a 77-level entry in COBOL line 41, and therein lies the problem. Look carefully at statement 41

```
77  WS-TOTAL-STUDENTS  PIC 999  COMP-3.
```

WS-TOTAL-STUDENTS was never initialized. Hence, the computer uses whatever happens to be in WS-TOTAL-STUDENTS at the time the program is executed. Insertion of a VALUE ZEROS clause would initialize our counter and eliminate the data exception. Let us further analyze the machine language instruction that "blew up." It referenced WS-TOTAL-STUDENTS as being 19 displaced from register 6. How and why?

The answer lies in the Data Division map of Figure 7.2. WS-TOTAL-STUDENTS is tied to BL = 3, which is subsequently linked to register 6 in Figure 7.3. Further, Figure 7.2 shows a displacement of 019 and a length of 2 for WS-TOTAL-STUDENTS. Indeed, these are the numbers appearing in the first operand of the Add Packed instruction. (Remember that a three-digit decimal number requires only two bytes if it is stored as a packed field. In addition, the length in the Add Packed instruction was 1, which is as it should be, since the length code in a machine language instruction is always *one less* than the actual length of a field.)

The STATE Option

One might logically, or perhaps hopefully, ask: Is this really necessary to determine the cause of an ABEND? We answer with an equivocal "maybe"

```
LOAD MODULE    GO

1C0CE0  4580F010 D4C1C9D5 D7D9D6C7 E5E2D9F1   0700989F F02407FF 90ECD00C 185D05F0   *..0.MAINPROGVSR1.........0*
1C0D00  000107FE 001C1B76 001C0CF8 001C0CF8   001C15B8 96021034 07FE41F0 001C1B36   *........8..8............0*
1C0D20  40614040 40406140 E2E3D6D7 4040F7F7   F3F4F04B F1F4F1F3 40C3D7E4 00000000   *.   .STOP  77340.1413 CPU*
1C0D40  40404040 D4C9D540 F0F14BF4 F9E2C5C3   40E2E3D6 D940E5C9 D9E340F1 00000000   *    MIN 01.49SEC STOR VIRT 1..*
1C0D60  F1F44BF0 F94BF0F8 C4C5C340 F666B840   F1F9F7F7 00000000 E6E240C2 C5C7C9D5   *14.09.08DEC 6. 1977....WS BEGIN*
1C0DA0  E24DC8C5 D9C59500 D5D640D5 D6400000   000C0000 00000000 C2C5D5D1 C1D4C9D5   *S HERE.NO NO ....BENJAMIN*
1C0DC0  6B40D340 404040F1 F4F0F0F0 F5F1F1F1   C1F3F2F2 F2C2F3F3 F3F3C3F3 F4F4F4C2   *.L 140051I1A3222B3333C3444B*
1C0DE0  F3F5F5F5 C2F34040 40404040 40404040   40404040 40000000 40000000 40404040   *3555B3          *
1C0E00  40404040 40404040 40404040 40404040   E2C3D9C9 D7E34040 40404040 40404040   *        TRANSCRIPT  *
1C0E20  40404040 40404040 40404040 40404040   40404040 40404040 40404040 40404040   *         *

LINES 1C0E40-1C0E60 SAME AS ABOVE

1C0E80  40D5C1D4 C57A8902 04C7C1E8 E204F3F3   F2F2F000 00404040 4040D4C1 D1D6D97A   * NAME....GAYS.3322....  MAJOR.*
1C0EA0  00000000 00000000 00404040 40404040   40404040 40404040 40404040 40404040   *..........   *
1C0EC0  40404040 40404040 40404040 40404040   40404040 40404040 40404040 40404040   *    *

LINE 1C0EE0 SAME AS ABOVE

1C0F00  40404040 40000000 40404040 40404040   4040C3D6 E4D9E2C5 7B404040 D9C5C4C9   *            COURSE.    CREDI*
1C0F20  E3E24040 C7D9C1C4 C5404040 40404040   40404040 40404040 40404040 40404040   *TS   GRADE    *
1C0F40  40404040 40404040 40404040 40404040   40404040 40404040 40404040 40404040   *    *

LINE 1C0F60 SAME AS ABOVE

1C0F80  40404040 40404040 40404040 40006DD4   40404040 40404040 40404040 40504FC9   *             .M       ..I*
1C0FA0  40404040 40404040 40C54040 40C54040   40404040 40404040 40404040 40404040   *     E       E   *
1C0FC0  40404040 40404040 40404040 40404040   40404040 40404040 40404040 40404040   *    *
```

Contents of locations
1C0DB1 - 1C0DB2 = '0000',
an invalid packed number

FIGURE 7.7 Partial Memory Dump for Example 1

Contents of location
1C1660 = '1C', a
packed 1

```
1C15A0  001C1BEC 001C1CB4 001C1CBE 00000000   00000000 60000000 001C4672 001C2EFA  *................*
1C15C0  001C3D12 001C4672 001C3D16 001C2F0A   001C3C9A 001C1CF2 001C4676 001C26E8  *..............Y.*
1C15E0  001C41E2 001C1820 001C19F8 001C1A08   001C1A78 001C1A88 001C1B20 001C1B30  *...S.....8......*
1C1600  001C1718 001C171E 001C172E 001C1740   001C1888 001C189A 001C18CC 001C1900  *................*
1C1620  001C192E 001C194E 001C196A 001C1942   001C1978 001C19C6 001C19F2 001C1A6C  *............F.2.*
1C1640  00AC17EA 001C1814 001C181A 001C117C   001C1230 001C1A03 001C1A88 001C1B30  *................*
1C1660  1C000100 0001F021 4B202000 0000000E   00000005 48004805 EF0700E8 C5E2D5D6  *....0.......YESNO*
1C1680  40E3D6C5 C1D340D7 D9D6C3C5 E2E2C5C4   407E4029 58F0C010 051F0000 006358F0  * TOTAL PROCESSED .O......O*

1C16A0  C01405EF 5810C094 D2011032 C0BC5840   1024D202 4011C019 5010D244 9200D244  *....K......K....K..*
1C16C0  5810C098 D2011032 C0BDD203 1060C0BF   58401024 D2024011 C0195010 D248920F  *....K...K.....K..K.*
1C16E0  D2489680 D2484110 D2440A13 58F0C014   05EF5810 C0941821 D2022021 C04958F0  *K...K...K..0....K..0*
1C1700  103005EF 5010D1F4 5870D1F4 D23C6020   70005850 C04C07F5 D2026010 C0C35800  *...J4.J4K...5K...C..*
1C1720  D2385000 D22C5800 C0505000 D2385820   C054D502 6010C0C3 07825810 C02C07F1  *K...K...K...N...C...1*
1C1740  5800D22C 5000D238 58F0C014 05EF58F0   C01C051F C0949110 10300550 47805000  *K.K.0...0......0.....*
1C1760  02020003 0D0001FC 0019FFFF 58F0C014   05EF5810 C0949110 10525020 104C5010  *...........0....K....*
1C1780  5830102C 910F300C 0550047E 50105820   104C4B20 10525020 104C5010 D2449240  *K..........0.....K...*
1C17A0  D2445810 C0985010 D2489240 D2489680   D2484110 D2440A14 5850D1B0 5050D1F4  *K...K...K...K...K...J4*
1C17C0  5820C094 5840C088 91012017 07145810   20149601 20171B44 43401006 4C401006  *K...K....J...J4...*
1C17E0  41004008 41101000 0A0A5820 C0985840   C08C9101 20170714 58102014 96012017  *.....................*
1C1800  1B444340 10054C40 10064100 40084110   10000A0A 58F0C014 05EF58F0 C02007FF  *.....O.......0....0..*
```

FIGURE 7.7 (Continued)

```
PROGRAM          MAINPROG
                                                            Nature of the ABEND

LAST PSW BEFORE ABEND = FF150007D01C1830    SYSTEM COMPLETION CODE = 0C7

LAST CARD NUMBER/VERB NUMBER EXECUTED  --  CARD NUMBER 000111/VERB NUMBER 01.

                                                      FLOW TRACE
MAINPROG 000099 000110                      COBOL statement in which ABEND occurred


                                            END OF COBOL DIAGNOSTIC AIDS
```

FIGURE 7.8 Illustration of the STATE Option

(i.e., there are other debugging aids which can sometimes lead to an answer more quickly). The most useful of these is the STATE option, which is requested at compile time. Specification of this option displays the last COBOL statement executed (i.e., the statement that probably caused the ABEND). Consider Figure 7.8.

As can be seen from Figure 7.8, COBOL statement 111 produced the ABEND. (This is the same conclusion that was reached by subtracting the Entry Point Address from the last 3 bytes in the PSW and relating the answer to the PMAP.) An experienced programmer would know immediately that an 0C7 can only be caused by an invalid packed field, and would conclude that one or both of the operands in the ADD statement was invalid. A quick inspection of the COBOL listing should immediately point to WS-TOTAL-STUDENTS. Thus, in this example at least, the detailed analysis of the dump is probably not necessary. There are, however, many situations where quick answers are not readily apparent, as shown in the next section.

EXAMPLE 7.2. DUMP READING

Figure 7.1a was revised to include a VALUE IS ZEROS clause for WS-TOTAL-STUDENTS in COBOL line 41. Insertion of this clause does not have any effect on either the Data or Procedure Division maps of Figures 7.2 and 7.4. A new run was made and the corrected program produced a transcript before another data exception occurred.

A good place to start is with the output of the STATE option shown in Figure 7.9. As can be seen, the data exception resulted during execution of the IF statement of COBOL line 147. At first glance, the computer seems to have erred (i.e., how can invalid decimal data occur during a comparison?) After some thought, and analysis of the Procedure Division map in Figure 7.4, we realize that the IF statement involves two numeric fields, ST-MAJOR-CODE (PIC 9(4)) and MAJOR-CODE (PIC 9(4)), and that the generated instructions include a compare packed instruction. We conclude that one or both operands are invalid. Experience suggests (1) invalid in-

```
PROGRAM          MAINPROG                        COBOL statement in
                                                 which ABEND occurred

LAST PSW BEFORE ABEND = FF150007E01C1A36    SYSTEM/COMPLETION CODE = 0C7

LAST CARD NUMBER/VERB NUMBER EXECUTED -- |CARD NUMBER 000147|/VERB NUMBER 01.

                                               ———————— FLOW TRACE ————————
MAINPROG |000154 000146 000154 000146 000154 000146 000154 000146 000154 000146|
```

Statement number of last 10 paragraphs
immediately preceding the ABEND   END OF COBOL DIAGNOSTIC AIDS

FIGURE 7.9 Illustration of the FLOW Option

coming data (e.g., a blank field for ST-MAJOR-CODE), (2) an invalid code in the majors table itself, or (3) a valid ST-MAJOR-CODE in the sense that it is a proper decimal number but invalid in that the code is not contained in the major table. Any of these is possible, and the STATE option did little to find the bug.

The FLOW Option

There is, however, another aid to consider before the dump. The FLOW option specifies the last n paragraphs which were executed prior to the ABEND (the value of n is entered at compile time). Figure 7.9 shows that the last 10 paragraphs executed alternated between statement 146, 030-FIND-MAJOR, and 154, 030-FIND-MAJOR-EXIT. We conclude, therefore, that the incoming value of ST-MAJOR-CODE was a valid decimal number. Further, after examining COBOL lines 82–91, we conclude that the code values in the table are all valid. Thus, the cause of the data exception was probably an incoming code, which is not present in the table. Analysis of the dump will confirm our conclusion and also identify the student causing the problem. Salient information is contained in Figures 7.10 and 7.11. We begin with the usual subtraction:

$$
\begin{array}{lll}
\text{Last three bytes of PSW} & = & \text{1C1A36} \\
- \text{ Entry Point Address} & = & - \text{ 1C0CF8} \\
\hline
\text{Relative location} & = & \text{D3E}
\end{array}
$$

The Procedure Division map of Figure 7.4 is used to determine that D3E falls within the IF statement of COBOL line 147. This, in turn, is within the COBOL routine to find an expanded value for MAJOR-NAME, given a ST-MAJOR-CODE. D3E points to the instruction that would have been executed if the data exception had not occurred. The instruction which actually caused the data exception is immediately before. Let us analyze the instruction at D38 in depth:

```
JOB ARTJHM22        STEP GO          TIME 140717     DATE 77340

COMPLETION CODE      SYSTEM = 0C7              ILC 6    INTC 0007

PSW AT ENTRY TO ABEND  071D2000 00│1C1A36│
                                   └─────┘
                                   Last three bytes of PSW

CDE

C9F020    ATR1 0B    NCDE 000000    ROC-RB 00C9EC38    NM GO       USE 01    EPA │1C0CF8│    ATR2 20    XL/MJ C9EE30
FFE500    ATR1 B9    NCDE FFE4D8    ROC-RB 00000000    NM IGG019BA  USE 08    EPA F67480     ATR2 20    XL/MJ FFE518
FFE4D8    ATR1 B8    NCDE FFA848    ROC-RB 00000000    NM IGG019BB  USE 08    EPA F67690     ATR2 20    XL/MJ FFE4F0
FF9A18    ATR1 B1    NCDE FF97F0    ROC-RB 00000000    NM IGG019CF  USE 09    EPA D4E618     ATR2 20    XL/MJ FF9A30
FF97F0    ATR1 B0    NCDE FFE460    ROC-RB 00000000    NM IGG019CL  USE 0A    EPA F37938     ATR2 20    XL/MJ FF9808
FFE460    ATR1 B8    NCDE FFE488    ROC-RB 00000000    NM IGG019AI  USE 10    EPA F67A90     ATR2 20    XL/MJ FFE478
                                                                              └──────┘
                                                                        Entry point address

REGS AT ENTRY TO ABEND

FLTR 0-6    0000000000000000    00D71D0000000000    0000000000000000    0116320001210D00    01163│0000D71B08│
                                                                                            └──────────────┘
                                                                                            Contents of
                                                                                            register 6

REGS 0-7    001C1888    501C1A0E    00000000    000000B6    001C1148    001C19F8    │001C0D98│    001FEA08
REGS 8-15   001C12B0    001C1B76    001C0CF8    001C0CF8    001C15B8    │001C1338│   001C1A12     001C3D16
                                                                        └────────┘
                                                                       Contents of
                                                                       register 13
```

FIGURE 7.10 Information Associated with Memory Dump of Example 2

```
                                              Incoming major code
1C0CE0  4580F010 D4C1C9D5 D7D9D6C7 E5E2D9F1   0700989F F02407FF   90ECD00C 185DD05F0   *....0.MAINPROGVSR1.....0*
1C0D00  000107FE 001C1B76 001C0CF8 001C0CF8   001C15B8 001C1338   96021034 07FE41F0   *.............8...8......0*
1C0D20  40404040 40404040 40F1F9F4 00000025   40F1F9F4 00000025   40F1F9F4 001C1B36   *...........8...8....194..*
1C0D40  D9D6E4E3 C9D5C540 E3D640C3 D6D4D7E4   E3C540C7 D9C1C4C5   40D7D6C9 40405C40   *ROUTINE TO COMPUTE GRADE POI..*
1C0D60  F1F44BF0 F34BF5F6 C4C5C340 40F66B40   F1F9F7F7 40404040   40D7D6C9 C5C7C9D5   *14.03.56DEC 6. 1977 WS BEGIN*
1C0D80  E240C8C5 D9C5000D 05D640D5 D640F3F6   C7002FC7 C8E3E27A   D4C9D3C7 D9D6D46B   *S HERE..NO NO 36G..GHTS.MILGROM.*
1C0DA0  40D44040 40404040 F7F7F7F0 F6F1F2F3   C1F2F4F5 F6C1F3F7   F8F9C1F4 F0F1F2C1   * M   77706123A2456A3789A4012A*
1C0DC0  F3F3F4F5 C2F3F6F7 F8C2F340 40404040   E2C3D9C9 D7E34040   40404040 40404040   *3345B3678B3*
1C0DE0  40404040 40404040 40404040 40404040   40404040 40000027   D7E34040 F0F1F2C1   *                            *
1C0E00  40404040 40404040 40404040 E3D9C1D5   E2C3D9C9 D7E34040   40404040 40404040   *             TRANSCRIPT     *
1C0E20  40404040 40404040 40404040 40404040   40404040 40404040   40404040 40404040   *                            *
LINE 1C0E40  SAME AS ABOVE
1C0E60  40404040 40404040 40404040 40404040   40404040 40404040   7B404040 D9C5C4C9   *                         CRE*
1C0E80  40D5C1D4 C57AC2C5 D5D1C1D4 C9D56B40   40404040 40D4C1   D1D6D97A   40404040   * NAME.BENJAMIN. L    MAJOR.*
1C0EA0  C2C9D6D3 D6C7E840 40404040 40404040   D3404040 4040D4C1   D1D6D97A   40404040   *BIOLOGY                     *
1C0EC0  40404040 40404040 40404040 40404040   40404040 40404040   40404040 40404040   *                            *
LINE 1C0EE0  SAME AS ABOVE
1C0F00  40404040 405C5C5C 40404040 40404040   40404040 40C3D9C5   7B404040 D9C5C4C9   *    ...              COURSE. CREDI*
1C0F20  E3E24040 C7D9C1C4 C5404040 40404040   E3E24040 E4D9E2C5   40404040 40404040   *TS GRADE*
1C0F40  40404040 40404040 40404040 40404040   40404040 40404040   40404040 40404040   *                            *
LINE 1C1060  SAME AS ABOVE
1C1080  40404040 40404040 40404040 40404040   40404040 40C2E840   40404040 40C2E840   *                          BY*
1C10A0  F1F2F3F4 C1C3C3D6 E4D5E3C9 D5C7F1F4   F0F0C2C9 D6D3D6C7   E8404040 F1F9F7F6   *1234ACCOUNTING1400BIOLOGY  1976*
1C10C0  C3C8C5D4 C9E2E3D9 E840F2F1 F0F0C3C9   E5C9D340 C5D5C740   F2F4F5F8 C54BC4C4   *CHEMISTRY 2100CIVIL ENG 2458E. D*
1C10E0  4B40D74B 4040F3F2 F4F5C5C3 D6D5D6D4   C9C3E240 F3F9F6F0   C6C9D5C1 D5C3C540   *. P. 3245ECONOMICS 3960FINANCE*
1C1100  4040F4F3 F2F1D4C1 D5C1C7C5 D4C5D5E3   F4F9F9F9 D4C1D9D2   C5E3C9D5 C7404040   * 4321MANAGEMENT4999MARKETING 54*
1C1120  F0F0E2E3 C1E3C9E2 E3C9C3C1 E260C3C1   E6E240C5 D5C4E240   C8C5D9C5 D9C1C7C5   *00STATISTICSS CAWS ENDS HERERAGE*
1C1140  40D9D6E4 00000000 00000000 00000000   051C3C9A 00000000   00000000 051C0D1E   * ROU........................*
1C1160  00000001 00000000 00000000 00000000   80000000 00000000   80000000 00000000   *............................*
1C1180  00000000 00000000 00410000 00000000   021FEA00 00000001   00090050 461C19F2   *............................*
1C11A0  801C1144 00A44800 00C9E60C 12F545A8   00F54400 06000001   28022828 00000000   *.......IW.. 5...5...........*
1C11C0  001FE888 001FEA58 001FEA08 00000050   00000001 00000000   00F5E0C8 00000000   *.......Y........5.H.........*
1C11E0  00000000 00000000 00000000 30000000   00000000 00800000   00000040 00000000   *............................*
1C1200  00000000 00000000 051C3C9A 001C0D1E   00000001 00000000   00000000 00000000   *............................*
```

Location 1C0DB8 - beginning of problem record

MILGROM. — Student causing data exception

Incoming major code

Table of major codes and values . 2

ENDS HERE

FIGURE 7.11 Partial Memory Dump for Example 2

```
1C1400  001C6808  00010F8A  01C5810   401C122C        061C3568  001C2DA8  20000036  001C2270    *..................................*
1C1420  401C11C6  001C16E8  00000002  601C298A        00C9EC60  00C9E978  001C287C  401C294A    *.F...Y........I...IZ..........*
1C1440  00035000  00005CD8  00000063                  9D6E0011  00060C40  E3000000  4040407B    *.....Q.....T...*
1C1460  F5F7F4F0  60C3C2F1  40C3D6D7  E8D9C9C7        C8E340C9  C2D440C3  D6D9D74B  40F1F9F7    *5740.CB1 COPYRIGHT IBM CORP. 197*
1C1480  F56BF2F4  F0F3F7F7  C9D2C6C3  C2D3F0F0        C9D2C6C3  C2D3F0F0  E5E2D9F1  F1D7F0F7    *5.240377IKFCBLOOIKFCBLOOVSR11P07*
1C14A0  90ECD00C  055047F0  55700000  00000000        00000000  00000000  00200020  00000000    *...............0..............*
1C14C0  01900028  00000000  00000000  00000000        001C0003  00000000  0E100024  00000000    *..............................*
1C14E0  001C1852  401C09E0  001C0CF8  000008A0        001C2DA8  E2E8E2D6  E4E34040  E3000000    *........8.......SYSOUT  T...*
1C1500  001C0D80  00000000  00080008  00000000        00280008  00000000  00140002  00000000    *..............................*
1C1520  0C000180  00400008  001FEA08                  001C12B0  001C0D98  00000000  00 07777F   *..................................*
1C1540  00000000  00000000  F0F34BF0  F0000000        00000000  00000000  001C0DE1  001C0DE5    *............03.00..........V.*
1C1560  001C0DE4  001C1A08  001C1A88  001C1B30        001C172E  001C1B30  001C1B30  001C117C    *.......U...................*
1C1580  8F1C1230  00000000  001C0DB8  801C0DAE        801C1230  00000000  0A000E3E  00000000    *..............................*
1C15A0  001C1BEC  001C1CB4  001C1CBE  00000000        00680022  00000000  001C4672  001C2EFA    *..............................*
1C15C0  001C3D12  001C4672  001C3D16  001C2F0A        001C3C9A  001C1CF2  001C4676  001C26E8    *............................Y*
```

Value of second operand beginning at location 1C1545

Value of first operand beginning at location 1C153D

FIGURE 7.11 (Continued)

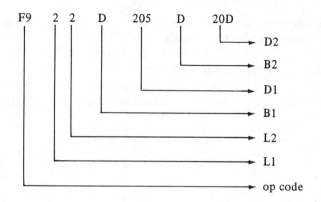

F9 is the op code for Compare Packed. This instruction compares the contents of two fields and establishes a condition code for a subsequent branch instruction. Both operands must be valid packed fields; else a data exception will occur.

The value of both operands is computed by adding the contents of register 13 and the appropriate displacements. Register 13 contains 1C1338. The displacements of the two operands are 205 and 20D, respectively. Thus, the first operand is contained in the three bytes beginning at location 1C153D. (*The length code in the machine instruction is always one less than the number of bytes in the field.*) In similar fashion, the second operand is contained in three bytes beginning at 1C1545 (1C1338 + 20D).

From the dump in Figure 7.11, the first operand is seen to contain 07777F, a valid packed field. The second contains 000000, an *invalid* packed number. Unfortunately, neither appears to shed too much light on the situation. In effect, we have determined the technical reason for the dump, but have not yet related the information to the source program.

The chapter began by stating that a dump, in and of itself, reveals nothing. We cannot overemphasize that point! In order to properly analyze a dump, one must also play detective: *list the suspects and gather evidence.* Analysis of the PSW and entry point address has shown that a data exception occurred within the routine to find a major from an incoming code. The dump has confirmed the presence of the data exception. Now identify the prime suspect, which is the student in memory at the time of the ABEND.

The Data Division map of Figure 7.2 shows that WS–STUDENT–RECORD is displaced 20 (in hex) bytes from Base Locator 3 (register 6). The incoming record begins therefore at location 1C0DB8 (1C0D98 + 20). Further analysis of Figure 7.11 shows the incoming student to be MILGROM, M and the incoming major code to be 7777.

The first operand (beginning at locations 1C153D) in the compare packed instruction was 07777F, which is nothing more than 7777 as a packed number. The program was able to find major codes for other students because transcripts have already printed, yet it could not find a major name corresponding to a code of 7777. *The only conclusion is that there is no major code of 7777!* (See COBOL lines 82-91 in Figure 7.1a, or examine the table as it appears in the dump.)

Now let us recreate what happened. The COBOL routine to find a major from a major code, is reproduced from Figure 7.1a:

```
      MOVE 1 TO WS-SUB.
      MOVE 'NO' TO WS-FOUND-MAJOR-SWITCH.
      PERFORM 030-FIND-MAJOR THRU 030-FIND-MAJOR-EXIT
          UNTIL WS-FOUND-MAJOR-SWITCH = 'YES'.
      .
      .
      .
  030-FIND-MAJOR.
      IF ST-MAJOR-CODE = MAJOR-CODE (WS-SUB)
          MOVE 'YES' TO WS-FOUND-MAJOR-SWITCH
          MOVE MAJOR-NAME (WS-SUB) TO HDG-MAJOR
      ELSE
          ADD 1 TO WS-SUB.
  030-FIND-MAJOR-EXIT.
      EXIT.
```

The table of major names has been established by VALUE clauses in COBOL lines 82-91. The table is 140 bytes long and is shown schematically as follows:

1	2	3	4	A	C	C	O	U	N	T	I	N	G	1	4	0	0	B	I	O	L	O	G	Y				1	9	7	6	C	H	E	M

. . . .	5	5	0	0	S	T	A	T	I	S	T	I	C	S

The COBOL code begins by initializing WS-SUB to 1. It compares the incoming code of 7777 to the first code in the table, which is 1234. If no match is found, it then increments WS-SUB by one and looks at the second code, and so on. Now consider what happened to MILGROM. The incoming code of 7777 was not found in the table. After WS-SUB reached 10 without finding a match, WS-SUB was incremented to 11 to look at the next entry in the table. (*We know that the table only has 10 entries, but the computer does not.*) Hence, it goes past the table, takes whatever is there, and subsequently encounters a data exception.

EXAMPLE 7.3.   DUMP READING

After Figure 7.1a was revised to include the VALUE clause for WS-TOTAL-STUDENTS and the invalid code for MILGROM was corrected, the program was rerun. Another data exception occurred, and the salient information is shown in Figure 7.12.

JOB ARTJHM22 ——— Job name

COMPLETION CODE SYSTEM = 0C7 ——— Completion code

STEP GO   TIME 140238   DATE 77340

PSW AT ENTRY TO ABEND 071D2000 00292C0E   ILC 6   INTC 0007

——— Last three bytes of PSW

CDE

Entry point address

C9F020	ATR1	0B	NCDE	000000	ROC-RB	00C9EC38	NM	GO	USE	01	EPA	290CF8	ATR2	20	XL/MJ C9EE30
FFE500	ATR1	B9	NCDE	FFE4D8	ROC-RB	00000000	NM	IGG019BA	USE	06	EPA	F67480	ATR2	20	XL/MJ FFE518
FFE4D8	ATR1	B8	NCDE	FFA848	ROC-RB	00000000	NM	IGG019BB	USE	06	EPA	F67690	ATR2	20	XL/MJ FFE4F0
FF9A18	ATR1	B1	NCDE	FF97F0	ROC-RB	00000000	NM	IGG019CF	USE	04	EPA	D4E618	ATR2	20	XL/MJ FF9A30
FF97F0	ATR1	B0	NCDE	FFE460	ROC-RB	00000000	NM	IGG019CL	USE	06	EPA	F37938	ATR2	20	XL/MJ FF9808
FFE460	ATR1	B8	NCDE	FFE488	ROC-RB	00000000	NM	IGG019AI	USE	02	EPA	F67A90	ATR2	20	XL/MJ FFE478

REGS AT ENTRY TO ABEND

FLTR 0-6   0000000000000000   0000000000000000   00981D0000000000   00BD0E0009D0D00   00BD0F0000981B08

REGS 0-7   00292A7E 5029282E 00000000 00000000 00290DD1 00000005 00292788 0029298F
REGS 8-15 00292990 00292CC2 002926E8 002929E0 00292798 00290DB8 00293D16

FIGURE 7.12 Information Associated with Memory Dump of Example 3

We begin as before; take the last three bytes of the PSW and subtract the Entry Point Address.

$$
\begin{array}{rcl}
\text{Last three bytes of PSW} & = & \text{292C0E} \\
-\text{ Entry Point Address} & = & -\text{ 290CF8} \\
\hline
\text{Relative location} & = & \text{1F16}
\end{array}
$$

Next, take 1F16 as the relative location within the program and go to the Procedure Division map of Figure 7.4. Unfortunately the relative locations stop well below 1F16, and hence we cannot find where we are in our program. The procedure which worked so well only a short time ago seems to have failed completely. Do not panic. The dump is still as useful as always; it must, however, be coaxed a little more to tell us what we need to know.

What should come immediately to mind is that we are executing a load module, comprised of two COBOL programs (a main program and a subprogram), which have been link-edited into a single executable program. Perhaps our problem lies in the subprogram and not in the main program. We can determine if this is the case by examining Figure 7.13.

Figure 7.13 is an OS linkage-editor map which lists all the Control Sections (CSECTs) comprising the load module. The first column lists the CSECT's name. The next column shows the origin (i.e., the relative location of each routine within the load module), and the last column shows the length of the routine in bytes (in hex). We can recognize MAINPROG and SUBRTN as the PROGRAM-ID's from Figure 7.1a and b (COBOL line 2 in each program). The remaining, rather strangely named, routines are IBM subroutines required by our COBOL program for I/O and other functions.

Recall from Figure 7.12 that the main program had an EPA of 290CF8. The subroutine, in turn, has an origin of 19F0 bytes past MAINPROG, and the relationship between these modules is shown schematically in Figure 7.14.

Now reconsider 1F16 the relative address where our program blew out. We can verify that the error did occur somewhere in the link-edit map of Figure 7.13, since 1F16 is less than 41E0, the origin of ILBOMSG (the last module shown). We scan the origins of Figure 7.13 (which are listed in ascending order) and find that the problem occurred in SUBRTN (i.e., the highest origin that does not exceed 1F16). We find where within SUBRTN by subtraction:

$$
\begin{array}{rcl}
\text{Location in load module} & = & \text{1F16} \\
-\text{ Origin in SUBRTN} & = & -\text{ 19F0} \\
\hline
\text{Relative location} & = & \text{526}
\end{array}
$$

CROSS REFERENCE TABLE

CONTROL SECTION   ENTRY

Annotations: PROGRAM-ID of main program → MAINPROG; PROGRAM-ID of subprogram → SUBRTN; Origin of subprogram → ILBOCOM0*

NAME	ORIGIN	LENGTH		NAME	LOCATION	NAME	LOCATION	NAME	LOCATION	NAME	LOCATION
MAINPROG	00	FC6									
ILBODSP	FC8	A28		ILBODSP0	FFA	ILBODSS0	FFA				
SUBRTN	19F0	6BB									
ILBOCOM0*	20B0	120		ILBOCOM	20B0						
ILBODBG *	21D0	DD0		ILBODBG0	2202	ILBODBG1	2206	ILBODBG2	220A	ILBODBG3	220E
				ILBODBG4	2212	ILBODBG5	2216	ILBODBG6	221A	ILBODBG7	221E
ILBOEXT *	2FA0	46		ILBOEXT0	2FA2						
ILBOFLW *	2FE8	500		ILBOFLW0	301A	ILBOFLW1	301E	ILBOFLW2	3022		
ILBOSPA *	34E8	454		ILBOSPA0	34EA	ILBOSPA1	34EE				
ILBOSRV *	3940	408		ILBOSRV0	397A	ILBOSR5	397A	ILBOSR3	397A	ILBOSR	397A
				ILBOSRV1	397E	ILBOSTP1	397E	ILBOST	3982	ILBOSTP0	3982
ILBOBEG *	3D48	C2		ILBOBEG0	3D7A						
ILBOCMM *	3E10	3CE		ILBOCMM0	3E42	ILBOCMM1	3E46				
ILBOMSG *	41E0	128		ILBOMSG0	4212						

LOCATION	REFERS TO SYMBOL	IN CONTROL SECTION		LOCATION	REFERS TO SYMBOL	IN CONTROL SECTION
8C0	ILBOSRV0	ILBOSRV		8C4	ILBODBG0	ILBODBG
8C8	ILBOFLW0	ILBOFLW		8CC	ILBOSR5	ILBOSRV
8D0	ILBOFLW1	ILBOFLW		8D4	ILBODBG4	ILBODBG
8D8	ILBOEXT0	ILBOEXT		8DC	ILBODSP0	ILBODSP
8E0	ILBOSRV1	ILBOSRV		8E4	SUBRTN	SUBRTN
8E8	ILBOSPA0	ILBOSPA		7F8	SUBRTN	SUBRTN
1CE8	ILBOSRV0	ILBOSRV		1CEC	ILBOCOMO	ILBOCOMO
1CF0	ILBOFLW0	ILBOFLW		1CF4	ILBODBG0	ILBODBG
1CF8	ILBOFLW1	ILBOFLW		1CFC	ILBOSR5	ILBOSRV
1D00	ILBOSRV1	ILBOSRV		1C58	ILBODBG4	ILBODBG
2E60	ILBOFLW0	ILBOFLW		2E64	ILBOCOMO	ILBOCOMO
2E68	ILBOTEF3	$UNRESOLVED(W)		2E6C	ILBOFLW2	ILBOFLW
2E74	ILBOTC00	$UNRESOLVED(W)		3C4C	ILBOCOM	$UNRESOLVED(W)
3C5C	ILBOSTT0	$UNRESOLVED(W)		3C50	ILBOCOMO	ILBOCOMO
3C54	ILBOBEG0	ILBOBEG		3C58	ILBOMSGO	ILBOMSG

FIGURE 7.13 Linkage-Editor Map

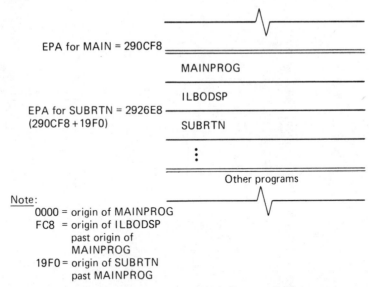

EPA for MAIN = 290CF8

MAINPROG

ILBODSP

EPA for SUBRTN = 2926E8
(290CF8 + 19F0)

SUBRTN

Other programs

Note:
    0000 = origin of MAINPROG
    FC8 = origin of ILBODSP
         past origin of
         MAINPROG
    19F0 = origin of SUBRTN
         past MAINPROG

FIGURE 7.14 Origins and Lengths of Main Program and Subprogram

Next, consider a partial Procedure Division map for SUBRTN, shown in Figure 7.15. 526 is contained within the COMPUTE statement, COBOL line 63. A good intuitive conclusion is that the incoming course data for a particular student are in error. The question is: Which student and which data?

The Linkage Section of the subprogram contains the 01 record, DATA–PASSED–FROM–MAIN, which in turn has the student name and course data. The CALL statement of the main program (COBOL lines 112–114 in Figure 7.1*a*) shows that the 01 record, WS–STUDENT–RECORD, corresponds to DATA–PASSED–FROM–MAIN in the subprogram (i.e., *the two 01 records, WS–STUDENT–RECORD (main program) and DATA–PASSED–FROM–MAIN (subprogram), occupy a single area in memory*). Hence, if we can locate either 01 record, we automatically have the other! (This "single" area is always part of the *calling* program; in other words, data names, defined in the Linkage Section of a *called* program exist elsewhere (i.e., in the calling program).)

Figure 7.16 is the Data Division map of the subprogram, which is similar to Figure 7.2, which contained the Data Division map for the main program. There is one *significant* difference, however; the entries in the Linkage Section of the subprogram are tied to a Base Linkage Locator (BLL). The simple procedure we used in the other examples will *not* work because there is no direct tie from the BLL to a corresponding register. Nor can one take the contents of register 6 and assume they point to Working-Storage for the main program. The program blew out in SUBRTN, not in the main program; hence, the registers displayed in Figure 7.12 are those of

FIGURE 7.15 Truncated Procedure Division Map for SUBRTN

COBOL Card #	COBOL Verb	Relative Location	Machine Instruction	Assembler Formats		
50	COMPUTE	0003D8	F2 72 D 1F8 6 000	PACK	1F8(8,13),000(3,6)	DNM=1-109 TS=01
		0003DE	F2 72 D 200 6 003	PACK	200(8,13),003(3,6)	DNM=1-135 TS=09
		0003E4	F0 30 D 204 0 003	SRP	204(4,13),003(0),0	TS=013
		0003EA	FD 51 D 202 D 1FE	DP	202(6,13),1FE(2,13)	TS=011
		0003F0	F8 73 D 200 D 202	ZAP	200(8,13),202(4,13)	TS=09
		0003F6	F0 35 D 204 0 03F	SRP	204(4,13),03F(0),5	TS=013
		0003FC	58 E0 D 210	L	14,210(0,13)	BLL=3
		000400	D3 22 E 000 D 205	UNPK	000(3,14),205(3,13)	DNM=1-201 TS=014
52	*005-RETURN-TO-MAIN					
55	*010-COMPUTE-QUALITY-POINTS					
		000440	PN=01	EQU	*	
		000440	58 F0 C 010	L	15,010(0,12)	V(ILBOFLW1)
		000446	05 1F	BALR	1,15	
		000448	00000037	DC	X'00000037'	
56	MOVE	00044A	92 F0 6 006	MVI	006(6),X'F0'	DNM=1-162
		00044E	58 E0 D 214	L	14,214(0,13)	BLL=4
59	IF	000452	41 40 E 018	LA	4,018(0,14)	DNM=1-393
		000456	48 30 6 007	LH	3,007(0,6)	DNM=1-185
		00045A	5C 20 C 058	M	2,058(0,12)	LIT+8
		00045E	1A 43	AR	4,3	
	· · · ·					
62	MOVE	0004FA	92 F1 6 006	MVI	006(6),X'F1'	DNM=1-162
63	COMPUTE	0004FE	GN=08	EQU	*	
		0004FE	58 E0 D 214	L	14,214(0,13)	BLL=4
		000502	41 40 E 019	LA	4,019(0,14)	DNM=1-421
		000506	48 30 6 007	LH	3,007(0,6)	DNM=1-185
		00050A	5C 20 C 058	M	2,058(0,12)	LIT+8
		00050E	1A 43	AR	4,3	
		000510	5B 40 C 058	S	4,058(0,12)	LIT+8
		000514	F2 70 D 200 6 006	PACK	200(8,13),006(1,6)	TS=09
		00051A	F2 70 D 1F8 4 000	PACK	1F8(8,13),000(1,4)	TS=01
		000520	FC 10 D 206 D 1FF	MP	206(2,13),1FF(1,13)	TS=015
		000526	F2 72 D 1F8 6 003	PACK	1F8(8,13),003(3,6)	TS=01
		00052C	FA 21 D 205 D 1FE	AP	205(3,13),1FE(2,13)	TS=014
		000532	F3 22 6 003 D 205	UNPK	003(3,6),205(3,13)	DNM=1-135
		000538	96 F0 6 005	OI	005(6),X'F0'	DNM=1-135+2
65	ADD	00053C	F2 70 D 200 4 000	PACK	200(8,13),000(1,4)	TS=09
		000542	F2 72 D 1F8 6 000	PACK	1F8(8,13),000(3,6)	TS=01
		000548	FA 21 D 205 D 1FE	AP	205(3,13),1FE(2,13)	TS=014
		00054E	F3 22 6 000 D 205	UNPK	000(3,6),205(3,13)	DNM=1-109
		000554	96 F0 6 002	OI	002(6),X'F0'	DNM=1-109+2
		000558	58 10 D 224	L	1,224(0,13)	VN=01
		00055C	07 F1	BCR	15,1	

Instruction at location 526

INTRNL NAME	LVL	SOURCE NAME
DNM=1-109	77	WS-TOTAL-CREDITS
DNM=1-135	77	WS-QUALITY-POINTS
DNM=1-162	77	WS-MULTIPLIER
DNM=1-185	77	WS-SUB
DNM=1-201	77	LS-CALCULATED-AVERAGE
DNM=1-232	01	DATA-PASSED-FROM-MAIN
DNM=1-266	02	ST-NAME
DNM=1-283	02	ST-MAJOR-CODE
DNM=1-306	02	ST-NUMBER-OF-COURSES
DNM=1-336	02	ST-COURSE-TABLE
DNM=1-364	03	ST-COURSE-NUMBER
DNM=1-393	03	ST-COURSE-GRADE
DNM=1-421	03	ST-COURSE-CREDITS

BASE	DISPL	INTRNL NAME	DEFINITION	USAGE
BL=1	000	DNM=1-109	DS 3C	DISP-NM
BL=1	003	DNM=1-135	DS 3C	DISP-NM
BL=1	006	DNM=1-162	DS 1C	DISP-NM
BL=1	007	DNM=1-185	DS 2C	COMP
BLL=3	000	DNM=1-201	DS 3C	DISP-NM
BLL=4	000	DNM=1-232	DS 0CL61	GROUP
BLL=4	000	DNM=1-266	DS 15C	DISP
BLL=4	00F	DNM=1-283	DS 4C	DISP-NM
BLL=4	013	DNM=1-306	DS 2C	DISP-NM
BLL=4	015	DNM=1-336	DS 0CL5	GROUP
BLL=4	015	DNM=1-364	DS 3C	DISP
BLL=4	018	DNM=1-393	DS 1C	DISP
BLL=4	019	DNM=1-421	DS 1C	DISP-NM

Base linkage locators

FIGURE 7.16 Data Division Map for SUBRTN

the subprogram and go nowhere fast. Give up? Don't! We have another trick up our sleeve.

Notice COBOL lines 35 and 36 of the main program in Figure 7.1*a*. We establish the literal WS BEGINS HERE at the start of Working-Storage for the main program and use this as a crutch (i.e., we begin at the start of the dump, Figure 7.17, and scan the alphabetic interpretation at the right-hand side of each line looking for WS BEGINS HERE. We then deduce that Working-Storage begins at hex location 290D98. Using the Data Division map for the main program, we see immediately that the student named BOROW, J had the incorrect data. Specifically credits were left blank for his first course, #666, in which he received a B, hence the data exception and ABEND. (The hex representation for a blank is 40, so that when credits is packed, the low-order digit (i.e., sign) of the resulting packed field will be 4. This is an invalid sign and will subsequently cause the ABEND.)

Before you object too strongly to the use of our crutch, consider the following:

1. It works, and consequently allows the reader to build confidence immediately. This is extremely important because dumps are often anathema even to the most ambitious applications programmer. Too often the response is a premature yell for help, which we are trying to avoid.

2. It substantiates more sophisticated means; obviously, there should be other ways to find Working-Storage, and indeed we proceed to cover both BL and BLL cells in the next section. Our crutch is a valuable way to verify these results.

Use of BL and BLL Cells

This section will corroborate conclusions drawn from WS BEGINS HERE. Figure 7.18 contains the memory map of the COBOL program, SUBRTN. It was produced by the compiler and contains displacements of work areas used by the compiler. One entry in Figure 7.18, the BLL cells, will help to identify the record in question.

Each BLL (Base Linkage Locator) cell contains an address that is used to locate entries in the Data Division map. BLL cells are analogous to BL cells except that they indicate parameters that were passed as arguments from another program. BL cells, on the other hand, are associated with data names originating in the program under consideration. In other words, any data name associated with a BLL cell was originally defined in *another* program, whereas any data name associated with a BL cell was defined in *this* program.

Figure 7.18 shows the displacement of the BLL cells to be 2B8. This means that the value of the first BLL cell will be found 2B8 bytes into the

LOAD MODULE   GO

Start of working-storage location 290D98 — Working-storage begins here

```
290CE0  4580F010 D4C1C9D5 D7D9D6C7 E5E2D9F1   90ECD00C 185D05F0            *..0.MAINPROGVSR1....0*
290D00  000107FE 00291B76 00290CF8 00290CF8   F02407FF 96021034 07FE41F0   *........8...80......0*
290D20  00000001 00000000 AC001001 05050000   00291B76 00291333 00291694 00291B36   *.....................*
290D40  922F5A53 40000008 062F5A98 60000104   0001AC00 00010505 06000000 40000400    *.....................*
290D60  F1F34BF5 F94BF5F2 C4C5C340 40F66B40   922F5A5F 40000008 082F5CD0 00000000    *13.59.52DEC  6. 1977...*
290D80  E240C8C5 D9C50006 D5D640E8 C5E2F3F0   F1F9F7F7 00000001 E6E240C2 C5C7C9D5    *S HERE..NO YES30.1977....WS BEGIN*
290DA0  C0002F00 0001AC00 0001AC00 C2D6D9D6   E66B40D1                               *..........BOROW. J*
290DC0  C240F7F7 F7C2F4F8 F8C3F4F9 F9F9F9C3    3960466B[ ]777B4888C4999C            *  3960466B[]777B4888C4999C*
290DE0  F4404040 40010505 40404040 40404040                                         *4*
290E00  E2C3D9C9 D7E3                                                                *TRANSCRIPT*
290E20  40404040 40404040 40404040 40404040                                         * *
```

ST-NAME begins here (290DB8)

Credits was left blank

```
LINE 290F60 SAME AS ABOVE
290F80  40404040 40404040 40404040 40000000   40404040 40404040 40F5F5F5            *                555*
290FA0  40404040 40F34040 40404040 40404040   40404040 40404040 404040C2            *    3          B*
290FC0  40404040 40404040 40404040 40404040   40404040 40404040 40404040            * *
LINE 290FE0 SAME AS ABOVE
291000  40404040 40404040 40404040 4000002C   40404040 40404040 40404040            * *
291020  40F34BF0 F0404040 C1E5C5D9 C1C7C57A   40F34BF0 F0404040 C1E5C5D9 C1C7C57A   *AVERAGE. 3.00  ...*
291040  40404040 40404040 40404040 40404040   40404040 40404040 40404040            * *
LINE 291060 SAME AS ABOVE
291080  40404040 40404040 40404040 40404040   40404040 40404040 40276000            *                ...*
2910A0  F1F2F3F4 C1C3C3D6 E4D5E3C9 D5C7F1F4   F0F0C2C9 D6D3D6C7 E8404040 F1F9F7F6   *1234ACCOUNTING1400BIOLOGY   1976*
2910C0  C3C8C5D4 C9E2E3D9 E840F2F1 F0F0C3C9   E5C9D340 C5D5C740 F2F4F5F8 C54B40C4   *CHEMISTRY 2100CIVIL ENG 2458E. D*
2910E0  4B40D74B 4040F3F2 F4F5C5C3 D6D5D6D4   C9C3E240 F3F9F6F0 C6C9D5C1 D5C3C540   *. P.  3245ECONOMICS 3960FINANCE *
```

FIGURE 7.17 Partial Memory Dump for Example 3

```
2914A0  60004140 60285040 60144140 602C5040   601C4140 60305040 6018D70B 60046004   *.......................P...*
2914C0  D71F6020 60204140 00000000 00000000   A1545040 60349102 B2604710 C17ED200   *P.............8.....A.K.*
2914E0  00291852 60293EBA 00290CF8 000008A0   00292DA8 E2E8E2D6 E4E34040 E3000008   *.............SYSOUT T...*
291500  00290D80 5000B2A8 5000B254 4000B378   D707B69C 00000000 B430B430 D77FB3A8   *....P............P.*
291520  B3ASD205 B414C512 4810B168 002CEA08   00000000 00000000 00000000 0003000C   *.K..E....03.00.K...*
291540  00000000 0001400F F0F34BF0 F099D201   00290DE4 00000000 00290DE1 00290DE5   *.....U........V.*
291560  00290DE4 00291A08 00291A88 00291B30   0029172E 00291A88 00291B30 0029117C   *.....K...........*
291580  3F291230 18D24120 00290DB8 80290DAE   80291230 10004780 0A000E3E 00000000   *.....K.........*
2915A0  00000EF4 00000FBC 00000FC6 D202B4B9   100147F0 C256D202 00294672 00292EFA   *....4.....FK...0B.K..*
2915C0  00293D12 00294672 00293D16 00292F0A   00293C9A 00291A88 00291CF2 002926E8   *...........2...Y*
2915E0  002941E2 00291820 002919F8 00291A08   00291A78 00291888 00291B20 00291B30   *..S.......8.....*
291600  00291718 0029171E 0029172E 00291740   00291888 0029189A 002918CC 00291900   *.............*
```

Value of BL = 3 for main program → 00290D98

```
292900  00000000 00000000 00000000 00000000   00000000 00000000 00000000 00000000   *.......................*
292920  00000000 00000000 00000000 00000000   00000000 00000001 00000001 00000000   *.......................*
292940  00000001 402909E0 00292926E8 000002D8  00292DA8 E2E8E2D6 E4E34040 E3FE0008   *.........Y...Q...SYSOUT T..*
292960  00292770 07F99110 C0184710 7B121854   06404144 00000000 59400D50 47808EC   *..9........Y......9.*
292980  D403C004 C0044780 B2CC955D 00292788   00000000 00000000 00000000 0000003F   *M.................*
2929A0  00000000 00000000 80290DAE 00290DB8   00000000 00290DD0 00292C46 00292A7E   *...............K.*
2929C0  0A00059A 00000000 00292D30 00292D99   00292DA3 53320014 41330000 D201D043   *.............K.*
2929E0  00294672 00292EFA 00293D12 00294672   00293D16 00292F0A 00294676 00292B28   *..........K...*
292A00  00292C46 00292A83 00292AAA 00292A7E   00292AB3 00292B62 00292B8E 00292BBA   *....W.....Y000.*
292A20  00292BE6 00292AF8 00292C46 0A326BE8   F0F0F000 01000001 00000005 584D0004   *....K...8...Y000.*
292A40  58504018 58504000 5050D214 58504004   5050D210 58F0C010 051F0000 002CD202   *...K....K.0....K.*
```

Value of BLL = 4 for the subprogram → 00290DB8

FIGURE 7.17 (Continued)

```
                MEMORY MAP

        TGT                         000B0

    SAVE AREA                       000B0
    SWITCH                          000F8
    TALLY                           000FC
    SORT SAVE                       00100
    ENTRY-SAVE                      00104
    SORT CORE SIZE                  00108
    RET CODE                        0010C
    SORT RET                        0010E
    WORKING CELLS                   00110
    SORT FILE SIZE                  00240
    SORT MODE SIZE                  00244
    PGT-VN TBL                      00248
    TGT-VN TBL                      0024C
    VCONPTR                         00250
    LENGTH OF VN TBL                00254
    LABEL RET                       00256
    CURRENT PRIORITY                00257
    DBG R14SAVE                     00258
    COBOL INDICATOR                 0025C
    A(INIT1)                        00260
    DEBUG TABLE PTR                 00264
    SUBCOM PTR                      00268
    SORT-MESSAGE                    0026C
    SYSOUT DDNAME                   00274
    RESERVED                        00275
    COBOL ID                        00276
    COMPILED POINTER                00278
    COUNT TABLE ADDRESS             0027C
    RESERVED                        00280
    DBG R11SAVE                     00288
    COUNT CHAIN ADDRESS             0028C
    PRBL1 CELL PTR                  00290
    RESERVED                        00294
    TA LENGTH                       00299
    RESERVED                        0029C
    OVERFLOW CELLS                  002A4
    BL CELLS                        002A4
    DECBADR CELLS                   002A8
    FIB CELLS                       002A8
    TEMP STORAGE                    002A8
    TEMP STORAGE-2                  002B8
    TEMP STORAGE-3                  002B8
    TEMP STORAGE-4                  002B8
    BLL CELLS                      [002B8]──Displacement of
    VLC CELLS                       002CC    BLL cells in
    SBL CELLS                       002CC    SUBRTN
    INDEX CELLS                     002CC
    SUBADR CELLS                    002CC
    ONCTL CELLS                     002D0
    PFMCTL CELLS                    002D0
    PFMSAV CELLS                    002D0
    VN CELLS                        002D4
    SAVE AREA =2                    002D8
    SAVE AREA =3                    002D8
    XSASW CELLS                     002D8
    XSA CELLS                       002D8
    PARAM CELLS                     002D8
    RPTSAV AREA                     002D8
    CHECKPT CTR                     002D8
    VCON TBL                        002D8
    DEBUG TABLE                     002D8
```

FIGURE 7.18 Memory Map of SUBRTN

SUBRTN program. Recall that the entry point of the entire module was 290CF8 and the origin of SUBRTN was 19F0. Thus, the first BLL cell is at location 2929A0 (290CF8 + 19F0 + 2B8). Each Base Linkage Locator is one word (four bytes) long. The Data Division map of Figure 7.16 indicates that ST–NAME is associated with BLL = 4. Thus, its value will be found in the four bytes beginning at 2929AC, at the start of the fourth word from 2929A0.

The dump in Figure 7.17 shows the value of BLL = 4 to be 290DB8 (only the three low-order bytes are used). This is the exact location of ST–NAME (since ST–NAME has a displacement of 000 in Figure 7.16) and contains BOROW, J. Note that the address obtained from BLL cells substantiates the conclusion drawn from WS BEGINS HERE. Hopefully, this will make some sense to you. If so, you are well on your way towards a real understanding of program linkages. If not, you are not alone, as many programmers become confused on first encountering BLL cells. Try re-reading the material and discussing it with a colleague. Eventually, it will all come clear.

The data name DATA–PASSED–FROM–MAIN in the subprogram of Figure 7.1*b* occupies the identical storage locations as WS–STUDENT–RECORD in the main program of Figure 7.1*a*. We have seen that the BLL cells are used to locate data names in the subprogram. We will now show how the BL cells can be used to identify data names in the main program. Recall that the Data Division map of the main program, Figure 7.2, showed that ST–NAME is displaced hex 20 bytes from BL = 3. To find the address of ST–NAME, we need the value of BL = 3. Figure 7.19 is a partial memory

```
                      MEMORY MAP
            TGT                        00640

       SAVE AREA                       00640
       SWITCH                          00688
       TALLY                           0068C
       SORT SAVE                       00690
       ENTRY-SAVE                      00694
       SORT CORE SIZE                  00698
                •
                •
                •
                •

       TA LENGTH                       00829
       RESERVED                        0082C
       OVERFLOW CELLS                  00834      Location of
       BL CELLS                        00834      BL cells
       DECBADR CELLS                   00840
       FIB CELLS                       00840
       TEMP STORAGE                    00840
       TEMP STORAGE-2                  00850
```

FIGURE 7.19 Partial Memory Map of Main Program

map of the main program. As can be seen, 834 is the displacement of the BL cells in the main program. The first BL cell for the main program is at location 29152C (290CF8 + 834). The value of the third BL cell is found in the four bytes beginning at location 291534 and is equal to 290D98. WS-STUDENT-RECORD begins therefore at location 290DB8 (290D98 + 20), which is the identical location of DATA-PASSED-FROM-MAIN in the subprogram. The circle of checks and double checks is complete.

THE SAVE AREA TRACE

At this point we have completely debugged three 0C7s using a variety of techniques. We now introduce one additional aid which, although not immediately necessary, may prove invaluable in the future. We are refer-ring to the SAVE AREA TRACE and the method by which control is passed from one program to another.

As the reader is well aware, there are 16 general-purpose registers which are constantly used by an executing program. Any time a program is called by another program, the called program is expected to save the registers of the calling program in an area known as a *save area*. The called program is then free to use and alter the 16 registers. When the called program returns control to the calling program, it must first restore the contents of the calling program's registers.

All this sounds very complicated but is made easier in practice by the fact that the COBOL compiler automatically generates the necessary instructions. (Assembler programmers must, on the other hand, explicitly code these instructions themselves. See the discussion in Chapter 11.) A brief knowledge of some of these linkage conventions may prove helpful in debugging. This is particularly true in modular systems where control is passed through several routines.

We will concern ourselves with only two conventions. Register 14 contains the return address (i.e., the place in the calling program (e.g., a COBOL main program) to which the called program (i.e., a COBOL sub-program) is to return control). Register 15 contains the entry point address (i.e., the place in the called program where execution is to begin). These points are clarified by Figure 7.20, which shows the SAVE AREA TRACE from the third 0C7.

Figure 7.20 shows the flow between programs in effect at the time of the ABEND. The first line is *always* associated with the main (sometimes only) COBOL program. The low return address, 010F8A, indicates a return address in the operating system which receives control when the COBOL program terminates. The entry point on the first line, 290CF8, is the entry point for the main COBOL program. The return address in the second save area, 29185C, is the place where control is to return in the main program

```
SAVE AREA TRACE

GO    WAS ENTERED VIA LINK                              Return point in supervisor   Entry point in the main
                                                                                            program

SA  2CEF68  WD1 00000000  HSA 00000000  LSA 00291338  RET 0001CF8A  EPA 01290CF8  R0  00C9EE38
            R1  002CEFF8  R2  002CEFF8  R3  5CC9E840  R4  00C9F2E0  R5  00C9EEF0  R6  00C9EE24
            R7  00C9F118  R8  00C9E818  R9  00C9EC60  R10 00C9E840  R11 00000000  R12 40F582E2

GO    WAS ENTERED VIA CALL
                                                       Return point in the          Entry point in the
                                                       main program                 subprogram

SA  291338  WD1 0030C4C2  HSA 002CEF68  LSA 00292798  RET 5029185C  EPA 002926E8  R0  00C9E8B0
            R1  00291588  R2  00291740  R3  00000005  R4  00290DE5  R5  002919F8  R6  00290D98
            R7  002CEA03  R8  00291220  R9  00291076  R10 00290CF8  R11 00220250  R12 00221550

GO    WAS ENTERED VIA CALL
                                                       Return point in the
                                                       subprogram

SA  292798  WD1 0030C4C2  HSA 002CEF68  LSA 00291338  RET 00292B32  EPA 00293D16  R0  00292A7E
            R1  50292B2E  R2  00000000  R3  00000004  R4  00291583  R5  00000001  R6  00292783
            R7  0029298F  R8  00292990  R9  00292CC2  R10 00292CC2  R11 002926E8  R12 002929E0
```

FIGURE 7.20 The SAVE AREA TRACE

after the subprogram has completed execution. Subtracting the entry point from the return address yields a relative address of B64, which can be found in the Procedure Division map of Figure 7.4.

Note well two instructions immediately above relative address B64. Location B5E contains a load instruction which places the address of SUBRTN into register 15. The next instruction at B62 is BALR 14,15, which puts the address of the next sequential instruction into register 14 and branches to the address contained in register 15. This demonstrates the linkage conventions exactly. Register 14 contains the return address (i.e., the first instruction to be executed when control is returned to the main program). Register 15 contains the first instruction in the called program (i.e., SUBRTN).

In similar fashion the subprogram itself is seen to call another program. Subtracting the EPA of the subprogram, 2926E8, from the return address of 292B32 yields a relative address of 44A in the subprogram. Consider the two instructions immediately above 44A in the Procedure Division map in Figure 7.15. The first, at 440, loads the address of ILB0FLW1, an IBM module associated with the FLOW option, into register 15. Recall that this option keeps track of the last n procedures executed prior to an ABEND, and evidently was called in this instance. The instruction at 444 is BALR 1,15, which branches to the address contained in register 15, and stores the address of the next sequential instruction in register 1. (The IBM routine will set register 14 to the return address which is four bytes past register 1. Register 1 therefore is seen to contain a parameter list.)

The SAVE AREA TRACE is always present in a dump and appears slightly before the registers at entry to ABEND. In our example it contained three levels of program flow, but it could contain many more! The trace is often used to determine program flow prior to an ABEND.

Summary

This chapter introduces ABEND debugging for COBOL programs. Attempted execution of the same COBOL program causes a data exception for three distinct reasons. The rudiments of a debugging procedure were established. *One takes the address contained in the PSW at the time of the ABEND, subtracts the entry point address, and determines the relative location within the COBOL program of the instruction causing the problem.* There are, however, numerous subtleties associated with the subtraction. First and foremost, a dump may reveal the technical reason for an ABEND (e.g., invalid decimal data), but it is up to the programmer to relate this information to the source listing and/or to the data. Second, the contents of the registers at the time of the ABEND may not coincide with the BL cells and the latter must be determined. The SAVE AREA TRACE was introduced as an additional technique. We hope that we have not falsely represented debugging as a "cookbook" procedure. It is anything but! A dump is a valuable tool in determining the cause and location of a bug, but it is only a tool. In the final analysis it is the programmer who somehow, perhaps by divine inspiration, is able to interpret the dump and find the answer.

In conclusion, there are many ways to debug the same problem and this allows programmers to use a variety of techniques. For example, we have a colleague who uses the SAVE AREA TRACE to the exclusion of almost everything else. Another makes extensive use of the STATE and FLOW options and uses a dump only as a last resort. The method you choose is up to you. More than likely, however, you will use a collection of techniques, for no method seems to work every time.

TRUE/FALSE EXERCISES

1. The PSW address refers directly to the instruction which produced the ABEND.
2. The last 6 bytes of the PSW contain the address referred to in question 1.
3. To begin solving an ABEND, one subtracts the PSW address from the EPA.
4. The Linkage Section of a subprogram does not allocate any additional memory.
5. A data exception (0C7 ABEND) will never be produced by a COBOL READ or MOVE instruction.
6. Datanames in a subroutine may be referenced by either BL or BLL cells, depending on where in the program they were defined.
7. Subtraction of the EPA from the PSW address will always yield an address contained in the main program.
8. Registers 14 and 15 have well-defined functions according to the standard linkage conventions.
9. The Procedure Division map is automatically produced for the programmer by the COBOL compiler.
10. The Data Division map ties all COBOL data names directly to a base register.

PROBLEMS

1. Take a COBOL program of your own and cause a data exception. Do it in two ways, first by failing to initialize a Working-Storage entry, then by improper input. Analyze the resulting dumps to pinpoint the errors. Better yet, exchange your dump with that of a partner and try to debug the other person's program.

2. Consider the COBOL programs of Figure 7.1a and b. List at least three "defensive" checks that could be included. Show the necessary COBOL code.

3. Explain how a data exception need not occur, even though a Working-Storage entry used as a counter was not initialized; specifically, consider the first example in this chapter, in which WS-TOTAL-STUDENTS was not set to zero. What would be the consequences of *not* getting a data exception, even if WS-TOTAL-STUDENTS was not initialized?

4. (a) Example 3 showed that a blank in a one-position numeric field causes a data exception if arithmetic is performed on that field. Assume that we define a four-position numeric field that is also used in arithmetic calculations. Further, assume that this four-position field has a valid low-order digit but is punched with leading (high-order) blanks. Will a data exception result? Why or why not?
   (b) Explain why an incoming numeric field (USAGE DISPLAY) will cause a data exception if a decimal point is actually punched in the field.

5. Consider the following COBOL entries:

   ```
   05   TOTAL-COUNTER      PIC S9(4)  COMP.
   ```

   and

   ```
   ADD 1 TO TOTAL-COUNTER.
   ```

   Explain why the ADD statement will *never* cause a data exception, even though TOTAL-COUNTER was never initialized. What can you say about the ultimate value of TOTAL-COUNTER (assuming that it was never initialized)?

6. (a) Consider COBOL line 41 of Figure 7.1a, in which WS-TOTAL-STUDENTS is initialized to zero (i.e., after the error has been found in Example 1). Would there be any difference in substituting the

statement MOVE ZEROS TO WS-TOTAL-STUDENTS in the MAINLINE paragraph of the Procedure Division? Why?

(b) Would there be any difference if COBOL lines 45 and 46 were removed in the subprogram of Figure 7.1*b*, provided that the clause VALUE IS ZEROS were added to COBOL lines 15 and 16? Why?

7. Use the COBOL listing, register assignments, and so on, from the chapter (Figures 7.1–7.4) to determine the cause of the ABEND in Figure 7.21. A series of leading questions (*which continue on page 203*) is provided.

(a) Analyze the completion code.
   (1) What is the completion code?
   (2) What does the completion code mean?

(b) Determine where the ABEND occurred.
   (3) What address is contained in the PSW?
   (4) At what location was the program loaded?
   (5) Subtract the address in part 4 from the one in part 3.
   (6) Is the relative location obtained in part 5 contained in the main program?
   (7) What is the origin of the subroutine within the load module?
   (8) Subtract the address in part 7 from the one in part 5.
   (9) To which program does the relative location in part 8 refer?
   (10) What machine instruction is at that location?
   (11) What is the actual machine address of the instruction in part 10?
   (12) What is the corresponding COBOL instruction?

(c) Examine the machine instruction that failed to execute. The instruction that actually produced the ABEND is the one immediately before the instruction determined in part 11.
   (13) What is the machine instruction that actually caused the ABEND?
   (14) What is its op code?
   (15) Which base register is associated with the first operand?
   (16) What is the displacement of the first operand?
   (17) What is the effective address of the first operand?
   (18) How many bytes are associated with the first operand? (Careful.)
   (19) What are the internal contents of the first operand? Are they valid as a decimal number?
   (20) Which base register is associated with the second operand?
   (21) What is the displacement of the second operand?
   (22) How many bytes are associated with the second operand?
   (23) What are the internal contents of the second operand? Are they valid as a decimal number?
   (24) Technically, why did the ABEND occur?

(d) Relate the technical cause of the ABEND to the COBOL program.

COMPLETION CODE   SYSTEM = 0CB

PSW AT ENTRY TO ABEND   071D0000 001D2AD8   ILC 6   INTC 000B

CDE

```
CCF140    ATR1 0B    NCDE 000000    ROC-RB 00CCE930    NM GO         USE 01    EPA 1D0CF8    ATR2 20    XL/MJ CCF018
FFE500    ATR1 B9    NCDE FFE4D8    ROC-RB 00000000    NM IGG019BA   USE 07    EPA F67480    ATR2 20    XL/MJ FFE518
FFE4D8    ATR1 B8    NCDE FFA848    ROC-RB 00000000    NM IGG019BB   USE 07    EPA F67690    ATR2 20    XL/MJ FFE4F0
FF7828    ATR1 B1    NCDE FF7828    ROC-RB 00000000    NM IGG019CF   USE 02    EPA D4E618    ATR2 20    XL/MJ FF7638
FF7620    ATR1 B0    NCDE FFE460    ROC-RB 00000000    NM IGG019CL   USE 02    EPA F37938    ATR2 20    XL/MJ FF7840
FFE460    ATR1 B8    NCDE FFE488    ROC-RB 00000000    NM IGG019AI   USE 03    EPA F67A90    ATR2 20    XL/MJ FFE478
```

SAVE AREA TRACE

GO   WAS ENTERED VIA LINK

```
SA  20EF68  WD1 00000000  HSA 00000000  LSA 001D1338  RET 00010F8A  EPA 011D0CF8  R0  00CCF150
            R1  0020EFF8   R2  00CCE790   R3  5CCCEAB8   R4  00CCF2E0   R5  00CCEEF0   R6  00CCEBB4
            R7  00CCF118   R8  00CCEA90   R9  00CCEC60   R10 00CCEAB8   R11 00000000   R12 40F582E2
```

GO   WAS ENTERED VIA CALL

```
SA  1D1338  WD1 0030C4C2  HSA 0020EF68  LSA 001D2798  RET 501D185C  EPA 001D26E8  R0  00CCE5F8
            R1  001D1588   R2  001D1740   R3  00000005   R4  001D0DE5   R5  001D19F8   R6  001D0D98
            R7  0020EA08   R8  001D12B0   R9  001D1B76   R10 001D0CF8   R11 001D0CF8   R12 001D15B8
```

GO   WAS ENTERED VIA CALL

```
SA  1D2798  WD1 0030C4C2  HSA 001D1338  LSA 0020EB48  RET 001D2B32  EPA 001D3D16  R0  001D2A7E
            R1  401D2B2E   R2  00000000   R3  00000004   R4  001D0DDB   R5  00000004   R6  001D2788
            R7  001D298F   R8  001D2990   R9  001D2CC2   R10 001D26E8   R11 001D26E8   R12 001D29E0
```

REGS AT ENTRY TO ABEND

```
FLTR 0-6   00000000000000000000  00000000000000000000  00000000000000000000  00000000000000000000

REGS 0-7    001D2C46  001D2A7E  00000000  00000000  00000004  00000005  001D2788  001D298F
REGS 8-15   001D2990  001D2CC2  001D26E8  001D29E0  001D2798  001D0DB8  001D0DB8  001D2AB8
```

FIGURE 7.21 Material for Problem 7

```
1D0CE0
1D0D00  4580F010 D4C1C9D5 D7D9D6C7 E5E2D9F1   0700989F F02407FF 90ECD00C 185D05F0   *...0.MAINPROGVSR1....0....0*
1D0D20  000107FE 001D1B76 001D0CF8 00000000   001D15B8 001D1694 96021034 07FE41F0   *........8...8........0*
1D0D40  00000000 00000000 00000000 00000000   00000000 000000C3 001D1338 001D1B36   *....................*
1D0D60  00000000 00000000 00000800 00000000   00C3FBE8 000000C3 00000000 00000000   *.............C.Y...C.C9H....*
1D0D80  F1F04BF0 F54BF4F3 D5D6E540 F2F66B40   F1F9FFF7 00000000 E6E240C2 C5C7C9D5   *10.05.43NOV 26. 1977...WS BEGIN*
1D0DA0  E240C8C5 D9C50006 D5D640E8 C5E2F3F0   C0002F98 00000390 E2D4C9E3 C86B40D1   *S HERE..NO YES30...SMITH.J*
1D0DC0  D6C8D540 40404043 F9F6F0F0   F0F4F6F6 C2F0FFF7 F7C2F0F8 F8F8C3F0 F9F9F9C3   *OHN 39600466B0777B0888C0999C*
1D0DE0  F0404040 40404040 40404040   E2C3D9C9 D7E34040 40000000 40404040            *0          TRANSCRIPT..*
1D0E00  40404040 40404040 E3D9C1D5   40404040 40404040 40404040 40404040            *                              *
1D0E20  40404040 40404040 40404040   40404040 40404040 40404040 40404040            *                              *
LINE 1D0E40 SAME AS ABOVE
1D0E60  40404040 40404040 40404040   40404040 40404040 40404040 40F0F1F5            *                              *
1D0E80  40D5C1D4 C57AC2C5 D5D1C1D4   D34040 40 40404040 4040 40D4C1 D1D6D97A 015     *.NAME.BENJAMIN. L        015*
1D0EA0  C2C9D6D3 D6C7E840 40404040   40404040 40404040 40404040 40404040            *BIOLOGY              MAJOR.*
1D0EC0  40404040 40404040 40404040   40404040 40404040 40404040 40404040            *                              *

       . . . . . . . . .

LINE 1D0F60 SAME AS ABOVE
1D0F80  40404040 40404040 40F59002   40404040 40404040 40404040 40F5F5F5            *            5..              555*
1D0FA0  40404040 40404040 40F34040   404040C2 40404040 40404040 40404040            *            3     B            *
1D0FC0  40404040 40404040 40404040   40404040 40404040 40404040 40404040            *                              *
LINE 1D0FE0 SAME AS ABOVE
1D1000  40404040 40404040 40404040   40404040 40404040 40404040 40404040            *                              *
1D1020  40404040 40404040 C1E5C5D9   40CCDDCC 40F34BF0 F0404040 40404040            *       AVERAGE. 3.00    ....  *
1D1040  40404040 40404040 40404040   40404040 40404040 40404040 40404040            *                              *
LINE 1D1060 SAME AS ABOVE
1D1080  40404040 40404040 40404040   40404040 40404040 40404040 40D6D7D4            *                         OPM*
1D10A0  F1F2F3F4 C1C3C3D6 E4D5E3C9   D5C7F1F4 F0F0C2C9 D6D3D6C7 E8404040 F1F9F7F6   *1234ACCOUNTING1400BIOLOGY 1976*
```

FIGURE 7.21 (Continued)

```
1D10C0  C3C8C5D4 C9E2E3D9 E840F2F1 F0F0C3C9   E5C9D340 C5D5C740 F2F4F5F8 C54B40C4   *CHEMISTRY 2100CIVIL ENG 2458E. D*
1D10E0  4B40D74B F2F4F5C3 F4F5C5C3 D6D5D6D4   C9C3E240 F3F9F6F0 C6C9D5C1 D5C3C540   *. P. 3245ECONOMICS 3960FINANCE *
1D1100  4040F4F3 F2F1D4C1 D5C1C7C5 D4C5D5E3   F4F9F9F9 D4C1D9D2 C5E3C9D5 C740F5F4   * 4321MANAGEMENT4999MARKETING 54*
1D1120  F0F0E2E3 C1E3C9E2 E3C9C3E2 C5C2C1E3   E6E240C5 D5C4E240 C8C5D9C5 87AE87B0   *00STATISTICSEBATWS ENDS HERE...*
1D1140  87B287B4 00000000 00000000 00000000   00000000 051D3C9A 051D0D1E 00000001   *................*

1D14C0  1000D49D 411E5B5C UU000000 00000000   5B5ED202 1000D49A 41EE5B61 001FA300   *...M............K..M..*
1D14E0  001D1852 601D3EBA 001D0CF8 000008A0   E2E8E2D6 E4E34040 E31F0008 001FA368   *...8.....8....SYSOUT T...*
1D1500  001DDD80 F322A7C3 D21595D5 001FA358   B3CA92D5 B3D0D200 0000300C 001FA368   *...3..CK.N....N....K...*
1D1520  D201A7CB 771596F0 A7CCD201 0020EA08   001D12B0 001D0D98 00000000 0000300C   *K....0..K........*
1D1540  0001400F F0F34BF0 F01FA398 00000000   00000000 00000000 001D0DE1 001D0DE5   *....03.00......V.*
1D1560  001DDDE4 001D1A08 001D1A88 001D1B30   00000000 001D0DE1 001D1B30 001D117C   *...U............*
1D1580  8F1D1230 D220D4B0 001D0DB8 801D0DAE   801D1A88 0AD00DB8 00000000 001D2EFA   *...K.M.........*
1D15A0  00000EF4 00000FBC 00000FBC 001D4672   F311D220 A7AC96F0 0AD00DFA 001D26E8   *...4....F..83.K...0....Y.*
1D15C0  001D3D12 001D4672 001D1820 001D1A08   001D3C9A 001D1CF2 001D4676 001D1B30   *.......8....K......0....2.*
1D15E0  001D41E2 001D1820 001D19F8 001D1A08   001D1A78 001D1A88 001D1B20 001D1B30   *..S.........8...........*
1D1600  001D1718 001D171E 001D172E 001D1740   001D1888 001D189A 001D18CC 001D1900   *................*

1D2900  00000000 00000000 00000000 00000000   00C8EAB0 000000A8 00000000 81D3F648   *..........P..H......L6.*
1D2920  00004FC0 01F5E430 00000000 000002D8   0000010C 00011EE0 14200003 05C8E200   *....5U.......Y....HS.*
1D2940  10000000 401D09E0 001D26E8 000002D8   001D2DA8 E2E8E2D6 E4E34040 E3000008   *......Q....SYSOUT T...*
1D2960  001D2770 00110000 00150005 18000E0C   00000000 00160001 18000E0C 00000000   *..............*
1D2980  00000000 00170000 00170001 001D2788   00000000 0000000F 00000000 0000000C   *............*
1D29A0  0A000059A 00000000 801D0DAE 001D0DB8   001D0DDF 001D0DDF 001D2C46 001D2C46   *...........H.U.HP*
1D29C0  0A000059A 00000000 001D2D30 001D2D99   001D2DA3 00C8DDE4 00C8D750 00000028   *.....H.U.HP...*
1D29E0  001D4672 001D2EFA 001D3D12 001D4672   001D3D16 001D2F0A 001D4676 001D2B28   *...............*
1D2A00  001D2C46 001D2A8A 001D2AAA 001D2A7E   001D2AB8 001D2B62 001D2B8E 001D2BBA   *...8..6.Y00.....*
1D2A20  001D2BE6 001D2AF8 001D2C46 F611DE8    F0F0F000 01000001 00000005 5840D004   *W..8...6.Y00......*
1D2A40  58404018 50504000 5050D214 58504004   5050D210 58F0C010 051F0000 002CD202   *....K....K.O...K.*
```

FIGURE 7.21 (Continued)

(25) Which data name *in the main program* contains the description of the invalid student record?

(26) Which base locator is associated with that data name?

(27) What is the displacement of the BL cells in the main program?

(28) Add the entry point address of the main program to the answer to part 27.

(29) What is contained at the four bytes beginning at the address found in part 28?

(30) What is the value of Base Locator 3?

(31) Which student had the invalid data? Identify his record in memory.

(e) Verify the solution using the BLL cells.

(32) Which data name in the subprogram contains the description of the invalid student record?

(33) Which Base Linkage Locator is associated with that data name?

(34) What is the displacement of the BLL cells in the subprogram?

(35) Add the Entry Point Address of the main program, plus the origin of the subprogram, plus the answer from question 34.

(36) What is contained at the 4 bytes beginning at the address found in part 35?

(37) What is the value of Base Linkage Locator 4?

(38) What is the relationship between the answers in questions 30 and 37?

(f) Using the SAVE AREA TRACE:

(39) What are the linkage conventions for registers 14 and 15?

(40) What is the entry point in the main program?

(41) What return address is specified in the first called program in the save area trace?

(42) Subtract the address in step 40 from that in step 41. Examine the assembler instruction in the main program immediately before this one and explain its significance.

Additional Exercises may be found in Appendix C, pages 323–345, which contains a COBOL program, two subprograms, a dump, and associated compiler aids (PMAPs, DMAPs, etc.). The appendix also provides a series of leading questions similar to those of problem 7. The reader may also be interested in Section VII of *A COBOL Book of Practice and Reference* by Robert Grauer (Prentice-Hall, 1981) for four additional problems.

8

ABEND Debugging
Without Dumps

Overview

The subtraction technique of finding the next sequential instruction, illustrated in Chapter 7, works in only a limited number of instances—i.e., when the instruction causing the problem is contained *within* the COBOL program. As likely as not, an ABEND occurs during execution of a routine entirely *outside* the COBOL program (e.g., during an I/O operation). Recall, for example, the large number of IBM-supplied routines contained in the linkage-editor map of Figure 7.13. Although the applications programmer has not written these modules, he or she is responsible for debugging problems in their use.

OS accomplishes the I/O function by monitoring a set of tables, directories, lists, queues, and so on, which control execution of the COBOL program. These items are collectively known as *control blocks*, and their net effect is to provide a complete description of the current program. They are displayed in the first few pages of a dump and are routinely avoided.

Most applications programmers know little about these control blocks other than the fact they exist. This is *not* a handicap in debugging if the ABEND is contained within the COBOL program (e.g., an 0C7). It may not even pose a problem when debugging data management ABENDs (i.e., errors in an I/O module), for the MVS operating system provides fairly lucid error messages. (This is in distinct contrast to earlier versions of OS, which contained more cryptic messages and which demanded more intimate knowledge of the system.)

DATA MANAGEMENT ABENDS

Data Management ABENDs occur when there is a conflict between a user's request for service and a data management routine. These errors are particularly irksome to the COBOL programmer because the problem is usually due to the data files provided, rather than to the program itself. Regardless of the reason, the competent individual *must* be able to resolve these errors. A knowledge of JCL and an ability to interpret the system messages are essential.

Figure 8.1 contains a COBOL listing which is used for the examples

```
00001          IDENTIFICATION DIVISION.
00002          PROGRAM-ID.        TWOFILES.
00003          AUTHOR.            R. GRAUER.
00004
00005          ENVIRONMENT DIVISION.
00006          CONFIGURATION SECTION.
00007          SOURCE-COMPUTER.   IBM-4341.
00008          OBJECT-COMPUTER.   IBM-4341.
00009
00010          INPUT-OUTPUT SECTION.
00011          FILE-CONTROL.
00012              SELECT INPUT-FILE-ONE ASSIGN TO UT-S-FILEONE.
00013              SELECT INPUT-FILE-TWO ASSIGN TO UT-S-FILETWO.
00014              SELECT MERGED-FILE    ASSIGN TO UT-S-MERGED.
00015
00016          DATA DIVISION.                          DDname of output file
00017          FILE SECTION.
00018          FD  INPUT-FILE-ONE
00019              LABEL RECORDS ARE STANDARD
00020              BLOCK CONTAINS 0 RECORDS
00021              RECORD CONTAINS 80 CHARACTERS
00022              DATA RECORD IS INPUT-RECORD-ONE.
00023
00024          01  INPUT-RECORD-ONE          PIC X(80).
00025
00026          FD  INPUT-FILE-TWO
00027              LABEL RECORDS ARE STANDARD
00028              BLOCK CONTAINS 0 RECORDS
00029              RECORD CONTAINS 80 CHARACTERS
00030              DATA RECORD IS INPUT-RECORD-TWO.
00031
00032          01  INPUT-RECORD-TWO          PIC X(80).
00033
```

FIGURE 8.1 Two-File Merge

```
00034          FD   MERGED-FILE
00035               LABEL RECORDS ARE STANDARD      ┌── Indicates blocksize will
00036               BLOCK CONTAINS 0 RECORDS        │   be entered in JCL
00037               RECORD CONTAINS 80 CHARACTERS
00038               DATA RECORD IS MERGED-RECORD.
00039
00040          01   MERGED-RECORD                   PIC X(80).
00041
00042          WORKING-STORAGE SECTION.
00043          01   FILLER                          PIC X(18)
00044               VALUE '* WS BEGINS HERE *'.
00045
00046          01   WS-INPUT-RECORD-ONE.
00047               05   FILLER                     PIC X(9).
00048               05   INPUT-ONE-ID               PIC X(9).
00049               05   INPUT-ONE-NAME             PIC X(20).
00050               05   INPUT-ONE-SALARY           PIC 9(6).
00051               05   INPUT-ONE-DEPARTMENT       PIC 9(4).
00052               05   INPUT-ONE-LOCATION         PIC X(10).
00053               05   FILLER                     PIC X(22).
00054
00055          01   WS-INPUT-RECORD-TWO.
00056               05   FILLER                     PIC X(9).
00057               05   INPUT-TWO-ID               PIC X(9).
00058               05   INPUT-TWO-NAME             PIC X(20).
00059               05   INPUT-TWO-SALARY           PIC 9(6).
00060               05   INPUT-TWO-DEPARTMENT       PIC 9(4).
00061               05   INPUT-TWO-LOCATION         PIC X(10).
00062               05   FILLER                     PIC X(22).
00063
00064          PROCEDURE DIVISION.
00065          005-MAINLINE.
00066               OPEN INPUT  INPUT-FILE-ONE
00067                           INPUT-FILE-TWO
00068                    OUTPUT MERGED-FILE.
00069               PERFORM 015-READ-FIRST-FILE.
00070               PERFORM 020-READ-SECOND-FILE.
00071               PERFORM 010-PROCESS-FILES
00072                    UNTIL INPUT-ONE-ID = HIGH-VALUES
00073                         AND INPUT-TWO-ID = HIGH-VALUES.
00074               CLOSE INPUT-FILE-ONE
00075                     INPUT-FILE-TWO
00076                     MERGED-FILE.
00077               STOP RUN.
00078
00079          010-PROCESS-FILES.
00080               IF INPUT-ONE-ID LESS THAN INPUT-TWO-ID
00081                    WRITE MERGED-RECORD FROM INPUT-RECORD-ONE
00082                    PERFORM 015-READ-FIRST-FILE
00083               ELSE
00084                    IF INPUT-TWO-ID LESS THAN INPUT-ONE-ID
00085                         WRITE MERGED-RECORD FROM INPUT-RECORD-TWO
00086                         PERFORM 020-READ-SECOND-FILE
00087                    ELSE
00088                         DISPLAY 'DUPLICATE IDS ' INPUT-ONE-ID
00089                         PERFORM 015-READ-FIRST-FILE
00090                         PERFORM 020-READ-SECOND-FILE.
00091
00092          015-READ-FIRST-FILE.
00093               READ INPUT-FILE-ONE INTO WS-INPUT-RECORD-ONE
00094                    AT END MOVE HIGH-VALUES TO INPUT-ONE-ID.
00095
00096          020-READ-SECOND-FILE.
00097               READ INPUT-FILE-TWO INTO WS-INPUT-RECORD-TWO
00098                    AT END MOVE HIGH-VALUES TO INPUT-TWO-ID.
```

FIGURE 8.1 (Continued)

in this chapter. The specifications call for two input files to be merged into a single output file. Both input files are assumed to be in sequence. However, if the same ID number appears on both files, a warning message should be issued, and neither record is to appear on the merged file.

The simplicity of the Procedure Division of Figure 8.1 is an elegant argument for structured programming. The program is driven by the nested IF statement of lines 80-90. Of equal importance, the logic is correct for all combinations of test data—e.g., if file one runs out of data first, or if file two runs out of data first, or if the files become empty simultaneously.

The program of Figure 8.1 failed on its initial attempt at execution. Figures 8.2a and 8.2b contain the execution JCL and associated JES messages, respectively. The ABEND was accompanied by a lengthy dump, but the error can be resolved by using Figure 8.2 exclusively. That is precisely the point of this chapter, namely *how to debug a data management ABEND without resorting to the associated dump.*

013-34 ABEND

The JES output in Figure 8.2b contains an error message, IEC141I, and an associated completion code, 013-34. The vendor manual, *OS/VS Message*

```
//JSC$3693      JOB (MAS526),JACKIE
//STEP1         EXEC PGM=IEBGENER
//SYSPRINT      DD SYSOUT=R
//SYSIN         DD DUMMY
//SYSUT2        DD DSN=&&FILEONE,DISP=(NEW,PASS),UNIT=SYSDA,
//              DCB=(LRECL=80,BLKSIZE=640,RECFM=FB),SPACE=(TRK,(1,1))
//SYSUT1        DD *
//STEP2         EXEC PGM=IEBGENER
//SYSPRINT      DD SYSOUT=R
//SYSIN         DD DUMMY
//SYSUT2        DD DSN=&&FILETWO,DISP=(NEW,PASS),UNIT=SYSDA,
//              DCB=(LRECL=80,BLKSIZE=640,RECFM=FB),SPACE=(TRK,(1,1))
//SYSUT1        DD *
//STEP3         EXEC COBVCLG
//COB.SYSLIB    DD DSN=MEN.PGM.JSC.RTG,DISP=SHR
//COB.SYSIN     DD DSN=MEN.PGM.JSC.RTG(TWOFILES),DISP=SHR
//GO.FILEONE    DD DSN=&&FILEONE,DISP=(OLD,PASS)
//GO.FILETWO    DD DSN=&&FILETWO,DISP=(OLD,PASS)
//GO.MERGED     DD DSN=&&MERGED,DISP=(NEW,PASS),UNIT=SYSDA,
//              DCB=(LRECL=80,RECFM=FB),SPACE=(TRK,(1))
//GO.SYSUDUMP   DD SYSOUT=R
```
          └─ DCB parameter omitted BLKSIZE information

FIGURE 8.2a Execution JCL (013-34)

```
17.23.57 JOB 1839    $HASP373 JSC$3693 STARTED - INIT 2 - CLASS A - SYS IPO1
17.24.23 JOB 1839    IEC141I 013-34,IGG0191A,JSC$3693,GO,MERGED,111,UMF111,
17.24.23 JOB 1839    IEC141I SYS83015.T172356.RA000.JSC$3693.MERGED
17.24.28 JOB 1839    IEF450I JSC$3693 GO STEP3 - ABEND S013 U0000 - TIME=17.24.27
17.24.29 JOB 1839    $HASP395 JSC$3693 ENDED
```
          └─ Error message indicates DDname of problem file

FIGURE 8.2b JES Messages (013-34)

Library VS2 System Codes, (*GC38 1008-6*), describes the problem as follows:

> *The error occurred during execution of an OPEN macro instruction. In the message text 013-rc associates this message with system completion code 013 and with return code rc.*

Reading further, a return code of 34 indicates that the *blocksize was not allocated*. This is the technical reason for the ABEND, and it has to be related to the program at hand. The JES output displays the job step and DDname where the problem occurred as GO and MERGED, respectively. The SELECT statement in Figure 8.1 ties the DDname MERGED to the programmer chosen file name MERGED-FILE.

MERGED-FILE is an output file, as indicated by the OPEN statement of lines 66-68. Its FD contained the clause, BLOCK CONTAINS 0 RECORDS (line 36), implying that the blocksize will be entered in the JCL at execution time. However, the DCB parameter of Figure 8.2*a* did not include the BLKSIZE subparameter. In other words, the system was told to allocate buffers, but was never provided with the buffer length. The solution is to include the BLKSIZE parameter in the execution JCL.

Note well that this ABEND was solved *without* reference to the dump. This does *not* mean that knowledge of dumps is unimportant, but rather less important than it once was. The ability to analyze system output should be regarded as another tool in the arsenal of the debugger. A quick solution was obtained only because of the preciseness of the system messages which identified the problem file.

013-20 ABEND

The COBOL program of Figure 8.1 was rerun with the jobstream of Figure 8.3*a*, producing the error message in Figure 8.3*b*. The error message and completion code are the same as previously, IEC141I and 013 respectively, but the *return code* is different. The vendor manual indicates that an 013-20 is attributable to:

> *An OPEN macro instruction was issued for a sequential data set, . . . but BLKSIZE is not a multiple of LRECL.*

In other words, the program ABENDed because of an unsuccessful OPEN for the file with DDname, MERGED, specifically a DCB conflict involving blocksize. The DD statement, GO.MERGED specified a blocksize of 600 which conflicts with the logical record length of 80. Hence the problem and solution; change the BLKSIZE parameter to a multiple of 80; e.g., 640.

```
1       //JSC$3691 JOB (MAS526),JACKIE
2       //STEP1         EXEC PGM=IEBGENER
3       //SYSPRINT      DD SYSOUT=R
4       //SYSIN         DD DUMMY
5       //SYSUT2        DD DSN=&&FILEONE,DISP=(NEW,PASS),UNIT=SYSDA,
        //              DCB=(LRECL=80,BLKSIZE=640,RECFM=FB),SPACE=(TRK,(1,1))
6       //SYSUT1        DD *
7       //STEP2         EXEC PGM=IEBGENER
8       //SYSPRINT      DD SYSOUT=R
9       //SYSIN         DD DUMMY
10      //SYSUT2        DD DSN=&&FILETWO,DISP=(NEW,PASS),UNIT=SYSDA,
        //              DCB=(LRECL=80,BLKSIZE=640,RECFM=FB),SPACE=(TRK,(1,1))
11      //SYSUT1        DD *
12      //STEP3         EXEC COBVCLG
13      XXCOBVCLG PROC OUT=R
14      XXCOB EXEC PGM=IKFCBL00,PARM=(LOAD,SUPMAP,LIB,'LINECNT=60',
        XX            'SXREF','PMAP','DMAP','STATE','FLOW=10','NOSEQ',
        XX            'BUF=63922','SIZE=217088')
15      XXSTEPLIB      DD DSN=SYS2.LINKLIB,DISP=SHR
16      XX             DD DSN=SYS1.COBLIB,DISP=SHR
17      XXSYSPRINT DD SYSOUT=&OUT
18      XXSYSPUNCH DD DUMMY
19      //COB.SYSLIB    DD DSN=MEN.PGM.JSC.RTG,DISP=SHR
        X/SYSLIB       DD DUMMY
20      XXSYSUT1       DD UNIT=3350,SPACE=(1024,(120,120)),DSN=&&SYSUT1
21      XXSYSUT2       DD UNIT=3350,SPACE=(1024,(120,120)),DSN=&&SYSUT2
22      XXSYSUT3       DD UNIT=3350,SPACE=(1024,(120,120)),DSN=&&SYSUT3
23      XXSYSUT4       DD UNIT=3350,SPACE=(1024,(120,120)),DSN=&&SYSUT4
24      XXSYSUT5       DD UNIT=3350,SPACE=(1024,(120,120)),DSN=&&SYSUT5
25      XXSYSLIN       DD DSN=&&OBJ,DISP=(MOD,PASS),UNIT=3350,
        XX             SPACE=(3040,(40,40)),
        XX             DCB=(BLKSIZE=3040,LRECL=80,RECFM=FBS,BUFNO=1)
26      //COB.SYSIN    DD DSN=MEN.PGM.JSC.RTG(TWOFILES),DISP=SHR
27      XXLKED EXEC PGM=HEWL,PARM='LIST,XREF,LET,MAP',COND=(5,LT,COB)
28      XXSYSLIN       DD DSN=&&OBJ,DISP=(OLD,DELETE)
29      XXSYSLMOD      DD DSN=&&LOD(X),DISP=(,PASS),UNIT=3350,DCB=BUFNO=1,
        XX             SPACE=(CYL,(1,1,1))
30      XXSYSLIB       DD DSN=SYS1.COBLIB,DISP=SHR
31      XXSYSUT1       DD UNIT=3350,SPACE=(1024,(120,120)),DCB=BUFNO=1,
        XX             DSN=&&SYSUT1
32      XXSYSPRINT DD SYSOUT=&OUT
33      XXGO EXEC PGM=*.LKED.SYSLMOD,COND=((5,LT,COB),(5,LT,LKED))
34      XXSTEPLIB      DD DSN=SYS1.COBLIB,DISP=SHR
35      XXSYSOUT       DD SYSOUT=&OUT
36      XXSYSOUC       DD SYSOUT=&OUT
37      XXSYSCOUNT     DD SYSOUT=&OUT
38      XXSYSDBOUT DD SYSOUT=&OUT
39      //GO.FILEONE    DD DSN=&&FILEONE,DISP=(OLD,PASS)
40      //GO.FILETWO    DD DSN=&&FILETWO,DISP=(OLD,PASS)
41      //GO.MERGED     DD DSN=&&MERGED,DISP=(NEW,PASS),UNIT=SYSDA,
        //              DCB=(LRECL=80,BLKSIZE=600,RECFM=FB),SPACE=(TRK,(1))
42      //GO.SYSUDUMP DD SYSOUT=R
```

└─ Blocksize is not a multiple of record length

FIGURE 8.3a Execution JCL (013-20)

```
17.44.32 JOB 2194  $HASP373 JSC$3691 STARTED - INIT  1 - CLASS A - SYS IP01
17.44.55 JOB 2194  IEC141I 013-20,IGG0191A,JSC$3691,GO,MERGED,111,UMF111,
17.44.55 JOB 2194  IEC141I SYS83017.T174432.RA000.JSC$3691.MERGED
17.44.58 JOB 2194  IEF450I JSC$3691 GO STEP3 - ABEND S013 U0000
17.44.59 JOB 2194  $HASP395 JSC$3691 ENDED
```

└─ Error message indicates DDname of problem file

FIGURE 8.3b JES Messages (013-20)

209

As with the previous example, the ABEND was corrected *without* referring to the dump, and in this case with no real reference even to the COBOL program. The process can be just as simple in practice *if one approaches problems with a positive mental attitude and an open mind.*

001-4 ABEND

Figure 8.4 contains the third, and last, attempt at executing the COBOL program of Figure 8.1. As can be seen from Figure 8.4*a*, temporary data sets are created in steps one and two for use as test files. The system messages in Figure 8.5 indicate that these steps executed successfully (Figure 8.5 is included to remind the reader that the system messages contain a wealth of information. See, for example, parts (g) through (r) of problem 4.) The COBOL program compiled and linked cleanly, but ABENDed in the GO

```
//JSC$3720      JOB (MAS526),JACKIE
//STEP1         EXEC PGM=IEBGENER
//SYSPRINT      DD SYSOUT=R
//SYSIN         DD DUMMY
//SYSUT2        DD DSN=&&FILEONE,DISP=(NEW,PASS),UNIT=SYSDA,
//              DCB=(LRECL=80,BLKSIZE=640,RECFM=FB),SPACE=(TRK,(1,1))
//SYSUT1        DD *
//STEP2         EXEC PGM=IEBGENER
//SYSPRINT      DD SYSOUT=R
//SYSIN         DD DUMMY
//SYSUT2        DD DSN=&&FILETWO,DISP=(NEW,PASS),UNIT=SYSDA,
//              DCB=(LRECL=80,BLKSIZE=640,RECFM=FB),SPACE=(TRK,(1,1))
//SYSUT1        DD *
//STEP3         EXEC COBVCLG
//COB.SYSLIB    DD DSN=MEN.PGM.JSC.RTG,DISP=SHR
//COB.SYSIN     DD DSN=MEN.PGM.JSC.RTG(TWOFILES),DISP=SHR
//GO.FILEONE    DD DSN=&&FILEONE,DISP=(OLD,PASS),UNIT=SYSDA,
//              DCB=(LRECL=80,BLKSIZE=640,RECFM=FB),SPACE=(TRK,(1,1))
//GO.FILETWO    DD DSN=&&FILETWO,DISP=(OLD,PASS),UNIT=SYSDA,
//              DCB=(LRECL=80,BLKSIZE=240,RECFM=FB),SPACE=(TRK,(1,1))
//GO.MERGED     DD DSN=&&MERGED,DISP=(NEW,PASS),UNIT=SYSDA,
//              DCB=(LRECL=80,BLKSIZE=640,RECFM=FB),SPACE=(TRK,(1))
//GO.SYSUDUMP   DD SYSOUT=R
```

└─DDname of problem file

FIGURE 8.4*a* Execution JCL (001-4)

```
17.52.53 JOB 2195   $HASP373 JSC$3720 STARTED - INIT  1 - CLASS A - SYS IP01
17.53.16 JOB 2195   IEC020I 001-4,JSC$3720,GO,FILETWO,135,UMF135,
17.53.16 JOB 2195   IEC020I SYS83017.T175253.RA000.JSC$3720.FILETWO
17.53.16 JOB 2195   IEC020I DCB EROPT=ABE OR AN INVALID CODE, AND/OR NO SYNAD EXIT SPECIFIED
17.53.20 JOB 2195   IEF450I JSC$3720 GO STEP3 - ABEND S001 U0000
17.53.21 JOB 2195   $HASP395 JSC$3720 ENDED
```

└─Error message indicates DDname of problem file

FIGURE 8.4*b* JES Messages (001-4)

```
IEF236I ALLOC. FOR JSC$3720 STEP1
IEF237I JES2 ALLOCATED TO SYSPRINT
IEF237I DMY   ALLOCATED TO SYSIN
IEF237I 135   ALLOCATED TO SYSUT2                    Step 1 executed cleanly
IEF237I JES2 ALLOCATED TO SYSUT1
IEF142I JSC$3720 STEP1 - STEP WAS EXECUTED - COND CODE 0000
IEF285I    JES2.JOB02195.S00103                          SYSOUT
IEF285I    SYS83017.T175253.RA000.JSC$3720.FILEONE        PASSED
IEF285I    VOL SER NOS= UMF135.
IEF285I    JES2.JOB02195.SI0101                           SYSIN
IEF373I STEP /STEP1    / START 83017.1752
IEF374I STEP /STEP1    / STOP 83017.1752 CPU    0MIN 00.20SEC SRB
IEF236I ALLOC. FOR JSC$3720 STEP2
IEF237I JES2 ALLOCATED TO SYSPRINT
IEF237I DMY   ALLOCATED TO SYSIN
IEF237I 135   ALLOCATED TO SYSUT2                    Step 2 executed cleanly
IEF237I JES2 ALLOCATED TO SYSUT1
IEF142I JSC$3720 STEP2 - STEP WAS EXECUTED - COND CODE 0000
IEF285I    JES2.JOB02195.S00104                          SYSOUT
IEF285I    SYS83017.T175253.RA000.JSC$3720.FILETWO        PASSED
IEF285I    VOL SER NOS= UMF135.
IEF285I    JES2.JOB02195.SI0102                           SYSIN
IEF373I STEP /STEP2    / START 83017.1752
IEF374I STEP /STEP2    / STOP 83017.1752 CPU    0MIN 00.19SEC SRB

  ⋱                                                 Compile executed cleanly
IEF237I 113   ALLOCATED TO SYSIN
IEF142I JSC$3720 COB STEP3 - STEP WAS EXECUTED - COND CODE 0000
IEF285I    SYS2.LINKLIB                                   KEPT
IEF285I    VOL SER NOS= UMF133.
IEF285I    SYS1.COBLIB                                    KEPT
IEF285I    VOL SER NOS= UMF133.

  ⋱
IEF373I STEP /COB     / START 83017.1752
IEF374I STEP /COB     / STOP 83017.1753 CPU    0MIN 01.96SEC SRB
IEF236I ALLOC. FOR JSC$3720 LKED STEP3
IEF237I 133   ALLOCATED TO SYSLIN
IEF237I 135   ALLOCATED TO SYSLMOD
IEF237I 133   ALLOCATED TO SYSLIB
IEF237I 131   ALLOCATED TO SYSUT1                    Link-edit executed cleanly
IEF237I JES2 ALLOCATED TO SYSPRINT
IEF142I JSC$3720 LKED STEP3 - STEP WAS EXECUTED - COND CODE 0000
IEF285I    SYS83017.T175253.RA000.JSC$3720.OBJ            DELETED
IEF285I    VOL SER NOS= UMF133.
IEF285I    SYS83017.T175253.RA000.JSC$3720.LOD            PASSED
IEF285I    VOL SER NOS= UMF135.

  ⋱
IEF237I 135   ALLOCATED TO FILEONE
IEF237I 135   ALLOCATED TO FILETWO
IEF237I 111   ALLOCATED TO MERGED            Cause of ABEND
IEF237I JES2 ALLOCATED TO SYSUDUMP
IEC020I 001-4,JSC$3720,GO,FILETWO,135,UMF135,
IEC020I SYS83017.T175253.RA000.JSC$3720.FILETWO
IEC020I DCB EROPT=ABE OR AN INVALID CODE, AND/OR NO SYNAD EXIT SPECIFIED
IEF472I JSC$3720 GO STEP3 - COMPLETION CODE - SYSTEM=001 USER=0000
IEF285I    SYS83017.T175253.RA000.JSC$3720.LOD            KEPT
IEF285I    VOL SER NOS= UMF135.
```

FIGURE 8.5 Partial System Output

step. The error message, IEC020I, and completion code, 001-4, are explained as follows:

Invalid value for EROPT parameter in the DCB and/or no error handling exit specified

Further analysis of the error messages pinpoints the problem DDname as FILETWO, which ties to INPUT-FILE-TWO in the COBOL program. In other words, there is a DCB conflict associated with this file, due perhaps to a wrong-length physical record.

Execution of IEBGENER in STEP2 of the execution JCL created the temporary data set &&FILETWO, with DCB characteristics of LRECL=80 and BLKSIZE=640. The associated DD statement in the GO step had corresponding values of 80 and 240 respectively. The ABEND was due to the fact that the blocksize specified with the COBOL program was too small to accommodate the actual file.

Many other ABENDs can be debugged as simply as the three in this chapter. Although space restrictions do not permit additional examples, we do include a list of common ABENDs as a reference.

COMMON ABENDS

This section contains a series of common ABENDs, with possible causes. The list is by no means complete, nor is it the last word on debugging. Numerous codes have been omitted, as well as reasons for ABENDing within a given code. The author does hope, however, that the list provides a useful starting place.

0C1:   Operation exception (i.e., an invalid operation code). Figure 6.7 on instruction formats shows that the first byte of any instruction is its op code. An operation exception results if this byte is unknown to the system.

Common causes:
1. A missing (or misspelled) DD statement (missing DD statements can sometimes be caused by an inadvertent duplication of an EXEC statement, where the duplicated statement would have no DD statements)
2. Attempting to read from a data set that has not been opened (e.g., a misplaced OPEN statement)
3. A subscript or index error which caused a portion of code to be overlaid, resulting in an attempt to "execute" data

Corrective action:

1. A very low address for the interrupt indicates that the error occurred in a data management routine rather than in the COBOL program per se. Check the JCL messages carefully for indication of missing DD statements.
2. If the JCL messages are not helpful, register 2 plus hex 28 should point to the TIOT offset of the DDname in question.
3. If the interrupt address is within the program (or close to it), chances are the 0C1 was caused by a subscript (or index) problem. A careful review of program logic is called for with particular attention to any routines which fill tables.

0C4: Protection exception—attempting to overwrite a protected area in storage.

Common causes:

1. Invalid subscript or index
2. Inclusion of a STOP RUN statement in the INPUT or OUTPUT PROCEDURE of the SORT verb.
3. Missing or misspelled DD statement
4. Block size and record size specified as equal in a variable length file

Corrective action:

1. An interrupt at a low address indicates a missing DD statement or attempt to read an unopened file.
2. If the interrupt is within the COBOL program, it is probably a subscript (index) error. A *thorough* review of program logic is required. Subscript errors are often the most difficult to find.

0C5: Addressing exception—an address has been calculated outside the bounds of available storage.

Common causes:

1. Invalid subscript or index
2. Attempting to close an already closed file
3. An attempt to reference an I/O area before READ or OPEN was issued
4. Improper exit from a performed routine. Remember that GO TO out of a PERFORM is strictly prohibited.

5. Invoking a subprogram with a Linkage Section but with no associated USING clause, or too few parameters, or parameters listed in the wrong order

Corrective action:

1. Review program logic to determine if a subscript error exists.
2. Register 1 contains the DCB address of the last referenced file. Register 14 should contain the next sequential instruction in the COBOL program.

0C6:   Specification exception—an address was generated which does not fall on the proper boundary.

Common causes:

1. Invalid subscript or index
2. Incorrect or missing DD statement
3. Improper exit from a performed routine. Remember that GO TO out of a PERFORM is strictly prohibited.

Corrective action:

1. Register 2 contains the DCB address of the last file referenced prior to the ABEND.
2. Review program logic to determine if a subscript error exists.

0C7:   Data exception (i.e., invalid "decimal" data). This error can result only after attempted execution of an instruction to process packed data. Specifically, the sign or digits of an operand in a decimal arithmetic, editing, or CVB instruction are invalid.

Common causes:

1. Failure to initialize a counter
2. Invalid incoming data (e.g., blanks, decimal points, or commas in a numeric field)
3. Exceeding a table via a subscript (index) error, causing a reference to invalid data. This can also result in an 0C4, 0C5, or 0C6.
4. Moving zeros or LOW-VALUES to a group field defined as numeric. (See Figure 6.4.)
5. An omitted or erroneous USAGE clause
6. Passing parameters between programs in the wrong order

Corrective action:

1. The subtraction technique of Chapter 7, or the STATE option will identify the COBOL statement causing the ABEND. The error may be immediately obvious, as in the case of an uninitialized counter or erroneous USAGE clause. If not, a check of the program's logic is necessary to determine if invalid data are referenced.
2. Register 2 will point to the DCB for the last referenced file.

0CB: Decimal Divide Exception (division by zero). This error results from attempted execution of a DP (Divide Packed) Assembler instruction where the divisor is zero.

Common causes:

1. A COBOL DIVIDE or COMPUTE statement has a divisor of zero. (See Chapter 7, Problem 7.)

Corrective action:

1. The STATE option can identify the COBOL statement in error. Review program logic to determine how the divisor is calculated.

001: An incorrectable input/output error which is sometimes attributable to DCB conflicts

Common causes:

1. Attempting to read from a file after the AT END condition has been encountered
2. A device malfunction, or a damaged (dirty) tape or disk
3. Wrong-length record of physical block

Corrective action:

1. Check the JCL messages for an indication of the file in question.
2. Register 2 points to the DCB.

013: Unsuccessful attempt to OPEN a file, usually due to a DCB conflict. An error message will appear in the JCL to indicate the exact nature of the error. The return code mentioned in the error message specifies the error.

Common causes (with return codes):

1. 18—System was unable to find specified member of a partitioned data set.

2. 20—BLKSIZE is not a multiple of LRECL.
3. 34—BLKSIZE not specified; the system knows it has to allocate buffers, but is unable to do so.
4. 60—BLKSIZE is not equal to LRECL for unblocked (i.e., RECFM = F) records.
5. 68—BLKSIZE specified as greater than 32,767.

Corrective action:

1. Check the JCL messages to determine the file in question. Look for any immediately obvious inconsistencies.
2. Register 2 contains the DCB address of the file in question. Use the table of DCB offsets to determine DCB information.

122:    Job canceled by operator for unspecified reason

Common causes:

1. Program in an apparent loop
2. Program is producing an "abnormal" number of error messages.
3. Program requested an unavailable resource
4. A "panic" job required immediate processing and needed resources assigned to your job.
5. A mistake on the part of operations

Corrective action:

1. It is definitely possible that nothing is wrong with your job. Accordingly, find out why the operator canceled. Make the necessary corrections and resubmit.

213:    An error in opening a file on a direct access device. Specifically, the system cannot locate the data set specified in the DSNAME parameter.

Common causes:

1. The DSNAME parameter is misspelled.
2. The wrong volume was specified.
3. The data set no longer exists because it was accidentally scratched.
4. The DISP parameter specified OLD or SHR for an output data set.

Corrective action:

1. Register 2 contains the DCB address. Add hex 28 to locate the two-byte TIOT offset. Determine the DDname from the TIOT offset.

2. Register 4 plus hex 64 contains the DSNAME as specified in the JCL.

3. Register 4 plus hex DA contains the volume serial number as specified in the JCL or catalog.

322:     CPU time limit for a step or job was exceeded.

Common causes:

1. An error in program logic causing an endless loop
2. A switch to a slower CPU
3. A switch to a different operating system
4. The time requested was insufficient.

Corrective action:

1. Check to see if a slower CPU was used. This can happen in large shops with multiple CPU's where for some reason your job was switched to a different CPU.

2. Review program logic to ensure that no endless loops are present. Structured programs will not contain 'traditional' loops—i.e., those induced by backward GO TO statements. However, they can well contain problems brought about by improper setting (resetting) of switches. Some advice: do *not* use the same switch for more than one purpose, and do use meaningful names— e.g., TRANSACTION-FILE-SWITCH as opposed to SWITCH-1.

3. The subtraction technique can be used to determine the next sequential instruction. This may be useful in determining the endless loop if one exists.

4. The READY TRACE statement and/or FLOW option may be useful in identifying the loop. Use of READY TRACE should be carefully controlled with ON and RESET TRACE statements to avoid use of needless volumes of paper.

513:     An attempt was made to open more than one data set on the same tape volume.

Common causes:

1. Attempting to open a second file before closing the first
2. Assignment of two data sets to the same tape device
3. Transferring data sets from direct access devices which may have more than one data set open simultaneously

Corrective action:

1. This type of error may be easily corrected at the source level. Examine all OPEN and associated CLOSE statements to determine where the problem exists.
2. The JCL allocation messages can also be studied to determine which devices are used for which files.
3. Register 2 contains the address of the DCB in question.

80A, 804: More storage was requested than is currently available in the region.

Common causes:

1. The REGION parameter was omitted and the installation's default is too small.
2. The REGION parameter on the JOB or EXEC statement did not specify sufficient storage. Realize that if REGION is specified on the JOB card, it *overrides* any subsequent specification on EXEC cards (i.e., the REGION parameter of EXEC statements is ignored).
3. Blocking factors were increased without corresponding increase in REGION parameter.

Corrective action:

1. Review JCL to ensure that REGION parameters are not omitted and/or overridden.

806: A requested program could not be found.

Common causes:

1. Missing JOBLIB or STEPLIB statements
2. Misspelled module name

Corrective action:

1. The system messages will typically contain the module name. (A list of commonly called I/O subroutines and their functions can be found in the programmer's guide by looking under ILB subroutines in the index.)
2. The address in register 12 plus 4 may point to the missing module.
3. Register 15 will contain 00000004 if the requested module could not be found in the private, job, or link library. It will contain 00000008 if an I/O error occurred in searching the directory of the indicated libraries.

813:   An error in label processing for tape. Specifically, the data set name on the header label does not match the specification in the JCL.

Common causes:

1. The DSNAME parameter is misspelled.
2. The wrong volume was called for and mounted.
3. The data set no longer exists.

Corrective action:

1. Add 64 to the address contained in register 4 to determine the DSNAME parameter in storage obtained from the DD statement.
2. Add 4 to the address contained in register 4 to determine the data set name as it appears on the header label. Attempt to resolve the conflict between this and the JCL entry from step 1. If more than a misspelling, a review of file logs, etc., is probably called for.

B37, D37, E37:   Space problems; insufficient space available for an output data set

Common causes:

1. An infinite loop containing a WRITE statement
2. The space requested was insufficient. This may happen if a secondary allocation was not specified in the SPACE parameter, or, if specified, it was not large enough to accommodate the data set.
3. Sufficient space was requested but was not available on the volume specified.

Corrective action:

1. The possibility of an infinite loop should be eliminated through review of program logic.
2. Check the SPACE parameter for a secondary allocation on the file in question. Register 2 plus hex 28 will supply the TIOT offset from where the DDname can be determined.
3. The DCB/DEB relationship can be used to determine the number of extents (i.e., secondary allocations) actually made. Register 2 plus hex 2D contains the DEB address of the file in question. The first byte of the fifth word in the DEB contains the number of extents used. If this value is less than 15, the system did not have sufficient space.

Summary ▬▬▬▬▬▬▬▬▬▬▬▬▬▬▬▬▬▬▬▬

The chapter discussed data management ABENDs. These errors occur *outside* the COBOL program where the simple subtraction technique of Chapter 7 is inapplicable. Accordingly, the execution JCL and associated system messages were used as the primary means of debugging—hence the chapter title "ABEND Debugging *Without* Dumps." The chapter concluded with a list of the most common ABENDs, reasons for their occurrences, and suggestions for their resolution.

Regardless of which technique you choose, *a dump reveals only the technical reason for the ABEND; the programmer must still relate this information to the source program and/or data.* Some individuals prefer to debug at the source level, others use dumps extensively, and most switch back and forth between the two. Either way, approach debugging with an open mind; suspect everything and eliminate nothing. The most difficult task is to maintain objectivity. Do not go in with preconceived ideas as to the problem. Know when you hit a dead end, and avoid rehashing the same ground. If one technique fails, leave it and try another.

Debugging is more art than science, in that there are no guaranteed debugging procedures, only debugging aids. A bug does not leap from the pages of a dump, but must be coaxed out by logic, perseverance, and even luck. In short, debugging is an incomparable source of frustration and satisfaction.

TRUE/FALSE EXERCISES

1. The subtraction technique of Chapter 7 is not likely to be helpful in resolving a data management ABEND.
2. Completion codes of 013, 213, 513, and 813 all relate to problems in a COBOL OPEN statement.
3. JCL and system messages are of no help in debugging a data management ABEND.
4. Detailed knowledge of control blocks is mandatory if one is to debug an 001 ABEND.
5. The subtraction technique of Chapter 7 is likely to produce fruitful results in debugging an 0CB ABEND.
6. A data management ABEND is very often caused by a condition external to the program, rather than by an error in programming logic.

7. Completion codes of B37, D37, and E37 are due to insufficient space for an output file.

8. An infinite loop, due to an error in programming logic, is likely to produce a 322 completion code.

9. The subtraction technique of Chapter 7 may be useful in solving a 322 completion code.

10. The system messages which accompany an 013 completion code identify the associated COBOL file name directly.

11. The system messages which accompany an 013 completion code identify the DDname of the problem file.

12. WS BEGINS HERE and the associated READ INTO or WRITE FROM statement is useless with a data management ABEND.

PROBLEMS

1. Modify a working COBOL program in an attempt to create as many of the ABENDs in the chapter summary as possible. Do you always obtain the expected result? Do the associated ABENDs provide a better appreciation for debugging? For the system messages?

2. The author makes the statement that data management ABENDs occur *outside* the COBOL program. How does this situation manifest itself with respect to the subtraction technique of Chapter 7?

3. Modify the program of Figure 8.1 to accommodate the following:

   (a) If duplicate ID numbers are detected (i.e., the same ID appears on both input files), the record with the *higher* salary is to be written to the merged file. However, if both records have the same salary, neither is to be written, and an error message is required.

   (b) The input files must be checked to ensure that records are in ascending sequence, and further that duplicate IDs are not present in the *same* file.

4. Figure 8.6 contains a modified Procedure Division for the original COBOL program of Figure 8.1. Figure 8.7 displays the associated JCL (with test data) and JES messages. Determine the cause of the ABEND with the aid of the following leading questions:

   (a) What is the completion code?
   (b) What does it mean?
   (c) What is the DDname of the problem data set? What is the associated COBOL file name?

```
00064              PROCEDURE DIVISION.
00065              005-MAINLINE.
00066                 OPEN INPUT  INPUT-FILE-ONE
00067                             INPUT-FILE-TWO
00068                    OUTPUT MERGED-FILE.
00069                 PERFORM 015-READ-FIRST-FILE.
00070                 PERFORM 020-READ-SECOND-FILE.
00071                 PERFORM 010-PROCESS-FILES
00072                    UNTIL INPUT-ONE-ID = HIGH-VALUES
00073                       AND INPUT-TWO-ID = HIGH-VALUES.
00074                 CLOSE INPUT-FILE-ONE
00075                       INPUT-FILE-TWO
00076                       MERGED-FILE.
00077                 STOP RUN.
00078
00079              010-PROCESS-FILES.
00080                 IF INPUT-ONE-ID LESS THAN INPUT-TWO-ID
00081                    WRITE MERGED-RECORD FROM INPUT-RECORD-ONE
00082                 ELSE
00083                    IF INPUT-TWO-ID LESS THAN INPUT-ONE-ID
00084                       WRITE MERGED-RECORD FROM INPUT-RECORD-TWO
00085                       PERFORM 020-READ-SECOND-FILE
00086                    ELSE
00087                       DISPLAY 'DUPLICATE IDS ' INPUT-ONE-ID
00088                       PERFORM 015-READ-FIRST-FILE
00089                       PERFORM 020-READ-SECOND-FILE.
00090
00091              015-READ-FIRST-FILE.
00092                 READ INPUT-FILE-ONE INTO WS-INPUT-RECORD-ONE
00093                    AT END MOVE HIGH-VALUES TO INPUT-ONE-ID.
00094
00095              020-READ-SECOND-FILE.
00096                 READ INPUT-FILE-TWO INTO WS-INPUT-RECORD-TWO
00097                    AT END MOVE HIGH-VALUES TO INPUT-TWO-ID.
```

FIGURE 8.6 Modified Procedure Division

(d) List three distinct reasons why the available space may be insufficient for an output data set.

(e) Which one of the reasons in part (d) is most likely due to a logic error?

(f) Examine the Procedure Division of Figure 8.6 and identify the reason for the ABEND.

Although the reader has presumably solved the dump, Figures 8.8 and 8.9 provide additional debugging aids which should reinforce the previous analysis. Accordingly:

(g) What was the last record read for INPUT-FILE-ONE?

(h) What was the last record read for INPUT-FILE-TWO?

(i) What does the FLOW option of Figure 8.9 indicate?

(j) Use the answers from parts (g), (h), and (i) to substantiate your earlier answer to part (f).

The system messages of Figure 8.10 should provide deeper understanding of the various data sets. Accordingly, the questions continue on page 226.

```
//JSC$3706     JOB (MAS526),JACKIE
//STEP1        EXEC PGM=IEBGENER
//SYSPRINT     DD SYSOUT=R
//SYSIN        DD DUMMY
//SYSUT2       DD DSN=&&FILEONE,DISP=(NEW,PASS),UNIT=SYSDA,
//             DCB=(LRECL=80,BLKSIZE=640,RECFM=FB),SPACE=(TRK,(1,1))
//SYSUT1       DD *
           100000000
           200000000
           300000000
           400000000
           500000000
           600000000
//STEP2        EXEC PGM=IEBGENER
//SYSPRINT     DD SYSOUT=R
//SYSIN        DD DUMMY
//SYSUT2       DD DSN=&&FILETWO,DISP=(NEW,PASS),UNIT=SYSDA,
//             DCB=(LRECL=80,BLKSIZE=640,RECFM=FB),SPACE=(TRK,(1,1))
//SYSUT1       DD *
           111111111
           222222222
           333333333
           444444444
           555555555
           666666666
//STEP3        EXEC COBVCLG,OUT=A
//COB.SYSLIB   DD DSN=MEN.PGM.JSC.RTG,DISP=SHR
//COB.SYSIN    DD DSN=MEN.PGM.JSC.RTG(TWOFILE2),DISP=SHR
//GO.FILEONE   DD DSN=&&FILEONE,DISP=(OLD,PASS),UNIT=SYSDA,
//             DCB=(LRECL=80,BLKSIZE=640,RECFM=FB)
//GO.FILETWO   DD DSN=&&FILETWO,DISP=(OLD,PASS),UNIT=SYSDA,
//             DCB=(LRECL=80,BLKSIZE=640,RECFM=FB)
//GO.MERGED    DD DSN=&&MERGED,DISP=(NEW,PASS),UNIT=SYSDA,
//             DCB=(LRECL=80,BLKSIZE=640,RECFM=FB),SPACE=(TRK,(1))
//GO.SYSUDUMP  DD SYSOUT=A
```

FIGURE 8.7a Execution JCL with Data (Problem 3)

```
17.55.42 JOB 2196    $HASP373 JSC$3706 STARTED - INIT  1 - CLASS A - SYS IP01
17.56.03 JOB 2196    IEC031I D37-04,IFG0554T,JSC$3706,GO,MERGED,131,UMF131,
17.56.03 JOB 2196    IEC031I SYS83017.T175542.RA000.JSC$3706.MERGED
17.56.06 JOB 2196    IEF450I JSC$3706 GO STEP3 - ABEND SD37 U0000
17.56.08 JOB 2196    $HASP395 JSC$3706 ENDED
```

FIGURE 8.7b JES Messages (Problem 3)

```
0B5FA0  90ECD00C 185D05F0 4580F010 E3E6D6C6   C9D3C5E2 E5E2D9F1 0700989F F02407FF   *........0..0.TWOFILESVSR1....0...*
0B5FC0  96021034 07FE41F0 000107FE 000B6C76   000B5FA0 000B5FA0 000B66C8 000B6450   *.......0............H....*
0B5FE0  000B67B4 000B6C36 00000000 00000000   00000000 00000000 00000000 00000000   *................................*
0B6000  00000000 00000000 00000000 00000000   00000000 00000000 00000000 00000000   *................................*
0B6020  00000000 00000000 F1F74BF5 F54BF4F7   D1C1D540 F1F76B40 F1F9F8F3 00000000   *........17.55.47JAN 17. 1983....*
0B6040  5C40E6E2 40C2C5C7 C9D5E240 C8C5D9C5   405C0000 00000000 40404040 40404040   *. WS BEGINS HERE .......*
0B6060  40F1F0F0 F0F2F0F0 F0F04040 40404040   40404040 40404040 40404040 40404040   *.100000000                      *
0B6080  40404040 40404040 40404040 40404040   40404040 40404040 40404040 40404040   *                                *
0B60A0  40404040 40404040 40404040 40404040   40F1F1F1 F1F1F1F1 F1F14040 40404040   *              111111111         *
0B60C0  40404040 40404040 40404040 40404040   40404040 40404040 40404040 40404040   *                                *
0B60E0  40404040 40404040 40404040 40404040   40404040 40404040 00000000 00000000   *........                .......*
0B6100  00000000 00000000 00000000 050B7C06   000B5FC6 00000001 00000021 00000000   *.............F...........*
0B6120  00000000 00000000 00000000 00000000   80000000 00000000 52000000 01190001   *................................*
0B6140  0002C7B8 002B4B35 050BA378 00004000   000BA1A8 460B8356 900B60FC 00904800   *..G.............G........*
0B6160  00986434 12F658F0 00BFA000 09000001   00090280 30013030 000BA258 000BA7E0   *.....6.0........6.0..............*
0B6180  000BA500 00000050 00000000 00000000   00CB8E68 05EF0700 00000000 00000000   *................................*
0B61A0  00000000 00000000 00000000 00900000   00000000 02000001 00500804 00000000   *.............0..................*
0B61C0  00000000 000B49F0 00000000 000B6BC0   00000000 00000000 00000000 00000000   *.......0........................*
0B61E0  00000000 00000000 00000000 00000000   00000000 00000000 00000000 000B8348   *................................*
0B6200  000B837A 000B837A 000B837A 00000000   00000000 00000000 00000000 00000000   *................................*
```

FIGURE 8.8 Partial Dump (Problem 4)

```
PROGRAM        TWOFILES

LAST PSW BEFORE ABEND = FF85003750C4B51A      SYSTEM COMPLETION CODE = D37

LAST CARD NUMBER/VERB NUMBER EXECUTED -- CARD NUMBER 000081/VERB NUMBER 01.

                                              FLOW TRACE
TWOFILES 000079 000079 000079 000079 000079 000079 000079 000079 000079 000079


                                      END OF COBOL DIAGNOSTIC AIDS
```

FIGURE 8.9 STATE and FLOW Options (Problem 4)

```
IEF236I ALLOC. FOR JSC$3706 STEP1
IEF237I JES2 ALLOCATED TO SYSPRINT
IEF237I DMY  ALLOCATED TO SYSIN
IEF237I 135  ALLOCATED TO SYSUT2
IEF237I JES2 ALLOCATED TO SYSUT1
IEF142I JSC$3706 STEP1 - STEP WAS EXECUTED - COND CODE 0000
IEF285I    JES2.JOB02196.S00103                    SYSOUT
IEF285I    SYS83017.T175542.RA000.JSC$3706.FILEONE  PASSED
IEF285I    VOL SER NOS= UMF135.
IEF285I    JES2.JOB02196.SI0101                    SYSIN
IEF373I STEP /STEP1   / START 83017.1755
IEF374I STEP /STEP1   / STOP  83017.1755 CPU    0MIN 00.19SEC SRB
IEF236I ALLOC. FOR JSC$3706 STEP2
IEF237I JES2 ALLOCATED TO SYSPRINT
IEF237I DMY  ALLOCATED TO SYSIN
IEF237I 135  ALLOCATED TO SYSUT2
IEF237I JES2 ALLOCATED TO SYSUT1
IEF142I JSC$3706 STEP2 - STEP WAS EXECUTED - COND CODE 0000
IEF285I    JES2.JOB02196.S00104                    SYSOUT
IEF285I    SYS83017.T175542.RA000.JSC$3706.FILETWO  PASSED
IEF285I    VOL SER NOS= UMF135.
IEF285I    JES2.JOB02196.SI0102                    SYSIN
IEF373I STEP /STEP2   / START 83017.1755
IEF374I STEP /STEP2   / STOP  83017.1755 CPU    0MIN 00.20SEC SRB
IEF236I ALLOC. FOR JSC$3706 COB STEP3
IEF237I 133  ALLOCATED TO STEPLIB
IEF237I 133  ALLOCATED TO
IEF237I JES2 ALLOCATED TO SYSPRINT
IEF237I DMY  ALLOCATED TO SYSPUNCH
IEF237I 113  ALLOCATED TO SYSLIB
IEF237I 113  ALLOCATED TO SYS00087
IEF237I 135  ALLOCATED TO SYSUT1
IEF237I 111  ALLOCATED TO SYSUT2
IEF237I 131  ALLOCATED TO SYSUT3
IEF237I 135  ALLOCATED TO SYSUT4
IEF237I 111  ALLOCATED TO SYSUT5
IEF237I 135  ALLOCATED TO SYSLIN
IEF237I 113  ALLOCATED TO SYSIN
IEF142I JSC$3706 COB STEP3 - STEP WAS EXECUTED - COND CODE 0000
IEF285I    SYS2.LINKLIB                            KEPT
IEF285I    VOL SER NOS= UMF133.
IEF285I    SYS1.COBLIB                             KEPT
IEF285I    VOL SER NOS= UMF133.
IEF285I    JES2.JOB02196.S00105                    SYSOUT
IEF285I    MEN.PGM.JSC.RTG                         KEPT
IEF285I    VOL SER NOS= UMF113.
```

FIGURE 8.10 System Messages for Problem 4

```
IEF285I    SYSCTLG.VUMF113                              KEPT
IEF285I    VOL SER NOS= UMF113.
IEF285I    SYS83017.T175542.RA000.JSC$3706.SYSUT1       DELETED
IEF285I    VOL SER NOS= UMF135.
IEF285I    SYS83017.T175542.RA000.JSC$3706.SYSUT2       DELETED
IEF285I    VOL SER NOS= UMF111.
IEF285I    SYS83017.T175542.RA000.JSC$3706.SYSUT3       DELETED
IEF285I    VOL SER NOS= UMF131.
IEF285I    SYS83017.T175542.RA000.JSC$3706.SYSUT4       DELETED
IEF285I    VOL SER NOS= UMF135.
IEF285I    SYS83017.T175542.RA000.JSC$3706.SYSUT5       DELETED
IEF285I    VOL SER NOS= UMF111.
IEF285I    SYS83017.T175542.RA000.JSC$3706.OBJ          PASSED
IEF285I    VOL SER NOS= UMF135.
IEF285I    MEN.PGM.JSC.RTG                              KEPT
IEF285I    VOL SER NOS= UMF113.
IEF373I STEP /COB      / START 83017.1755
IEF374I STEP /COB      / STOP  83017.1755 CPU    0MIN 01.93SEC SRB
IEF236I ALLOC. FOR JSC$3706 LKED STEP3
IEF237I 135   ALLOCATED TO SYSLIN
IEF237I 111   ALLOCATED TO SYSLMOD
IEF237I 133   ALLOCATED TO SYSLIB
IEF237I 131   ALLOCATED TO SYSUT1
IEF237I JES2 ALLOCATED TO SYSPRINT
IEF142I JSC$3706 LKED STEP3 - STEP WAS EXECUTED - COND CODE 0000
IEF285I    SYS83017.T175542.RA000.JSC$3706.OBJ          DELETED
IEF285I    VOL SER NOS= UMF135.
IEF285I    SYS83017.T175542.RA000.JSC$3706.LOD          PASSED
IEF285I    VOL SER NOS= UMF111.
IEF285I    SYS1.COBLIB                                  KEPT
IEF285I    VOL SER NOS= UMF133.
IEF285I    SYS83017.T175542.RA000.JSC$3706.SYSUT1       DELETED
IEF285I    VOL SER NOS= UMF131.
IEF285I    JES2.JOB02196.S00106                         SYSOUT
IEF373I STEP /LKED     / START 83017.1755
IEF374I STEP /LKED     / STOP  83017.1756 CPU    0MIN 00.57SEC SRB
IEF236I ALLOC. FOR JSC$3706 GO STEP3
IEF237I 111   ALLOCATED TO PGM=*.DD
IEF237I 133   ALLOCATED TO STEPLIB
IEF237I JES2 ALLOCATED TO SYSOUT
IEF237I JES2 ALLOCATED TO SYSOUC
IEF237I JES2 ALLOCATED TO SYSCOUNT
IEF237I JES2 ALLOCATED TO SYSDBOUT
IEF237I 135   ALLOCATED TO FILEONE
IEF237I 135   ALLOCATED TO FILETWO
IEF237I 131   ALLOCATED TO MERGED
IEF237I JES2 ALLOCATED TO SYSUDUMP
IEC031I D37-04,IFG0554T,JSC$3706,GO,MERGED,131,UMF131,
IEC031I SYS83017.T175542.RA000.JSC$3706.MERGED
IEF472I JSC$3706 GO STEP3 - COMPLETION CODE - SYSTEM=D37 USER=0000
IEF285I    SYS83017.T175542.RA000.JSC$3706.LOD          KEPT
IEF285I    VOL SER NOS= UMF111.
IEF285I    SYS1.COBLIB                                  KEPT
IEF285I    VOL SER NOS= UMF133.
IEF285I    JES2.JOB02196.S00107                         SYSOUT
IEF285I    JES2.JOB02196.S00108                         SYSOUT
IEF285I    JES2.JOB02196.S00109                         SYSOUT
IEF285I    JES2.JOB02196.S00110                         SYSOUT
IEF285I    SYS83017.T175542.RA000.JSC$3706.FILEONE      PASSED
IEF285I    VOL SER NOS= UMF135.
IEF285I    SYS83017.T175542.RA000.JSC$3706.FILETWO      PASSED
IEF285I    VOL SER NOS= UMF135.
IEF285I    SYS83017.T175542.RA000.JSC$3706.MERGED       PASSED
IEF285I    VOL SER NOS= UMF131.
```

FIGURE 8.10 (Continued)

```
IEF285I    JES2.JOB02196.S00111                              SYSOUT
IEF373I STEP /GO      / START 83017.1756
IEF374I STEP /GO      / STOP  83017.1756 CPU     0MIN 02.04SEC SRB
IEF237I 135  ALLOCATED TO SYS00001
IEF285I    SYS83017.T175607.RA000.JSC$3706.R0000001         KEPT
IEF285I    VOL SER NOS= UMF135.
IEF285I    SYS83017.T175542.RA000.JSC$3706.FILEONE          DELETED
IEF285I    VOL SER NOS= UMF135.
IEF237I 135  ALLOCATED TO SYS00003
IEF285I    SYS83017.T175607.RA000.JSC$3706.R0000003         KEPT
IEF285I    VOL SER NOS= UMF135.
IEF285I    SYS83017.T175542.RA000.JSC$3706.FILETWO          DELETED
IEF285I    VOL SER NOS= UMF135.
IEF237I 111  ALLOCATED TO SYS00005
IEF285I    SYS83017.T175607.RA000.JSC$3706.R0000005         KEPT
IEF285I    VOL SER NOS= UMF111.
IEF285I    SYS83017.T175542.RA000.JSC$3706.LOD              DELETED
IEF285I    VOL SER NOS= UMF111.
IEF237I 131  ALLOCATED TO SYS00007
IEF285I    SYS83017.T175607.RA000.JSC$3706.R0000007         KEPT
IEF285I    VOL SER NOS= UMF131.
IEF285I    SYS83017.T175542.RA000.JSC$3706.MERGED           DELETED
IEF285I    VOL SER NOS= UMF131.
IEF375I JOB /JSC$3706/ START 83017.1755
IEF376I JOB /JSC$3706/ STOP  83017.1756 CPU     0MIN 04.93SEC SRB
```

FIGURE 8.10 (Continued)

(k) What is the condition code associated with STEP1?

(l) What is the name of the data set created in STEP1 and passed forward to subsequent steps?

(m) How does the answer to part (l) relate to the JCL DSN parameter? To the job name? To the date and time of execution?

(n) What is the ultimate disposition of the data set from part (l)? How is this consistent with the original JCL specifications?

(o) Answer parts (l), (m) and (n) for the data set created in STEP2.

(p) What is the name of the data set created in the LKED step? What is its significance? Its ultimate disposition?

(q) What is the first data set deleted in the LKED step? What is its significance? Where did it originate?

(r) Explain the significance of JSC$3706, GO, MERGED, 131, and UMF131, all of which appeared in the original error message of Figure 8.7b (and/or Figure 8.10).

Insight Into the COBOL Compiler

The COBOL compiler is a remarkably sophisticated program that translates COBOL into machine language. Unfortunately, many practicing programmers know little more about the compiler. While such knowledge is unnecessary in terms of being able to write a COBOL program, it is invaluable in raising the overall capabilities of the individual.

The compiler-generated instructions to add two COMPUTATIONAL fields are different from those which add two COMPUTATIONAL-3 fields. Further, if COBOL operands are of different data types and/or decimal alignment, additional machine instructions are generated to convert and/or shift the data. How does this relate to COBOL, since the programmer is permitted to mix data types or decimal alignments in the same COBOL instruction? The compiler, and not the programmer, is responsible for generating proper machine code to convert, shift, and do arithmetic. If the programmer is "lazy" or unaware, the compiler will bail him out. The

227

COBOL programmer can, however, simplify the job of the compiler and thereby ensure more efficient machine code by specifying appropriate data types, decimal alignments, etc. That is the focus of this chapter. We shall examine in close detail machine language instructions generated by the COBOL compiler and see how apparently insignificant changes in COBOL code produce very different machine instructions. We shall show that even brief consideration of machine characteristics results in more efficient COBOL code and a *better understanding of the COBOL logic.*

The chapter begins with elementary coverage of some Assembler instructions. (We assume the material on instruction formats and machine architecture from Chapter 6 has been well digested.) A superficial level is maintained, for the present objective is to establish a link between COBOL and Assembler and not to provide in-depth coverage of BAL coding. After the necessary Assembler has been covered, we shall concoct a COBOL program in which the Procedure Division consists entirely of ADD instructions for different data types, signs, and decimal alignments. We shall then examine the procedure and data division maps associated with this program to accomplish our objective.

CONVERSION INSTRUCTIONS

The reader may refer to Chapter 6 to review instruction formats and the addressing scheme. We shall begin with two instructions that convert from character to packed format and packed to character format, the PACK and UNPK instructions, respectively. First the PACK instruction:

```
Name                Pack
Mnemonic op code    PACK
Machine op code     F2
Type                SS
Assembler format    PACK D1(L1,B1),D2(L2,B2)
```

Essentially, the PACK instruction packs the data in the second operand, and moves the result into the first operand. The contents of the second operand are unchanged.

EXAMPLE 9.1

```
PACK   FIELDA,FIELDB
```

	FIELDA				FIELDB			
Before execution:	??	??	??		F1	F2	F3
After execution:	00	12	3F		F1	F2	F3

Observe that, since FIELDA was larger than necessary, high-order zeros are generated. The initial contents of FIELDA, i.e., the receiving field, are overwritten, and the final contents of FIELDB—i.e., the sending field—are not changed.

The UNPK (unpack) instruction is the reverse of the PACK instruction in that a packed field is converted to character format:

```
Name                Unpack
Mnemonic op code    UNPK
Machine op code     F3
Type                SS
Assembler format    UNPK D1(L1,B1),D2(L2,B2)
```

EXAMPLE 9.2

```
UNPK  FIELDC,FIELDD
```

Before execution: FIELDC | ?? | ?? | ?? | FIELDD | 32 | 1F |

After execution: FIELDC | F3 | F2 | F1 | FIELDD | 32 | 1F |

As before, the final contents of the sending field—i.e., FIELDD—are unchanged, and the initial contents of the receiving field—i.e., FIELDC— are destroyed. Further note that the receiving field is larger than the sending field to accommodate the expanded results of the unpacking operation.

Next, consider two instructions that convert binary data to decimal (i.e., packed) format, and decimal data to binary, the convert to decimal and convert to binary instructions:

```
Name                Convert to binary
Mnemonic op code    CVB
Machine op code     4F
Type                RX
Assembler format    CVB R1,D2(X2,B2)
```

The convert to binary (CVB) instruction requires that the second operand be 8 bytes long (a double word) and in packed format. The result of the conversion is stored in the general register specified as R1.

EXAMPLE 9.3

```
CVB  8,FIELDC
```

Before execution: FIELDC | 00 | 00 | 00 | 00 | 00 | 00 | 12 | 3C |

Register 8 | ?? | ?? | ?? | ?? |

After execution: FIELDC

| 00 | 00 | 00 | 00 | 00 | 00 | 12 | 3C |

Register 8

| 00 | 00 | 00 | 7B |

Note: $(123)_{10} = (7B)_{16}$.

The convert to decimal (CVD) instruction works in reverse; i.e., it takes the binary contents of a general-purpose register, converts it to decimal, and stores the result in the 8 byte packed field specified in the instruction.

Name	Convert to decimal
Mnemonic op code	CVD
Machine op code	4E
Type	RX
Assembler format	CVD R1,D2(X2,B2)

EXAMPLE 9.4

CVD   6,RESULT

Before execution: Register 6

| 00 | 00 | 00 | 23 |

RESULT

| ?? | ?? | ?? | ?? | ?? | ?? | ?? | ?? |

After execution: Register 6

| 00 | 00 | 00 | 23 |

Note: $(23)_{16} = (35)_{10}$.

RESULT

| 00 | 00 | 00 | 00 | 00 | 00 | 03 | 5C |

Execution of the CVD instruction leaves the contents of the designated register unchanged. The original contents of the register are converted to a packed number and stored in the second operand.

INSTRUCTIONS THAT MOVE DATA

Data are constantly transferred from storage to a register, or from a register to storage. In this section two instructions are introduced, but there are several others in the complete instruction set.

Load instructions bring data from a storage location to a register, while store instructions transfer data from a register to storage. A load instruction does not alter the initial contents of the storage address. A store instruction does not change the contents of a register. We shall consider two instructions that manipulate a full word.

Name	Load
Mnemonic op code	L
Machine op code	58
Type	RX
Assembler format	L R1,D2(X2,B2)

EXAMPLE 9.5

```
L   5,FIELDA
```

Before execution:	Register 5	??	??	??	??	FIELDA	00	00	00	01
After execution:	Register 5	00	00	00	01	FIELDA	00	00	00	01

After the load instruction has been executed, the contents of FIELDA (a full word) are unchanged. The initial contents of register 5 have been replaced by the contents of FIELDA.

The store instruction causes the contents of a register to be placed in storage. The contents of the register are unaltered, and what was originally in storage is overwritten.

```
Name                Store
Mnemonic op code    ST
Machine op code     50
Type                RX
Assembler format    ST  R1,D2(X2,B2)
```

EXAMPLE 9.6

```
ST   6,FIELDB
```

Before execution:	Register 6	00	00	12	34	FIELDB	??	??	??	??
After execution:	Register 6	00	00	12	34	FIELDB	00	00	12	34

ADD INSTRUCTIONS

Any one of several BAL instructions can be used to add data depending on the length, type, and location of the operands. The add packed (AP) instruction is for decimal data with both operands in storage. The add full word (A) instruction is for binary data when one operand is contained in a register and the other in a full word in storage. Consider the add packed instruction:

```
Name                Add packed
Mnemonic op code    AP
Machine op code     FA
Type                SS
Assembler format    AP  D1(L1,B1),D2(L2,B2)
```

The contents of the second operand are added to the contents of the first operand, and the results are placed in the first operand. Both fields must be valid decimal fields—i.e., packed; otherwise a data exception will occur. The sum is in packed format, and its sign is stored in the low-order byte of the first operand.

EXAMPLE 9.7

```
AP   FIELDA,FIELDB
```

Before execution:	FIELDA	01	23	4C		FIELDB	05	67	8C
After execution:	FIELDA	06	91	2C		FIELDB	05	67	8C

The initial contents of the first operand are overwritten, and the contents of the second operand are unchanged.

The add full word instruction adds (in binary) the contents of a full word in storage, to the contents of a register, and places the results in the designated register.

Name	Add full word
Mnemonic op code	A
Machine op code	5A
Type	RX
Assembler format	A R1,D2(X2,B2)

EXAMPLE 9.8

```
A   5,FIELDC
```

Before execution:	Register 5	00	00	00	07		FIELDC	00	00	00	01
After execution:	Register 5	00	00	00	08		FIELDC	00	00	00	01

The contents of FIELDC, a full word in storage, are added to the value of register 5, and the result is placed in register 5. (Note that both operands are in hex.) The initial contents of register 5 are destroyed, and the contents of FIELDC are unaltered.

COBOL FROM THE VIEWPOINT OF BAL

The intent of Figure 9.1 is to illustrate a variety of COBOL and corresponding object formats for different data types, lengths, signs, decimal alignments, etc. The Working-Storage section defines 12 data names that are

```
00001          IDENTIFICATION DIVISION.
00002          PROGRAM-ID.      COBOLBAL.
00003          AUTHOR.          R. GRAUER.
00004
00005          ENVIRONMENT DIVISION.
00006          CONFIGURATION SECTION.
00007          SOURCE-COMPUTER.  IBM-4341.
00008          OBJECT-COMPUTER.  IBM-4341.
00009
00010          DATA DIVISION.
00011          WORKING-STORAGE SECTION.
00012          01  COMPUTATIONAL-FIELDS.
00013              05  BINARY-FIELD-ONE          PIC S9(3)   USAGE COMP.
00014              05  BINARY-FIELD-TWO          PIC S9(5)   USAGE COMP.
00015              05  BINARY-FIELD-UNSIGNED     PIC  9(3)   USAGE COMP.
00016              05  BINARY-FIELD-WITH-POINT   PIC S9(3)V9 USAGE COMP.
00017
00018          01  DISPLAY-FIELDS.
00019              05  ZONED-DECIMAL-FIELD-ONE   PIC S9(3)   USAGE DISPLAY.
00020              05  ZONED-DECIMAL-FIELD-TWO   PIC S9(5)   USAGE DISPLAY.
00021              05  ZONED-DECIMAL-UNSIGNED    PIC  9(3)   USAGE DISPLAY.
00022              05  ZONED-DECIMAL-WITH-POINT  PIC S9(3)V9 USAGE DISPLAY.
00023
00024          01  PACKED-FIELDS.
00025              05  PACKED-FIELD-ONE          PIC S9(3)   USAGE COMP-3.
00026              05  PACKED-FIELD-TWO          PIC S9(5)   USAGE COMP-3.
00027              05  PACKED-FIELD-UNSIGNED     PIC  9(3)   USAGE COMP-3.
00028              05  PACKED-FIELD-WITH-POINT   PIC S9(3)V9 USAGE COMP-3.
00029
00030          PROCEDURE DIVISION.
00031
00032          ****************************************************************
00033          *          COMPARISON OF ADD INSTRUCTIONS FOR ALL             *
00034          *              COMBINATIONS OF DATA TYPES                     *
00035          *          ALL DATA NAMES ARE SIGNED                          *
00036          *          ALL DATA NAMES HAVE SIMILAR DECIMAL ALIGNMENTS     *
00037          ****************************************************************
00038
00039          *          COMBINE SIMILAR DATA TYPES
00040
00041              ADD BINARY-FIELD-ONE TO BINARY-FIELD-TWO.
00042              ADD ZONED-DECIMAL-FIELD-ONE TO ZONED-DECIMAL-FIELD-TWO.
00043              ADD PACKED-FIELD-ONE TO PACKED-FIELD-TWO.
00044
00045          *          COMBINING PACKED FIELDS WITH ZONED DECIMAL FIELDS
00046
00047              ADD PACKED-FIELD-ONE TO ZONED-DECIMAL-FIELD-ONE.
00048              ADD ZONED-DECIMAL-FIELD-ONE TO PACKED-FIELD-ONE.
00049
00050          *          COMBINING PACKED FIELDS WITH BINARY FIELDS
00051
00052              ADD PACKED-FIELD-ONE TO BINARY-FIELD-ONE.
00053              ADD BINARY-FIELD-ONE TO PACKED-FIELD-ONE.
00054
00055          *          COMBINING ZONED DECIMAL FIELDS WITH BINARY FIELDS
00056
00057              ADD ZONED-DECIMAL-FIELD-ONE TO BINARY-FIELD-ONE.
00058              ADD BINARY-FIELD-ONE TO ZONED-DECIMAL-FIELD-ONE.
00059
00060          ****************************************************************
00061          *     COMPARISON OF ADD INSTRUCTIONS FOR SIMILAR DATA TYPES   *
00062          *     ONE OPERAND IN UNSIGNED                                 *
00063          *     ALL DATA NAMES HAVE SIMILAR DECIMAL ALIGNMENTS          *
00064          ****************************************************************
```

FIGURE 9.1 COBOL Listing to Illustrate Efficiency Considerations

```
00065
00066            ADD ZONED-DECIMAL-UNSIGNED TO ZONED-DECIMAL-FIELD-ONE.
00067            ADD ZONED-DECIMAL-FIELD-ONE TO ZONED-DECIMAL-UNSIGNED.
00068            ADD BINARY-FIELD-UNSIGNED TO BINARY-FIELD-ONE.
00069            ADD BINARY-FIELD-ONE TO BINARY-FIELD-UNSIGNED.
00070            ADD PACKED-FIELD-UNSIGNED TO PACKED-FIELD-ONE.
00071            ADD PACKED-FIELD-ONE TO PACKED-FIELD-UNSIGNED.
00072
00073        ****************************************************************
00074        *     COMPARISON OF ADD INSTRUCTIONS FOR SIMILAR DATA TYPES    *
00075        *     ALL DATA NAMES ARE SIGNED                                *
00076        *     ALL DATA NAMES HAVE DIFFERENT DECIMAL ALIGNMENTS         *
00077        ****************************************************************
00078
00079            ADD ZONED-DECIMAL-WITH-POINT TO ZONED-DECIMAL-FIELD-ONE.
00080            ADD ZONED-DECIMAL-FIELD-ONE TO ZONED-DECIMAL-WITH-POINT.
00081            ADD BINARY-FIELD-WITH-POINT TO BINARY-FIELD-ONE.
00082            ADD BINARY-FIELD-ONE TO BINARY-FIELD-WITH-POINT.
00083            ADD PACKED-FIELD-WITH-POINT TO PACKED-FIELD-ONE.
00084            ADD PACKED-FIELD-ONE TO PACKED-FIELD-WITH-POINT.
00085
00086            STOP RUN.
```

FIGURE 9.1 (Continued)

used in various combinations in the Procedure Division. Of primary interest in this example is the machine language code generated from the COBOL statements. In the ensuing sections, we shall consider only a few of the COBOL statements in Figure 9.1, but the reader is well advised to consider the entire listing as an exercise.

Figure 9.2 shows the Data Division map, Figure 9.3 the literal pool and register assignment, and Figure 9.4 a truncated Procedure Division map for Figure 9.1.

Data Division Map

Figure 9.2 is the Data Division map or glossary. A partial explanation of the various entries begins on page 236, but the reader is referred to the *IBM COBOL Programmer's Guide* for a more detailed description.

INTRNL NAME	LVL	SOURCE NAME	BASE	DISPL	INTRNL NAME	DEFINITION	USAGE
DNM=1-032	01	COMPUTATIONAL-FIELDS	BL=1	000	DNM=1-032	DS 0CL10	GROUP
DNM=1-065	02	BINARY-FIELD-ONE	BL=1	000	DNM=1-065	DS 2C	COMP
DNM=1-091	02	BINARY-FIELD-TWO	BL=1	002	DNM=1-091	DS 4C	COMP
DNM=1-117	02	BINARY-FIELD-UNSIGNED	BL=1	006	DNM=1-117	DS 2C	COMP
DNM=1-148	02	BINARY-FIELD-WITH-POINT	BL=1	008	DNM=1-148	DS 2C	COMP
DNM=1-181	01	DISPLAY-FIELDS	BL=1	010	DNM=1-181	DS 0CL15	GROUP
DNM=1-209	02	ZONED-DECIMAL-FIELD-ONE	BL=1	010	DNM=1-208	DS 3C	DISP-NM
DNM=1-241	02	ZONED-DECIMAL-FIELD-TWO	BL=1	013	DNM=1-241	DS 5C	DISP-NM
DNM=1-274	02	ZONED-DECIMAL-UNSIGNED	BL=1	018	DNM=1-274	DS 3C	DISP-NM
DNM=1-306	02	ZONED-DECIMAL-WITH-POINT	BL=1	01B	DNM=1-306	DS 4C	DISP-NM
DNM=1-340	01	PACKED-FIELDS	BL=1	020	DNM=1-340	DS 0CL10	GROUP
DNM=1-366	02	PACKED-FIELD-ONE	BL=1	020	DNM=1-366	DS 2P	COMP-3
DNM=1-392	02	PACKED-FIELD-TWO	BL=1	022	DNM=1-392	DS 3P	COMP-3
DNM=1-418	02	PACKED-FIELD-UNSIGNED	BL=1	025	DNM=1-418	DS 2P	COMP-3
DNM=1-449	02	PACKED-FIELD-WITH-POINT	BL=1	027	DNM=1-449	DS 3P	COMP-3

FIGURE 9.2 Data Division Map

LITERAL POOL (HEX)

00328 (LIT+0)   000A0000   0000000A

PGT	00308
OVERFLOW CELLS	00308
VIRTUAL CELLS	00308
PROCEDURE NAME CELLS	00320
GENERATED NAME CELLS	00320
DCB ADDRESS CELLS	00324
VNI CELLS	00324
LITERALS	00328
DISPLAY LITERALS	00330

REGISTER ASSIGNMENT

REG 6   BL =1

WORKING-STORAGE STARTS AT LOCATION 000A0 FOR A LENGTH OF 00030.

FIGURE 9.3 Literal Pool and Register Assignment

```
41   ADD   000330                        START   EQU
           000330   48 30 6 000                   LH    • • •  DNM=1-65
           000334   5A 30 6 002                   A            DNM=1-91
           000338   50 30 6 002                   ST           DNM=1-91
42   ADD   00033C   F2 72 D 208 6 010             PACK         TS=01          DNM=1-208
           000342   F2 74 D 210 6 013             PACK         TS=09          DNM=1-241
           000348   FA 32 D 20C D 215             AP           TS=05          TS=014
           00034E   F3 43 6 013 D 20C             UNPK         DNM=1-241      TS=05
43   ADD   000354   FA 21 6 022 6 020             AP           DNM=1-392      DNM=1-366
47   ADD   00035A   F2 72 D 210 6 010             PACK         TS=09          DNM=1-208
           000360   FA 21 D 215 6 020             AP           TS=014         DNM=1-366
           000366   F3 22 6 010 D 215             UNPK         DNM=1-208      TS=014
48   ADD   00036C   F2 72 D 210 6 010             PACK         TS=09          DNM=1-208
           000372   FA 11 6 020 D 216             AP           DNM=1-366      TS=015
52   ADD   000378   F8 71 D 210 6 020             ZAP          TS=09          DNM=1-366
           00037E   4F 30 D 210                   CVB          TS=09
           000382   4A 30 6 000                   AH           DNM=1-65
           000386   40 30 6 000                   STH          DNM=1-65
53   ADD   00038A   48 30 6 000                   LH           DNM=1-65
           00038E   4E 30 D 210                   CVD          TS=09
           000392   FA 11 6 020 D 216             AP           DNM=1-366      TS=015
57   ADD   000398   F2 72 D 210 6 010             PACK         TS=09          DNM=1-208
           00039E   4F 30 D 210                   CVB          TS=09
           0003A2   4A 30 6 000                   AH           DNM=1-65
           0003A6   40 30 6 000                   STH          DNM=1-65
58   ADD   0003AA   F2 72 D 210 6 010             PACK         TS=09          DNM=1-208
           0003B0   48 30 6 000                   LH           DNM=1-65
           0003B4   4E 30 D 208                   CVD          TS=01
           0003B8   FA 21 D 20D D 216             AP           TS=06          TS=015
           0003BE   F3 22 6 010 D 20D             UNPK         DNM=1-208      TS=06
66   ADD   0003C4   F2 72 D 210 6 018             PACK         TS=09          DNM=1-274
           0003CA   F2 72 D 208 6 010             PACK         TS=01          DNM=1-208
           0003D0   FA 21 D 215 D 20E             AP           TS=014         TS=07
           0003D6   F3 22 6 010 D 215             UNPK         DNM=1-208      TS=014
67   ADD   0003DC   F2 72 D 210 6 010             PACK         TS=09          DNM=1-208
           0003E2   F2 72 D 208 6 018             PACK         TS=01          DNM=1-274
           0003E8   FA 21 D 215 D 20E             AP           TS=014         TS=07
           0003EE   F3 22 6 018 D 215             UNPK         DNM=1-274      TS=014
           0003F4   96 F0 6 01A                   OI           DNM=1-274+2
```

FIGURE 9.4 Procedure Division Map

```
68    ADD      0003F8  48 30 6 006          LH • • •     DNM=1-117
               0003FC  4A 30 6 000          AH           DNM=1-65
               000400  40 30 6 000          STH          DNM=1-65
69    ADD      000404  48 30 6 000          LH           DNM=1-65
               000408  4A 30 6 006          AH           DNM=1-117
               00040C  10 33                LPR
               00040E  40 30 6 006          STH          DNM=1-117
70    ADD      000412  FA 11 6 020 6 025    AP           DNM=1-366      DNM=1-418
71    ADD.     000418  FA 11 6 025 6 020    AP           DNM=1-418      DNM=1-366
               00041E  96 0F 6 026          OI           DNM=1-418+1
79    ADD      000422  F2 73 D 210 6 01B    PACK         TS=09          DNM=1-306
               000428  F2 72 D 208 6 010    PACK         TS=01          DNM=1-208
               00042E  F0 20 D 20D 0 001    SRP          TS=06
               000434  FA 22 D 215 D 20D    AP           TS=014         TS=06
               00043A  F1 76 D 210 D 210    MVO          TS=09          TS=09
               000440  F3 22 6 010 D 215    UNPK         DNM=1-208      TS=014
80    ADD      000446  F2 72 D 210 6 010    PACK         TS=29          INM=1-22E
               00044C  F2 73 D 208 6 01B    PACK         TS=01          DNM=1-306
               000452  F0 20 D 215 0 001    SRP          TS=014
               000458  FA 22 D 215 D 20D    AP           TS=014         TS=06
               00045E  F3 32 6 01B D 215    UNPK         DNM=1-306      TS=014
81    ADD      000464  48 30 6 000          LH           DNM=1-65
               000468  4C 30 C 020          MH           LIT+0
               00046C  4A 30 6 008          AH           DNM=1-148
               000470  18 23                LR
               000472  8E 20 0 020          SRDA         LIT+4
               000476  5D 20 C 024          D            LIT+4
               00047A  40 30 6 000          STH          DNM=1-65
82    ADD      00047E  48 30 6 000          LH           DNM=1-65
               000482  4C 30 C 020          MH           LIT+0
               000486  4A 30 6 008          AH           DNM=1-148
               00048A  40 30 6 008          STH          DNM=1-148
83    ADD      00048E  F8 71 D 210 6 020    ZAP          TS=09          DNM=1-366
               000494  F0 20 D 215 0 001    SRP          TS=014
               00049A  FA 22 D 215 6 027    AP           TS=014         DNM=1-449
               0004A0  F1 76 D 210 D 210    MVO          TS=09          TS=09
               0004A6  F8 11 6 020 D 216    ZAP          DNM=1-366      TS=014+1
84    ADD      0004AC  F8 71 D 210 6 020    ZAP          TS=29          DNM=1-366
               0004B2  F0 20 D 215 0 001    SRP          TS=014
               0004B8  FA 22 6 027 D 215    AP           DNM=1-449      TS=014
               0004BE  94 0F 6 027          NI           DNM=1-449
86    STOP     0004C2  58 F0 C 010          L            V(ILBODBG4)
               0004C6  05 EF                BALR
               0004C8                GN=01  EQU
               0004C8  58 F0 C 014          L            V(ILBOSRV1)
               0004CC  07 FF                BCR
               0004CE  4110020741000080     DC
               0004D6  8900001816100A0D     DC
               0004DE  58 F0 C 018          L            GN=01
               0004E2  07 FF                BCR
               0004E4  50 D0 5 008   INIT2  ST
```

FIGURE 9.4 (Continued)

Entries in the Data Division Map are explained as follows:

Internal name — The internal name generated by the compiler and used in the object code listing to represent data names in the source program.

Level number — A normalized level number, in that the first level for any hierarchy is always kept at 01 but the other levels are incremented by 1. Levels 66, 77, and 88 are unaffected. Thus the level numbers in the Data Division map need not match those in the Data Division.

Source name Data name as it appears in the source program.

Base Contains information about the base register used for each data name. In general, every file has its own base locator. In our example all data names have a base locator of 1, which is tied to register 6 in Figure 9.3.

Displ Indicates the displacement, in hexadecimal, from the base register for each data name.

Definition Defines storage requirements for each data item in Assembler-like terminology. Observe the various storage assignments and how they correspond to the specific COBOL USAGE and PICTURE clauses.

Usage Indicates the usage of the data name as defined in the COBOL program.

Literal Pool and Register Assignment

Figure 9.3 contains the literal pool and register assignment for Figure 9.1. The literal pool lists the collection of literals in the program. It includes those specified by the programmer as in a MOVE statement and those generated by the compiler, e.g., those needed for decimal alignment. Use of these literals is made clearer in the section on nonaligned fields. The PGT, or program global table, contains the remaining addresses and literals used by the object program. Its use is not discussed further. The register assignment shows that BL 1 (base locator 1) is assigned to general register 6.

Procedure Division Map

The abbreviated Procedure Division map (Figure 9.4) contains information about the generated object code. Reading from left to right, we see:

1. Compiler-generated statement number
2. The COBOL verb referenced in the statement number under item 1
3. The relative location, in hexadecimal, of the object instruction
4. The actual object code instruction
5. Compiler-generated information about the operands

COBOL ADD INSTRUCTIONS
WITH SIMILAR DATA TYPES

Display to Display:

We return to Figure 9.1 and shall examine three COBOL add state-ments and generated object code. In each example both operands are signed, of the same data type, and have identical decimal alignment. Consider first COBOL statement 42, as well as statements 19 and 20 in the Working-Storage section.

```
ADD ZONED-DECIMAL-FIELD-ONE TO ZONED-DECIMAL-FIELD-TWO.

05  ZONED-DECIMAL-FIELD-ONE  PIC S9(3)  USAGE DISPLAY.

05  ZONED-DECIMAL-FIELD-TWO  PIC S9(5)  USAGE DISPLAY.
```

From the Procedure Division map, we extract four lines associated with COBOL statement 42:

```
42 ADD F2 72 D 208 6 010   PACK...TS=01      DNM=1-208
       F2 74 D 210 6 013   PACK...TS=09      DNM=1-241
       FA 32 D 20C D 215   AP  ...TS=05      TS=014
       F3 43 6 013 D 20C   UNPK...DNM=1-241 TS=05
```

The COBOL programmer is adding two numeric fields. However, since the fields are DISPLAY—i.e., stored as zoned decimal numbers—they must first be packed, and then after the addition, the sum must be unpacked. The first object instruction packs DNM = 1-208, i.e., ZONED-DECIMAL-FIELD-ONE (check the data division map), into a temporary storage area 8 bytes in length. In like manner, DNM = 1-241, i.e., ZONED-DECIMAL-FIELD-TWO, is packed into TS = 09, also a temporary storage area of 8 bytes. Notice how the length, base register, and displacement match the data division map. The contents of the two temporary storage areas are then added via the add packed instruction, and finally the sum is unpacked into DNM = 1-241, i.e., ZONED-DECIMAL-FIELD-TWO. (Observe the length codes associated with each instruction.)

Packed to Packed:

Consider now COBOL statement 43 and its relevant Working-Storage entries (lines 25 and 26).

```
ADD PACKED-FIELD-ONE TO PACKED-FIELD-TWO.

05  PACKED-FIELD-ONE   PIC S9(3)  USAGE COMP-3.

05  PACKED-FIELD-TWO   PIC S9(5)  USAGE COMP-3.
```

This time only a single add packed instruction is generated by the compiler:

```
43   ADD   FA 21 6 022 6 020   AP...DNM=1-392   DNM=1-366
```

Observe that the operands DNM = 1–392 and DNM = 1–366 correspond to PACKED-FIELD-TWO and PACKED-FIELD-ONE, respectively. Further note the displacement for each operand, 022 and 020, and the correspondence in the Data Division map. Finally, the sum of the add packed instruction is stored in the first operand, i.e., DNM = 1–392 corresponding to PACKED-FIELD-TWO, as intended by the COBOL programmer. Compare this single instruction to the four instructions and 24 bytes of code required in the previous example. The saving is realized because the operands are defined as packed fields by the programmer; hence, there is no need for the compiler to pack and subsequently unpack.

Binary to Binary:

Addition of two binary operands is illustrated in COBOL statement 41 with the relevant Working-Storage entries defined in statements 13 and 14.

```
ADD BINARY-FIELD-ONE TO BINARY-FIELD-TWO.

05   BINARY-FIELD-ONE   PIC S9(3)   USAGE COMP.

05   BINARY-FIELD-TWO   PIC S9(5)   USAGE COMP.
```

Object instructions generated by the compiler are shown:

```
41   ADD   48 30 6 000   LH...DNM=1-65
           5A 30 6 002   A ...DNM=1-91
           50 30 6 002   ST...DNM=1-91
```

Since we are dealing with binary operands, the add packed instruction is no longer appropriate. Instead the compiler generates either an AH (add half-word) or A (add full-word) instruction depending on the size of the binary operands. The LH (load half-word) instruction brings BINARY-FIELD-ONE into register 3. The A (add full word) instruction adds the value of BINARY-FIELD-TWO to register 3. Finally, the store instruction moves the contents of register 3 to BINARY-FIELD-TWO.

Careful analysis of this section shows how three apparently similar COBOL instructions in Figure 9.1, statements 41, 42, and 43, produce vastly different object instructions. In each instance, the programmer was adding a three-position signed field to a five-position signed field of similar data type and decimal alignment. Addition of two COMPUTATIONAL-3 fields required one instruction (6 bytes); addition of two DISPLAY fields took four instructions (24 bytes); and addition of two COMPUTATIONAL fields took three instructions (12 bytes).

COBOL ADD INSTRUCTIONS
WITH DISSIMILAR DATA TYPES

We shall concentrate on combinations of packed and binary data and leave the reader to work through other examples in Figure 9.1.

Binary to Decimal:

BINARY-FIELD-ONE is added to PACKED-FIELD-ONE in COBOL statement 53. Both fields are defined as signed three-digit fields with no decimal point, as shown:

```
    ADD BINARY-FIELD-ONE TO PACKED-FIELD-ONE.

05  BINARY-FIELD-ONE   PIC S9(3)   USAGE COMP.

05  PACKED-FIELD-ONE   PIC S9(3)   USAGE COMP-3.
```

Since a binary field is added to a packed field, it is necessary first to convert the binary data to packed data. Consider the three machine language statements generated:

```
53  ADD  48 30 6 000        LH ...DNM=1-65
         4E 30 D 210        CVD...TS=09
         FA 11 6 020 D 216  AP ...DNM=1-366   TS=015
```

BINARY-FIELD-ONE (i.e., DNM = 1-65) is loaded into register 3 via the load half-word instruction. Next it is converted to a packed field and stored on a double word boundary by the CVD instruction. Finally, the newly created packed field is added to DNM = 1-366, i.e., PACKED-FIELD-ONE, and the results are stored there.

Decimal to Binary:

COBOL statement 52 is identical to statement 53, except that the results are stored in the binary field. The reasoning in the Assembler sequence is analogous to the previous example.

```
52  ADD  F8 71 D 210 6 020  ZAP...TS=09       DNM=1-366
         4F 30 D 210        CVB...TS=09
         4A 30 6 000        AH ...DNM=1-65
         40 30 6 000        STH...DNM=1-65
```

The CVB instruction must operate on a double-word boundary, and since PACKED-FIELD-ONE is only 2 bytes in length, it is necessary to fill the high-order bytes of the double-word with zeros. The ZAP (zero and add packed) instruction takes the second operand DNM = 1-366, i.e., PACKED-FIELD-ONE, moves it to a double word boundary, and fills the high-order bytes with binary zeros. The newly moved decimal field is then converted to binary and stored in register 3. BINARY-FIELD-ONE is added to the contents of register 3, with the sum remaining in register 3. The sum is finally stored in BINARY-FIELD-ONE via the STH. Seem complicated? Yes, it is, but that is exactly the point. It is unnecessarily complex because the COBOL programmer, perhaps inadvertently, is adding a packed field to a binary field. Compare the four instructions and 18 bytes of code in this example to the single add packed instruction needed for addition of two decimal fields.

ADDITION OF SIMILAR DATA TYPES WITH AN UNSIGNED OPERAND

Packed to Packed:

A numeric field in COBOL should be preceded by an "S" if it is to contain potentially negative numbers. Consider COBOL statement 71 and relevant Working-Storage entries, lines 25 and 27.

```
        ADD PACKED-FIELD-ONE TO PACKED-FIELD-UNSIGNED.

    05  PACKED-FIELD-ONE        PIC S9(3)       USAGE COMP-3.

    05  PACKED-FIELD-UNSIGNED   PIC 9(3)        USAGE COMP-3.
```

The generated instructions are

```
71  ADD  FA 11 6 025 6 020  AP...DNM=1-418    DNM=1-366
         96 0F 6 026         OI...DNM=1-418+1
```

The add packed instruction works exactly as the one generated by COBOL statement 43, considered earlier in the addition of packed fields. DNM = 1-418 is two bytes in length and stored in bytes 025 and 026 displaced from register 6. The AP instruction always produces a sign of "C" (plus) or "D" (minus) and stores it in the low-order byte of the sum, in this case byte 026 displaced from register 6.

The OI (or immediate) instruction is an SI instruction that takes the value of the "I" operand, "0F," and does a bit-by-bit *logical or* upon the storage address, altering the value of the storage location DNM = 1-418 + 1 (base register 6, displaced by 026). In effect, it changes the sign from either "C" or "D" to "F" while the rest of the field remains undisturbed. Thus, since PACKED-FIELD-UNSIGNED was declared unsigned, an OI instruction was generated to remove the sign. This is not true in COBOL statement 70, as shown:

```
ADD PACKED-FIELD-UNSIGNED TO PACKED-FIELD-ONE.
```

Generated instructions:

```
70  ADD  FA 11 6 020 6 025  AP...DNM=1-366  DNM=1-418
```

Here the sum is stored in PACKED-FIELD-ONE, which was declared as a signed field. Thus, there is only a single AP instruction generated, and the sign remains intact.

Binary to Binary:

Similar reasoning holds for binary operands, except a different instruction is used to remove the sign. Recall that the sign of a binary number is stored in the high-order bit. (A "0" indicates a positive number, and a "1" indicates a negative number stored in two's complement.) If the receiving field is unsigned, then an LPR (load positive register) instruction is generated in the series of instructions. Consider COBOL statement 69 and its relevant Working-Storage entries.

```
ADD BINARY-FIELD-ONE TO BINARY-FIELD-UNSIGNED.

05  BINARY-FIELD-ONE        PIC S9(3)  USAGE COMP.

05  BINARY-FIELD-UNSIGNED   PIC 9(3)   USAGE COMP.
```

The generated instructions are

```
69  ADD  48 30 6 000  LH ...DNM=1-65
         4A 30 6 006  AH ...DNM=1-117
         10 33        LPR...
         40 30 6 006  STH...DNM=1-117
```

These instructions parallel those generated for COBOL statement 41, except that an AH (add half-word) and STH (store half-word) are generated in lieu of an A (add full-word) and ST (store full-word), respectively. Why? Further note the instruction LPR 3,3 after the addition. The effect of this instruction is to load the absolute value of register 3 into register 3, thereby destroying a minus sign if it were present.

COBOL statement 68 also involves an unsigned operand, except that it is not the receiving field; hence, there is no LPR instruction, and the generated code is comparable to that of COBOL statement 41.

ADDING OPERANDS THAT ARE NOT ALIGNED

The addition of operands with nonsimilar decimal alignment produces extensive and often confusing object code. COBOL statements 79 to 84 in Figure 9.1 illustrate several combinations for nonaligned fields. However, only statement 82 is covered in detail, as the others require introduction of several new instructions that go beyond the scope of this chapter. The reader should also realize that as complicated as the object instructions appear, they would be substantially more involved if different data types were mixed in the same instruction.

Consider COBOL statement 82 and relevant Working-Storage entries, statements 13 and 16.

```
        ADD BINARY-FIELD-ONE TO BINARY-FIELD-WITH-POINT.

05   BINARY-FIELD-ONE          PIC S9(3)     USAGE COMP.

05   BINARY-FIELD-WITH-POINT   PIC S9(3)V9   USAGE COMP.
```

The generated object code is

```
82   ADD   48 30 6 000   LH ...DNM=1-65
           4C 30 C 020   MH ...LIT+0
           4A 30 6 008   AH ...DNM=1-148
           40 30 6 008   STH...DNM=1-148
```

Let us first consider conceptually what is and is not required. Both operands are binary, so there is no need for conversion of data type; both operands are signed, and thus no instructions need be generated to remove the sign. However, the decimal alignments are different, and they must first be made identical before addition can occur. BINARY-FIELD-WITH-POINT is the receiving field with an implied decimal point, which in effect makes it larger by a factor of 10 than BINARY-FIELD-ONE; thus BINARY-FIELD-ONE will be multiplied by 10 prior to addition. (Note the presence of a divide instruction in the Assembler sequence for COBOL statement 81 in which the same two operands are combined but where BINARY-FIELD-ONE is the receiving field.)

First, DNM = 1-65 (i.e., BINARY-FIELD-ONE) is loaded into register 3. The contents of register 3 are then multiplied by the contents of a half-word, beginning at LIT + 0, which equals "000A" in hexadecimal and "10" in decimal (see Figure 9.3). The results of the multiplication are stored in register 3. Next, DNM = 1-148 (i.e., BINARY-FIELD-WITH-POINT) is added to the contents of register 3, and the sum is placed in register 3. Finally, the contents of register 3 are stored in BINARY-FIELD-WITH-POINT.

As can be seen from this example, the combination of nonaligned fields in a source program necessitates the generation of extra instructions in the object program. COBOL statements 79 to 84 present a sufficient variety of new BAL instructions to acquaint the reader with alignment logic. In actual practice, situations arise in which incompatible formats are unavoidable. In such instances one must comply with the "specs" as given, and efficiency considerations are shunted aside.

Summary

The following Assembler instructions were introduced as background for efficiency considerations:

PACK   Pack
UNPK   Unpack
CVB   Convert to binary
CVD   Convert to decimal
L   Load (full-word)
ST   Store (full-word)
AP   Add packed
A   Add (full-word)

Next, a COBOL program, consisting of ADD statements using various combinations of data types and decimal alignments, was used to illustrate basic workings of the COBOL compiler. The Procedure and Data Division maps, register assignments, and literal pool were examined in detail. Several sets of COBOL and generated object instructions were compared. Initially, both operands in the COBOL instruction were of the same data type and sign, and were similarly aligned. Subsequently, these restrictions were removed to consider combinations of packed and binary data, nonaligned binary fields, and unsigned binary and decimal fields.

The COBOL listing of Figure 9.1 and its associated output can be used to provide intuitive justification for some commonplace efficiency considerations. These include the following:

1. Where possible, arithmetic should be performed on packed fields, i.e., those defined as COMPUTATIONAL-3. Arithmetic should not

be performed on zoned decimal fields—i.e., those with no clause or with USAGE IS DISPLAY—as additional instructions are required to convert these fields to packed data prior to arithmetic. With respect to Figure 9.1, the statement

```
ADD PACKED-FIELD-ONE TO PACKED-FIELD-TWO
```

is preferable to

```
ADD DISPLAY-FIELD-ONE TO DISPLAY-FIELD-TWO.
```

As can be seen from Figure 9.1, addition of packed fields requires one instruction, addition of binary fields takes three instructions, and addition of zoned decimal fields, four.

2. Regardless of what usage is specified, all data names in the same instruction should contain the same number of decimal places. Thus the statement

```
ADD PACKED-FIELD-ONE TO PACKED-FIELD-TWO
```

is preferable to

```
ADD PACKED-FIELD-ONE TO PACKED-FIELD-WITH-POINT.
```

The second statement, involving addition of two operands with different numbers of decimal places, requires additional machine instructions to align the data prior to the arithmetic.

3. The receiving operand, whether packed, binary, or display, should always be signed. Omission of the sign in the picture clause causes an extra instruction that removes the sign generated as the result of the arithmetic operation. Further, omission of a sign in the picture clause of the receiving data name could cause algebraic errors in cases where negative numbers could legitimately be present. Thus the statement

```
ADD PACKED-FIELD-ONE TO PACKED-FIELD-TWO
```

is preferable to

```
ADD PACKED-FIELD-ONE TO PACKED-FIELD-UNSIGNED.
```

4. Arithmetic should be performed on fields with like usage clauses to avoid conversion from one format to another; thus the statement

```
ADD PACKED-FIELD-ONE TO PACKED-FIELD-TWO
```

is superior to

```
ADD PACKED-FIELD-ONE TO BINARY-FIELD-ONE.
```

In reviewing these suggestions, the reader must remember they are only guidelines and consequently cannot be implemented 100% of the time. Since the problem specifications may, in and of themselves, prohibit implementation, the guidelines must be subservient to the problem itself. Second, all suggestions are based solely on the number of generated machine instructions. Thus the alternative with fewer instructions is presumed superior in that it requires less storage.

In conclusion, the COBOL programmer can and does function with no knowledge of the machine. However, a little knowledge in this area goes a long way toward genuine understanding of debugging and efficiency considerations. We hope this point has been effectively made. We have found that the best COBOL programmers are those who also know, or at least have a fundamental understanding of, Assembler.

TRUE/FALSE EXERCISES

1. A load instruction changes the contents of a register.
2. A store instruction does not change the contents of a storage location.
3. DISPLAY data must be packed before they can be added.
4. Data must be in binary format before they can be added.
5. The COBOL programmer is not permitted to mix data types in the same COBOL instruction.
6. An add half-word instruction could be used in conjunction with packed data.
7. The CVD instruction converts binary data to packed format.
8. The CVB instruction changes the contents of a register.
9. The PACK instruction must operate on two fields of identical length.
10. The AP instruction has only one length field.
11. AP (add packed) is a storage-to-storage instruction.
12. The CVB instruction works directly on DISPLAY data.
13. The addition of two COMPUTATIONAL-3 fields requires fewer machine instructions than does the addition of two DISPLAY fields.
14. A minimum of four machine instructions is required to add two DISPLAY fields.
15. The COBOL programmer is not permitted to combine data names of different decimal alignments in the same instruction.

16. Regardless of the data types involved, object code is more efficient if COBOL operands have identical decimal alignments.

17. If both a signed and unsigned operand appear in the same COBOL instruction, the answer will be unsigned.

18. If both COMP and COMP-3 operands appear in the same COBOL statement, the answer will be in packed format.

PROBLEMS

1. Consider the Data Division map of Figure 9.2. Show how the displacement and definition columns are consistent with the definitions in the Working-Storage section of Figure 9.1.

2. Consider the object instructions generated for COBOL statement 42. Show that the length codes in both the machine and Assembler instructions are consistent with the definitions in Working-Storage. Also show consistency of base registers and displacement between the machine and Assembler instructions.

3. Consider the following COBOL statement:

```
ADD COMP3-DATA-NAME TO DISPLAY-DATA-NAME.
```

where

```
05   COMP3-DATA-NAME  PICTURE IS S9(4)
         USAGE IS COMPUTATIONAL-3.
```

and

```
05   DISPLAY-DATA-NAME  PICTURE IS S9(4).
```

are the definitions for the respective data names. The following statements were found in a corresponding Procedure Division map:

```
F2 F3 3168 A009
FA F2 3168 A021
F3 3F A009 3168
```

(a) Where is the compiler work area? How many bytes does it contain?

(b) What is the location associated with each COBOL data name? (Do not guess, but explain how the structure of the COBOL and BAL ADD statements gives you an unambiguous answer.)

4. Given the Data Division entries

```
05   FIELD-A   PIC 9(3)    VALUE 456.
05   FIELD-B   PIC 9(3)    VALUE 123.
05   FIELD-C   PIC S9(3)   VALUE -100.
05   SUM1      PIC 9(3)    VALUE 0.
05   SUM2      PIC S9(3)   VALUE 0.
05   SUM3      PIC S9(3)   VALUE 25.
05   SUM4      PIC 9(4)    VALUE 25.
```

and the Procedure Division entries

```
ADD FIELD-A   FIELD-B GIVING SUM1.
ADD FIELD-A   FIELD-B GIVING SUM2.
ADD FIELD-C TO SUM3.
ADD FIELD-C TO SUM4.
```

   (a) Explain why SUM1 would print as 579 but SUM2 might print as 57I.
   (b) Explain why SUM3 would retain the value -75, but SUM4 would become +75. *Hint:* Remember the Or Immediate instruction.

5. Given the following Data Division entries:

```
01   FIRST-SET-OF-COUNTERS.
     05   COUNTER-A   DISPLAY   PIC 9(3).
     05   COUNTER-B   DISPLAY   PIC 9(3).
     05   COUNTER-C   DISPLAY   PIC 9(3).

01   SECOND-SET-OF-COUNTERS.
     05   COUNTER-D   COMP      PIC S9(4).
     05   COUNTER-E   COMP      PIC S9(4).
     05   COUNTER-F   COMP      PIC S9(4).

01   THIRD-SET-OF-COUNTERS.
     05   COUNTER-G   COMP-3    PIC 9(5).
     05   COUNTER-H   COMP-3    PIC 9(5).
     05   COUNTER-I   COMP-3    PIC 9(5).
```

Is there anything 'wrong' with the following?

   (a) MOVE ZEROS TO FIRST-SET-OF-COUNTERS.
   (b) MOVE ZEROS TO SECOND-SET-OF-COUNTERS.
   (c) MOVE ZEROS TO THIRD-SET-OF-COUNTERS.

An Assembler Subset

The reader is assumed to be familiar with fundamental Assembler concepts (Chapter 6), the use of Assembler in ABEND debugging (Chapter 7), and the various instruction formats as they relate to COBOL efficiency considerations (Chapter 9). The present chapter substantially enlarges the Assembler coverage by introducing a working subset of approximately 50 instructions.

One should approach this chapter with two objectives: First, to gain sufficient insight into Assembler as to be able to use the vendor manual intelligently should the need arise; second, to develop further the link between COBOL and Assembler. A third objective, realizable after completing the *next* chapter, is to develop the ability to read and understand simple Assembler programs, and/or to undertake elementary programming assignments.

The discussion is informal in nature. The presentation of individual instructions aims at intuitive understanding rather than detailed description of every subtlety. Hence, the chapter does not teach Assembler programming per se, but tries instead to instill an overall appreciation for the language.

We begin with coverage of the arithmetic operations, emphasizing the distinction between packed and binary data, and between half-word, full-word, and register operands. We introduce various move instructions and discuss relative addressing. We also cover the load and store instructions, again stressing the difference between half-word and full-word operands. We present several compare instructions, and discuss the extended mnemonics and the relationship to the condition code. The logical operations to manipulate bits within a byte are introduced. We cover the symbolic instruction formats and show various techniques for establishing a loop. Finally, the important "Techniques of the Trade" section shows common uses of various instructions.

ARITHMETIC INSTRUCTIONS

There are several Assembler instructions for each arithmetic operation. Figure 10.1, for example, shows four different instructions for addition: AP, AH, A, and AR. The choice depends on the *type* and *location* of the data on which the instruction is to operate. *All arithmetic instructions take the value of the first operand, perform the indicated operation using the second operand, and put the result in the first operand.* The instruction AP A,B, for example, takes the value of B, adds it to A, and puts the result in A. (The Assembler instruction AP A,B corresponds to the COBOL instruction ADD B TO A.)

Arithmetic is performed on either packed or binary data. (It may also be done in floating point, but that is not discussed further.) Binary operands may be located in registers, half-words, or full-words; thus there are three different binary add instructions, depending on the location of the data. However, there is only a single instruction to add packed data, as both operands in the Add Pack instruction are located in storage.

Examples 10.1a and 10.1b illustrate the Add Pack instruction, in which both operands contain packed data of variable length, from 1 to 16 bytes. Recall that the sign of a packed field is stored in the low-order 4 bits, with C and D denoting positive and negative numbers, respectively. The result of example 10.1b, which adds plus 10 and minus 25, is a minus 15, which is stored in the first operand.

Examples 10.1c and 10.1d add a half- and full-word, respectively, to the designated register. Both the AH and A instructions operate on *binary* data in which the sign of a number is indicated by its high-order bit (zero indicates a positive number, and one implies a negative quantity, stored

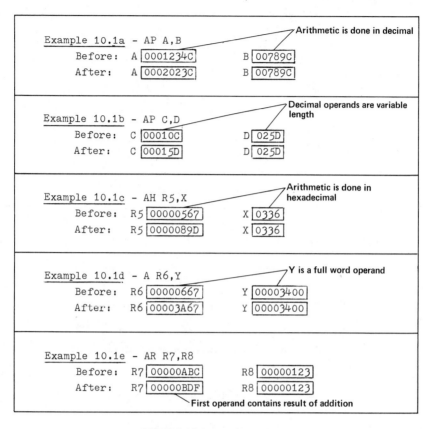

FIGURE 10.1 Add Instructions

in two's complement form). Note well that the result of example 10.1c (0000089D) is a positive *binary* number; also, that the result of example 10.1d is a valid binary number (00003A67), although it would be invalid as a packed field.

Example 10.1e operates on binary data, with both operands contained in registers. The instruction AR R7,R8 takes the contents of register 7, adds the contents of register 8, and leaves the result in register 7. Note well the use of binary (i.e., hexadecimal) arithmetic in examples 10.1c, d, and e.

Figure 10.2 illustrates the subtract instructions and closely parallels Figure 10.1. There is definite correspondence between SP, SH, S, and SR, and their counterparts from Figure 10.1. Be well aware that SH and S operate on a half- and full-word, respectively. Observe also that the result of example 10.2e, hexadecimal Fs (or binary 1s), is absolutely correct. Subtracting 1 from zero produces a minus 1, which is stored in two's complement notation as hexadecimal Fs.

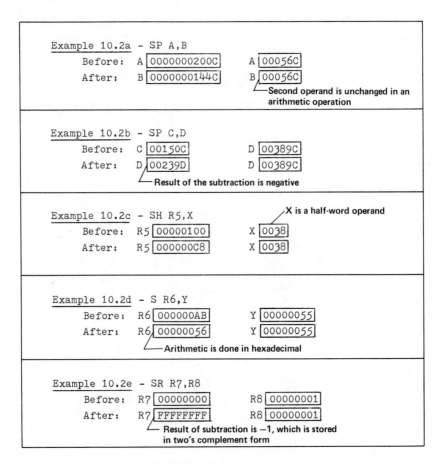

FIGURE 10.2 Subtract Instructions

The results of the multiplication in examples 10.3*a*, *b*, and *c*, are straightforward and require no further explanation. (The Multiply Packed instruction does involve a subtlety with leading zeros, and the reader is referred to the subsequent Techniques of the Trade section.) Examples 10.3*d* and 10.3*e* involve *even-odd register pairs* to accommodate 64-bit results. To better understand the need for the extra register, let us digress briefly to discuss a basic concept in multiplication. If an N digit number is multiplied by an M digit number, the product will contain N+M digits. For example, multiplication of the *two*-digit number 42, by the *three*-digit number 567, produces a *five*-digit answer, 23,814.

Consider now example 10.3*d*, M R4,Y. One would expect the contents of register 4 to be multiplied by the full word Y, with the result stored in register 4. That is *not*, however, what happens because the product produced by two 32-bit numbers (register 4 and a full word Y) requires 64 bits.

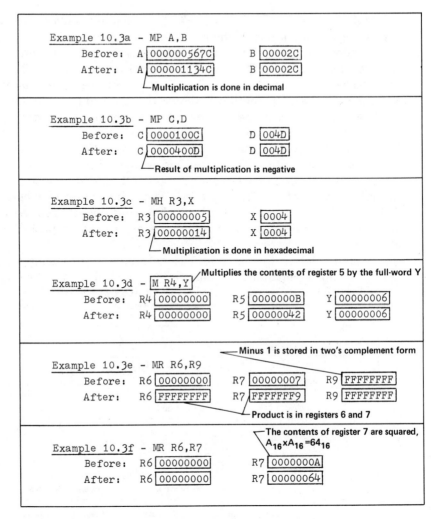

FIGURE 10.3 Multiply Instructions

The multiply full-word instruction specifies an *even* register, register 4, of an *even-odd register pair*, registers 4 and 5. It multiplies the contents of the *odd* register, register 5, by the contents of the full word Y and stores the result in registers 4 and 5. The multiplication takes place in binary. Hence, multiplication of the hexadecimal numbers B and 6 produces the hexadecimal result 42—i.e., $(11 \times 6 = 66)_{10}$, which equals $(B \times 6 = 42)_{16}$.

The MR instructions in examples 10.3e and f also utilize the even-odd concept. Example 10.3e multiplies the contents of register 7 by the contents of register 9 and stores the result in registers 6 and 7. In this case, plus 7 is multiplied by minus 1 (remember the two's complement notation), and the result is a minus 7. Example 10.3*f* effectively squares the initial contents of register 7 and stores the result in registers 6 and 7.

Division is illustrated by Figure 10.4. (Note well that there is no divide-half-word instruction.) The divide packed instruction DP A,B divides A by B and leaves the answer in A. Since division involves both a quotient and a remainder, further explanation is required. Accordingly, the receiving field is broken in two, *with the number of bytes in the remainder equal to the number of bytes in the divisor. The remainder occupies the rightmost portion of the first operand, and the quotient is put into the leftmost portion.*

In example 10.4*a* a five-byte field is divided by a two-byte field. This in turn produces a two-byte remainder and a three-byte quotient in the right and left portions of the first operand. Sixty divided by 18 yields a quotient of 3 and a remainder of 6. Both dividend and divisor must be packed initially, and both quotient and remainder are stored as packed fields with valid signs.

Example 10.4*b* divides plus 104 by minus 9, producing a quotient of minus 11 and a remainder of plus 5. Observe also that the length of the remainder (one byte) corresponds to the length of the divisor.

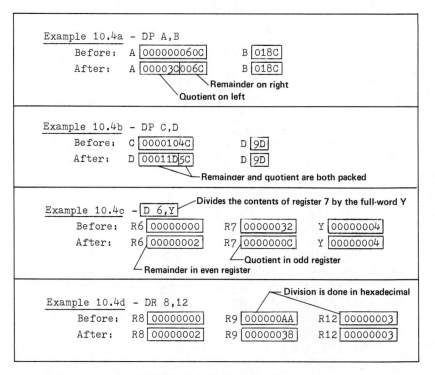

FIGURE 10.4 Divide Instructions

Examples 10.4*c* and 10.4*d* utilize an even-odd register pair, with the quotient and remainder in the odd and even registers, respectively. In both cases, the contents of the odd register, in the even-odd pair, are divided by the second operand. All arithmetic is done in binary (hexadecimal). Thus, in example 10.4*c*, $(32 \div 4 = C \text{ remainder } 2)_{16}$, which equals $(50 \div 4 = 12 \text{ remainder } 2)_{10}$.

MOVE INSTRUCTIONS

The Move Character (MVC) instruction moves data from the second operand to the first. The contents of the second operand are unchanged, and the contents of the first operand are overwritten. Data are moved *one byte at a time, from left to right, according to the length of the first operand.* MVC is an SS instruction, with a single length code, allowing a maximum of 256 bytes to be moved at one time. (There is also an MVCL, Move Character *Long*, instruction which can move more than 256 bytes, and which is not discussed further.)

Move Immediate (MVI) is an SI instruction which moves a *single* byte of data *contained in the instruction itself*, to the designated storage location. Examples of both MVC and MVI instructions are shown in Figure 10.5. (A question mark implies that the contents of a particular byte are immaterial to the example.)

Example 10.5*a* moves B to A, one byte at a time, from left to right. The contents of B are unchanged (unless A and B overlap), and the initial contents of A are immaterial. The instruction did *not* specify the length of the move, which defaults to the length of the receiving field—i.e., A. (It is purely by coincidence that the receiving and sending fields have the same length.)

Example 10.5*b* explicitly specifies that only three bytes are affected. The move takes place from *left to right*, and the fourth byte of the receiving field is unchanged. Note well that the lengths of the two operands are different from each other, and also different from the length of the move itself.

Example 10.5*c* specifies a length of two and, in addition, that the receiving field begins one byte past E; i.e., at E+1. Both the first and last bytes of the receiving field are unaffected by the move.

Example 10.5*d* moves H to G. The length of the move is not explicitly specified, and it defaults to the length of the receiving field. Accordingly, a total of 5 bytes will be moved, beginning with the leftmost byte of H. However, since the sending field is only three bytes in length, the next two *contiguous* locations—i.e., the first two bytes of I—are moved as well. This

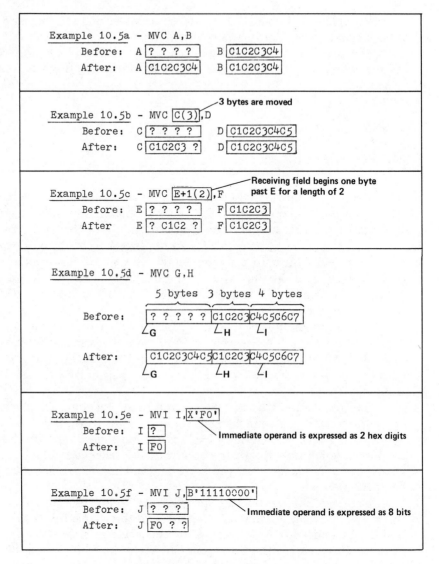

FIGURE 10.5 Move Instructions

in turn may lead to unintended results. The author strongly suggests therefore *that the length of a move be explicitly coded in any MVC instruction.*

Examples 10.5*e* and 10.5*f* illustrate the MVI instruction which moves a single byte. The latter is specified as two hex characters in example 10.5*e*, and as eight bits in example 10.5*f*. Observe also that if the receiving field is more than one byte in length, as in example 10.5*f*, the leftmost byte receives the move.

LOAD AND STORE INSTRUCTIONS

A *load* instruction brings the contents of a storage location into a register. *The initial contents of the register are immaterial, and the contents of the storage location are unchanged as a result of the instruction.* Consider Figure 10.6, which illustrates various load instructions.

Example 10.6a loads a *full-word* (four bytes) into register 3. Example 10.6b loads a *half-word* into register 4; i.e., the contents of *two* bytes, at locations X and X+1, are put into the *low*-order two bytes of register 4, and the high-order bytes are zero-filled. Example 10.6c is also a load half-word instruction, but it references location X+1, rather than X. Hence, the value of locations X+1 and X+2 are put into the low-order bytes of register 5. *Note well that the contents of the four bytes beginning at location X are unchanged as a result of examples a, b, and c.*

Example 10.6d is a *load address* instruction which puts the *address* of a dataname, rather than its value, into a register. Given that X is at hexadecimal address 556677, the value of register 6 will be 00556677 as a result of example 10.6d. Recall that all addresses are 24 bits; hence, the

```
Example 10.6a - L R3,X
    Before:  R3 [ ? ? ? ? ]    X [C1C2C3C4]
    After:   R3 [C1C2C3C4]     X [C1C2C3C4]


Example 10.6b - LH R4,X
    Before:  R4 [ ? ? ? ? ]    X [C1C2C3C4]
    After:   R4 [0000C1C2]     X [C1C2C3C4]


Example 10.6c - LH R5,X+1
    Before:  R5 [ ? ? ? ? ]    X [C1C2C3C4]
    After:   R5 [0000C2C3]     X [C1C2C3C4]


Example 10.6d - LA R6,X
    Before:  R6 [ ? ? ? ? ]    X [C1C2C3C4]
    After:   R6 [00556677]     X [C1C2C3C4]
```

Note: X is defined as a full-word, beginning at the hexadecimal address 556677 (see example 10.6d). A question mark indicates that the contents of a given location are immaterial as opposed to unknown.

FIGURE 10.6 Load Instructions

```
Example 10.7a - ST R5,X
    Before:   R5 |01234567|    X |? ? ? ?|
    After:    R5 |01234567|    X |01234567|


Example 10.7b - STH R5,Y
    Before:   R5 |01234567|    Y |? ?|
    After:    R5 |01234567|    Y |4567|


Example 10.7c - STH R5,Z+1
    Before:   R5 |01234567|    Z |? ? ?|
    After:    R5 |01234567|    Z |? 4567|
```

Note: A question mark indicates that the contents of a given
location are immaterial rather than unknown.

FIGURE 10.7 Store Instructions

high-order byte of the specified register is always 00 as a result of a load address instruction. (This will change under MVS/XA.)

A *store* instruction is the opposite of a load; i.e., it puts the contents of a register into storage. *The initial contents of the storage location are immaterial, and the value of the register is unchanged as a result of the instruction.* (A store instruction is one of the few Assembler instructions which changes the value of the *second* operand.) Consider Figure 10.7.

Example 10.7*a* stores the contents of register 5 into the full word X. Example 10.7*b* stores the *two* low-order (i.e., rightmost) bytes of register 5 into the half-word Y. Example 10.7*c* also stores the two low-order bytes of register 5, in locations Z+1 and Z+2, leaving location Z alone. Note well that the contents of register 5 are unchanged as a result of examples *a*, *b*, and *c*.

Load and Store Multiple

A "normal" load or store instruction utilizes a single register; e.g., L R4,X loads register 4 with the contents of the *full-word* X. A load or store multiple instruction specifies a *range* of registers; i.e., the instruction LM R4,R7,X loads registers 4 *through* 7, beginning with the contents of the full-word X. The situation is shown schematically in Figure 10.8.

As can be seen from Figure 10.8, the four bytes (i.e., full-word) beginning at location X are loaded into register 4; the full-word at X+4 is put into register 5, the full-word at X+8 into register 6, and the full-word at X+12 into register 7.

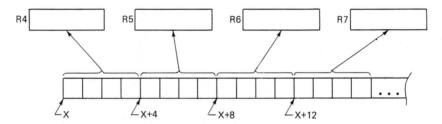

FIGURE 10.8 The LM Instruction (LM R4, R7, X)

The designated registers sometimes "wrap around" register 0—e.g., LM R14,R2,A. The latter instruction loads registers 14, 15, 0, 1, and 2 with successive full-words beginning at location A. The instruction LM R14,R12,TAG fills *15* registers (i.e., registers 14, 15, 0, 1, ... 12) with successive full-words from storage.

A Store Multiple instruction is the opposite of a Load Multiple; i.e., it puts the contents of consecutive registers into storage. Hence, the instruction STM R6,R8,B fills 12 bytes (i.e., 3 full-words) beginning at B with the contents of registers 6, 7, and 8. Wrap-around is also possible; i.e., STM 14,12,C stores the contents of *15* registers.

COMPARE INSTRUCTIONS

A compare instruction evaluates two quantities, and indicates whether the first is less than, equal to, or greater than the second. These results are *mutually exclusive* (i.e., only one condition can occur at a given time) and *collectively exhaustive* (i.e., one of the three conditions must occur). *The first operand is always compared to the second.* Hence, if A is less than B, the instruction Compare A,B will return a *low* condition. If the instruction were reversed—i.e., Compare B,A, and A were still less than B—then a high condition results. (Remember, the first operand is compared to the second.)

CLC is the mnemonic op code for *Compare Logical Character*. It is an SS instruction and compares two fields of *equal* length up to a maximum of 256 bytes. Figure 10.9 illustrates the CLC instruction. In example 10.9*a*, the character string 123 (F1F2F3 in hexadecimal) is compared to the string 126, resulting in the expected low condition. In example 10.9*b*, a *packed* plus one (1C) is compared to a *packed* minus one (1D), producing a *low* condition. The latter result may be somewhat surprising until we realize that the compare logical operation functions on a bit-by-bit basis, and ignores any numeric signs. If one is dealing with numeric rather than character data, a compare packed (CP) instruction should be used instead, as was done in example 10.9*c*. Compare packed evaluates the sign and produces a high result when plus 1 is compared to minus 1.

```
Example 10.9a - CLC X,Y
      X F1F2F3              Y F1F2F6

      Result: A low condition as X is less than Y
```

```
Example 10.9b - CLC PLUS1,MINUS1
      PLUS1 001C            MINUS1 001D

      Result: A low condition as PLUS1 is less than MINUS1
              on a bit by bit basis
```

```
Example 10.9c - CP PLUS1,MINUS1
      PLUS1 001C            MINUS1 001D

      Result: A high condition as Compare Packed accounts for a
              numeric sign; hence PLUS1 is algebraically greater
              than MINUS1
```

```
Example 10.9d - C R3,MINUS1
      R3 00000001           MINUS1 FFFFFFFF

      Result: A high condition as the comparison is a binary
              comparison and accounts for signed numbers
```

```
Example 10.9e - CL R3,MINUS1
      R3 00000001           MINUS1 FFFFFFFF

      Result: A low condition as CL does a logical comparison
              which ignores signed numbers
```

FIGURE 10.9 Compare Instructions

Similar considerations apply to binary operands as well, as can be seen by contrasting examples 10.9*d* and 10.9*e*. C by itself is an *arithmetic* operation and distinguishes between plus and minus numbers; CL is a *logical* operation and looks merely at the bit configurations. Note well the different results produced by examples 10.9*d* and 10.9*e*.

TRANSFER OF CONTROL

A computer executes instructions sequentially as they occur in storage. When the normal sequence of execution is altered—i.e., when the computer fetches the next instruction to be executed from somewhere other than the next sequential location—a *transfer of control* is said to occur.

There are two kinds of transfer of control instructions: *conditional* and *unconditional*. The latter corresponds to a COBOL GO TO statement; i.e., control is transferred regardless of any particular condition. On the other hand, a *conditional* transfer takes place only when a pre-existing circumstance is satisfied.

A conditional transfer of control is achieved by first comparing two quantities and then branching (or not), based on the results of that comparison. Consider the COBOL statement:

```
IF HOURS-WORKED > 40
    GO TO OVERTIME-CALCULATIONS.
```

The generated Assembler statements would include both a *compare* and a *conditional branch;* i.e., HOURS–WORKED would be compared to 40, and a subsequent branch to OVERTIME–CALCULATIONS executed if and only if HOURS–WORKED were greater than 40.

The Assembler programmer may use any of a number of instructions to indicate when a branch is to take place. These include:

BH	Branch High
BL	Branch Low
BE	Branch Equal
BNH	Branch Not High
BNL	Branch Not Low
BNE	Branch Not Equal
B	Branch (Unconditionally)

Collectively, these seven instructions encompass all possible conditions. (A branch on a "less than or equal" condition is equivalent to a "branch not high."). Note well the last mnemonic: B by itself denotes an *unconditional* transfer of control. A *conditional* transfer of control is preceded by a compare instruction of the form COMPARE A,B in which *the first operand (A) is compared to the second operand (B)*. The result of a compare instruction sets a *condition code* to one of three values: *high* if A is greater than B, *equal* if A equals B, and *low* if A is less than B. A subsequent conditional branch will achieve the desired transfer of control. For example, the sequence:

```
        COMPARE A,B
        BH TAG
NEXT    .
        .
        .
```

transfers control to TAG if A is greater than B, and executes NEXT if A is not greater than B.

A compare instruction merely sets the condition code. (The *condition code* is formally defined as bits 34 and 35 of the PSW. The condition code therefore has four possible values: 00, 01, 10, and 11.) The condition code is set to 00 if the quantities being compared are equal, to 01 if the comparison is low, and to 10 if the comparison is high. (The condition code cannot be set to 11 as the result of a comparison. However, other kinds of instructions also set the condition code. Any arithmetic operation, for example, has four possible outcomes; e.g., the result of an addition can be zero, negative, positive, or cause an overflow, which correspond to condition code settings of 00, 01, 10, and 11, respectively.)

All mnemonic branch instructions have the *same* machine op code, which is related to the condition code setting, and a generated mask, as shown in Figure 10.10.

Extended mnemonic	Mask				Branch on Condition	
	00 (=)	01 (<)	10 (>)	11		
BE	1	0	0	0	BC	8
BNE	0	1	1	1	BC	7
BL	0	1	0	0	BC	4
BNL	1	0	1	1	BC	11
BH	0	0	1	0	BC	2
BNH	1	1	0	1	BC	13
B	1	1	1	1	BC	15
NOP	0	0	0	0	BC	0

FIGURE 10.10 Extended Mnemonic Instructions

The four possible settings of the condition code are grouped together to form a mask. A branch not equal, for example, takes place if the condition code has any one of three values: 01, 10, or 11 (i.e., if the mask has a decimal value of 7). In similar fashion, a branch equal corresponds to a branch on a mask value of 8; branch low to a value of 4, etc. Note well that an unconditional branch takes place regardless of the value of the condition code, and is equivalent to a branch on a mask of 15. A NOP (no operation) implies that a branch is never to occur and corresponds to a branch on condition zero.

Given Figure 10.10, one should realize that the BC instruction with appropriate mask is equivalent to an extended mnemonic; e.g., BC 8,TAG is identical to BE TAG. When actually coding in Assembler, most people prefer the extended mnemonic. However, the generated machine language instruction reflects the BC op code, and hence there is a need to understand Figure 10.10. (See problem 1, parts (16), (17), and (18) in Chapter 11.)

The BC instruction is closely related to another instruction, BCR; i.e., *the single instruction BC 8,TAG is equivalent to the pair of instructions LA 9,TAG and BCR 8,9.* BC 8,TAG branches to the address TAG if the condition is met. An equivalent way to accomplish the same thing is first to load the address of TAG into a register, and then branch to the address contained in that register.

BIT MANIPULATION

A primary reason for using Assembler language in lieu of a higher-level language is the ability to manipulate bits within a byte. To that end, the programmer is often concerned with the *logical* operations And, Or, and Exclusive Or, which are defined in Figure 10.11. The left-hand side of Figure 10.11 shows the four possible bit combinations. The right-hand entry defines the value of the logical operation for the particular combination.

| Bit Combinations | | Logical Operations | | |
A	B	A OR B	A AND B	A XOR B
0	0	0	0	0
0	1	1	0	1
1	0	1	0	1
1	1	1	1	0

FIGURE 10.11 Definition of Logical Operations
(Or, And, Exclusive Or)

In order for the operation A or B to be considered true, either A must equal 1, or B must equal 1, or both. In Figure 10.11, A OR B is true in every instance, except when A and B are both zero.

A AND B requires that both A and B equal 1 in order to be true; hence, A AND B is true in only the last instance of the table.

A XOR B requires that A equal 1, or B equal 1, but *not* both. A XOR B is true when A and B assume different values, and false when they have the same value.

As we shall learn later in the chapter, the logical operations have some uses which are most immediately apparent. The exclusive or operation, for example is often used to initialize fields to zero and/or to reverse the setting of a binary switch. The logical or is most often used to remove the sign of a packed field after an arithmetic operation. We shall discover also that there are several forms of the logical instructions, depending on the location of the operands—e.g., in registers, storage, etc.

Test Under Mask

The Test Under Mask Instruction is a type of compare instruction in which bits within a byte are examined. It utilizes the SI instruction format and consequently operates on a single byte of storage. A maximum of 8 bits are evaluated in a given TM instruction. Consider, for example, TM FIELDA, B'11000000'.

The TM instruction contains a *binary literal*, in this case 11000000, known as a *mask*, which indicates which bits in the designated byte are to be evaluated. In this example, it is the two leftmost bits (i.e., they are the only mask bits set to one) within the byte FIELDA. The designated bits are each compared to one and the condition code is set appropriately. The TM instruction is followed by a branch instruction of the form:

BO   Branch if all designated bits are 1

BZ   Branch if all designated bits are 0

BM   Branch if the designated bits are mixed—i.e., a combination of 1's and 0's

BNO   Branch if the designated bits are not 1's—i.e., they are zeros or mixed

Consider, for example, the following series of instructions:

```
        TM FIELDB,B'00001111'
        BZ TAG1
        BO TAG2
NEXT    .
        .
        .
```

The low-order four bits in FIELDB are each compared to 1. If all four of these bits are zero, control is transferred to TAG1; if all four are one, control is transferred to TAG2. If the bits are mixed—i.e., a combination of zeros and ones—execution continues with NEXT.

It is also possible to express the mask as two hex characters, rather than as an eight-bit binary string. Hence, one could have coded TM FIELDB, X'0F' in lieu of TM FIELDB,B'00001111'.

SYMBOLIC INSTRUCTION FORMATS

Appendix A lists the Assembler instruction set in alphabetical order, and in addition contains the *symbolic instruction format* for each instruction; e.g., the Move Character (MVC) instruction has the format D1(L,B1),D2(B2). In order to appreciate the significance of this information, consider the instruction MVC A,B which moves field B to field A, one byte at a time, from left to right. (The length of the move is determined by the length of field A.) When a programmer codes MVC A,B he or she *implicitly relies on the Assembler to generate base registers and displacements for fields A and B, as well as to determine the length of the move.*

It is also possible to specify this information *explicitly* by utilizing the *symbolic instruction format*, as shown in Figure 10.12.

Implicit Specification:	MVC	A,B
Symbolic Format:	MVC	D1(L,B1),D2(B2)
Example of Explicit Specification:	MVC	200(10,5),100(6)

FIGURE 10.12 The MVC Instruction

Recall from Figure 6.7 that in the symbolic instruction format, L denotes the length code, B_1 and D_1 denote the base register and displacement for the first operand, and B_2 and D_2 denote similar values for the second operand. Thus, the explicit specification of Figure 10.12 indicates that the first operand (A) is displaced 200 bytes from register 5, that the second operand (B) is displaced 100 bytes from register 6, and that the length of the move is 10 bytes. Normally, there is no need for explicit specification. The programmer most likely, and more conveniently, codes MVC A,B and trusts in the assembler to calculate the necessary base registers and displacements. However, certain applications—e.g., *table lookups*—mandate its use.

Table Lookups

A table lookup—e.g., the conversion of an incoming code to an expanded value—is a frequent application in any language. Figure 10.13 illustrates one way to accomplish a *sequential* table lookup in COBOL; Figure 10.14 depicts the associated storage allocation. (The reader should have no difficulty with either figure, but the following COBOL reference is provided: *Structured Methods Through COBOL*, R. Grauer, Prentice-Hall, Englewood Cliffs, NJ, 1983.)

```
01  TABLE-PROCESSING-ELEMENTS.
    05  TITLE-SUB               PIC 99       VALUE ZERO.
    05  FOUND-TITLE-SWITCH      PIC X(3)     VALUE SPACES.

01  TITLE-VALUES.
    05  FILLER                  PIC X(15)    VALUE '010ACCOUNTANT'.
    05  FILLER                  PIC X(15)    VALUE '015ANALYST'.
    .
     .
      .
    05  FILLER                  PIC X(15)    VALUE '896TECHNICIAN'.

01  TITLE-CODES-AND-VALUES REDEFINES TITLE-VALUES.
    05  TITLE-TABLE OCCURS 10 TIMES.
        10  TITLE-CODE          PIC X(3).
        10  TITLE               PIC X(12).
.
 .
  .
PROCEDURE DIVISION.
.
 .
  .
    MOVE 'NO' TO FOUND-TITLE-SWITCH.
    MOVE 1 TO TITLE-SUB.
    PERFORM FIND-TITLE
        UNTIL FOUND-TITLE-SWITCH = 'YES'.
NEXT-PARAGRAPH.
.
 .
  .
FIND-TITLE.
    IF TITLE-CODE (TITLE-SUB) = INCODE
        MOVE TITLE (TITLE-SUB) TO PRINT-LINE
        MOVE 'YES' TO FOUND-TITLE-SWITCH
    ELSE
        IF TITLE-SUB = 10
            MOVE 'UNKNOWN' TO PRINT-LINE
            MOVE 'YES' TO FOUND-TITLE-SWITCH
        ELSE
            ADD 1 TO TITLE-SUB.
```

FIGURE 10.13 Table Lookup in COBOL

TITLE-CODES-AND-VALUES						
TITLE-TABLE (1)		TITLE-TABLE (2)			TITLE-TABLE (10)	
CD(1)	TITLE(1)	CD(2)	TITLE(2)		CD(10)	TITLE(10)
0 1 0	A C C O U N T A N T	0 1 5	A N A L Y S T	• • •	8 9 6	T E C H N I C I A N

FIGURE 10.14 COBOL Table Allocation

```
            SR     R5,R5                          First operand is displaced 0 bytes
            LA     R6,TABLE                       from register 6, and is 3 bytes long
LOOP        CLC    0(3,R6),INCODE
            BE     MATCH
            AH     R5,ONE                          Checks that table size is not exceeded
            C      R5,=F'10'
            BE     NOMATCH                         Equivalent to COBOL entry,
            A      R6,FIFTEEN                       ADD 1 TO SUBSCRIPT
            B      LOOP
NOMATCH     MVC    REPORT(12),=C'UNKNOWN'
            B      NEXT
MATCH       MVC    REPORT(12),3(R6)
NEXT
             .
             .
ONE         DC     H'1'
FIFTEEN     DC     F'15'                           Defines TABLE as a 150 byte
TABLE       DS     0CL150                          group item
            DC     CL15'010ACCOUNT'
            DC     CL15'015ANALYST'
             .
             .
            DC     CL15'896TECHNICIAN'
```

FIGURE 10.15 Table Lookup in Assembler

Figures 10.15 and 10.16 are the Assembler counterparts to Figures 10.13 and 10.14, respectively. An understanding of the Assembler routine is facilitated by comparison to the parallel COBOL statements. Figure 10.15 uses two registers for the lookup procedure. Register 5 monitors the number of times through the loop. Register 6 steps through the table comparing the various table entries to the incoming value. The procedure begins by initializing register 5 to zero; i.e., the loop has been executed zero times. Register 6 is initialized with the address of the table.

The CLC instruction is in symbolic format. It compares INCODE to a three byte-field, which begins at the address in register 6 plus a displacement of zero. An equality causes a branch to a symbolic MVC instruction which moves the expanded value to a print line. The expanded value is the second operand in the MVC instruction, and begins three bytes past register 6—i.e., 3(R6). The length of the move is 12 bytes.

If the CLC instruction returns an inequality, register 5 is incremented by one, and the value of register 5 is compared to 10 (the maximum number of times through the loop). An equality here implies an invalid code and a branch to NOMATCH. If the loop has not been executed 10 times, register 6 is incremented by 15 (the length of a table entry consisting of a three-byte

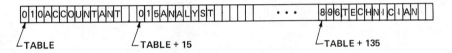

FIGURE 10.16 Assembler Table Allocation

code and 12-byte expanded value), and the loop is reexecuted with the next code in the table; in other words, register 6 points to the current code in the table, and is analogous to the COBOL entry TITLE–SUB.

Figure 10.15 also illustrates the Assembler DC instruction. *A DC (Define Constant) statement is analogous to a COBOL Data Division entry with both a Picture and a Value clause.* Observe, for example, the definition of ONE and FIFTEEN as a half- and full-word, respectively. The variation is only for illustration; i.e., both constants could have been either half-words or full-words. Consistency must, however, be maintained with the associated add instructions; e.g., definition of a half-word (ONE) requires an AH (Add Half-word) instruction. The DC statement may also be omitted in favor of defining the *literal* directly in the instruction itself, as was done in the compare instruction.

The table itself is defined with a DS (Define Storage) statement as DS 0CL150. DS is analogous to a COBOL entry with a Picture clause, but *without* a VALUE clause; i.e., Define Storage merely allocates space for 150 bytes. The leading zero implies that this 150-byte entry will be *redefined* by subsequent DC statements.

Figure 10.17 illustrates a superior implementation of the table lookup procedure utilizing the BCT (Branch on Count) instruction as the *last* statement of the loop. The BCT instruction subtracts one from the designated register and compares the result to zero. If it is not zero, control is transferred to the specified tag—i.e., to LOOP. If, however, the result is zero, execution continues with the next sequential instruction. The loop is established by initializing register 5 with the maximum number of iterations prior to the first execution. (See "Techniques of the Trade" section for further explanation.)

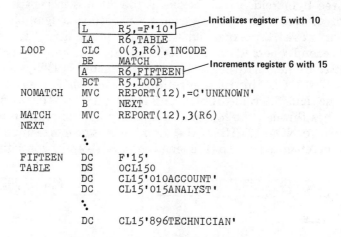

```
                                        ┌── Initializes register 5 with 10
               ┌─────┬──────────────┐
               │ L   │ R5,=F'10'    │
               └─────┴──────────────┘
                 LA    R6,TABLE
        LOOP     CLC   0(3,R6),INCODE
                 BE    MATCH           ┌── Increments register 6 with 15
               ┌─────┬──────────────┐
               │ A   │ R6,FIFTEEN   │
               └─────┴──────────────┘
                 BCT   R5,LOOP
        NOMATCH  MVC   REPORT(12),=C'UNKNOWN'
                 B     NEXT
        MATCH    MVC   REPORT(12),3(R6)
        NEXT
                   ⋱

        FIFTEEN  DC    F'15'
        TABLE    DS    0CL150
                 DC    CL15'010ACCOUNT'
                 DC    CL15'015ANALYST'
                   ⋱

                 DC    CL15'896TECHNICIAN'
```

FIGURE 10.17 Table Lookup in Assembler/II

```
                LA      R5,10 ┐──── Initializes Register 5 with 10
                LA      R6,TABLE
LOOP            CLC     0(3,R6),INCODE
                BE      MATCH
                LA      R6,15(R6) ┐──── Increments Register 6 with 15
                BCT     R5,LOOP
NOMATCH         MVC     REPORT(12),=C'UNKNOWN'
                B       NEXT
MATCH           MVC     REPORT(12),3(R6)
NEXT
                ⋱

TABLE           DS      0CL150
                DC      CL15'010ACCOUNTANT'
                DC      CL15'015ANALYST'
                ⋱

                DC      CL15'896TECHNICIAN'
```

FIGURE 10.18 Table Lookup in Assembler/III

Figure 10.18 is a slightly modified version of Figure 10.17, but it is the way an Assembler programmer would most likely code the table lookup procedure. Figure 10.18 uses the *Load Address* instruction (reader, that is not a mistake) to initialize register 5 and increment register 6. This rather strange use of Load Address depends on the symbolic form of the instruction and is explained in detail in the "Techniques of the Trade" section.

TECHNIQUES OF THE TRADE

The chapter has so far presented the mechanics of many basic instructions in traditional fashion. Now we focus on how these instructions are actually used to accomplish routine programming tasks. Accordingly, we discuss 14 "techniques of the trade" which review much of the preceding material from the chapter, and which are summarized below:

♦ Getting registers to appear in a cross-reference listing
♦ Subtracting 1 from a register
♦ Setting a register to zero
♦ Incrementing a register
♦ Initializing a register with a constant
♦ Establishing a loop
♦ Establishing a COBOL PERFORM
♦ Zeroing out a storage location
♦ Reversing two fields
♦ Reversing bits in a byte
♦ Eliminating the sign of a packed field

- ◆ Establishing a base register
- ◆ Multiplying two packed fields
- ◆ Clearing a print line

Getting Registers to Appear in a Cross-Reference Listing

Example:

```
R0    EQU   0
   .
   .
   .
R15   EQU   15
```

Effect:

```
Allows the registers to be referenced by R0, R1,...R15,
respectively, and causes same to appear in a cross-reference
listing.
```

A typical Assembler program contains multiple references to the registers, and it is extremely helpful to be able to identify all instructions which refer to a given register. Consider, for example, the instruction BCTR 10,11, which references registers 10 and 11.

A cross-reference listing contains an *alphabetized* list of all datanames within a program, but does not list references to numeric constants. The EQU statement equates a dataname to a constant and causes the former to appear in a cross-reference listing. For example, R0 EQU 0 allows R0 to be used in place of a numeric zero. The situation is illustrated in Figure 11.3.

Subtracting 1 from a Register

Example:

```
BCTR R9,R0
```

Effect:

```
Subtracts 1 from the contents of register 9
```

The BCTR instruction subtracts one from the contents of the first register and compares the result to zero. If the result is not zero, it branches to the address in the second register, unless it is register zero.

Whenever register 0 is specified as the second register in an instruction, its address is ignored. Accordingly, the instruction BCTR R9,R0 subtracts one from register 9 and continues execution with the next sequential instruction. The branch to the address in register 0 is *never* taken.

Setting a Register to Zero

Example:

```
SR R6,R6
```

Effect:

```
Sets the contents of register 6 to zero
```

The easiest, and most obvious, way to initialize a register to zero is to subtract the register from itself.

Incrementing a Register

Example:

```
LA R5,2(R5)
```

Effect:

```
Increments the contents of register 5 by 2
```

The Load Address instruction, in addition to its primary function, is used to increment and/or initialize the contents of a register. Typically, the Load Address instruction is coded LA R5,TAG, which causes the address of TAG to be loaded into the designated register.

The general format of this RX instruction is LA R1,D2(X2,B2) which implies that the address is computed by summing three numbers: the address of a base register (B2), the address of an index register (X2), and a displacement (D2). In the address portion of the instruction LA R5,(R0,R5) register 0 corresponds to the index register (X2) and register 5 corresponds to the base register (B2). *Register 0, however, is always ignored*, so that the effective address is the sum of only two numbers (B2 and D2) rather than three. Since register 0 is not used, it need not be specified; i.e., *one may code LA R5,2(R5) as equivalent to LA R5,2(R0,R5)*.

Consider the effect of LA R5,2(R5). The computed address is the sum of the address in register 5 plus a displacement of 2, and the result is placed into register 5. In other words, LA R5,2(R5) adds 2 to the contents of register 5; i.e., it increments the contents of register 5 by 2.

Initializing a Register with a Constant

Example:

```
LA R5,2
```

Effect:

```
Initializes the contents of register 5 to 2
```

Extending the previous discussion, consider the instruction LA R5, 2(R0,R0). Register 0 is specified as both the base and index register—i.e., B2 and X2 in the symbolic format—*and is ignored in both instances.* Hence, one may code LA R5,2 as equivalent to LA R5,2(R0,R0).

The address which is loaded into register 5 reduces to the specified displacement; in effect, register 5 is initialized to 2.

Establishing a Loop

Example:

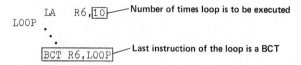

Effect:

```
The instructions in the body of the loop are executed 10 times.
```

Establishment of a loop in any language requires that one initialize a counter, increment it, compare it to a final value, and branch accordingly. Establishment of a loop in Assembler is accomplished by coding a Load Address instruction immediately before the body of the loop, and a BCT instruction as the *last* instruction in the loop. In the example shown, register 6 is initialized to 10 (the number of times the loop is to be executed). The last statement in the loop, BCT R6,LOOP, subtracts 1 from register 6, and compares the result to zero. If the contents of register 6 are not zero, control is transferred to the specified address—i.e., to LOOP. If, however, the contents of register 6 are zero, control is transferred to the next sequential instruction, effectively terminating the loop.

The reader should be convinced that the example shown will execute the instructions in the body of the loop exactly 10 times.

Establishing a COBOL PERFORM

Example:

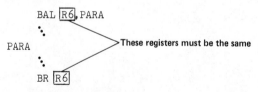

The Branch and Link instruction stores the contents of the next sequential instruction—i.e., the return point—in register 6, and transfers control to the address designated as PARA. The *last* statement of the routine designated as PARA is an unconditional branch to the address contained in register 6. (The single Branch and Link instruction may be replaced by the combination of a Load Address and Branch and Link Register—i.e., LA R7,PARA followed by BALR R6,R7.)

Zeroing out a Storage Location

Example:

```
XC A,A
```

Effect:

```
Sets storage location A to binary zeros
```

The exclusive or operation was defined in Figure 10.11. Recall that the results of A exclusive or B will be 1 if A is equal to 1, or B is equal to 1, but not both; i.e., if both A and B are equal to 1, then A exclusive or B is zero. Accordingly, when a field exclusive ors itself, the result is always zero.

Reversing Two Fields

Example:

```
XC A,B
XC B,A
XC A,B
```

Effect:

```
Reverses the contents of storage locations A and B
```

The "normal" way to switch the contents of two locations in any language is with three move instructions; for example:

```
MVC TEMP,A
MVC A,B
MVC B,TEMP
```

The same effect can be achieved in Assembler with three exclusive or instructions. Consider Figure 10.19.

At first glance, it may seem that nothing but confusion is gained by the technique of Figure 10.19. After all, we still need three instructions to

	A	B
Initial Values	0000 1111	1111 0000
After XC A,B	1111 1111	1111 0000
After XC B,A	1111 1111	0000 1111
After XC A,B	1111 0000	0000 1111

FIGURE 10.19 Use of Exclusive Or to Switch Fields

reverse two fields. However, the MVC instructions require the use of an intermediate field, TEMP, which is avoided with the three exclusive or instructions. Since both MVC and XC are SS instructions with a single length code, one can save up to 256 bytes of storage by using the latter technique. This is not significant in today's era of megabyte machines, but was truly necessary in the early days of the 360.

Reversing Bits in a Byte

Example:

```
XI FIELDA,B'11111111'
```

Effect:

```
Reverses the bits in FIELDA
```

Extending the preceding discussion of exclusive or, the results of an exclusive or operation against binary ones always reverse the initial value. Consider:

```
             FIELDA       1111 0000
             Binary 1's   1111 1111
Result of Exclusive OR    0000 1111
```

This technique is used to reverse bits in a byte, as when reversing the value of a switch. Note also that one could specify XI FIELDA,X'FF' as equivalent to XI FIELDA,B'11111111'; i.e., the hex characters FF are equivalent to the binary string 11111111.

Eliminating the Sign of a Packed Field

Example:

```
OI FIELD,X'F0'
```

Effect:

```
Changes the high-order 4 bits of the designated byte
to a hexadecimal 'F'
```

Incoming numeric data are typically read in character format, necessitating that such fields be packed before arithmetic, and unpacked after. Consider the effect of the following sequence of instructions:

```
PACK WORKA,A
PACK WORKB,B
AP   WORKA,WORKB
UNPK ANSWER,WORKA
```

Assume, for example, that the initial values of A and B are 123 and 456 respectively, or F1F2F3 and F4F5F6 in hexadecimal. WORKA and WORKB assume values of 123F and 456F after packing, and WORKA becomes 579C after the addition. (A packed operation always produces a sign of C or D.) Unpacking WORKA into ANSWER produces F5F7C9 which would print as 57*I* rather than 579 as intended. A fifth instruction, OI ANSWER+2,X'F0' is required to eliminate the sign—i.e., to convert C9 to F9.

The reader may want to review the PMAP of Figure 9.4 with respect to the OI instruction. He or she may also want to review the effect of signed numeric fields in COBOL (see problem 4 in Chapter 9).

Establishing a Base Register

Example:

```
BALR R10,R0
USING *,R10
```

Effect:

```
Designates register 10 as a base register and establishes
a base address
```

The BALR instruction loads the address of the next sequential instruction into the first register and branches to the address in the second register. The instruction BALR R10,R0 loads the address of the next sequential instruction into register 10 *but does not branch*, as register 0 is always ignored.

USING is an assembler language control statement which does *not* generate machine language instructions. Its function is to inform the assembler that the designated register is to be used as the base register in computing storage addresses according to the base/displacement addressing scheme. The asterisk implies that the current value of the location counter will be in the base register at execution time (hence the need for the preceding BALR instruction).

Multiplying Two Packed Fields

Example:

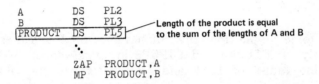

```
A          DS    PL2
B          DS    PL3
PRODUCT    DS    PL5          Length of the product is equal
                              to the sum of the lengths of A and B
             ∴
           ZAP   PRODUCT,A
           MP    PRODUCT,B
```

Effect:

```
Multiplies the packed fields, A and B, and leaves the
result in PRODUCT
```

The MP (Multiply Packed) instruction is simple in concept; e.g., MP X, Y multiplies X by Y and leaves the result in X. There is one significant restriction, however, in that *the first operand must contain a number of bytes of leading zeros equal to the length of the second operand.* For example, if the second operand is two bytes in length, then the first operand must contain at least two bytes of leading zeros. (This restriction is imposed to ensure that the product will always fit in the first operand; e.g., if a two-digit number is multiplied by a three-digit number, the product is a five-digit number.)

In order to multiply two packed fields, one should define the length of the product as the *sum of the lengths of the fields to be multiplied.* The ZAP (Zero and Add Packed) instruction zeros out the PRODUCT field, and then adds field A; i.e., in effect, it loads A into PRODUCT, leaving the necessary high-order zeros. The MP instruction will then work as intended.

Clearing a Print Line

Example:

```
MVI PRTR,X'40'
MVC PRTR+1(132),PRTR
```

Effect:

```
Moves spaces to a 133 position field (the first byte of
which is PRTR)
```

The instruction MVC A,B moves B to A, one byte at a time, from left to right, according to the length specified in A. In order to clear a print line one uses the MVI instruction in combination with an MVC. After the MVI instruction is executed, the value of PRTR is a blank—i.e., a hexadecimal '40'. The value of PRTR is then moved to PRTR+1, then PRTR+1 is moved to PRTR+2, PRTR+2 to PRTR+3, and so on for 132 bytes. The situation is shown schematically:

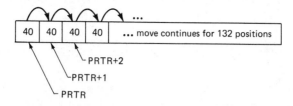

Summary

The chapter presented approximately 50 Assembler instructions. The intent was to develop an overall appreciation for Assembler, rather than a detailed proficiency in individual instructions. Accordingly, several basic operations were covered, including: arithmetic (add, subtract, multiply, and divide), load, store, compare, branch, move, and logical (or, and, exclusive or). All examples stressed the difference between packed and binary data, and for the latter, the difference between register, fullword, and halfword operands. The chapter concluded with an important "techniques of the trade" section which showed how many of the instructions are applied in practice.

TRUE/FALSE EXERCISES

1. The instruction MR R6,R6 squares the contents of register 6.

2. The instruction BCT R5,TAG *always* branches to the instruction at TAG.

3. LA R5,0(R5,R5) doubles the contents of register 5.

4. All assembler instructions change the contents of the *first* operand.

5. The instruction LM R14,R2,ADDRESS will change the value of five registers.

6. ZAP frequently precedes an MP instruction.

7. BC 8 and the extended mnemonic BE are equivalent.

8. The instruction MVC 2(3,4),5(6) moves a total of three bytes.

9. The instruction MVI BYTE(2),X'40' is syntactically correct.

10. A BCT instruction is typically the first instruction in a loop.

11. The MVI instruction moves a maximum of 256 bytes.

12. A, S, M, and D all operate on a register and a full-word.

13. AH, SH, MH, and DH all operate on a register and a half-word.

14. The AP instruction can reference a field with a maximum length of 256 bytes.

15. A compare instruction sets the value of the condition code and branches appropriately.

16. An assembler DS instruction is the equivalent of a COBOL VALUE clause.

17. The logical or instruction may be used to reverse the value of a switch.

18. The condition code in the PSW has four possible settings.

19. The condition code is changed only as the result of a compare instruction.

20. The results of a CLC and a CP instruction on the same fields will always be identical.

21. Numeric fields can be printed correctly *immediately* after decimal operations.

22. Arithmetic can only be done in registers.

23. A logical compare instruction does not take the sign of a numeric field into account.

24. The TM instruction can test a maximum of eight bits.

25. The mask in a TM instruction may be expressed as two hex characters.

PROBLEMS

1. Given the initial values:

```
A:   01234C
B:   2C
C:   00305C
D:   0000002D
E:   056D
F:   100C
```

Indicate the value of the receiving field *after* each of the following instructions has been executed. In each case, refer to the *initial* value above. In addition, state which instructions, if any, will cause problems in execution and/or compilation.

(a) DP C,B
(b) AP A,B
(c) MP A,B
(d) MP D,A
(e) AP A(2),B
(f) SP F,B
(g) AP E,F

2. Given the initial values:

```
Register 2:    00000000
Register 3:    0000020A
Register 4:    0000ABCD
Register 5:    FFFFFFFF
        X:     00000003
        Y:     0005
```

Indicate the value of the receiving field *after* each of the following instructions has been executed. In each case, refer to the *initial* value above. In addition, state which instructions, if any, will cause problems in execution and/or compilation.

(a) AR R3,R4
(b) M   R2,X
(c) MH R4,X
(d) MR R3,R4
(e) A   R5,X
(f) D   R2,X
(g) DH R2,X
(h) S   X,Y
(i) MR R2,R3

3. Given the initial values:

```
        A:     123C
        B:     567D
        C:     7C
Register 3:    00000000
Register 4:    80000000
```

Indicate the value of the condition code after each of the following instructions has been executed. In addition, state which instructions, if any, will cause problems in execution and/or compilation.

(a)	CLC	A,B
(b)	CP	A,B
(c)	CP	A(2),C(1)
(d)	CLC	A(2),C(1)
(e)	CH	R3,B
(f)	CR	R3,R4
(g)	CLR	R3,R4
(h)	CP	A(1),C
(i)	CLC	A(1),C

4. Given the initial values:

```
FIELDA:   F0
FIELDB:   C6
FIELDC:   FF
FIELDD:   56789A
FIELDE:   0000
```

Indicate the value of the receiving field *after* each of the following instructions has been executed. In each case, refer to the *initial* value above. In addition, state which instructions, if any, will cause problems in execution and/or compilation.

(a)	XI	FIELDA,X'FF'
(b)	OI	FIELDB,B'11110000'
(c)	NI	FIELDC,X'00'
(d)	XC	FIELDD,FIELDD
(e)	OI	FIELDC(1),X'F0'
(f)	XC	FIELDE(2),FIELDD(3)

5. Assume that A, B, C, D, and E are defined in *contiguous* storage locations with initial contents as follows:

```
A:   F0F1F2F3
B:   F4F5
C:   F6F7F8F9
D:   C6C7C8
E:   D5D6D7D8D9
```

Indicate the contents of the receiving field after each one of the following instructions has been executed. In each instance, refer to the *initial* contents of both operands. Finally, indicate which, if any, instructions will cause problems in execution.

(a)	MVC	A,D
(b)	MVC	A,E
(c)	MVC	A(3),D
(d)	MVC	C,D(4)

(e)   MVC   B,C+2
(f)   MVC   C+1(3),E+2
(g)   MVI   B+1,X'40'
(h)   MVI   B+1,=X'40'
(i)   MVI   B+1(1),X'40'

6. Given the initial values:

```
FIELDA:        000000000000123C
FIELDB:        000000000000008D
FIELDC:        789C
FIELDD:        F1F2F3F4F5F6F7F8
Register 2:    FFFFFF00
Register 3:    00000ABC
```

Indicate the value of the receiving field *after* each of the following instructions has been executed. Assume that ANS1, ANS2, ANS3, and ANS4 have been defined via DS statements to be as long as necessary. Recall that the CVB, CVD, PACK, and UNPK instructions were discussed in Chapter 9. Finally, indicate which instructions, if any, will cause problems in execution.

(a)   CVB   R2,FIELDA
(b)   CVB   R3,FIELDB
(c)   UNPK   ANS1,FIELDC
(d)   PACK   ANS2,FIELDD
(e)   CVD   R2,ANS3
(f)   CVD   R3,ANS4
(g)   CVB   R4,FIELDC
(h)   CVB   R5,FIELDD

7. Given the initial values:

```
A:        C1C2C3C4
B:        C5C6
C:        C7C8
D:        D1D2D3D4
Register 5:    01234567
Register 6:    89ABCDEF
```

Indicate the value of the receiving field *after* each of the following instructions has been executed. In each case, refer to the *initial* value above. Assume that A, B, C, and D occupy contiguous locations. Also assume that W, X, Y, and Z are defined as contiguous full-words initialized to binary zeros.

(a)   L   R2,A
(b)   LH   R2,A
(c)   L   R3,B

(d)   LM   R2,R4,A
(e)   STH   R5,W
(f)   ST   R5,W
(g)   STH   R5,W+2
(h)   STM   R5,R6,Y

8. State the effects of the following instructions, or pairs of instructions.

(a)   BCTR   R6,R0

(b)   XR   R5,R5

(c)   LA   R10,15

(d)   LA   R10,2(R10)

(e)   LA   R10,5(R10,R10)

(f)   XC   C,D
      XC   D,C
      XC   C,D

(g)   LA   R5,PARA
      BALR   R6,R5

(h)   BAL   R6,PARA

(i)   BC   0,TAG

(j)   BC   15,TAG

(k)   BC   8,TAG

(l)   XI   BYTE,X'FF'

(m)   MVI   PRTR,X'40'
      MVC   PRTR+1(132),PRTR

(n)   OI   NUMBER,X'F0'

9. Compare the *binary* op codes of the instructions AP, AH, A, AR. What do they have in common? Does a similar relationship exist for the other arithmetic operations? Can you make a general statement about the function of bits 4–7 in an op code?

What are the first two bits in the op code of an RR instruction? Of an SS instruction? What do the op codes of AP, SP, MP, and DP have in common? AR, SR, MR, and DR? A, S, M, and D? Can you make a general statement about the function of bits 0 and 1 in an op code?

10. Indicate whether the following SS instructions have one length code or two: AP, SP, MP, and DP; CLC and MVC; NC, OC, and XC; PACK, UNPK, and CP. Can you see any general pattern to determine whether an SS instruction has one length code or two?

11. The extended mnemonics associated with the TM instruction (BO, BZ, BM, and BNO) are also variations of the BC instruction. This is because the TM instruction sets the condition code in the PSW as follows:

Condition code	Meaning
0	Mask bits are all zero
1	Mask bits are all a mixture of zeros and ones
2	—
3	Masked bits are all ones

Derive equivalent BC instructions for BO, BZ, BM, and BNO.

12. Derive the appropriate symbolic instructions from the following machine language statements:

(a) D23171238456
(b) FA3123456789
(c) 4A304100
(d) 1ABC

In essence, you are working backwards; i.e., one normally codes symbolically and the Assembler generates the machine language instruction. You may find it necessary to refer to Figure 6.7, which depicts the instruction formats. Realize also that the component parts of a machine language instruction appear in *different* order than the symbolic counterparts, also that the length codes are different (they are off by 1), and finally that each numeric op code has a mnemonic counterpart which can be obtained from Appendix A.

13. Do you have any preference for using *literals* in an instruction, versus defining the associated constant elsewhere in the program; i.e., which do you prefer:

```
        A    R6,=F'15'
```

versus

```
        A    R6,FIFTEEN
        .
        .
        .
FIFTEEN DC   F'15'
```

Is there a COBOL analogy? On a related note, can you explain why the equal sign is sometimes required and sometimes omitted; i.e., *why are both of the following compare instructions correct?*

```
CLI  FIELDA,C'1'
CLC  FIELDB,=C'1'
```

11

Assembler Language Programming

Overview

Chapter 10 presented a BAL subset of some 50 instructions which were discussed in isolation, without regard for writing a complete program. In this chapter, we incorporate the individual instructions into a finished product. We begin, therefore, with presentation of a working program, and cover the macros necessary for simple I/O—namely, OPEN, CLOSE, GET, and PUT. We cover the DCB macro, its relationship to the supporting JCL, and the DC and DS statements to describe record layouts.

The second half of the chapter contains a complete discussion of *linkage conventions.* We define the special role of registers 0, 1, 13, 14, and 15, describe what happens when a subroutine is called, and emphasize that the 16 general-purpose registers are used by any executing program, be it written in COBOL, BAL, or the Operating System itself. *The primary objective of this latter section is to increase the competence of the COBOL pro-*

grammer by making him or her more aware of precisely what happens when a COBOL program invokes a subroutine.

We begin with consideration of a completed program.

A BAL PROGRAM

The author has always advocated that programming in any language is best learned through *early* exposure to the machine.   Accordingly, we move rather quickly to the Assembler listing of Figure 11.1. Although the reader

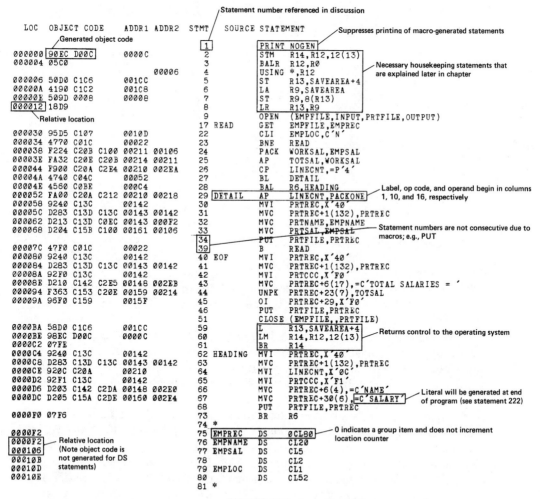

FIGURE 11.1 Assembler Listing

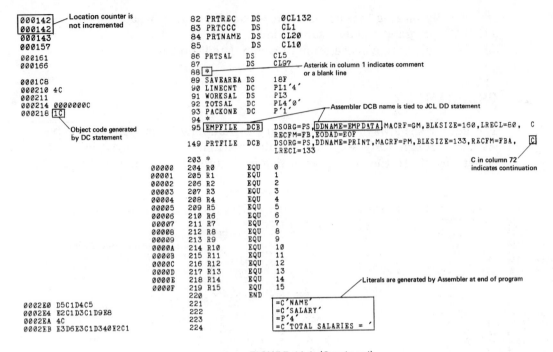

```
000142 ┐  Location counter is          82 PRTREC    DS   0CL132
000142 ┘  not incremented              83 PRTCCC    DS   CL1
000143                                 84 PRTNAME   DS   CL20
000157                                 85           DS   CL10
000161                                 86 PRTSAL    DS   CL5
000166                                 87           DS   CL97 ← Asterisk in column 1 indicates comment
                                       88 *                     or a blank line
0001C8                                 89 SAVEAREA  DS   18F
000210 4C                              90 LINECNT   DC   PL1'4'
000211                                 91 WORKSAL   DS   PL3
000214 0000000C                        92 TOTSAL    DC   PL4'0'
000218 1C                              93 PACKONE   DC   P'1'
                                       94 *              ┌ Assembler DCB name is tied to JCL DD statement
          Object code generated        95 EMPFILE   DCB  DSORG=PS,DDNAME=EMPDATA,MACRF=GM,BLKSIZE=160,LRECL=80,  C
          by DC statement                                RECFM=FB,EODAD=EOF
                                      149 PRTFILE   DCB  DSORG=PS,DDNAME=PRINT,MACRF=PM,BLKSIZE=133,RECFM=FBA,  C
                                                         LRECL=133
                                      203 *                                      C in column 72
                               00000  204 R0        EQU  0                       indicates continuation
                               00001  205 R1        EQU  1
                               00002  206 R2        EQU  2
                               00003  207 R3        EQU  3
                               00004  208 R4        EQU  4
                               00005  209 R5        EQU  5
                               00006  210 R6        EQU  6
                               00007  211 R7        EQU  7
                               00008  212 R8        EQU  8
                               00009  213 R9        EQU  9
                               0000A  214 R10       EQU  10
                               0000B  215 R11       EQU  11
                               0000C  216 R12       EQU  12
                               0000D  217 R13       EQU  13
                               0000E  218 R14       EQU  14
                               0000F  219 R15       EQU  15
                                      220           END
0002E0 D5C1D4C5                        221               =C'NAME'
0002E4 E2C1D3C1D9E8                    222               =C'SALARY'
0002EA 4C                              223               =P'4'
0002EB E3D6E3C1D340E2C1                224               =C'TOTAL SALARIES = '
```

Literals are generated by Assembler at end of program

FIGURE 11.1 (Continued)

is certainly not expected to know the ramifications of every single instruction, he or she should be able to develop an intuitive understanding of the overall program. That is our initial objective.

The processing specifications are merely to read an incoming file and print selected records (those with an N in column 28), four to a page. In addition, the salaries of all selected records are to be summed and printed at the end of the job. Figure 11.2 contains test data and corresponding output to clarify these requirements.

The first eight lines of Figure 11.1 appear at the start of *any* program and have no relationship with specific processing requirements. The very first statement, PRINT NOGEN, instructs the Assembler to suppress the printing of any machine language instructions which are generated by a macro.

A *macro* is an Assembler statement which expands into one or more machine language instructions. Consider, for example, the PUT macro in statement 34, and note that statement 39 is immediately underneath; i.e., *the statement numbers which appear in the listing are not consecutive.* In other words, the PUT macro generated machine language statements 35, 36, 37, and 38, *but these are not shown.* (The author suggests that the beginner *always* include a PRINT NOGEN statement because he or she is not likely to

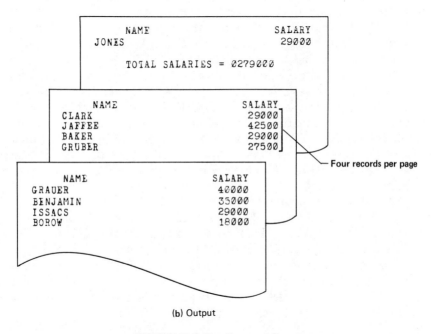

(a) Test Data

(b) Output

FIGURE 11.2 Test Data and Output

understand the generated sequence of instructions.) Examine Figure 11.1 to find other macros whose generated instructions are also suppressed—e.g., OPEN, GET, CLOSE, and DCB in statements 9, 17, 51, and 95, respectively.

Statements 2 through 8 are labeled housekeeping, and serve two important functions. First, they establish register 12 (an *arbitrary* choice) as a base register for use in the base/displacement addressing scheme. Second, they adhere to the normal linkage conventions and establish various save areas for use by calling and/or called programs. For the time being, realize simply that the machine has only one set of 16 general-purpose registers, and further that these registers must be shared by all programs which are executing concurrently. Accordingly, the first responsibility of any program gaining control is to save the registers of the calling program; the last thing it must do prior to returning control is restore the calling program's registers. (The COBOL programmer does not do this explicitly, as the compiler generates the necessary machine language instructions.) This function must be carried out, however, in Assembler—hence, the housekeeping at the beginning of the program and the restoration at the end (statements 59–61). These instructions should be accepted on faith for the present, but they are explained in abundant detail in the latter portion of the chapter.

The OPEN macro in statement 9 begins the "Procedure Division" of the Assembler program. It opens EMPFILE as input, and PRTFILE as output. These files are further defined in the DCB macros (analogous to COBOL FDs) of lines 95 and 149, respectively. EMPFILE is a sequential file; i.e., *Data Set Organization* (DSORG) is specified as *Physically Sequential* (PS). It is tied to the DD statement EMPDATA which provides information on the physical whereabouts of the file. Put another way, *the Assembler DCB statement ties a programmer-chosen filename (EMPFILE) to a DDname*, and functions the same way as the SELECT statement in COBOL. The DCB also describes the file's physical characteristics, and incorporates functions of the COBOL FD; e.g., logical records are 80 bytes, the blocksize is 160, and the file contains Fixed Block records. The file will be accessed in the Get Move (GM) mode, which corresponds to a COBOL READ INTO statement. Finally, control will pass to the label EOF when the end of file (*End Of Device ADdress*) is reached.

The DCB for PRTFILE is similar in concept, but specifies a macro format of Put Move (PM) corresponding to the COBOL WRITE FROM statement. It omits the EODAD parameter, as PRTFILE is an output rather than an input file. It also specifies RECFM as FBA, in which the A indicates the use of standard carriage control characters for a printer.

The main processing loop begins with the GET statement of line 17, which corresponds directly to a COBOL READ; i.e.,

```
GET EMPFILE,EMPREC
```

is equivalent to

```
READ EMPFILE INTO EMPREC
    AT END GO TO EOF.
```

Note well that the Assembler filename, EMPFILE, has been previously defined in a DCB macro (line 95, which also specified EOF as the end-of-file address), and further that the file was opened in line 9. EMPREC is an 80-byte work area, defined in lines 75–80, and is equivalent to the COBOL statements:

```
01  EMPREC.
    05  EMPNAME     PIC X(20).
    05  EMPSAL      PIC X(5).
    05  FILLER      PIC XX.
    05  EMPLOC      PIC X.
    05  FILLER      PIC X(52).
```

The Assembler DS (Define Storage) statement allocates space for a dataname and corresponds to a COBOL PICTURE clause. The statement EMPNAME DS CL20 defines EMPNAME as a character string of length 20 bytes. Note that EMPNAME begins at relative location F2 within the program, and that the next entry EMPSAL begins at relative location 106. (Subtracting F2 from 106 yields a hexadecimal 14, which is equivalent to 20 in decimal; i.e., the Assembler allocated 20 bytes for EMPNAME.) Observe also that EMPREC is defined as 0CL80, where the zero indicates the equivalent of a COBOL group item. Hence, the location counter is not incremented for EMPREC, so that both EMPREC and EMPNAME begin at relative location F2.

After a record has been read in line 17, the value of EMPLOC is compared to N by the CLI statement of line 22. If EMPLOC is *not* equal to N, control returns to line 17, and another record is read. If, on the other hand, EMPLOC is equal to N, the record is selected, and control passes to the next sequential instruction. The incoming salary of the selected record is packed into a work area (line 24), and the salary counter is incremented (line 25). A test is made for the heading routine, after which a detail line is written.

The logic for the heading routine parallels what one would expect to see in COBOL. A line counter is tested prior to writing each detail line. If it equals a predetermined value, then a heading routine is "performed" via a BAL instruction, as was described in the "Techniques of the Trade" section in Chapter 10. Note well that the heading routine resets LINECNT to zero (line 64), and that writing a detail line increments LINECNT by 1 (line 29). Observe also that there are four records per page in the output of Figure 11.2.

Lines 30–34 build and subsequently write a detail line. The output area is first cleared in lines 30 and 31 (as in "Techniques of the Trade" in Chapter 10). EMPNAME and EMPSAL are moved to the print line by individual MVC statements. Finally, an output line is produced by the PUT statement of line 34, which references PRTFILE and PRTREC, defined in line 149 and lines 82–87, respectively. An unconditional branch is executed in line 39 to read the next record.

The "end-of-file" routine extends from statement 40 to 61. The total line is written, the files are closed, and control returns to the operating system.

The reader is urged to attempt problems 1, 7, and 8, which consider this program further.

Cross-Reference Listing

A Cross-Reference Listing is available as an option of the Assembler process. Figure 11.3*a* contains a cross-reference for datanames and labels, and Figure 11.3*b* a cross reference for literals. Both figures list five columns: SYMBOL, LEN, VALUE, DEFN, and REFERENCES. Consider now Figure 11.3*a*.

All datanames and/or labels are listed in *alphabetical* order under the SYMBOL column. The entry under LEN specifies the length in bytes—e.g., LINECNT is a one-byte field, PRTNAME contains 20 bytes, and so on. (Verify these values by referring to the definition of LINECNT and PRT-NAME in lines 90 and 84 of Figure 11.1.)

VALUE indicates the value of the location counter where the entry is defined, and DEFN the corresponding statement number. As can be seen from Figure 11.3*a*, LINECNT was defined in statement 90 at a relative location of 210 within the program. Again, these values should be verified from Figure 11.1.

REFERENCES list all the statement numbers which refer to the particular entry. LINECNT, for example, was coded in lines 26, 29, and

```
                            CROSS-REFERENCE


SYMBOL    LEN    VALUE   DEFN    REFERENCES

DETAIL    00006  00000052 00229  00027
EMPFILE   00004  0000021C 00099  00013 00018 00055
EMPLOC    00001  0000001D 00079  00022
EMPNAME   00020  000000F2 00075  00032
EMPREC    00080  000000F2 00075  00019
EMPSAL    00005  00000106 00077  00024 00033
EOF       00004  00000080 00040  00117
HEADING   00004  000000C4 00052  00028
LINECNT   00001  00000210 00090  00026 00029 00064
PACKONE   00001  0000021B 00093  00029
PRTCCC    00001  00000142 00083  00042 00055
PRTFILE   00004  0000027C 00153  00015 00035 00047 00057 00069
PRTNAME   00020  00000143 00084  00032
PRTREC    00132  00000142 00082  00030 00031 00031 00036 00040 00041 00041 00043 00044 00045 00048 00062 00063 00063 00066
                                 00067 00070
PRTSAL    00005  00000161 00086  00033
READ      00004  00000022 00018  00023 00039
R2        00001  00042200 00204  00003
R12       00001  0000000C 00215  00002 00003 00004 00050
R13       00001  0000000D 00217  00005 00007 00008 00059
R14       00001  0000000E 00218  00002 00066 00061
R6        00001  00000006 00210  00026 00073
R9        00001  00000009 00213  00006 00007 00008
SAVEAREA  00004  000001C8 00089  00005 00006 00059
TOTSAL    00004  00000214 00092  00025 00044
WORKSAL   00003  00000211 00091  00024 00025
```

LINECNT is a 1 byte field, defined at a value of 210 of the location counter, which corresponds to statement number 90. It is referenced by statements 26, 29, and 64

Includes labels and datanames

FIGURE 11.3*a* Datanames and Labels

```
                                        LITERAL CROSS-REFERENCE


SYMBOL      LEN     VALUE    DEFN     REFERENCES

=C'NAME'    00004  000002E0  00221   00066
=C'SALARY'
            00006  000002E4  00222   00067
=P'4'       00001  000002EA  00223   00025
=C'TOTAL SALARIES = '
            00017  000002EB  00224   00043
```

All literals were defined by the Assembler at the end of the program (see Figure 11.1)

FIGURE 11.3*b* Literals

FIGURE 11.3 Cross Reference Listings

64. It is not uncommon for a few datanames to have a large number of references, even in small programs—e.g., PRTREC. Note also the appearance of the registers in the cross-reference—e.g., R12, R13, R14, etc., which was achieved through the EQU statements in Figure 11.1 (see "Techniques of the Trade" in Chapter 10).

Requirements of the Coding Sheet

Specific information about the coding sheet is necessary if one is to attempt actual programming. An Assembler statement consists of one to four entries: Name (or label), Operation (op code), Operand(s), and Comments.
Consider statement 29 of Figure 11.1.

```
DETAIL    AP    LINECNT,PACKONE
```

The *statement label*, e.g., DETAIL, *must* begin in column 1. A label consists of 1 to 8 characters, the first of which is alphabetic. No blanks or special characters (other than @, #, or $) are allowed within the name. The *operation* (or macro name) (e.g., AP) is coded in columns 10–14. The operands (e.g., LINECNT) begin in column 16. One or two operands are present, depending on the instruction. Operands are separated by commas, and no space is permitted after the comma. *Comments* are permitted on any Assembler statement and are separated from the last operand by at least one space. (No comments appear in statement 29.) A comment may also appear on a line by itself, provided that an asterisk is coded in column 1. Blank lines are not permitted within an Assembler listing; the same effect may be achieved, however, by coding an asterisk in column 1 and leaving the rest of the line blank—e.g., statement 88.)
Free form coding is also permitted. That is, the operation need not begin in column 10. It may appear in column 2 if no label is present, or follow one space immediately after a label. In similar fashion, operands need not begin in column 16, but can follow one space after the operation. The author *does not* recommend this style and suggests that *uniform* columns be used, as was done in Figure 11.1.
The DCB statements of lines 95 and 149 are *continued* on a second line. The first line of each statement ends in column 71, and contains a non-blank character in column 72 to signal continuation. The second line begins in column 16, and is blank in column 72.

LINKAGE CONVENTIONS

The discussion associated with Figure 11.1 made only brief mention of the housekeeping at the beginning of the program and the return of control to the operating system at its conclusion. The underlying theory, however, is extremely important in understanding the relationship among programs. Although the concepts are quite complex, the material will become clearer as you reread it and/or get some practice.

The Basic Concept

Every executing program, be it the operating system, a BAL program, or a COBOL application, uses the same 16 general-purpose registers. It is essential, therefore, when multiple programs are active simultaneously, that one program preserve the contents of another's registers. If, for example, a COBOL program calls a BAL subroutine, the first thing the latter must do is save the contents of the calling program's registers. Then, when the subroutine has completed execution, it must restore the COBOL program's registers prior to returning control. Otherwise, the calling program will not operate correctly.

To facilitate the transfer of control between programs, and to ensure that the process is uniform within an installation, a series of standard linkage conventions has been established. These conventions require that each program establish its own 18-word *save area* to hold the general-purpose registers and other information. In addition, they set aside particular registers for specific purposes as follows:

Register	Purpose
15	Entry Point Address of the Call*ed* Program (i.e., the subroutine)
14	Return Address in the Call*ing* Program (i.e., the main program)
13	Address of the 18-word save area
0 and 1	Pass arguments between programs; register 0 is used to pass a single parameter and register 1 the address of a parameter list

The layout of the 18-word save area is shown in Figure 11.4. The first word (four bytes) is *not* used. The second and third words contain the address of the call*ing* and call*ed* programs' save areas, respectively. Hence, if program A calls program B, which in turn calls program C, the save area of the middle program, B, is linked to both A and C.

Implementation in COBOL

Every object program, regardless of its source programming language, uses the *same* linkage convention and save area concepts. The Assembler programmer has the responsibility to establish *explicitly* the save area and

Save area ———

Save area + 4 ———

Save area + 8 ———

Not Used
Address of calling program's save area
Address of called program's save area
R14
R15
R0
R1
R2
R3
R4
R5
R6
R7
R8
R9
R10
R11
R12

FIGURE 11.4 The 18-Word Save Area

necessary linkages (as was done by the housekeeping portion of Figure 11.1). In a higher-level language, however, the compiler automatically generates code to do the necessary work. In a later section, we examine in depth the standard Assembler housekeeping routine. First, however, it is useful to return to COBOL to discern how these concepts are implemented automatically. Consider Figure 11.5, the Save Area Trace, which was discussed earlier in Chapter 7 (as Figure 7.20).

Figure 11.5 shows the flow between programs in effect at the time of the ABEND. The first line is *always* associated with the main (sometimes only) COBOL program. The low return address, 010F8A, indicates a return address in the operating system which receives control when the COBOL program is finished executing. The entry point on the first line, 290CF8, is

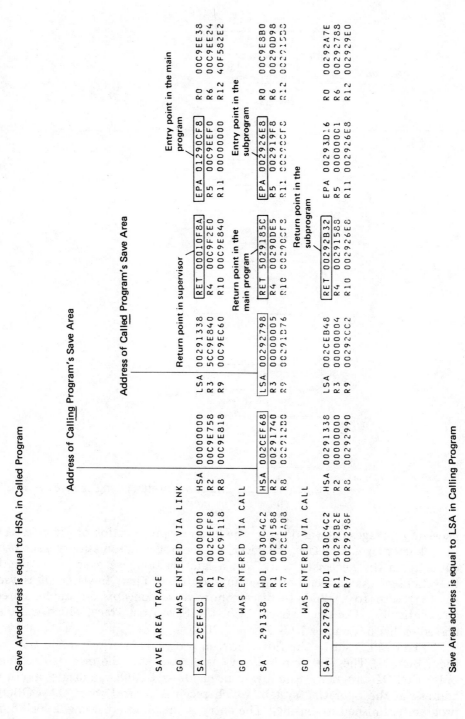

FIGURE 11.5 The SAVEAREA Trace

the entry point for the main COBOL program. The return address in the second save area, 29185C, is the place where control is to return in the main program after the subprogram has completed execution. Subtracting the entry point from the return address yields a relative address of B64, which can be found in the Procedure Division map of Figure 11.6 (and was studied as Figure 7.4).

Note well two instructions immediately above relative address B64. Location B5E contains a load instruction which places the address of SUBRTN into register 15. The next instruction at B62 is BALR 14,15, which puts the address of the next sequential instruction into register 14 and branches to the address contained in register 15. This demonstrates the linkage conventions exactly. Register 14 contains the return address (i.e., the first instruction to be executed when control is returned to the main program). Register 15 contains the first instruction in the called program (i.e., SUBRTN).

The first six Assembler instructions for the COBOL CALL of line 112 in Figure 11.6 illustrate the special role of register 1. Register 1 contains the address of the parameter list, which in turn contains the address of each dataname passed between programs. The first two LA (Load Address) instructions are for DNM=1-434 and DNM=1-381. A quick check of the DMAP in Figure 7.2 will show that these compiler names correspond to the COBOL datanames WS-STUDENT-RECORD and WS-GRADE-AVERAGE which appear in the CALL statement itself. The Or Immediate instruction is used to signify the end of the parameter list, and the final LA instruction puts the address of the list itself into register 1.

The next instruction loads the *external* address (a VCON, in Assembler terminology) of the subroutine ILBODBG4 into register 15. BALR 14,15 stores the address of the next sequential instruction into register 14 (i.e., it establishes a return address as per standard register usage), *and* branches to the address contained in register 15 (the entry point of the subroutine, again as per standard register usage). ILBODBG4 is an IBM debugging module mandated by the presence of the STATE and/or FLOW options. It is an external subroutine in that it is not mentioned explicitly in the COBOL program. Its address is resolved at link-edit time (note its presence in the link-edit map of Figure 7.13). The second set of Load and Branch and Link instructions transfer control to the COBOL subroutine SUBRTN, after establishing a suitable return point via register 14.

Implementation in Assembler

The preceding discussion defined the contents of the 18-word save area common to all programs, and described the roles assigned to various registers in enacting the standard linkage conventions. It showed how COBOL automatically performs these functions for the programmer, and presented an

Instructions to build parameter list

```
112  CALL

     000B3C   41 10 6 020        LA    1,020(0,6)          DNM=1-434
     000B40   50 10 D 250        ST    1,250(0,13)         PRM=1
     000B44   41 10 6 016        LA    1,016(0,6)          DNM=1-381
     000B48   50 10 D 254        ST    1,254(0,13)         PRM=2
     000B4C   96 80 D 254        OI    254(13),X'80'       PRM=2
     000B50   41 10 D 250        LA    1,250(0,13)         PRM=1
     000B54   58 F0 C 014        L     15,014(0,12)        V(ILBODBG4)
     000B58   05 EF              BALR  14,15
     000B5A   96 40 D 049        OI    049(13),X'40'
     000B5E   58 F0 C 024        L     15,024(0,12)        V(SUBRTN   )
     000B62   05 EF              BALR  14,15
     000B64   94 BF D 049        NI    049(13),X'BF'
     000B68   40 F0 D 05C        STH   15,05C(0,13)
     000B6C   58 F0 D 1B8        L     15,1B8(0,13)
     000B70   50 D0 F 080        ST    13,080(0,15)
117  MOVE 000B74  D2 01 6 00E C 0A9   MVC   00E(2,6),0A9(12)    DNM=1-307   LIT+1
118  MOVE 000B7A  D2 02 6 013 C 0C6   MVC   013(3,6),0C6(12)    DNM=1-347   LIT+30
```

Address of external subroutine is loaded into register 15; the branch is affected by BALR 14,15

FIGURE 11.6 COBOL Conformity to BAL Linkage Conventions

intuitive approach to understanding the material. This section formalizes the discussion by explicitly describing the steps taken by the Assembler programmer. The material is perhaps the most complex in the entire book, but by now the reader should be well prepared to handle it.

Let us begin with Figure 11.7, which reviews the layout of the save area, and the concept of calling and called programs. Three save areas are displayed for the operating system and the COBOL main and subprograms. The save areas are *chained together* by the addresses contained in the second and third words of each. Specifically, the second word contains the address of the *calling* program's save area, and may be viewed as a *backward* pointer. The third word contains the address of the *called* program's save area, and is a *forward* pointer. The reader should review the actual numbers in the Save Area Trace of Figure 11.5, and see that the real addresses are completely consistent with the more theoretical view of Figure 11.7.

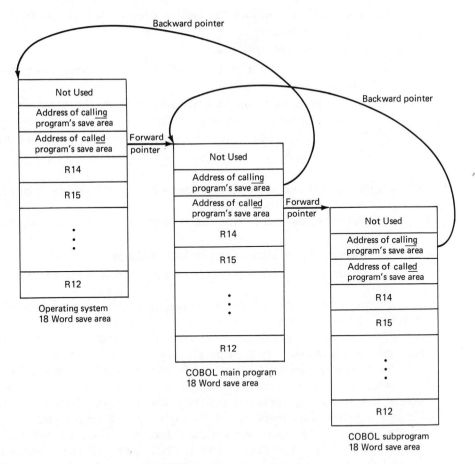

FIGURE 11.7 Chained Save Areas

The Assembler programmer must explicitly load the various save areas and registers with the appropriate contents. Accordingly, both *calling* and *called* program have well-defined responsibilities, which are listed:

Responsibilities of the Calling Program:

1. Build a parameter list using register 1
2. Put the address of its own save area into register 13
3. Put the entry point address of the subroutine into register 15
4. Put its return address into register 14
5. Branch to the address in register 15

Responsibilities of the Called Program Upon Entry:

1. Store the contents of the *calling* program's registers in the *calling* program's save area
2. Establish its own addressability
3. Store the address of the *calling* program's save area in the second word of its own save area
4. Store the address of its own save area in the third word of the *calling* program's save area
5. Put the address of its own save area into register 13 for a subsequent call

Responsibilities of the Called Program Before Returning Control:

1. Restore register 13 with the address of the *calling* program's save area
2. Restore the registers of the *calling* program
3. Return to the *calling* program via the address in register 14

Figure 11.8 outlines how these responsibilities are accomplished. It shows skeletal code for an Assembler program, which is viewed as *both a called and a calling program.* (An Assembler program is *always* a called program, as it is invoked by the operating system.)

When the program of Figure 11.8 gains control, register 13 points to the addresses of the operating system's save area. The program begins by saving the operating system's registers via a Store Multiple instruction. Fifteen registers (i.e., registers 14 through 12) are saved, beginning in the fourth word of the operating system's save area (i.e., 12 bytes displaced from register 13). The BALR and USING instructions designate register 12 as a base register and establish addressability. The first Store instruc-

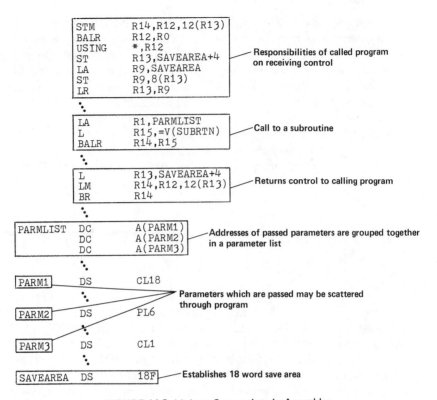

```
STM     R14,R12,12(R13)
BALR    R12,R0
USING   *,R12                   Responsibilities of called program
ST      R13,SAVEAREA+4          on receiving control
LA      R9,SAVEAREA
ST      R9,8(R13)
LR      R13,R9


LA      R1,PARMLIST
L       R15,=V(SUBRTN)          Call to a subroutine
BALR    R14,R15


L       R13,SAVEAREA+4
LM      R14,R12,12(R13)         Returns control to calling program
BR      R14


PARMLIST  DC    A(PARM1)
          DC    A(PARM2)        Addresses of passed parameters are grouped together
          DC    A(PARM3)        in a parameter list


PARM1     DS    CL18
                                Parameters which are passed may be scattered
                                through program
PARM2     DS    PL6


PARM3     DS    CL1


SAVEAREA  DS    18F             Establishes 18 word save area
```

FIGURE 11.8 Linkage Conventions in Assembler

tion saves the address of the operating system's save area in the second word of this program's save area—i.e., SAVEAREA+4. The Load Address and second Store instruction put the address of this program's save area into the third word of the operating system's save area. Finally, the Load Register instruction puts the address of the current save area into register 13. (The LR instruction could have been replaced with LA R13,SAVEAREA. However, since register 9 already contains the save area address, the LR instruction is preferred.) Note well that these instructions appeared earlier, in the housekeeping portion of Figure 11.1.

Three instructions are required to return control to the operating system. The Load instruction places the address of the operating system's save area into register 13. The Load Multiple is the reverse of the initial Store Multiple and restores the operating system's registers. Finally, control is returned to the operating system by branching to the address in register 14. These instructions also appeared earlier, in Figure 11.1.

Figure 11.8 also illustrates how to call a subroutine. The address of PARMLIST is first placed into register 1. PARMLIST is a tag, defined elsewhere in the program, which contains the *address of the first parameter.*

The address of all other parameters follow immediately, although the parameters themselves may be scattered. (This is only one of several techniques to pass arguments to a subprogram, but it is the simplest.) Once the parameter list has been established, the external address of the subroutine is put into register 15. The BALR 14,15 instruction establishes a return point and simultaneously branches to the called program.

This concludes the discussion on linkage conventions, save areas, and the transfer of control between programs. The intent was to present the theory in detail, and show its application in both COBOL and Assembler. Very few application programmers truly understand all that is behind Figure 11.8; if you can, then you should be in for a distinguished career.

Summary

The primary objective of this chapter was to enable the reader to develop a complete Assembler program. To that end, we introduced the necessary macros for simple I/O: OPEN, CLOSE, GET, PUT, and DCB. We covered basic rules of the coding sheet, and examined the Assembler output in detail. Although debugging was not discussed explicitly, *the reader is urged to do problems 7 and 8, which contain ABEND and syntactical exercises, respectively.* The debugging procedure closely follows the COBOL exercises of Chapter 7.

The discussion on linkage conventions, save areas, and subroutine calls is vital. The material, while difficult, does become easier to grasp, especially as one gains experience in a commercial environment. Eventually, one does in fact see the "big picture" and the overall relationship between COBOL and Assembler.

Finally, the BAL instruction set itself can be effectively reviewed by treating groups of related instructions and establishing general patterns. Accordingly, we will summarize the 60-odd instructions covered so far by developing a set of summary tables. The objective is not to make the reader proficient in Assembler per se, but rather to develop an overall appreciation for the language. We begin with Figure 11.9, a summary of the arithmetic instructions.

Realize from Figure 11.9 that the *first* letter of the mnemonic op code indicates the nature of the instruction; i.e., A, S, M, and D denote addition, subtraction, multiplication, and division, respectively. The *ending* letter indicates the type and location of the operands. R as in AR, implies binary data in registers; H, as in AH, indicates a half word binary operand; P, as in AP, implies packed data; and no ending letter, as in A, a full-word binary operand.

Operation	Packed data	Binary data Half-word	Full-word	Registers
Addition	AP	AH	A	AR
Subtraction	SP	SH	S	SR
Multiplication	MP	MH	M	MR
Division	DP	—	D	DR

FIGURE 11.9 Summary of Arithmetic Instructions

Similar observations hold for the logical operations of Figure 11.10. N, O, and X correspond to the logical operations, and, or, and exclusive or, respectively. (The letter A was already used for addition, hence N was selected for the logical and). There are no half-word operations; i.e., NH, OH, and XH do *not* exist. Full-word operations are denoted by a single letter—e.g., N, O, and X. The register-to-register instructions end with the letter R—i.e., NR, OR, and XR.

Operation	Instruction type SS	SI	RR	RX
And	NC	NI	NR	N
Or	OC	OI	OR	O
Exclusive Or	XC	XI	XR	X

FIGURE 11.10 Summary of Logical Instructions

Logical operations also have an "immediate" format not found in the arithmetic instructions, where one operand is contained in the instruction itself. NI, OI, and XI are all Storage Immediate (SI) instruction types. Finally, NC, OC, and XC indicate storage-to-storage or character-oriented instructions.

Figure 11.11 extends the discussion to the compare instructions. C by itself is an *arithmetic* compare in which the sign of the operands is taken into account. CP is used for packed data, CR for binary data in registers, CH for binary data in a register and a half-word, and C for binary data in a register and a full-word. Observe the complete consistency with the earlier tables.

CL denotes a *logical* compare instruction in which the algebraic sign is ignored. (Two letters, CL, are assigned to indicate the nature of the operation. C was already taken for the arithmetic compare, and L will be used subsequently for load instructions—hence, the need for a two-letter combination.) The third and last letter indicates the type and location of

	Instruction type				
Operation	SS	SI	RR	RX (Full-word)	RX (Half-word)
Arithmetic Compare	CP	—	CR	C	CH
Logical Compare	CLC	CLI	CLR	CL	—

FIGURE 11.11 Summary of Compare Instructions

the operands. CLI implies an immediate operand and an SI instruction format; CLR indicates both operands are in registers, CL a register–full-word operation, and CLC a storage-to-storage (or character-oriented) operation. Again, note the consistency with the previous tables.

Figure 11.12 contains over 20 additional instructions. Although it is more difficult to derive sets of instructions with general rules, some relationships are still possible. L and ST denote the load and store operations, respectively. (S by itself was used for subtraction.) L, LH, LR, ST, and STH follow the earlier conventions for full-word, half-word, and register-to-register operations, respectively. (There is no need for an STR operation, in that LR accomplishes that function exactly.) LM and STM indicate load and store operations involving *multiple* registers, and LA is in a class by itself.

Operation	Mnemonics
Load	L, LH, LR, LM, LA
Store	ST, STH, STM
Move	MVC, MVI, MVCL
Data Conversion	PACK, UNPK, CVB, CVD
Branch	(BCT, BCTR), (BAL, BALR), (BC, BCR)
Extended Mnemonics	B, BH, BL, BE, BNH, BNL, BNE, BO, BZ, BM

FIGURE 11.12 Miscellaneous Instructions

MV is the mnemonic for move. MVC and MVI adhere to the previous observations and imply storage-to-storage, and storage-immediate operations, respectively. PACK, UNPK, CVB, and CVD are reasonable mnemonics with no overall pattern.

Six branch instructions are listed and divided into three pairs: branch and count, branch and link, and branch. Each pair includes an RR instruction type, denoted by the ending R in the op code, in which the destination address is contained in a register. The ten extended mnemonics are all variations of the BC instruction.

The reader may be reasonably expected to be familiar with a working subset of the language and, further, to have an overall appreciation for Assembler. He or she should be comfortable with a COBOL PMAP, at least to the extent of being able to consult a reference manual for detailed information on individual instructions. Last, and most important, the reader should have obtained a truer sense of the relationship between COBOL and Assembler.

TRUE/FALSE EXERCISES

1. A macro generates one or more machine language instructions.
2. A COBOL programmer should explicitly define the save area for his or her program.
3. An Assembler programmer should explicitly define the save area for his or her program.
4. The instruction BAL 14,15 is typically used to branch to a subroutine.
5. The instruction BR 14 is typically the last statement executed in a subprogram.
6. The Assembler macros GET and PUT are analogous to the COBOL READ and WRITE statements, respectively.
7. In Assembler, one can access a file before it is open.
8. An Assembler programmer will commonly establish any of the 16 general-purpose registers as a base register.
9. Register 0 is used to pass a parameter list.
10. The Assembler DCB ties the programmer-chosen file name to a JCL DDname.
11. DC and DS are equivalent instructions.
12. The save area contains 18 full words.
13. A "VCON" and an "ADCON" are equivalent.
14. The first word of the save area contains the address of the calling program's save area.
15. The entry INREC DS 0CL80 does *not* increment the location counter, and is analogous to a COBOL group item.
16. USING *,R12 is sufficient in and of itself to establish register 12 as a base register.
17. USING and PRINT NOGEN are examples of macros.
18. Blank lines are permitted within an Assembler program.
19. The Assembler DCB combines functions of the COBOL FD and SELECT statements.

20. The OPEN statement ties Assembler file names to JCL DD statements.
21. Statement labels begin in column 1.
22. Operands generally begin in column 10.
23. Blanks are not permitted within an Assembler statement.
24. Blanks are not permitted between operands in an Assembler statement.
25. Statement numbers in an Assembler listing are not consecutive if PRINT NOGEN is specified.

PROBLEMS

1. A good deal of understanding about the assembly process can be gained simply by observing generated object code and associated information. Accordingly, answer the following questions pertaining to Figure 11.1:

   (a) With respect to the CLI instruction of line 22:
       (1) What is the generated object code? Divide the object code into its component parts.
       (2) At what relative location does the instruction begin?
       (3) What kind of instruction is CLI—i.e., SS, RR, etc? How many bytes does that type of instruction contain?
       (4) At what relative location does the instruction *after* CLI begin?
       (5) What is the EBCDIC translation for the letter N?
       (6) What is in the second byte of the CLI object code? Is this consistent with the SI instruction format?
       (7) What is the relative location of the dataname EMPLOC? What value appears in the ADDR1 column of the CLI instruction?
       (8) What is the initial value assigned to register 12? How is this accomplished?
       (9) What is the storage address in the object code of the CLI instruction? Is this consistent with the answers to parts 7 and 8?
   (b) With respect to the MVC instruction in line 66:
       (10) What is the generated object code? Divide the object code into its component parts.
       (11) What value did the programmer code for the length code? What value was generated in the machine language instruction? Why are the answers different?
       (12) What is the relative location of the second operand? What is the entry under the ADDR2 column of line 66?
       (13) What is the relative location of PRTREC? Of PRTREC+6? What is the entry under the ADDR1 column of line 66?
       (14) Given that register 12 is initialized to 6, what displacement is

necessary to reference the first operand (PRTREC+6)? What are the base/displacement entries in the machine language instruction for the first operand?

(15) At what relative location does the MVC instruction begin? What is the length of an MVC instruction? At what location does the next instruction begin?

(c) With respect to the branch instructions:

(16) What op code was generated for the BNE, BL, and B mnemonics of lines 23, 27, and 39, respectively?

(17) Why are the op codes from part 16 all the same? How does the generated object code distinguish the various instructions from each other?

(18) What is the value of the mask for the BNE, BL, and B extended mnemonics? Are these values consistent with those in Figure 10.10?

(19) At what relative location does the AP instruction labeled DETAIL (line 29) begin? How does the base/displacement generated for the instruction BL DETAIL (line 27) correspond? What is the entry under ADDR1 in line 27?

(d) With respect to literals, DS and DC statements, and generated object code:

(20) What object code is generated by the DC statement of line 90? Of line 92? Why are the lengths of these fields different?

(21) Why is no object code generated for a DS statement?

(22) Why is object code generated for individual instructions (e.g., the CLI and MVC statements of parts (a) and (b)), but not for macros?

(23) Where is object code for the literal "NAME", which was defined in line 66, generated? Verify that the object code does in fact correspond to the EBCDIC translation of NAME. What is the entry in the ADDR2 column of line 66?

2. This problem describes the so-called "register-14 trick" for debugging both COBOL and/or Assembler programs. The standard debugging procedure requires that one subtract the entry point address from the PSW address in order to determine the last instruction which was executed prior to the ABEND. Although the technique works much of the time, it fails on occasion, especially if the ABEND occurred in a data management routine. The "register-14 trick" suggests that one use the address in register 14 in lieu of the PSW address. Explain the rationale behind this often helpful technique.

3. Among the IBM utilities not studied in Chapters 4 and 5 is the one line program IEFBR14. This well-used utility consists of the *single* Assembler statement BR R14. Despite its brevity, the utility has several uses: e.g.,

to allocate space for a direct access data set or PDS directory, and to delete a data set. Describe the rationale behind this program and how it accomplishes all that it does.

4. A common error, made by beginning Assembler programmers, is *inadvertently* to code B 14 rather than BR 14 as the last executable statement. This in turn produces an 0C5 ABEND—i.e., an address exception. Why? (Hint: The instruction B 14 produces the following object code 47 F0 0 014.)

5. Code the Assembler DS statements to produce results equivalent to the COBOL entries:

```
01  INPUT-RECORD.
    05  IN-NAME.
        10   LAST         PIC X(15).
        10   FIRST        PIC X(10).
        10   MIDDLE       PIC X.
    05  FILLER           PIC X(10).
    05  DATE-OF-BIRTH.
        10   MONTH        PIC 99.
        10   DAY          PIC 99.
        10   YEAR         PIC 99.
```

6. Review the "Techniques of the Trade" section which concluded Chapter 10. Do these instructions make more sense in view of Figure 11.1? How many of these techniques were used in the example program?

7. Figure 11.13 contains a dump which resulted when the Assembler program of Figure 11.1 executed with a different set of test data. With the aid of the following leading questions, determine why the dump occurred. (Note well that the debugging procedure is very similar to the technique used for COBOL programs. Questions continue on page 309.)

    (a) Analyze the completion code:
        (1) What is the completion code?
        (2) What does the completion code mean?
    (b) Determine where the ABEND occurred:
        (3) What address is contained in the PSW?
        (4) At what location was the program loaded?
        (5) Subtract the address in part 4 from the one in part 3.
        (6) What machine language instruction is at that location? Underline the instruction in memory.
    (c) Examine the machine language instruction that failed to execute. The instruction which actually caused the ABEND is the one immediately before the instruction determined in part 6.
        (7) What is the machine instruction that actually caused the ABEND?

```
JOB JSC$4014          STEP GO           TIME 182653    DATE 83017    ID = 000    CPUID = 020131524341

COMPLETION CODE       SYSTEM = 0C7

PSW AT ENTRY TO ABEND   078D0200 000B5D44    ILC 6    INTC 0007


CDE

97F000     NCDE 00000000   RBP 009ACB08   NM GO        EPA 000B5D00   XL/MJ 009AD2C0   USE 00010000   ATTR 0B20000
FD7790     NCDE 00FD74C0   RBP 00000000   NM IGG019DK  EPA 00F7D2F0   XL/MJ 00FD77B0   USE 00020000   ATTR B122000
FD7DC0     NCDE 00FD7460   RBP 00000000   NM IGG019AQ  EPA 00BFA000   XL/MJ 00FD7DE0   USE 00020000   ATTR B122000
FD7370     NCDE 00FD7310   RBP 00000000   NM IGG019DJ  EPA 00C17138   XL/MJ 00FD7390   USE 00070000   ATTR B122000


REGS AT ENTRY TO ABEND

   FLTR 0-6    0000000000000000   0000000000000000   0000000000000000   0000000000000000

   REGS 2-7    000B5DF2   009A0610   00000040   009A0634   009AC770   800B5D52   FD000000
   REGS 8-15   000B5EC8   00971880   00000000   009ACEF8   400B5D06   000B5EC8   000B5D30   12C17144
```

FIGURE 11.13 Dump for Problem 7

307

ACTIVE LOAD MODULES

```
LFA/JPA MODULE       GO
0B5D00  90EC D00C  05C050D0  C1C64190  C1C2509D   *...........AF..AB...R....*
0B5D20  0A134110  C2164100  C2EC58F0  103005EF    *...B...B...0...NA...2.B.A.*
0B5D40  C20EC20B  F900C20A  C2E44740  C04C4560    *.B.B.9.B.BU....B..A.K.A.*
0B5D60  9240C13C  D204C15B  C1004110  C13CD210    *A.K.A..K.A...B..A..0A.*
0B5D80  9240C13C  D283C13D  C13C92F0  C13CD210    *.A.K.A..0A.K.A.BV3.A.B..0A.*
0B5DA0  C2764100  C13C58F0  103005EF  4510C0B2    *.B....A.0....A.....AF..*
0B5DC0  D00C07FE  9240C13C  D283C13D  C13C920C    *.B....A.K.A...B..1A.K.A.*
0B5DE0  C2DB4110  C2764100  C13C58F0  103005EF    *.B...B..A..0...6LAVOR*
0B5E00  40404040  40404040  40404040  42D54040    *....N*
0B5E20  4040F4C2  C5D5D1C1  D4C9D540  40404040    *05 BENJAMIN*
0B5E40  F0F540C2  F0F04040  40404040  40404040    *35000*
0B5E60  42F3F5F0  F0F04040  40404040  40404040
0B5E80  40404040  40404040  40404040  40404040

LINE 0B5EA0 SAME AS ABOVE.

0B5EC0  40404040  00000000  000B4FB2  000B5DF2   *..........A....2*
0B5EE0  000B5DF2  00000040  009A0634  009A2610   *.........G.......*
0B5F00  000B51C8  00000000  009ACEF8  400B5D05   *...H....8....A...*
0B5F20  00000000  00000000  00750020  00000000
0B5F40  92000000  00405000  00983F88  12C17144   *......A......*
0B5F60  00034E48  000B4A10  000B49C0  00000050
0B5F80  00000000  00050050  00983F08  92017150   *......A...*
0B5FA0  94000000  00000000  000B4795  000000265
0B5FC0  000B4CE0  000B4795  0D8B84CE3 D6E3C1D3    *.TOTAL SALARIES.*
0B5FE0  DC1D4C5   E2C1D3C1  D9E84CE3 D6E3C1D3     *NAME.SALARY.TOTAL SALARIES*

LFA/JPA MODULE       IGG019AQ
BFA200  90EFD040  18BF47F0  80220C7   C7F0F1F9    *.......0..IGG019AQ*
BFA220  F7F49108  203C4710  807E5833  00004133    *.74.............*
BFA240  47480052  41130004  41100001 0A0147F0     *......0......*
BFA260  00002A37  12FF4780  80A205EF  582D0028     *......0......*
BFA280  1B024111  00000A37 91082030  471080A2      *......0......*
BFA2A0  07FF9120  20304780  80389106  22304780
```

FIGURE 11.13 (Continued)

(8) What is its op code?

(9) Which base register is associated with the first operand?

(10) What is the displacement of the first operand?

(11) What is the effective address of the first operand?

(12) How many bytes are associated with the first operand? (Careful.)

(13) What are the internal contents of the first operand? Are they valid as a decimal number?

(14) Which base register is associated with the second operand?

(15) What is the displacement of the second operand?

(16) What is the effective address of the second operand?

(17) What is the entry under ADDR2 for the instruction determined in part 7?

(18) Add the Entry Point Address (EPA) from part 4 to the answer from part 17.

(19) Compare the answers from parts 16 and 18. Can you make any general statements about this relationship?

(20) Why is the address in register 12 exactly 6 bytes past the Entry Point Address?

(21) How many bytes are associated with the second operand?

(22) What are the internal contents of the second operand? Are they valid as a decimal number?

(23) Technically, why did the ABEND occur?

(d) Relate the technical cause of the ABEND to the Assembler program.

(24) What is the relative location of EMPNAME within the Assembler program?

(25) Add the answer from part 24 to the EPA (Entry Point Address) from part 4.

(26) Which employee was being processed at the time the ABEND occurred? Underline the entire record in memory.

(27) What is the value of EMPSAL for the invalid employee record?

(28) Why did the ABEND occur in statement 25, which referenced WORKSAL, rather than statement 24, which referenced EMPSAL directly?

8. Figure 11.14 contains a modified version of Figure 11.1. Find and correct all syntactical errors. Is any object code generated for instructions which are in error?

```
                                    1          PRINT NOGEN
000000 90EC D00C      0000C         2          STM   R14,R12,12(13)
000004 05C0                         3          BALR  R12,R0
                      00006         4          USING *,R12
000006 50D0 C1C6      001CC         5          ST    R13,SAVEAREA+4
00000A 4190 C1C2      001C8         6          LA    R9,SAVEAREA
00000E 509D 0008      00008         7          ST    R9,8(R13)
000012 18D9                         8          LR    R13,R9
```

FIGURE 11.14 Assembler Listing with Diagnostics

```
                                      9              OPEN    (EMPFILE,INPUT,PRTFILE,OUTPUT)
                                     17 READ         GET     EMPFILE,EMPREC
000030 0000 0000      0010D          22              CLI     EMPLOC(1),C'N'
         *** ERROR ***
000034 4770 C01C      00022          23              BNE     READ
000038 F224 C20B C100 00211 00106    24              PACK    WORKSAL,EMPSAL
00003E FA32 C20E C20B 00214 00211    25              AP      TOTSAL,WORKSAL
000044 F900 C20A C2D6 00210 002DC    26              CP      LINECNT,=P'4'
00004A 0000 0000      00000          27              BL      DETAILS
         *** ERROR ***
00004E 0000 0000      000C4          28              BAL     R6,HEADING
         *** ERROR ***
000052 FA00 C20A C20E 00210 00214    29 DETAIL       AP      LINECNT,PACKONE
000058 9240 C13C      00142          30              MVI     PRTREC,X'40'
00005C D283 C13D C13C 00143 00142    31              MVC     PRTREC+1(132),PRTREC
000062 0000 0000 0000 00000 000F2    32              MVC     PRTNAME,EMPNAME(20)
         *** ERROR ***
000068 D204 C15B C100 00161 00106    33              MVC     PRTSAL,EMPSAL
                                     34              PUT     PRTFILE,PRTREC
00007C 47F0 C01C      00022          39              B       READ
000080 9240 C13C      00142          40 EOF          MVI     PRTREC,X'40'
000084 D283 C13D C13C 00143 00142    41              MVC     PRTREC+1(132),PRTREC
00008A 92F0 C13C      00142          42              MVI     PRTCCC,X'F0'
00008E D210 C142 C2D7 00148 002DD    43              MVC     PRTREC+6(17),=C'TOTAL SALARIES = '
000094 F363 C153 C20E 00159 00214    44              UNPK    PRTREC+23(7),TOTSAL
00009A 96F0 C159      0015F          45              OI      PRTREC+29,X'F0'
                                     46              PUT     PRTFILE,PRTREC
                                     51              CLOSE   (EMPFILE,,PRTFILE)
0000BA 58D0 C1C6      001CC          59              L       R13,SAVEAREA+4
0000BE 98EC D00C      0000C          60              LM      R14,R12,12(13)
0000C2 07FE                          61              BR      R14
0000C4 9240 C13C      00142          62 HEADING      MVI     PRTREC,X'40'
0000C8 D283 C13D C13C 00143 00142    63              MVC     PRTREC+1(132),PRTREC
0000CE 920C C20A      00210          64              MVI     LINECNT,X'0C'
0000D2 92F1 C13C      00142          65              MVI     PRTCCC,X'F1'
0000D6 D203 C142 C2D2 00148 002D8    66              MVC     PRTREC+6(4),=C'NAME'
0000DC 0000 0000 0000 00160 00000    67              MVC     PRTREC+30(6),='SALARY'
         *** ERROR ***
                                     68              PUT     PRTFILE,PRTREC
0000F0 07F6                          73              BR      6
                                     74 *
0000F2                               75 EMPREC       DS      0CL80
0000F2                               76 EMPNAME      DS      CL20
000106                               77 EMPSAL       DS      CL5
00010B                               78              DS      CL2
00010D                               79 EMPLOC       DS      CL1
00010E                               80              DS      CL52
                                     81 *
000142                               82 PRTREC       DS      0CL132
000142                               83 PRTCCC       DS      CL1
000143                               84              DS      CL20
000157                               85              DS      CL10
000161                               86 PRTSAL       DS      CL5
000166                               87              DS      CL97
                                     88 *
0001C8                               89 SAVEAREA DS         18F
000210 4C                            90 LINECNT      DC      PL1'4'
000211                               91 WORKSAL      DS      PL3
000214                               92 TOTSAL       DC      PL4
         *** ERROR ***
000214 1C                            93 PACKONE      DC      P'1'
                                     94 *
                                     95 EMPFILE      DCB     DSORG=PS,DDNAME=EMPDATA,MACRF=GM,BLKSIZE=160,LRECL=80,
                                    149                      RECFM=FB,EODAD=EOF
         *** ERROR ***
                                    150 PRTFILE      DCB     DSORG=PS,DDNAME=PRINT,MACRF=PM,BLSIZE=133,RECFM=FBA,     C
         *** ERROR ***
                                    204                      LRECL=133
         *** ERROR ***
                                    205 *
                       00000        206 R0           EQU     0
                       00001        207 R1           EQU     1
                       00002        208 R2           EQU     2
                       00003        209 R3           EQU     3
                       00004        210 R4           EQU     4
                       00005        211 R5           EQU     5
                       00007        212 R7           EQU     7
                       00008        213 R8           EQU     8
                       00009        214 R9           EQU     9
                       0000A        215 R10          EQU     10
                       0000B        216 R11          EQU     11
                       0000C        217 R12          EQU     12
```

FIGURE 11.14 (Continued)

```
                    0000D   218 R13      EQU   13
                    0000E   219 R14      EQU   14
                    0000F   220 R15      EQU   15
                            221          END
0002D8 D5C1D4C5             222                =C'NAME'
0002DC 4C                   223                =P'4'
0002DD E3D6E3C1D340E2C1     224                =C'TOTAL SALARIES = '
```

ASSEMBLER DIAGNOSTICS AND STATISTICS

```
STMT  ERROR CODE   MESSAGE
  22  IF0228    RELOCATABLE DISPLACEMENT IN MACHINE INSTRUCTION NEAR OPERAND COLUMN 9
  27  IF0188    DETAILS IS AN UNDEFINED SYMBOL
  28  IF0188    R6 IS AN UNDEFINED SYMBOL
  32  IF0188    PRTNAME IS AN UNDEFINED SYMBOL
  32  IF0228    RELOCATABLE DISPLACEMENT IN MACHINE INSTRUCTION NEAR OPERAND COLUMN 19
  32  IF0230    BASE REGISTER NUMBER GREATER THAN 15 NEAR OPERAND COLUMN 19
  67  IF0161    INVALID LITERAL NEAR OPERAND COLUMN 14
  92  IF0178    SYNTAX ERROR NEAR OPERAND COLUMN 4
  92  IF0178    SYNTAX ERROR NEAR OPERAND COLUMN 4
  92  IF0178    SYNTAX ERROR NEAR OPERAND COLUMN 4
 149  IF0054    INVALID OPERATION CODE
 150  IF0092    KEYWORD PARAMETER BLSIZE UNDEFINED IN MACRO DEFINITION
 204  IF0054    INVALID OPERATION CODE

NUMBER OF STATEMENTS FLAGGED IN THIS ASSEMBLY =    9
HIGHEST SEVERITY WAS   12
```

FIGURE 11.14 (Continued)

9. Write an Assembler language program to calculate the value of X, using the following formula and values:

$$X = (A+B)*C$$

and

$$A = 100, B = 200, C = 50$$

Use packed constants—e.g., A DC PL3'100'. In the same program, calculate the value for Y, where:

$$Y = (D-E)/F$$

and

$$D = 300, E = 150, F = 20$$

Use character constants this time—e.g., D DC CL3'300'. Finally, use binary instructions to calculate the value of Z, where:

$$Z = (G+H)*(I+J)$$

and

G = 10, H = 20, I = 30, J = 40

Use binary constants—e.g., G DC H '10'. Leave Z in register 3. Use MH as multiply. After your computations, cause your program to dump and locate all constants, plus the program itself, in memory.

Assembler Formats

MACHINE INSTRUCTIONS

NAME	MNEMONIC	OP CODE	FOR-MAT	OPERANDS
Add (c)	AR	1A	RR	R1,R2
Add (c)	A	5A	RX	R1,D2(X2,B2)
Add Decimal (c)	AP	FA	SS	D1(L1,B1),D2(L2,B2)
Add Halfword (c)	AH	4A	RX	R1,D2(X2,B2)
Add Logical (c)	ALR	1E	RR	R1,R2
Add Logical (c)	AL	5E	RX	R1,D2(X2,B2)
AND (c)	NR	14	RR	R1,R2
AND (c)	N	54	RX	R1,D2(X2,B2)
AND (c)	NI	94	SI	D1(B1),I2
AND (c)	NC	D4	SS	D1(L,B1),D2(B2)
Branch and Link	BALR	05	RR	R1,R2
Branch and Link	BAL	45	RX	R1,D2(X2,B2)
Branch on Condition	BCR	07	RR	M1,R2
Branch on Condition	BC	47	RX	M1,D2(X2,B2)
Branch on Count	BCTR	06	RR	R1,R2
Branch on Count	BCT	46	RX	R1,D2(X2,B2)
Branch on Index High	BXH	86	RS	R1,R3,D2(B2)
Branch on Index Low or Equal	BXLE	87	RS	R1,R3,D2(B2)
Clear I/O (c,p)	CLRIO	9D01	S	D2(B2)
Compare (c)	CR	19	RR	R1,R2
Compare (c)	C	59	RX	R1,D2(X2,B2)
Compare and Swap (c)	CS	BA	RS	R1,R3,D2(B2)
Compare Decimal (c)	CP	F9	SS	D1(L1,B1),D2(L2,B2)
Compare Double and Swap (c)	CDS	BB	RS	R1,R3,D2(B2)
Compare Halfword (c)	CH	49	RX	R1,D2(X2,B2)
Compare Logical (c)	CLR	15	RR	R1,R2
Compare Logical (c)	CL	55	RX	R1,D2(X2,B2)
Compare Logical (c)	CLC	D5	SS	D1(L,B1),D2(B2)
Compare Logical (c)	CLI	95	SI	D1(B1),I2
Compare Logical Characters under Mask (c)	CLM	BD	RS	R1,M3,D2(B2)
Compare Logical Long (c)	CLCL	0F	RR	R1,R2
Convert to Binary	CVB	4F	RX	R1,D2(X2,B2)
Convert to Decimal	CVD	4E	RX	R1,D2(X2,B2)
Diagnose (p)		83		Model-dependent
Divide	DR	1D	RR	R1,R2
Divide	D	5D	RX	R1,D2(X2,B2)
Divide Decimal	DP	FD	SS	D1(L1,B1),D2(L2,B2)
Edit (c)	ED	DE	SS	D1(L,B1),D2(B2)
Edit and Mark (c)	EDMK	DF	SS	D1(L,B1),D2(B2)
Exclusive OR (c)	XR	17	RR	R1,R2
Exclusive OR (c)	X	57	RX	R1,D2(X2,B2)
Exclusive OR (c)	XI	97	SI	D1(B1),I2
Exclusive OR (c)	XC	D7	SS	D1(L,B1),D2(B2)
Execute	EX	44	RX	R1,D2(X2,B2)
Halt I/O (c,p)	HIO	9E00	S	D2(B2)
Halt Device (c,p)	HDV	9E01	S	D2(B2)
Insert Character	IC	43	RX	R1,D2(X2,B2)
Insert Characters under Mask (c)	ICM	BF	RS	R1,M3,D2(B2)
Insert PSW Key (p)	IPK	B20B	S	
Insert Storage Key (p)	ISK	09	RR	R1,R2
Load	LR	18	RR	R1,R2
Load	L	58	RX	R1,D2(X2,B2)
Load Address	LA	41	RX	R1,D2(X2,B2)
Load and Test (c)	LTR	12	RR	R1,R2
Load Complement (c)	LCR	13	RR	R1,R2
Load Control (p)	LCTL	B7	RS	R1,R3,D2(B2)
Load Halfword	LH	48	RX	R1,D2(X2,B2)
Load Multiple	LM	98	RS	R1,R3,D2(B2)
Load Negative (c)	LNR	11	RR	R1,R2
Load Positive (c)	LPR	10	RR	R1,R2
Load PSW (n,p)	LPSW	82	S	D2(B2)
Load Real Address (c,p)	LRA	B1	RX	R1,D2(X2,B2)
Monitor Call	MC	AF	SI	D1(B1),I2
Move	MVI	92	SI	D1(B1),I2
Move	MVC	D2	SS	D1(L,B1),D2(B2)
Move Long (c)	MVCL	0E	RR	R1,R2
Move Numerics	MVN	D1	SS	D1(L,B1),D2(B2)
Move with Offset	MVO	F1	SS	D1(L1,B1),D2(L2,B2)

MACHINE INSTRUCTIONS (Contd)

NAME	MNEMONIC	OP CODE	FOR-MAT	OPERANDS
Move Zones	MVZ	D3	SS	D1(L,B1),D2(B2)
Multiply	MR	1C	RR	R1,R2
Multiply	M	5C	RX	R1,D2(X2,B2)
Multiply Decimal	MP	FC	SS	D1(L1,B1),D2(L2,B2)
Multiply Halfword	MH	4C	RX	R1,D2(X2,B2)
OR (c)	OR	16	RR	R1,R2
OR (c)	O	56	RX	R1,D2(X2,B2)
OR (c)	OI	96	SI	D1(B1),I2
OR (c)	OC	D6	SS	D1(L,B1),D2(B2)
Pack	PACK	F2	SS	D1(L1,B1),D2(L2,B2)
Purge TLB (p)	PTLB	B20D	S	
Read Direct (p)	RDD	85	SI	D1(B1),I2
Reset Reference Bit (c,p)	RRB	B213	S	D2(B2)
Set Clock (c,p)	SCK	B204	S	D2(B2)
Set Clock Comparator (p)	SCKC	B206	S	D2(B2)
Set CPU Timer (p)	SPT	B208	S	D2(B2)
Set Prefix (p)	SPX	B210	S	D2(B2)
Set Program Mask (n)	SPM	04	RR	R1
Set PSW Key from Address (p)	SPKA	B20A	S	D2(B2)
Set Storage Key (p)	SSK	08	RR	R1,R2
Set System Mask (p)	SSM	80	S	D2(B2)
Shift and Round Decimal (c)	SRP	F0	SS	D1(L1,B1),D2(B2),I3
Shift Left Double (c)	SLDA	8F	RS	R1,D2(B2)
Shift Left Double Logical	SLDL	8D	RS	R1,D2(B2)
Shift Left Single (c)	SLA	8B	RS	R1,D2(B2)
Shift Left Single Logical	SLL	89	RS	R1,D2(B2)
Shift Right Double (c)	SRDA	8E	RS	R1,D2(B2)
Shift Right Double Logical	SRDL	8C	RS	R1,D2(B2)
Shift Right Single (c)	SRA	8A	RS	R1,D2(B2)
Shift Right Single Logical	SRL	88	RS	R1,D2(B2)
Signal Processor (c,p)	SIGP	AE	RS	R1,R3,D2(B2)
Start I/O (c,p)	SIO	9C00	S	D2(B2)
Start I/O Fast Release (c,p)	SIOF	9C01	S	D2(B2)
Store	ST	50	RX	R1,D2(X2,B2)
Store Channel ID (c,p)	STIDC	B203	S	D2(B2)
Store Character	STC	42	RX	R1,D2(X2,B2)
Store Characters under Mask	STCM	BE	RS	R1,M3,D2(B2)
Store Clock (c)	STCK	B205	S	D2(B2)
Store Clock Comparator (p)	STCKC	B207	S	D2(B2)
Store Control (p)	STCTL	B6	RS	R1,R3,D2(B2)
Store CPU Address (p)	STAP	B212	S	D2(B2)
Store CPU ID (p)	STIDP	B202	S	D2(B2)
Store CPU Timer (p)	STPT	B209	S	D2(B2)
Store Halfword	STH	40	RX	R1,D2(X2,B2)
Store Multiple	STM	90	RS	R1,R3,D2(B2)
Store Prefix (p)	STPX	B211	S	D2(B2)
Store Then AND System Mask (p)	STNSM	AC	SI	D1(B1),I2
Store Then OR System Mask (p)	STOSM	AD	SI	D1(B1),I2
Subtract (c)	SR	1B	RR	R1,R2
Subtract (c)	S	5B	RX	R1,D2(X2,B2)
Subtract Decimal (c)	SP	FB	SS	D1(L1,B1),D2(L2,B2)
Subtract Halfword (c)	SH	4B	RX	R1,D2(X2,B2)
Subtract Logical (c)	SLR	1F	RR	R1,R2
Subtract Logical (c)	SL	5F	RX	R1,D2(X2,B2)
Supervisor Call	SVC	0A	RR	I
Test and Set (c)	TS	93	S	D2(B2)
Test Channel (c,p)	TCH	9F00	S	D2(B2)
Test I/O (c,p)	TIO	9D00	S	D2(B2)
Test under Mask (c)	TM	91	SI	D1(B1),I2
Translate	TR	DC	SS	D1(L,B1),D2(B2)
Translate and Test (c)	TRT	DD	SS	D1(L,B1),D2(B2)
Unpack	UNPK	F3	SS	D1(L1,B1),D2(L2,B2)
Write Direct (p)	WRD	84	SI	D1(B1),I2
Zero and Add Decimal (c)	ZAP	F8	SS	D1(L1,B1),D2(L2,B2)

---

c. Condition code is set.
n. New condition code is loaded.

p. Privileged instruction.
x. Extended precision floating-point.

Floating-Point Instructions

NAME	MNEMONIC	OP CODE	FORMAT	OPERANDS
Add Normalized, Extended (c,x)	AXR	36	RR	R1,R2
Add Normalized, Long (c)	ADR	2A	RR	R1,R2
Add Normalized, Long (c)	AD	6A	RX	R1,D2(X2,B2)
Add Normalized, Short (c)	AER	3A	RR	R1,R2
Add Normalized, Short (c)	AE	7A	RX	R1,D2(X2,B2)
Add Unnormalized, Long (c)	AWR	2E	RR	R1,R2
Add Unnormalized, Long (c)	AW	6E	RX	R1,D2(X2,B2)
Add Unnormalized, Short (c)	AUR	3E	RR	R1,R2
Add Unnormalized, Short (c)	AU	7E	RX	R1,D2(X2,B2)
Compare, Long (c)	CDR	29	RR	R1,R2
Compare, Long (c)	CD	69	RX	R1,D2(X2,B2)
Compare, Short (c)	CER	39	RR	R1,R2
Compare, Short (c)	CE	79	RX	R1,D2(X2,B2)
Divide, Long	DDR	2D	RR	R1,R2
Divide, Long	DD	6D	RX	R1,D2(X2,B2)
Divide, Short	DER	3D	RR	R1,R2
Divide, Short	DE	7D	RX	R1,D2(X2,B2)
Halve, Long	HDR	24	RR	R1,R2
Halve, Short	HER	34	RR	R1,R2
Load and Test, Long (c)	LTDR	22	RR	R1,R2
Load and Test, Short (c)	LTER	32	RR	R1,R2
Load Complement, Long (c)	LCDR	23	RR	R1,R2
Load Complement, Short (c)	LCER	33	RR	R1,R2
Load, Long	LDR	28	RR	R1,R2
Load, Long	LD	68	RX	R1,D2(X2,B2)
Load Negative, Long (c)	LNDR	21	RR	R1,R2
Load Negative, Short (c)	LNER	31	RR	R1,R2
Load Positive, Long (c)	LPDR	20	RR	R1,R2
Load Positive, Short (c)	LPER	30	RR	R1,R2
Load Rounded, Extended to Long (x)	LRDR	25	RR	R1,R2
Load Rounded, Long to Short (x)	LRER	35	RR	R1,R2
Load, Short	LER	38	RR	R1,R2
Load, Short	LE	78	RX	R1,D2(X2,B2)
Multiply, Extended (x)	MXR	26	RR	R1,R2
Multiply, Long	MDR	2C	RR	R1,R2
Multiply, Long	MD	6C	RX	R1,D2(X2,B2)
Multiply, Long/Extended (x)	MXDR	27	RR	R1,R2
Multiply, Long/Extended (x)	MXD	67	RX	R1,D2(X2,B2)
Multiply, Short	MER	3C	RR	R1,R2
Multiply, Short	ME	7C	RX	R1,D2(X2,B2)
Store, Long	STD	60	RX	R1,D2(X2,B2)
Store, Short	STE	70	RX	R1,D2(X2,B2)
Subtract Normalized, Extended (c,x)	SXR	37	RR	R1,R2
Subtract Normalized, Long (c)	SDR	2B	RR	R1,R2
Subtract Normalized, Long (c)	SD	6B	RX	R1,D2(X2,B2)
Subtract Normalized, Short (c)	SER	3B	RR	R1,R2
Subtract Normalized, Short (c)	SE	7B	RX	R1,D2(X2,B2)
Subtract Unnormalized, Long (c)	SWR	2F	RR	R1,R2
Subtract Unnormalized, Long (c)	SW	6F	RX	R1,D2(X2,B2)
Subtract Unnormalized, Short (c)	SUR	3F	RR	R1,R2
Subtract Unnormalized, Short (c)	SU	7F	RX	R1,D2(X2,B2)

B

MVS JCL Reference Summary

The JOB Statement

//Name	Operation	Operand	P/K	Comments
//jobname	JOB	([account number] [,additional accounting information,...])	P	Identifies accounting information. Can be made mandatory.
		$\left[ADDRSPC = \left\{ \begin{array}{l} VIRT \\ REAL \end{array} \right\} \right]$	K	Requests storage type.
		[CLASS=jobclass]	K	Assigns a job class to each job.
		[COND=((code,operator),...)]	K	Specifies test for a return code.
		[GROUP=group name]	K	Specifies a group associated with a RACF-defined user.
		[MSGCLASS=output class]	K	Assigns an output class for the job.
		$\left[MSGLEVEL = \left(\begin{array}{c} 0 \\ 1 \\ 2 \end{array} \right) \left[\begin{array}{c} ,0 \\ ,1 \end{array} \right] \right)$	K	Specifies what job output is to be written.
		[NOTIFY=user identification]	K	Requests a message be sent to a time-sharing terminal.
		[PASSWORD=(password [,new password])]	K	Specifies a password for a RACF-defined user.
		[PERFORM=n]	K	Specifies the performance group a job belongs to.
		[programmer's name]	P	Identifies programmer. Can be made mandatory.
		[PRTY=priority]	K	Specifies a job's priority.
		$\left[RD = \left\{ \begin{array}{l} R \\ RNC \\ NC \\ NR \end{array} \right\} \right]$	K	Specifies restart facilities to be used.
		[REGION=valueK]	K	Specifies amount of storage space.
		$\left[RESTART = \left(\left\{ \begin{array}{l} * \\ stepname \\ stepname.procstepname \end{array} \right\} [,checkid] \right) \right]$	K	Specifies restart facilities for deferred restart.
		$\left[TIME = \left\{ \begin{array}{l} ([minutes] [,seconds]) \\ 1440 \end{array} \right\} \right]$	K	Assigns a job a CPU time limit.
		$\left[TYPRUN = \left\{ \begin{array}{l} HOLD \\ JCLHOLD \\ SCAN \\ COPY \end{array} \right\} \right]$	K	Holds a job in job queue, scans JCL for syntax errors, or copies the input deck to SYSOUT.
		[USER=userid]	K	Identifies a RACF-defined user.

Legend:

P   Positional parameter.
K   Keyword parameter
{ }   Choose one.
[ ]   Optional; if more than one line is enclosed, choose one or none.

FIGURE B.1

318

The EXEC Statement

//Name	Operation	Operand	P/K	Comments
// [stepname]	EXEC	[ACCT [.procstepname] = (accounting information, ...)]	K	Accounting information for step.
		[ADDRSPC [.procstepname] = $\begin{Bmatrix} \text{VIRT} \\ \text{REAL} \end{Bmatrix}$]	K	Requests storage type.
		[COND [.procstepname] = ($\begin{Bmatrix} \text{(code, operator)} \\ \text{(code, operator, stepname)} \\ \text{(code, operator, stepname.procstepname)} \end{Bmatrix}$, ... [,] $\begin{bmatrix} \text{EVEN} \\ \text{ONLY} \end{bmatrix}$)]	K	Specifies a test for a return code.
		[DPRTY [.procstepname] = ([value1] [,value2])]	K	Specifies dispatching priority for a job step.
		[DYNAMNBR [.procstepname] =n]	K	Specifies dynamic allocation.
		[PARM [.procstepname] =value]	K	Passes variable information to a program at execution time.
		[PERFORM [.procstepname] =n]	K	Specifies a performance group for a job.
		[PGM= $\begin{Bmatrix} \text{program name} \\ \text{*.stepname.ddname} \\ \text{*.stepname.procstepname.ddname} \end{Bmatrix}$]	P	Identifies program.
		[[PROC=] procedure name]	P	Identifies a cataloged or instream procedure.
		[RD [.procstepname] = $\begin{Bmatrix} \text{R} \\ \text{RNC} \\ \text{NC} \\ \text{NR} \end{Bmatrix}$]	K	Specifies restart facilities to be used.
		[REGION [.procstepname] =valueK]	K	Specifies amount of storage space.
		[TIME [.procstepname] = $\begin{Bmatrix} \text{([minutes] [,seconds])} \\ \text{1440} \end{Bmatrix}$]	K	Assigns step CPU time limit.

Legend:

K   Keyword parameter.
P   Positional parameter.
{}   Choose one.
[]   Optional; if more than one line is enclosed, choose one or none.

FIGURE B.2

The DD Statement

//Name	Oper- ation	Operand	P/K	Comments
//[ddname procstepname. ddname] ,	DD	[*]	P	Defines data set in the input stream.
		AMP=⎧ AMORG , 'BUFND=number' , 'BUFNI=number' , 'BUFSP=number' , 'CROPS= { RCK' NCK' NRE' NRC' } , 'OPTCD= { I' L' IL' } , 'RECFM= { F' FB' V' VB' } , 'STRNO=number' , 'SYNAD=modulename' , TRACE ⎫	K	Completes the access method control block (ACB) for VSAM data sets.
		[BURST= { Y } { N }]	K	Specifies whether or not paper output is to go to the Burster-Trimmer-Stacker of the 3800.
		[CHARS=(table name [, table name . . .])]	K	Specifies character arrangement table(s) to be used when printing on the 3800.
		[CHKPT=EOV]	K	For checkpoint at end of volume.
		[COPIES=(nnn [, (group value, group value . . .)])]	K	Requests multiple copies (and grouping, for the 3800 only) of the output data set.
		[DATA]	P	Defines data set in the input stream.
		[DCB=(list of attributes) DCB=({ dsname *.ddname *.stepname.ddname *.stepname.procstepname.ddname } [, list of attributes])]	K	Completes the data control block (used for all data sets except VSAM).
		[DDNAME=ddname]	K	Postpones the definition of a data set.
		[DEST=destination]	K	Specifies a destination for the output data set.
		DISP=([NEW OLD SHR MOD ,] [, DELETE , KEEP , PASS , CATLG , UNCATLG] [, DELETE , KEEP , CATLG , UNCATLG])	K	Assigns a status, disposition, and conditional disposition to the data set.
		[DLM=delimiter]	K	Assigns delimiter other than /*.

FIGURE B.3

The DD Statement (con't)

//Name	Oper-ation	Operand	P/K	Comments
// [ddname procstepname. ddname]	DD	[DSID=(id[,V])]	K	Indicates to a diskette reader that data is to be merged into the JCL stream at this point or specifies the name to be given to a SYSOUT data set written on a diskette.
		{ DSNAME } = { dsname DSN } = { dsname(member name) dsname(generation number) dsname(area name) &&dsname &&dsname(member name) &&dsname(area name) *.ddname *.stepname.ddname *.stepname.procstepname.ddname }	K	Assigns a name to a new data set or to identify an existing data set.
		[DUMMY]	P	Bypasses I/O operations on a data set (BSAM and QSAM).
		[DYNAM]	P	Specifies dynamic allocation.
		[FCB=(image-id [,ALIGN ,VERIFY])]	K	Specifies forms control information. The FCB parameter is ignored if the data set is not written to a 3211 or 1403 printer.
		[FLASH=(overlay name [,count])]	K	Identifies the forms overlay to be used on the 3800.
		[FREE= { END CLOSE }]	K	Specifies dynamic deallocation.
		[HOLD= { YES NO }]	K	Specifies whether output processing is to be deferred or processed normally.
		LABEL=([data set seq #] [,SL ,SUL ,AL ,AUL ,NSL ,NL ,BLP ,LTM ,] [,PASSWORD ,NOPWREAD ,] [,IN ,OUT] [EXPDT=yyddd ,RETPD=nnnn])	K	Supplies label information.
		[MODIFY=(module name [,trc])]	K	Specifies a copy modification module that is to be loaded into the 3800.
		[MSVGP=(id [,ddname])]	K	Identifies a mass storage group for a mass storage system (MSS) device.
		[OUTLIM=number]	K	Limits the number of logical records you want included in the output data set.

FIGURE B.3 (Continued)

The DD Statement (con't)

//Name	Oper-ation	Operand	P/K	Comments
// [ddname procstepname. ddname]	DD	[PROTECT=YES]	K	Requests RACF protection for tape volumes or for direct access data sets.
		[QNAME=process name]	K	Specifies the name of a TPROCESS macro which defines a destination queue for messages received by means of TCAM.
		SPACE=({ TRK / CYL / blocklength } ,(primary quantity [,secondary quantity] [,directory / ,index]) [,RLSE] [,CONTIG / ,MXIG / ,ALX] [,ROUND])	K	Assigns space on a direct access volume for a new data set.
		SPACE=(ABSTR,(primary quantity,address [,directory / ,index]))	K	Assigns specific tracks on a direct access volume for a new data set.
		[SUBSYS = (subsystem name [,parm1 [,parm2] ... [,parm254]])]	K	Specifies the subsystem that will process both the data set and the specified parameters.
		[SYSOUT=(class name [,program name] [,form name / ,code name])]	K	Assigns an output class to an output data set.
		[TERM=TS]	K	Identifies a time-sharing user.
		[UCS=(character set code [,FOLD] [,VERIFY])]	K	Requests a special character set for a 3211 or a 1403 printer.
		[UNIT=({ unit address / device type / user-assigned group name } [,unit count / ,P] [,DEFER]) / UNIT=AFF=ddname]	K	Provides the system with unit information.
		[{ VOLUME / VOL } =([PRIVATE] [,RETAIN] [,volume seq number] [,volume count] [,] [SER=(serial number,...) / REF=dsname / REF=*.ddname / REF=*.stepname.ddname / REF=*.stepname.procstepname.ddname])]	K	Provides the system with volume information.

Legend:

P   Positional parameter.
K   Keyword parameter.
|| Choose one.

[ ] Enclosing subparameter, indicates that subparameter is optional; if more than one line is enclosed, choose one or more.

FIGURE B.3 (Continued)

322

Supplementary Debugging Exercise

This exercise parallels the debugging exercise of Chapter 7, and is intended to review the concepts of debugging in a subprogram. In order to clarify the presentation, the list of associated figures is summarized:

Answer the following questions:

1. What is the completion code?
2. What does the completion code mean?
3. What address is contained in the PSW?
4. At what location was the program loaded?
5. Subtract the address in part 4 from the one in part 3.
6. In *which* program is the relative location from part 5?
7. What is the origin of SUBRTN2 within the load module?
8. Subtract the address in part 7 from the one in part 5.
9. What machine instruction is at that location?
10. Underline the instruction from part 9 in memory.
11. What is the corresponding COBOL instruction?
12. What is the machine instruction that actually caused the ABEND?
13. What is its op code?
14. Which base register is associated with the first operand?
15. What is the displacement of the first operand?
16. What is the effective address of the first operand?
17. How many bytes are associated with the first operand?
18. What are the internal contents of the first operand? Are they valid as a decimal number?
19. Which base register is associated with the second operand?
20. What is the displacement of the second operand?
21. How many bytes are associated with the second operand?
22. What is the effective address of the second operand?
23. What are the internal contents of the second operand? Are they valid as a decimal number?
24. Technically, why did the ABEND occur?
25. Which data name *in the main program* contains the description of the invalid student record?

26. Which BLL cell is associated with that data name?

27. What is the displacement of the BLL cells in the main program?

28. Add the entry point address of the main program to the answer to part 27.

29. What is contained at the four bytes beginning at the address found in part 28?

30. What is the value of Base Linkage Locator 3?

31. Which student had the invalid data? Identify his record in memory.

32. Which field is invalid in the student record?

33. Can you think of any reason why BLL cells (rather than BL cells) are specified in the main program for SORT-RECORD?

34. Which data name in the subprogram contains the description of the invalid field?

35. Which Base Linkage Locator is associated with that data name?

36. What is the displacement of the BLL cells in the subprogram?

37. Add the Entry Point Address of the main program, plus the origin of SUBRTN2, plus the answer from question 36.

38. What is contained at the 4 bytes beginning at the address found in part 37?

39. What is the value of Base Linkage Locator 3?

40. What is the address of LS–SCHOOL–CODE?

41. What is the value of LS–SCHOOL–CODE?

42. What was the value of Baker's school code in the incoming record (see Figure C.1)?

43. What is the hexadecimal representation of a period?

44. Use the PMAP of the main program to explain how the incoming period in Baker's record was converted to a hex 'FB'.

45. Could WS BEGINS HERE have been used in conjuction with the RE-TURN verb? Would this have facilitated the debugging procedure?

46. Examine the CALL statement of line 216 in the PMAP of Figure C.5, and explain how COBOL adheres to the linkage conventions for registers 14 and 15.

The reader may also refer to Chapter 3 of Robert Grauer's *Structured Methods Through COBOL* (Prentice-Hall, Englewood Cliffs, NJ, 1983) for a thorough explanation of the COBOL elements in the main and subprograms. In addition, Chapter 9 of the same reference contains a modified version which covers debugging at the source level.

```
100000000ALBERT        A  0159MSTA1059118Y0151002200330044045013
200000000BROWN         B  0258FSTA1089275N0251002200330044004111344 43
233300000BAKER         B  0457FEEN. 070275N02511134443
300000000CHARLES       C  0658MHIS2109286Y10050135033504350535063
```

FIGURE C.1 Data

```
00001          IDENTIFICATION DIVISION.
00002          PROGRAM-ID.    MAINPROG.
00003          AUTHOR.        R. GRAUER.
00004
00005          ENVIRONMENT DIVISION.
00006          CONFIGURATION SECTION.
00007          SOURCE-COMPUTER.       IBM-4341.
00008          OBJECT-COMPUTER.       IBM-4341.
00009
00010          INPUT-OUTPUT SECTION.
00011          FILE-CONTROL.
00012              SELECT STUDENT-FILE
00013                  ASSIGN TO UT-S-STUD.
00014              SELECT PRINT-FILE
00015                  ASSIGN TO UT-S-PRINT.
00016              SELECT SORT-FILE
00017                  ASSIGN TO UT-S-SORTWORK.
00018
00019          DATA DIVISION.
00020          FILE SECTION.
00021          FD  STUDENT-FILE
00022              LABEL RECORDS ARE STANDARD
00023              BLOCK CONTAINS O RECORDS
00024              RECORD CONTAINS 80 CHARACTERS
00025              DATA RECORD IS STUDENT-RECORD.
00026          01  STUDENT-RECORD              PIC X(80).
00027
00028          FD  PRINT-FILE
00029              LABEL RECORDS ARE STANDARD
00030              RECORD CONTAINS 133 CHARACTERS
00031              DATA RECORD IS PRINT-LINE.
00032          01  PRINT-LINE                  PIC X(133).
00033
00034          SD  SORT-FILE
00035              RECORD CONTAINS 80 CHARACTERS
00036              DATA RECORD IS SORT-RECORD.
00037          01  SORT-RECORD.
00038              05   SRT-SOC-SEC-NUMBER     PIC X(9).
00039              05   SRT-NAME-AND-INITIALS.
00040                   10   SRT-LAST-NAME     PIC X(18).
00041                   10   SRT-INITIALS      PIC XX.
00042              05   SRT-DATE-OF-BIRTH.
00043                   10   SRT-BIRTH-MONTH   PIC 99.
00044                   10   SRT-BIRTH-YEAR    PIC 99.
00045              05   SRT-SEX               PIC X.
00046              05   SRT-MAJOR-CODE        PIC X(3).
00047              05   SRT-SCHOOL-CODE       PIC 9.
00048              05   SRT-CUMULATIVE-CREDITS  PIC 9(3).
00049              05   SRT-CUMULATIVE-POINTS   PIC 9(3).
00050              05   SRT-UNION-MEMBER      PIC X.
00051              05   SRT-SCHOLARSHIP       PIC 999.
00052              05   SRT-COURSES-THIS-SEMESTER
00053                   OCCURS 6 TIMES.
00054                   10   SRT-COURSE-NUMBER   PIC XXX.
00055                   10   SRT-COURSE-CREDITS  PIC 9.
00056              05   SRT-GRADE-POINT-AVERAGE  PIC 9V999.
00057              05   FILLER                PIC X(4).
00058
00059          WORKING-STORAGE SECTION.
00060          01  FILLER                     PIC X(27)
00061              VALUE 'WS-MAIN PROGRAM BEGINS HERE'.
00062
00063          01  PROGRAM-SUBSCRIPTS.
00064              05   WS-COURSE-SUB         PIC S9(4)   COMP.
00065
00066          01  PROGRAM-SWITCHES.
00067              05   WS-DATA-REMAINS-SWITCH   PIC X(3) VALUE SPACES.
00068              05   WS-END-OF-SORT-FILE-SW   PIC X(3) VALUE SPACES.
00069
```

FIGURE C.2 Main Program COBOL Listing

```
00070        01   WS-STUDENT-RECORD.
00071             05   STU-SOC-SEC-NUMBER          PIC X(9).
00072             05   STU-NAME-AND-INITIALS.
00073                  10   STU-LAST-NAME          PIC X(18).
00074                  10   STU-INITIALS           PIC XX.
00075             05   STU-DATE-OF-BIRTH.
00076                  10   STU-BIRTH-MONTH         PIC 99.
00077                  10   STU-BIRTH-YEAR          PIC 99.
00078             05   STU-SEX                     PIC X.
00079             05   STU-MAJOR-CODE              PIC X(3).
00080             05   STU-SCHOOL-CODE             PIC 9..
00081             05   STU-CUMULATIVE-CREDITS      PIC 9(3).
00082             05   STU-CUMULATIVE-POINTS       PIC 9(3).
00083             05   STU-UNION-MEMBER            PIC X.
00084             05   STU-SCHOLARSHIP             PIC 999.
00085             05   STU-COURSES-THIS-SEMESTER
00086                  OCCURS 6 TIMES.
00087                  10   STU-COURSE-NUMBER       PIC XXX.
00088                  10   STU-COURSE-CREDITS      PIC 9.
00089             05   FILLER                      PIC X(8).
00090
00091        01   WS-SUBROUTINE-PARAMETERS.
00092             05   WS-MAJOR-CODE               PIC X(3).
00093             05   WS-MAJOR-VALUE              PIC X(15).
00094             05   WS-SCHOOL-CODE              PIC 9.
00095             05   WS-SCHOOL-VALUE             PIC X(12).
00096
00097        01   WS-PASSED-COURSE-TABLE.
00098             05   CODE-AND-VALUE OCCURS 6 TIMES.
00099                  10   PASSED-COURSE-CODE      PIC X(3).
00100                  10   PASSED-COURSE-VALUE     PIC X(12).
00101
00102        01   WS-AGE                           PIC 99V9.
00103
00104        01   DATE-WORK-AREA.
00105             05   TODAYS-YEAR                 PIC 99.
00106             05   TODAYS-MONTH                PIC 99.
00107             05   TODAYS-DAY                  PIC 99.
00108
00109        01   PROFILE-LINE-ONE.
00110             05   FILLER                      PIC X      VALUE SPACES.
00111             05   FILLER                      PIC X(21) VALUE SPACES.
00112             05   FILLER                      PIC X(31)
00113                  VALUE 'S T U D E N T   P R O F I L E S'.
00114             05   FILLER                      PIC X(80) VALUE SPACES.
00115
00116        01   ASTERISK-LINE.
00117             05   FILLER                      PIC X      VALUE SPACES.
00118             05   FILLER                      PIC X(80) VALUE ALL '*'.
00119             05   FILLER                      PIC X(32) VALUE SPACES.
00120
00121        01   PROFILE-LINE-TWO.
00122             05   FILLER                      PIC X(3)   VALUE SPACES.
00123             05   FILLER                      PIC X(6)    VALUE 'NAME: '.
00124             05   PL2-NAME                    PIC X(18).
00125             05   FILLER                      PIC X      VALUE SPACES.
00126             05   FILLER                      PIC X(5)    VALUE 'AGE: '.
00127             05   PL2-AGE                     PIC Z9.9.
00128             05   FILLER                      PIC X(18) VALUE SPACES.
00129             05   FILLER                      PIC X(13)
00130                  VALUE 'SOC SEC NUM: '.
00131             05   PL2-SOC-SEC-NUMBER          PIC 999B99B9999.
00132             05   FILLER                      PIC X(54)  VALUE SPACES.
00133
00134        01   PROFILE-LINE-THREE.
00135             05   FILLER                      PIC X(3)   VALUE SPACES.
00136             05   FILLER                      PIC X(7)   VALUE 'MAJOR: '.
00137             05   PL3-MAJOR                   PIC X(15) VALUE SPACES.
00138             05   FILLER                      PIC X(3)   VALUE SPACES.
00139             05   FILLER                      PIC X(20)
00140                  VALUE 'GRADE POINT AVERAGE '.
```

FIGURE C.2 (Continued)

```
00141              05   PL3-GRADE-POINT-AVERAGE    PIC 9.99.
00142              05   FILLER                     PIC X(3)    VALUE SPACES.
00143              05   FILLER                     PIC X(8)    VALUE 'SCHOOL:
00144              05   PL3-SCHOOL                 PIC X(12)   VALUE SPACES.
00145              05   FILLER                     PIC X(58)   VALUE SPACES.
00146
00147         01   PROFILE-LINE-FOUR.
00148              05   FILLER                     PIC X(20)   VALUE SPACES.
00149              05   FILLER                     PIC X(22)
00150                   VALUE 'COURSES THIS SEMESTER'.
00151              05   FILLER                     PIC X(91)   VALUE SPACES.
00152
00153         01   PROFILE-LINE-FIVE.
00154              05   FILLER                     PIC X(22)   VALUE SPACES.
00155              05   FILLER                     PIC X(18)
00156                   VALUE 'COURSE     CREDITS'.
00157              05   FILLER                     PIC X(93)   VALUE SPACES.
00158
00159         01   PROFILE-LINE-SIX.
00160              05   FILLER                     PIC X(18)   VALUE SPACES.
00161              05   PL6-COURSE                 PIC X(12).
00162              05   FILLER                     PIC X(5)    VALUE SPACES.
00163              05   PL6-CREDITS                PIC 9.
00164              05   FILLER                     PIC X(97)   VALUE SPACES.
00165
00166         PROCEDURE DIVISION.
00167         SORTING SECTION.
00168         0000-MAINLINE.
00169             SORT SORT-FILE
00170                 DESCENDING KEY SRT-GRADE-POINT-AVERAGE
00171                 INPUT PROCEDURE A-PROCESS-INPUT-FILE
00172                 OUTPUT PROCEDURE B-PREPARE-REPORTS.
00173             STOP RUN.
00174
00175         A-PROCESS-INPUT-FILE SECTION.
00176         A100-MAINLINE.
00177             OPEN INPUT STUDENT-FILE.
00178             READ STUDENT-FILE INTO WS-STUDENT-RECORD
00179                 AT END MOVE 'NO' TO WS-DATA-REMAINS-SWITCH.
00180             PERFORM A200-READ-STUDENT-RECORDS
00181                 UNTIL WS-DATA-REMAINS-SWITCH = 'NO'.
00182             CLOSE STUDENT-FILE.
00183             GO TO A300-EXIT.
00184
00185         A200-READ-STUDENT-RECORDS.
00186             MOVE WS-STUDENT-RECORD TO SORT-RECORD.
00187             COMPUTE SRT-GRADE-POINT-AVERAGE
00188                 = SRT-CUMULATIVE-POINTS / SRT-CUMULATIVE-CREDITS.
00189             RELEASE SORT-RECORD.
00190             READ STUDENT-FILE INTO WS-STUDENT-RECORD
00191                 AT END MOVE 'NO' TO WS-DATA-REMAINS-SWITCH.
00192
00193         A300-EXIT.
00194             EXIT.
00195
00196         B-PREPARE-REPORTS SECTION.
00197         B100-MAINLINE.
00198             OPEN OUTPUT PRINT-FILE.
00199             RETURN SORT-FILE
00200                 AT END MOVE 'YES' TO WS-END-OF-SORT-FILE-SW.
00201             PERFORM B200-PROCESS-SORTED-RECORDS
00202                 UNTIL WS-END-OF-SORT-FILE-SW = '._S'.
00203             CLOSE PRINT-FILE.
00204             GO TO B500-EXIT.
00205
00206         B200-PROCESS-SORTED-RECORDS.
00207             IF SRT-GRADE-POINT-AVERAGE > 3.00 OR = 3.00
00208                 PERFORM B300-EXPAND-CODES
00209                 PERFORM B400-PRINT-STUDENT-PROFILE.
00210             RETURN SORT-FILE
00211                 AT END MOVE 'YES' TO WS-END-OF-SORT-FILE-SW.
```

FIGURE C.2 (Continued)

```
00212
00213          B300-EXPAND-CODES.
00214              MOVE SRT-MAJOR-CODE TO WS-MAJOR-CODE.
00215              MOVE SRT-SCHOOL-CODE TO WS-SCHOOL-CODE.
00216              CALL 'SUBRTN2'
00217                  USING WS-SUBROUTINE-PARAMETERS.
00218              MOVE SPACES TO WS-PASSED-COURSE-TABLE.
00219              PERFORM B350-BUILD-COURSE-TABLE
00220                  VARYING WS-COURSE-SUB FROM 1 BY 1
00221                      UNTIL WS-COURSE-SUB > 6
00222                          OR SRT-COURSE-NUMBER (WS-COURSE-SUB) = SPACES.
00223              CALL 'SUBRTN1'
00224                  USING WS-PASSED-COURSE-TABLE.
00225
00226          B350-BUILD-COURSE-TABLE.
00227              MOVE SRT-COURSE-NUMBER (WS-COURSE-SUB)
00228                  TO PASSED-COURSE-CODE (WS-COURSE-SUB).
00229
00230          B400-PRINT-STUDENT-PROFILE.
00231              WRITE PRINT-LINE FROM PROFILE-LINE-ONE
00232                  AFTER ADVANCING PAGE.
00233
00234              MOVE SRT-LAST-NAME TO PL2-NAME.
00235              MOVE SRT-SOC-SEC-NUMBER TO PL2-SOC-SEC-NUMBER.
00236              ACCEPT DATE-WORK-AREA FROM DATE.
00237              COMPUTE WS-AGE = TODAYS-YEAR - SRT-BIRTH-YEAR
00238                          + (TODAYS-MONTH - SRT-BIRTH-MONTH) / 12.
00239              MOVE WS-AGE TO PL2-AGE.
00240              WRITE PRINT-LINE FROM PROFILE-LINE-TWO
00241                  AFTER ADVANCING 2 LINES.
00242
00243              MOVE WS-MAJOR-VALUE TO PL3-MAJOR.
00244              MOVE SRT-GRADE-POINT-AVERAGE TO PL3-GRADE-POINT-AVERAGE.
00245              MOVE WS-SCHOOL-VALUE TO PL3-SCHOOL.
00246              WRITE PRINT-LINE FROM PROFILE-LINE-THREE
00247                  AFTER ADVANCING 2 LINES.
00248
00249              WRITE PRINT-LINE FROM PROFILE-LINE-FOUR
00250                  AFTER ADVANCING 2 LINES.
00251
00252              WRITE PRINT-LINE FROM PROFILE-LINE-FIVE
00253                  AFTER ADVANCING 2 LINES.
00254
00255              PERFORM B450-WRITE-COURSE-LINE
00256                  VARYING WS-COURSE-SUB FROM 1 BY 1
00257                      UNTIL WS-COURSE-SUB > 6
00258                          OR PASSED-COURSE-VALUE (WS-COURSE-SUB) = SPACES.
00259
00260              WRITE PRINT-LINE FROM ASTERISK-LINE
00261                  AFTER ADVANCING 3 LINES.
00262
00263          B450-WRITE-COURSE-LINE.
00264              MOVE PASSED-COURSE-VALUE (WS-COURSE-SUB) TO PL6-COURSE.
00265              MOVE SRT-COURSE-CREDITS (WS-COURSE-SUB) TO PL6-CREDITS.
00266              WRITE PRINT-LINE FROM PROFILE-LINE-SIX
00267                  AFTER ADVANCING 1 LINE.
00268
00269          B500-EXIT.
00270              EXIT.
```

FIGURE C.2 (Continued)

INTRNL NAME	LVL	SOURCE NAME	BASE	DISPL	DEFINITION
DNM=1-392	FD	STUDENT-FILE	DCB=01		
DNM=1-418	01	STUDENT-RECORD	BL=1	000	DS 80C
DNM=1-442	FD	PRINT-FILE	DCB=02		
DNM=1-466	01	PRINT-LINE	BL=2	000	DS 133C
DNM=1-486	SD	SORT-FILE			
DNM=2-000	01	SORT-RECORD	BLL=3	000	DS 0CL80
DNM=2-024	02	SRT-SOC-SEC-NUMBER	BLL=3	000	DS 9C
DNM=2-052	02	SRT-NAME-AND-INITIALS	BLL=3	009	DS 0CL20
DNM=2-086	03	SRT-LAST-NAME	BLL=3	009	DS 18C
DNM=2-109	03	SRT-INITIALS	BLL=3	01B	DS 2C
DNM=2-131	02	SRT-DATE-OF-BIRTH	BLL=3	01D	DS 0CL4
DNM=2-161	03	SRT-BIRTH-MONTH	BLL=3	01D	DS 2C
DNM=2-186	03	SRT-BIRTH-YEAR	BLL=3	01F	DS 2C
DNM=2-210	02	SRT-SEX	BLL=3	021	DS 1C
DNM=2-227	02	SRT-MAJOR-CODE	BLL=3	022	DS 3C
DNM=2-251	02	SRT-SCHOOL-CODE	BLL=3	025	DS 1C
DNM=2-276	02	SRT-CUMULATIVE-CREDITS	BLL=3	026	DS 3C
DNM=2-308	02	SRT-CUMULATIVE-POINTS	BLL=3	029	DS 3C
DNM=2-339	02	SRT-UNION-MEMBER	BLL=3	02C	DS 1C
DNM=2-365	02	SRT-SCHOLARSHIP	BLL=3	02D	DS 3C
DNM=2-390	02	SRT-COURSES-THIS-SEMESTER	BLL=3	030	DS 0CL4
DNM=2-428	03	SRT-COURSE-NUMBER	BLL=3	030	DS 3C
DNM=2-458	03	SRT-COURSE-CREDITS	BLL=3	033	DS 1C
DNM=3-000	02	SRT-GRADE-POINT-AVERAGE	BLL=3	048	DS 4C
DNM=3-033	02	FILLER	BLL=3	04C	DS 4C
DNM=3-044	01	FILLER	BL=3	000	DS 27C
DNM=3-058	01	PROGRAM-SUBSCRIPTS	BL=3	020	DS 0CL2
DNM=3-089	02	WS-COURSE-SUB	BL=3	020	DS 2C
DNM=3-115	01	PROGRAM-SWITCHES	BL=3	028	DS 0CL6
DNM=3-144	02	WS-DATA-REMAINS-SWITCH	BL=3	028	DS 3C
DNM=3-176	02	WS-END-OF-SORT-FILE-SW	BL=3	02B	DS 3C
DNM=3-203	01	WS-STUDENT-RECORD	BL=3	030	DS 0CL80
DNM=3-238	02	STU-SOC-SEC-NUMBER	BL=3	030	DS 9C
DNM=3-266	02	STU-NAME-AND-INITIALS	BL=3	039	DS 0CL20
DNM=3-303	03	STU-LAST-NAME	BL=3	039	DS 18C
DNM=3-326	03	STU-INITIALS	BL=3	04B	DS 2C
DNM=3-348	02	STU-DATE-OF-BIRTH	BL=3	04D	DS 0CL4
DNM=3-378	03	STU-BIRTH-MONTH	BL=3	04D	DS 2C
DNM=3-403	03	STU-BIRTH-YEAR	BL=3	04F	DS 2C
DNM=3-430	02	STU-SEX	BL=3	051	DS 1C
DNM=3-447	02	STU-MAJOR-CODE	BL=3	052	DS 3C
DNM=3-471	02	STU-SCHOOL-CODE	BL=3	055	DS 1C
DNM=4-000	02	STU-CUMULATIVE-CREDITS	BL=3	056	DS 3C
DNM=4-032	02	STU-CUMULATIVE-POINTS	BL=3	059	DS 3C
DNM=4-063	02	STU-UNION-MEMBER	BL=3	05C	DS 1C
DNM=4-089	02	STU-SCHOLARSHIP	BL=3	05D	DS 3C
DNM=4-114	02	STU-COURSES-THIS-SEMESTER	BL=3	060	DS 0CL4
DNM=4-152	03	STU-COURSE-NUMBER	BL=3	060	DS 3C
DNM=4-182	03	STU-COURSE-CREDITS	BL=3	063	DS 1C
DNM=4-213	02	FILLER	BL=3	078	DS 8C
DNM=4-227	01	WS-SUBROUTINE-PARAMETERS	BL=3	080	DS 0CL31
DNM=4-264	02	WS-MAJOR-CODE	BL=3	080	DS 3C
DNM=4-287	02	WS-MAJOR-VALUE	BL=3	083	DS 15C
DNM=4-311	02	WS-SCHOOL-CODE	BL=3	092	DS 1C
DNM=4-335	02	WS-SCHOOL-VALUE	BL=3	093	DS 12C

REGISTER ASSIGNMENT

```
REG 6    BL =3
REG 7    BL =1
REG 8    BL =2
```

WORKING-STORAGE STARTS AT LOCATION 000A0 FOR A LENGTH OF 004B8.

FIGURE C.3 Truncated DMAP for Main Program and Register Assignments

331

TGT	00820
SAVE AREA	00820
SWITCH	00868
TALLY	0086C
SORT SAVE	00870
ENTRY-SAVE	00874
SORT CORE SIZE	00878
RET CODE	0087C
SORT RET	0087E
WORKING CELLS	00880
SORT FILE SIZE	009B0
SORT MODE SIZE	009B4
PGT-VN TBL	009B8
TGT-VN TBL	009BC
RESERVED	009C0
LENGTH OF VN TBL	009C4
LABEL RET	009C6
RESERVED	009C7
DBG R14SAVE	009C8
COBOL INDICATOR	009CC
A(INIT1)	009D0
DEBUG TABLE PTR	009D4
SUBCOM PTR	009D8
SORT-MESSAGE	009DC
SYSOUT DDNAME	009E4
RESERVED	009E5
COBOL ID	009E6
COMPILED POINTER	009E8
COUNT TABLE ADDRESS	009EC
RESERVED	009F0
DBG R11SAVE	009F8
COUNT CHAIN ADDRESS	009FC
PRBL1 CELL PTR	00A00
RESERVED	00A04
TA LENGTH	00A09
RESERVED	00A0C
PCS LIT PTR	00A14
DEBUGGING	00A18
CD FOR INITIAL INPUT	00A1C
OVERFLOW CELLS	00A20
BL CELLS	00A20
DECBADR CELLS	00A2C
FIB CELLS	00A2C
TEMP STORAGE	00A30
TEMP STORAGE-2	00A48
TEMP STORAGE-3	00A58
TEMP STORAGE-4	00A58
BLL CELLS	00A58
VLC CELLS	00A64
SBL CELLS	00A64
INDEX CELLS	00A64
SUBADR CELLS	00A64

FIGURE C.4 Memory Map of Main Program

```
211  MOVE
     001180  D2 02 6 02B C 224   GN=016    MVC   02B(3,6),224(12)    DNM=3-176    LIT+204
     001186  58 10 D 284                   L     1,284(0,13)         VN=04
     00118A  07 F1                         BCR   15,1

213  *B300-EXPAND-CODES                    EQU   *
                                  PN=06

214  MOVE
     00118C  58 E0 D 240                   L     14,240(0,13)        BLL=3
     001190  D2 02 6 080 E 022             MVC   080(3,6),022(14)    DNM=4-264    DNM=2-227

215  MOVE
     001196  D2 00 6 092 E 025             MVC   092(1,6),025(14)    DNM=4-311    DNM=2-251
     00119C  96 F0 6 092                   OI    092(6),X'F0'        DNM=4-311

216  CALL
     0011A0  41 10 6 080                   LA    1,080(0,6)          DNM=4-227
     0011A4  50 10 D 2C4                   ST    1,2C4(0,13)         PRM=1
     0011A8  96 80 D 2C4                   OI    2C4(13),X'80'       PRM=1
     0011AC  41 10 6 2C4                   LA    1,2C4(0,13)         PRM=1
     0011B0  96 40 D 049                   OI    049(13),X'40'
     0011B4  58 F0 C 020                   L     15,020(0,12)        V(SUBRTN2 )
     0011B8  05 EF                         BALR  14,15
     0011BA  94 BF D 049                   NI    049(13),X'BF'
     0011BE  40 F0 D 05C                   STH   15,05C(0,13)
     0011C2  58 F0 D 1B8                   L     15,1B8(0,13)
     0011C6  50 D0 F 080                   ST    13,080(0,15)

218  MOVE
     0011CA  92 40 6 0A0                   MVI   0A0(6),X'40'        DNM=4-360
     0011CE  D2 58 6 0A1 6 0A0             MVC   0A1(89,6),0A0(6)    DNM=4-360+1  DNM=4-360

219  PERFORM
     0011D4  58 00 D 29C                   ST    0,29C(0,13)         VN=07
     0011D8  50 00 D 264                   ST    0,264(0,13)         PSV=7
     0011DC  D2 01 6 020 C 15B             MVC   020(2,6),15B(12)    DNM=3-89     LIT+3
     0011E2  58 10 C 09C                   L     1,09C(0,12)         GN=018
     0011E8  07 F1               GN=019    BCR   15,1
                                           EQU   *
```

FIGURE C.5 Truncated PMAP for Main Program

```
00C01            IDENTIFICATION DIVISION.
00002            PROGRAM-ID.    SUBRTN1.
00003            AUTHOR.        R. GRAUER.
00004
00005            ENVIRONMENT DIVISION.
00006            CONFIGURATION SECTION.
00007            SOURCE-COMPUTER.       IBM-4341.
00008            OBJECT-COMPUTER.       IBM-4341.
00009
00010            INPUT-OUTPUT SECTION.
00011            FILE-CONTROL.
00012                SELECT COURSE-FILE
00013                    ASSIGN TO UT-S-COURSE.
00014
00015            DATA DIVISION.
00016            FILE SECTION.
00017            FD  COURSE-FILE
00018                LABEL RECORDS ARE STANDARD
00019                BLOCK CONTAINS O RECORDS
00020                RECORD CONTAINS 80 CHARACTERS
00021                DATA RECORD IS COURSE-RECORD.
00022            01  COURSE-RECORD.
00023                05  IN-COURSE-CODE          PIC X(3).
00024                05  IN-COURSE-VALUE         PIC X(15).
00025                05  FILLER                  PIC X(62).
00026
00027            WORKING-STORAGE SECTION.
00028            01  FILLER                      PIC X(22)
00029                VALUE 'WS SUBRTN1 BEGINS HERE'.
00030
00031            01  WS-COURSE-TABLE.
00032                05  COURSES OCCURS 1 TO 50 TIMES
00033                    DEPENDING ON WS-NUMBER-OF-COURSES
00034                    ASCENDING KEY IS COURSE-CODE
00035                    INDEXED BY COURSE-INDEX.
00036                    10  COURSE-CODE          PIC X(3).
00037                    10  COURSE-VALUE         PIC X(15).
00038
00039            01  PROGRAM-SWITCHES.
00040                05  WS-ALREADY-EXECUTED-SWITCH PIC X(3)   VALUE 'NO'.
00041                05  END-OF-COURSE-FILE-SWITCH  PIC X(3)   VALUE SPACES.
00042
00043            01  COUNTERS-AND-SUBSCRIPTS.
00044                05  WS-NUMBER-OF-COURSES     PIC 9(3)   VALUE ZEROS.
00045                05  COURSE-SUB               PIC S9(4) COMP.
00046
00047            LINKAGE SECTION.
00048            01  PASSED-PARAMETERS.
00049                05  PASSED-COURSE-TABLE OCCURS 6 TIMES.
00050                    10  LS-CODE              PIC X(3).
00051                    10  LS-VALUE             PIC X(12).
00052
00053            PROCEDURE DIVISION
00054                USING PASSED-PARAMETERS.
```

FIGURE C.6 SUBRTN1 COBOL Listing

```
00055          0010-MAINLINE.
00056              IF WS-ALREADY-EXECUTED-SWITCH = 'NO'
00057                  MOVE 'YES' TO WS-ALREADY-EXECUTED-SWITCH
00058                  PERFORM 0080-INITIALIZE-COURSE-TABLE.
00059
00060              PERFORM 0030-EXPAND-COURSE-CODE
00061                  VARYING COURSE-SUB FROM 1 BY 1
00062                      UNTIL COURSE-SUB > 6
00063                          OR LS-CODE (COURSE-SUB) = SPACES.
00064
00065          0020-RETURN-TO-MAIN.
00066              EXIT PROGRAM.
00067
00068          0030-EXPAND-COURSE-CODE.
00069              SEARCH ALL COURSES
00070                  AT END
00071                  MOVE 'UNKNOWN' TO LS-VALUE (COURSE-SUB)
00072                  WHEN COURSE-CODE (COURSE-INDEX) = LS-CODE (COURSE-SUB)
00073                      MOVE COURSE-VALUE (COURSE-INDEX) TO LS-VALUE (COURSE-SUB).
00074
00075          0080-INITIALIZE-COURSE-TABLE.
00076              OPEN INPUT COURSE-FILE.
00077              READ COURSE-FILE
00078                  AT END MOVE 'YES' TO END-OF-COURSE-FILE-SWITCH.
00079              PERFORM 0090-READ-COURSE-FILE
00080                  VARYING COURSE-INDEX FROM 1 BY 1
00081                      UNTIL END-OF-COURSE-FILE-SWITCH = 'YES'.
00082              CLOSE COURSE-FILE.
00083
00084          0090-READ-COURSE-FILE.
00085              IF WS-NUMBER-OF-COURSES > 50
00086                  DISPLAY 'ERROR - COURSE TABLE EXCEEDED'
00087                  MOVE 'YES' TO END-OF-COURSE-FILE-SWITCH
00088              ELSE
00089                  ADD 1 TO WS-NUMBER-OF-COURSES
00090                  MOVE IN-COURSE-CODE TO COURSE-CODE (COURSE-INDEX)
00091                  MOVE IN-COURSE-VALUE TO COURSE-VALUE (COURSE-INDEX).
00092
00093              READ COURSE-FILE
00094                  AT END MOVE 'YES' TO END-OF-COURSE-FILE-SWITCH.
```

FIGURE C.6 (Continued)

```
00001                    IDENTIFICATION DIVISION.
00002                    PROGRAM-ID.   SUBRTN2.
00003                    AUTHOR.       R. GRAUER.
00004
00005                    ENVIRONMENT DIVISION.
00006                    CONFIGURATION SECTION.
00007                    SOURCE-COMPUTER.      IBM-4341.
00008                    OBJECT-COMPUTER.      IBM-4341.
00009
00010                    DATA DIVISION.
00011                    WORKING-STORAGE SECTION.
00012                    01  FILLER                       PIC X(22)
00013                        VALUE 'WS SUBRTN2 BEGINS HERE'.
00014
00015                    01  SCHOOL-TABLE-AND-VALUES.
00016                        05  SCHOOL-VALUES.
00017                            10 FILLER   PIC X(12)     VALUE 'BUSINESS'.
00018                            10 FILLER   PIC X(12)     VALUE 'LIBERAL ARTS'.
00019                            10 FILLER   PIC X(12)     VALUE 'ENGINEERING'.
00020                            10 FILLER   PIC X(12)     VALUE 'EDUCATION'.
00021
00022                        05  SCHOOL-TABLE REDEFINES SCHOOL-VALUES.
00023                            10  SCHOOL-NAME OCCURS 4 TIMES  PIC X(12).
00024
00025                        COPY TEMP.
00026 C                 01  MAJOR-VALUES.
00027 C                     05  FILLER       PIC X(18)     VALUE 'STASTATISTICS'.
00028 C                     05  FILLER       PIC X(18)     VALUE 'FINFINANCE'.
00029 C                     05  FILLER       PIC X(18)     VALUE 'MANMANAGEMENT'.
00030 C                     05  FILLER       PIC X(18)     VALUE 'EDPDATA PROC'.
00031 C                     05  FILLER       PIC X(18)     VALUE 'ENGENGLISH'.
00032 C                     05  FILLER       PIC X(18)     VALUE 'BIOBIOLOGY'.
00033 C                     05  FILLER       PIC X(18)     VALUE 'ECOECONOMICS'.
00034 C                     05  FILLER       PIC X(18)     VALUE 'EENELECTRICAL ENG'.
00035 C                     05  FILLER       PIC X(18)     VALUE 'MENMECHANICAL ENG'.
00036 C                     05  FILLER       PIC X(18)     VALUE 'ELEELEMENTARY ED'.
00037 C                     05  FILLER       PIC X(18)     VALUE 'SEESECONDARY ED'.
00038 C                     05  FILLER       PIC X(18)     VALUE 'SPESPECIAL ED'.
00039 C
00040 C                 01  WS-MAJOR-TABLE REDEFINES MAJOR-VALUES.
00041 C                     05  MAJORS OCCURS 12 TIMES
00042 C                         INDEXED BY MAJOR-INDEX.
00043 C                         10  MAJOR-CODE            PIC X(3).
00044 C                         10  MAJOR-VALUE           PIC X(15).
00045                    01  COUNTERS-AND-SUBSCRIPTS.
00046                        05  MAJOR-SUB                PIC S9(4) COMP.
00047
00048                    LINKAGE SECTION.
00049                    01  PASSED-PARAMETERS.
00050                        05  LS-MAJOR-CODE            PIC X(3).
00051                        05  LS-MAJOR-VALUE           PIC X(15).
00052                        05  LS-SCHOOL-CODE           PIC 9.
00053                        05  LS-SCHOOL-VALUE          PIC X(12).
00054
00055                    PROCEDURE DIVISION
00056                        USING PASSED-PARAMETERS.
00057
00058                    0010-MAINLINE.
00059                        SET MAJOR-INDEX TO 1.
00060                        SEARCH MAJORS
00061                          AT END MOVE 'UNKNOWN' TO LS-MAJOR-VALUE
00062                          WHEN LS-MAJOR-CODE = MAJOR-CODE (MAJOR-INDEX)
00063                            MOVE MAJOR-VALUE (MAJOR-INDEX) TO LS-MAJOR-VALUE.
00064
00065                        IF LS-SCHOOL-CODE > 0 AND < 5
00066                            MOVE SCHOOL-NAME (LS-SCHOOL-CODE) TO LS-SCHOOL-VALUE
00067                        ELSE
00068                            MOVE 'UNKNOWN' TO LS-SCHOOL-VALUE.
00069
00070                    0020-RETURN-TO-MAIN.
00071                        EXIT PROGRAM.
```

FIGURE C.7 SUBRTN2 COBOL Listing

INTRNL NAME	LVL	SOURCE NAME	BASE	DISPL	INTRNL NAME	DEFINITION
DNM=1-078	01	FILLER	BL=1	000	DNM=1-078	DS 22C
DNM=1-089	01	SCHOOL-TABLE-AND-VALUES	BL=1	018	DNM=1-089	DS 0CL48
DNM=1-125	02	SCHOOL-VALUES	BL=1	018	DNM=1-125	DS 0CL48
DNM=1-151	03	FILLER	BL=1	018	DNM=1-151	DS 12C
DNM=1-165	03	FILLER	BL=1	024	DNM=1-165	DS 12C
DNM=1-179	03	FILLER	BL=1	030	DNM=1-179	DS 12C
DNM=1-193	03	FILLER	BL=1	03C	DNM=1-193	DS 12C
DNM=1-207	02	SCHOOL-TABLE	BL=1	018	DNM=1-207	DS 0CL48
DNM=1-232	03	SCHOOL-NAME	BL=1	018	DNM=1-232	DS 12C
DNM=1-253	01	MAJOR-VALUES	BL=1	048	DNM=1-253	DS 0CL216
DNM=1-278	02	FILLER	BL=1	048	DNM=1-278	DS 18C
DNM=1-292	02	FILLER	BL=1	05A	DNM=1-292	DS 18C
DNM=1-306	02	FILLER	BL=1	06C	DNM=1-306	DS 18C
DNM=1-320	02	FILLER	BL=1	07E	DNM=1-320	DS 18C
DNM=1-334	02	FILLER	BL=1	090	DNM=1-334	DS 18C
DNM=1-348	02	FILLER	BL=1	0A2	DNM=1-348	DS 18C
DNM=1-362	02	FILLER	BL=1	0B4	DNM=1-362	DS 18C
DNM=1-376	02	FILLER	BL=1	0C6	DNM=1-376	DS 18C
DNM=1-390	02	FILLER	BL=1	0D8	DNM=1-390	DS 18C
DNM=1-404	02	FILLER	BL=1	0EA	DNM=1-404	DS 18C
DNM=1-418	02	FILLER	BL=1	0FC	DNM=1-418	DS 18C
DNM=1-432	02	FILLER	BL=1	10E	DNM=1-432	DS 18C
DNM=1-446	01	WS-MAJOR-TABLE	BL=1	048	DNM=1-446	DS 0CL216
DNM=1-473	01	MAJOR-INDEX			DNM=1-473	
DNM=1-491	02	MAJORS	BL=1	048	DNM=1-491	DS 0CL18
DNM=2-000	03	MAJOR-CODE	BL=1	048	DNM=2-000	DS 3C
DNM=2-023	03	MAJOR-VALUE	BL=1	04B	DNM=2-023	DS 15C
DNM=2-047	01	COUNTERS-AND-SUBSCRIPTS	BL=1	120	DNM=2-047	DS 0CL2
DNM=2-083	01	MAJOR-SUB	BL=1	120	DNM=2-083	DS 2C
DNM=2-102	01	PASSED-PARAMETERS	BLL=3	000	DNM=2-102	DS 0CL31
DNM=2-132	02	LS-MAJOR-CODE	BLL=3	000	DNM=2-132	DS 3C
DNM=2-155	02	LS-MAJOR-VALUE	BLL=3	003	DNM=2-155	DS 15C
DNM=2-179	02	LS-SCHOOL-CODE	BLL=3	012	DNM=2-179	DS 1C
DNM=2-203	02	LS-SCHOOL-VALUE	BLL=3	013	DNM=2-203	DS 12C

FIGURE C.8 Truncated DMAP for SUBRTN2

```
63 MOVE  00048E  D5 02 E 000 F 000        CLC  000(3,14),000(15)   DNM=2-132              DNM=2-0
         000494  07 72                    BCR  7,2
         000496  41 40 6 04B              LA   4,04B(0,6)          DNM=2-23
         00049A  5A 40 D 228              A    4,220(0,13)         INX=1
         00049E  50 40 D 228              ST   4,228(0,13)         SBS=2
         0004A2  58 F0 D 228              L    15,228(0,13)        DNM=2-155              DNM=2-23
         0004A6  D2 0E E 003 F 01C        MVC  003(15,14),000(15)  GN=04
         0004AC  58 10 C 01C              L    1,01C(0,12)
         0004B0  07 F1                    BCR  15,1
                          GN=05           EQU  *
         0004B2  41 00 0 012              LA   0,012(0,0)
         0004B6  5A 00 D 220              A    0,220(0,13)         INX=1
         0004BA  50 00 D 220              ST   0,220(0,13)         INX=1
         0004BE  10 00                    LPR  0,0
                          GN=01           EQU  *
         0004C0  41 00 0 0C6              LA   0,0C6(0,0)
         0004C4  59 00 D 220              C    0,220(0,13)         INX=1
         0004C8  58 F0 C 014              L    15,014(0,12)        GN=02
         0004CC  07 4F                    BCR  4,15
         0004CE  58 10 C 018              L    1,018(0,12)
         0004D2  07 F1                    BCR  15,1                GN=03
65 IF                     GN=04           EQU  *
         0004D4  58 E0 D 218              L    14,218(0,13)        BLL=3
         0004D8  F2 70 D 208 E 012        PACK 208(8,13),012(1,14) TS=01                 DNM=1-232
         0004DE  F9 00 D 20F C 030        CP   20F(1,13),030(1,12) TS=08                 LIT+0
         0004E4  58 F0 C 024              L    15,024(0,12)        GN=06
         0004E8  07 DF                    BCR  13,15
         0004EA  F2 70 D 208 E 012        PACK 208(8,13),012(1,14) TS=01                 DNM=2-179
         0004F0  F9 00 D 20F C 031        CP   20F(1,13),031(1,12) TS=08                 LIT+1
         0004F6  58 F0 C 024              L    15,024(0,12)        GN=06
         0004FA  07 AF                    BCR  10,15
66 MOVE  0004FC  41 40 6 018              LA   4,018(0,6)          DNM=1-232
         000500  F2 70 D 208 E 012        PACK 208(8,13),012(1,14) TS=01                 DNM=2-179
         000506  4F 30 D 208              CVB  3,208(0,13)         TS=01
```

FIGURE C.9 Truncated PMAP for SUBRTN2

```
TGT                                001C8

    SAVE AREA                      001C8
    SWITCH                         00210
    TALLY                          00214
    SORT SAVE                      00218
    ENTRY-SAVE                     0021C
    SORT CORE SIZE                 00220
    RET CODE                       00224
    SORT RET                       00226
    WORKING CELLS                  00228
    SORT FILE SIZE                 00358
    SORT MODE SIZE                 0035C
    PGT-VN TBL                     00360
    TGT-VN TBL                     00364
    RESERVED                       00368
    LENGTH OF VN TBL               0036C
    LABEL RET                      0036E
    RESERVED                       0036F
    DBG R14SAVE                    00370
    COBOL INDICATOR                00374
    A(INIT1)                       00378
    DEBUG TABLE PTR                0037C
    SUBCOM PTR                     00380
    SORT-MESSAGE                   00384
    SYSOUT DDNAME                  0038C
    RESERVED                       0038D
    COBOL ID                       0038E
    COMPILED POINTER               00390
    COUNT TABLE ADDRESS            00394
    RESERVED                       00398
    DBG R11SAVE                    003A0
    COUNT CHAIN ADDRESS            003A4
    PRBL1 CELL PTR                 003A8
    RESERVED                       003AC
    TA LENGTH                      003B1
    RESERVED                       003B4
    PCS LIT PTR                    003BC
    DEBUGGING                      003C0
    CD FOR INITIAL INPUT           003C4
    OVERFLOW CELLS                 003C8
    BL CELLS                       003C8
    DECBADR CELLS                  003CC
    FIB CELLS                      003CC
    TEMP STORAGE                   003D0
    TEMP STORAGE-2                 003D8
    TEMP STORAGE-3                 003D8
    TEMP STORAGE-4                 003D8
    BLL CELLS                      003D8
    VLC CELLS                      003E8
    SBL CELLS                      003E8
    INDEX CELLS                    003E8
    SUBADR CELLS                   003EC
    ONCTL CELLS                    003F4
```

FIGURE C.10 Memory Map for SUBRTN2

F64-LEVEL LINKAGE EDITOR OPTIONS SPECIFIED LIST,XREF,LET,MAP
      DEFAULT OPTION(S) USED - SIZE=(196608,65536)

CONTROL SECTION

NAME	ORIGIN	LENGTH
MAINPROG	00	16C6
SUBRTN1	16C8	E30
SUBRTN2	24F8	640
ILBOCOMO*	2B38	16D
ILBODTE *	2CA8	202
ILBOEXT *	2EB0	68
ILBOQIO *	2F18	7FC
ILBOSMG *	3718	D78
ILBOSPA *	4490	6C4
ILBOSRV *	4B58	4A4
ILBOBEG *	5000	188
ILBOCMM *	5188	399
ILBOCVB *	5528	428
ILBODSP *	5950	A08
ILBOMSG *	6358	100
ILBOSCH *	6458	40A
ILBOSDB *	6868	42C
ILBOWTB *	6C98	11A

LOCATION	REFERS TO SYMBOL	IN CONTROL SECTION	LOCATION	REFERS TO SYMBOL	IN CONTROL SECTION
B40	ILBOSRVO	ILBOSRV	B44	ILBOQIOI	ILBOQIO
B48	ILBOSR5	ILBOSRV	B4C	ILBOSMGO	ILBOSMG
B50	ILBOSRV1	ILBOSRV	B54	ILBOEXT1	ILBOEXT
B58	ILBOQIOO	ILBOQIO	B5C	ILBOSPAO	ILBOSPA
B60	SUBRTN2	SUBRTN2	B64	SUBRTN1	SUBRTN1

CROSS REFERENCE TABLE

ENTRY

NAME	LOCATION	NAME	LOCATION	NAME	LOCATION	NAME	LOCATION
ILBOCOM	2B38						
ILBODTEO	2CAA	ILBODTE1	2CAE	ILBODTE2	2CB2	ILBODTE3	2CB6
ILBODTE4	2CBA						
ILBOEXTO	2EB2	ILBOEXT1	2EB6				
ILBOQIOO	2F1A	ILBOQIOI	2F1E				
ILBOSMGO	371A						
ILBOSPAO	4492	ILBOSPA1	4496	ILBOSPA2	449A		
ILBOSRVO	4B62	ILBOSR5	4B62	ILBOSR3	4B62	ILBOSR	4B62
ILBOSRV1	4B66	ILBOSTP1	4B66	ILBOST	4B66	ILBOSTPO	4B6A
ILBOBEGO	5002						
ILBOCMMO	518A	ILBOCMM1	518E				
ILBOCVBO	552A	ILBOCVB1	552E				
ILBODSPO	5952	ILBODSSO	5952				
ILBOMSGO	635A						
ILBOSCHO	645A						
ILBOSDBO	686A						
ILBOWTBO	6C9A						

FIGURE C.11 Link-Edit Map

```
JOB JSC$0736          STEP GO              TIME 174140    DATE 82085       ID = 000       CPUID = 00013152434      PAGE 0001

COMPLETION CODE          SYSTEM = 0C7

PSW AT ENTRY TO ABEND   078D2000 000B7C24        ILC 6    INTC 0007


CDE

9AC8B8      NCDE 00000000   RBP 00967DB0   NM X                EPA 000B5248   XL/MJ 009ACB20   USE 00010000   ATTR 0B20000
97B028      NCDE 009AC8B8   RBP 0097EC60   NM ICEMON           EPA 000BC030   XL/MJ 009677B0   USE 00010000   ATTR 0B20000
967D70      NCDE 0097B028   RBP 00967818   NM ICECRO           EPA 000C2018   XL/MJ 009AC0C8   USE 00010000   ATTR 0B20000
FD99A0      NCDE 00FD9850   RBP 00000000   NM IGG019DJ         EPA 00C16928   XL/MJ 00FD99C0   USE 00040000   ATTR B122000
FCD280      NCDE 00FCD2B0   RBP 00000000   NM IGG019DK         EPA 00F7D2F0   XL/MJ 00FCD2A0   USE 00030000   ATTR B122000


REGS AT ENTRY TO ABEND

FLTR 0-6    0000000000000000   0000000000000000   0000000000000000

REGS 0-7    000000C6   000000C6   000B7BF2   0000000C   000B78A9   0000000000000000   000B5368   000B7B0F
REGS 8-15   000B7B10   000B7D1A   000B7740   000B7740   000B7B40   000B7908   000B5368   000B78A9
```

FIGURE C.12 Dump

341

ACTIVE LOAD MODULES

```
LPA/JPA MODULE    X
0B5240  0700989F F02407FF 90ECD00C 185D05F0  4580F010 D4C1C9D5 D7D9D6C7 E5E2D9F1  *........0....).0...MAINPROGVSR1*
0B5260  00B5D088 000B5A68 000B5FB4 000B6832  000107FE 000B6872 000B5248 000B5248  *........O.....O................*
0B5280  00000000 00000000 00000000 00000000  00000000 00000000 00000000 00000000  *..............................*
0B52A0  00000000 00000000 00000000 000B5CA8  F1F74BF4 F04BF0F8 D4C1D940 F2F66B40  *.............*...17.40.08MAR 26.*
0B52C0  F1F9F8F2 00000000 00000000 C1C9D540  D7D9D6C7 D9C1D440 C2C5C7C9 D5E240C8  *1982......WS.MAIN PROGRAM BEGINS H*
0B52E0  C5D9C500 00000000 E6E260D4 00000000  D5D6400C 40F0F6F5 F8D4C8C9 E2F2F1F0  *ERE.......WS-M...NO   C 0658MHIS210*
0B5300  F0C3C8C1 D9D3C5E2 40404040 00000000  404040C3 F8D4C8C9 40404040 00000000  *0CHARLES........ C  30000000*
0B5320  F9F2F8F6 E8F1F0F0 F5F0F1F3 F5F0F1F3  40F0F6F5 F8D4C8C9 F5F0F6F3 F5F0F6F3  *9286Y10050135043 50535063*
0B5340  F0F0F0F5 F0F0F0F6 C5C5D5C5 D3C5C3E3  D9C9C3C1 D340C5D5 C7400000 00000000  *00050006EENELECTRICAL ENG*
0B5360  00000000 00000000 00000000 00000000  00000000 00000000 00000000 00000000  *..............................*
           LINES 0B53A0-0B53C0 SAME AS ABOVE
0B53E0  00000000 00000000 00000000 00000000  00000000 00000000 00000000 40404040  *..............................*
0B5400  40404040 40404040 4040E240 4040E240  E340E440 C440E540 D5E240D7 4040D740  *R O F I L E S   S T U D E N T  P*
0B5420  D9C1D640 C640C2C5 D340D340 40404040  40404040 40404040 40404040 40404040  *..............................*
0B5440  40404040 40404040 40404040 40404040  40404040 40404040 40404040 40404040  *..............................*
0B5460  40404040 40404040 40404040 40404040  40404040 40404040 40404040 40000000  *..............................*
0B5480  5C5C5C5C 5CC5C5C5 5C5C5C5C 5CC5C5C5  5C5C5C5C 5CC5C5C5 5C5C5C5C 5CC5C5C5  *..............................*
0B54A0  5C5C5C5C 5CC5C5C5 5C5C5C5C 5CC5C5C5  5C5C5C5C 5CC5C5C5 5C5C5C5C 5CC5C5C5  *..............................*
0B54C0  5C5C5C5C 5CC5C5C5 5C5C5C5C 5C3C5C5C  5C404040 404040D5 C1D4C57A 40404040  *.............NAME..*
0B54E0  40404040 40404040 40404040 40404040  00000000 404040D5 C1D4C57A 00404040  *............AGE.*
0B5500  40000000 00000000 00000000 404040E2  00000040 C1C7C57A 00404040 00404040  *..........SOC SEC NUM....*
0B5520  40404040 00000000 00000000 404040E2  D6C340E2 C5C340D5 E4D47A40 00000000  *....MAJOR....GRAD*
0B5540  40404040 40404040 40404040 40404040  40404040 E4D47A40 40404040 40404040  *......................*
0B5560  40404040 40404040 40404040 40404040  40404040 40404040 40404040 40000000  *..E POINT AVERAGE ....SCHOOL.*
0B5580  40404040 C1D1D6D9 7AA04040 40404040  40404040 404040E2 C7D9C1C4 7A404040  *..MAJOR...........GRAD*
0B55A0  C540D7D6 C9D5E340 C1E5C5D9 C1C7C540  404040E2 C3C8D6D6 D340D37A 40404040  *E POINT AVERAGE ....SCHOOL.*
0B55C0  40404040 40404040 40404040 40404040  40404040 40404040 40404040 40404040  *..............................*
           LINE 0B55E0 SAME AS ABOVE
0B5600  40404040 40000000 00000000 40404040  40404040 40404040 40404040 C3D6E4D9  *................................COUR*
0B5620  E2C5E240 40E2C5D4 40404040 C5E2E3C5  D9404040 D7404040 40404040 40404040  *SES THIS SEMESTER*
0B5640  40404040 40404040 40404040 40404040  40404040 40404040 40404040 40404040  *..............................*
           LINE 0B5660 SAME AS ABOVE
0B5680  40404040 40404040 40404040 40000000  40404040 40C3D6E4 D9E2C540 40404040  *....COURSE*
0B56A0  40404040 40404040 40C3D6C3 E4D9E2C5  40C3D9C5 C4C9E3E2 40404040 40404040  *....COURSE ... CREDITS*
0B56C0  40404040 40404040 40404040 40404040  40404040 40404040 40404040 40404040  *..............................*
           LINE 0B56E0 SAME AS ABOVE
0B5700  40404040 40404040 40404040 40404040  40404040 40404040 40404040 40404040  *..............................*
0B5720  40404040 40000000 40400000 00000000  40404040 40404040 40404000 40404040  *..............................*
0B5740  40404040 40404040 40404040 40404040  40404040 40404040 40404040 40404040  *..............................*
           LINE 0B5760 SAME AS ABOVE
0B5780  40404040 40404040 40404040 40404040  40404040 40404040 40404040 40000000  *..............................*
```

FIGURE C.12 (Continued)

342

FIGURE C.12 (Continued)

```
OB77C0  00000000 000B7B20 F1F74BF4 F14BF1F0   D4C1D940 F2F66B40 F1F9F8F2 00000000   *....17.41.10MAR 26, 1982.*
OB77E0  E6E240E2 E4C2D9E3 D5F240C2 C5C7C9D5   E240C8C5 D9C50000 C2E4E2C9 D5C5E2E2   *WS SUBRTN2 BEGINS HERE..BUSINESS*
OB7800  40404040 40404040 D3C9C2C5 D9C1D340   C1D9E3E2 C5D5C7C9 D5C5C5D9 C9D5C740   *     LIBERAL ARTSENGINEERING EDUC*
OB7820  C1E3C9D6 D5404040 E2E3C1E2 E3C1E3C9   E2E3C9C3 E2404040 40C0C6C9 D5C6C9D5   *ATION    STASTATISTICS    FINFIN*
OB7840  C1D5C3C5 40404040 40404040 D4C1D5D4   C1D5C1C7 C5D4C5D5 E3404040 40C0C5C4   *ANCE        MANMANAGEMENT      ED*
OB7860  D7C4C1E3 C140D7D9 D6C34040 40404040   C5D5C7C5 D5C7D3C9 E2C84040 40404040   *PDATA PROC      ENGENGLISH      *
OB7880  40404040 D6C2C9D6 D3D6C7E8 40404040   C5C3D6C5 C3D6D5D6 D4C9C3E2 D4C9C3E2   *    BIOBIOLOGY    ECOECONOMICS.*
OB78A0  40404040 40C0C5C5 D5C5D3C5 C3E3D9C9   C3C1D3C0 C5D5C740 D4C5D5D4 D4C9C3E2   *     EENELECTRICAL ENG MENMECHA*
OB78C0  D5C9C3C1 D340C5D5 C740C5D3 C5C5D3C5   D4C5D5E3 C1D9E840 C5C440E2 C5C5E2D7   *NICAL ENG ELEELEMENTARY ED  SEES*
OB78E0  C5C3D6D5 C4C1D9E8 40C5C440 40404040   E2D7C5E2 D7C5C3C9 C1D3404 0 40404040   *ECONDARY ED  SPESPECIAL ED*
OB7900  00000000 00000000 00000000 00000000   00000000 00000000 00000000 00000000   *                                *
OB7920  00000000 00000000 00000000 00000000   00000000 00000000 00000000 00000000   *                                *
OB7940  00000000 00000000 00000000 00000000   2002A04B 00000000 000B7B80 00000000   *                                *
OB7960  00000000 00000000 00000000 00000000   00000000 00000000 00000000 00000000   *                                *

LINES  OB7980-OB7A80  SAME AS ABOVE

OB7AA0  00000000 00000000 00000000 00000000   00000000 00000000 00000000 00000000   *                                *
OB7AC0  000B7D80 E2E8E2D6 E4E34040 40404040   000B7740 C380E2E8 00000000 00000000   *SYSOUT        C         H       *
OB7AE0  00000000 00000000 00000000 00000000   00000000 00000000 00000000 00000000   *                                *
OB7B00  00000000 000B77E0 000B78A6 800B5368   000B78A9 000000BF 00000000 00000000   *                                *
OB7B20  000B9DAE 000B7C7C 000B7B9C 000B7C00   000B7BB6 000B7C14 00000000 00000000   *                                *
OB7B40  000B9DAA 000B7C7C 0C5C0000 0000000C   E4D5D2D5 D6E6D500 00000000 00000000   *                  UNKNOWN.       *
OB7B60  000B7BF2 5050D218 1B005810 D2205810   C01007F1 58E0D218 00000000 00000000   *            2             .K.    *
OB7B80  5840D004 58504000 5810C01C 07F14140   60485A40 D2205040 58E0D218 .K.        *K.      K     1     K.    *
OB7BA0  D206E003 E00AD206 E0774140 07724140   604B5A40 D2205040 604B5A40 D2205040   *K. K. OK N. O      1     K. K.   *
OB7BC0  D2245820 D21858F0 001258F0 00125A00   D2205000 D2201000 .K. O. 1. K.2. K. 9.      *K.OK N. O     1     K.2.K. 9.*
OB7BE0  D22858F0 E003F000 074F5810 58E0D218   F27 0D208 E012F900 .K. F. K. O. 2.K. 9.K. O.  *K. OK. K. O. 1. K.2.K. 9.*
OB7C00  41000006 5900D220 074F5810 C03158F0   C02407AF 41406018 K. F. K. O. 2.K. 9.K. O.    *K. F. K. O. 2.K. 9.K. OK.*
OB7C20  58F0C030 57DFF270 D208E012 F900D20F   5B40C034 58F0D224 D20BE013 .2.K. O. K. OK.K.   *2.K. O. 2.K. 9.K. OK.K.*
OB7C40  F270D208 D2085C20 C0341A43 5B40D224   58F0D224 E01BE01A 9110D048 .O. 1. K.K. K.      *O. 1. K.K. K.*
OB7C60  F0005810 58E0D218 D206E013 C0389240   E01AD203 D01458E0 .OJ. O. O.                  *O. OJ. O. O.*
OB7C80  58F0C02C 071F58F0 D1B0900E D05C58D0   D004980C 900EF048 D0OC07FE .O. O. OJ. O. O.    *O. O. OJ. O. O.*
OB7CA0  41100207 41000080 89000018 16100A0D   58F0D1B0 05F09110 D04847E0 .O. O. O. J. O. O.  *O. O. O. J. O. O.*
OB7CC0  F00E58F0 C00807FF 48F0D05C 58D0D004   980CD014 58E0D00C 07FE5000 .O. O. O.           *O. O. O.*
OB7CE0  D00450E0 D0549120 D04847E0 F02E5820   D04947E0 F02E9604 200058F0 .O. OO. O. O.        *O. OO. O. O.*
OB7D00  203841F0 F00407FF 94EFD048 58F0C000   05EF1200 07899610 9120D048 .O. J. K.           *O. J. K.*
OB7D20  47E0F016 5800B048 982DB050 58E0D054   07FE9620 D0484160 C00C4170 .K.                 *K.*
OB7D40  C0300670 05505840 10001E4B 50401000   87165000 41600004 417 0D207 .K.                *K.*
OB7D60  51005800 80001200 47801010 1E0B5000   80008786 D20058E0 D05407FE ILBONTRO.           *ILBONTRO.*
OB7D80  80000000 000B5A68 C9D3C2D6 D5E3D9F0   00000000 D20058E0 00000000 .K.                 *K.*
OB7DA0  00000000 00000000 00000000 00000000   00000000 000B9DAA 00000000 00000000   *                                *
```

FIGURE C.12 (Continued)

```
0D1760  5BF0F7F3  F6404040  40404040  4040E2E3  C5D740C7  D6404040  40404040  40404040  *.0736      STEP GO        *
0D1780  40404OE3  C9D4C540  F1F7F4F1  F4F04040  40C4C1E3  C540F8F2  F0F8F540  40404040  * .  TIME 174140    DATE 82085  I*
0D17A0  C4407E40  40D7C1C7  C540F0F0  F4F24040  40007D00  40404040  40404040  40404040  *D .  000    ............. *
0D17C0  40404040  40404040  00404040  F4F24040  40007D00  40404040  40404040  40404040  * .  PAGE 0042  ..........*
0D17E0  40404040  40404040  40404040  40404040  40404040  40404040  40404040  40404040  *                          *
        LINES 0D1800-0D1820 SAME AS ABOVE
0D1840  40404040  40404040  40404040  4040007D  C4F1F7F6  F0404040  F0F4F0F4  F5C2C6F0  *  ....0D1760    5BF0*
0D1860  C6F7C6F3  40C6F6F4  F0F4F0F4  F040F4F0  F4F0F4F0  F4F040F4  F0F4F0F4  F2C5F340  *F7F3 F6404040 40404040 4040E2E3*
0D1880  40404OC3  F5C4F7F4  F0C3F740  C4F6F640  F4F0F4F0  40F4F0F4  F0F4F0F4  F040F4F0  *    C5D740C7 D6404040 40404040 40*
0D18A0  F4F0F4F0  F4F04040  405C4BF0  F7F3F640  40404040  E2E3C5D7  40F4F0F4  40C7D640  *404040    .0736      STEP GO*
0D18C0  40404040  40404040  40405C00  7D000040  F0C4F1F7  F8F04040  40F4F0F4  F0F4F0C5  *          ....0D1780    404040E*
0D18E0  F340C3F9  C4F4C3F5  40C3F5F4  F0C6F7C6  F4C6F140  C6F4C6F0  F4F04040  40404040  *3 C9D4C540 F1F7F4F1 F4F04040*
0D1900  F4F0C3F4  C3F1C5F3  40C3F5F4  F0C6F8C6  C6F5F440  C6F8C6F5  F4F04040  F0F4F0F4  *40C4C1E3 C540F8F2 F0F8F540 40404040*
0D1920  F0C3F940  40405C40  4040E3C9  D4C540F1  F0404040  CAC1E3C5  40F8F2F0  40F8F2F0  *0C9    TIME 174140    DATE 820*
0D1940  F8F54040  4040C95C  007D0000  40F0C4F1  40404040  4040C3F4  4040F7C5  4040C6F4  *85    I .    0D17A0    C4407E40 F*
0D1960  F0C6F0C6  F4C6F040  F0F4F0F4  F0F4F0F4  F0404040  F4F04040  F4F0F4F0  F4F0F4F0  *0F0F040 00404040 40404040 404*
0D1980  F4C6F0C6  F0C6F0C6  F4C6F040  F0F4F0F4  F0F4F0F4  F0F4F0F4  C6F0C6F4  F0404040  *4F0F4 F0F4F0F4 F0404040 40F4F0F4*
0D19A0  40404O05C  F0C6F0C6  F4F04040  40404040  40F4F0F4  F0404040  40404040  40404040  *404 . 0F0F040 00404040 40404040*
0D19C0  40F4F0F4  5C000000  00000000  00000000  000BFB28  000D2D70  000D2E18  000D2D1C  *                          *
0D19E0  000D2D1C  000D2D1C  00000000  00000000  00000000  00000000  00000000  00000000  *                          *
0D1A00  00000000  00000000  00000000  00000000  00000000  00000000  00000000  00000000  *                          *
        LINES 0D1A20-0D2CA0 SAME AS ABOVE
0D2CC0  00000000  00000000  F2F3F3F3  F0F0F0F0  F0C2C1D2  C5D94040  40404040  40404040  * ....2330000000BAKER     *
0D2CE0  40404OC2  40F0F4F5  F7C6C5C5  D54BF0F7  F0F2F7F5  D5F0F2F5  F1F1F1F3  F4F4F4F3  * B 0457FEEN.070275N02511134443*
0D2D00  40404040  40404040  40404040  40404040  F3F9F2F8  F0F0F0F6  00000000  00FDFFF0  *39280006 . . . . . . . .0*
0D2D20  F1F0F0F0  F0F0F0F0  F0C1D3C2  C5D9E340  40404040  40404040  404040C1  40F0F1F5  *100000000ALBERT      A 015*
0D2D40  F9D4E2E3  C1F1F0F5  F9F1F1F8  E8F0F1F5  F1F0F0F2  F2F0F0F3  F3F0F0F4  F4F0F0F4  *9MSTA1059118Y01510022003300440004*
0D2D60  F5F0F1F3  40404040  F2F0F0F0  F0F0F0F6  00FCF760  F2F0F0F0  F0C2D9D6  F9F2F7F5  *5013    20000006 . 7.200000000BR0*
0D2D80  E6D54040  40404040  40404040  404040C2  40F0F2F5  F8C6E2E3  C1F1F0F8  F9F2F7F5  *WN    B 0258FSTA1089275*
0D2DA0  D5F0F2F5  F1F0F0F2  F2F0F0F3  F3F0F0F4  F4F0F0F4  F1F1F1F3  F4F4F4F3  F3F0F8F9  *N0251002200330044004111344433089*
0D2DC0  F0F0F0F6  00FC6D70  F2F3F3F3  F0F0F0F0  F0C2C1D2  C5D94040  40404040  40404040  *0006 . . .2330000000BAKER*
0D2DE0  40404OC2  40F0F4F5  F7C6C5C5  D54BF0F7  F0F2F7F5  D5F0F2F5  F1F1F1F3  F4F4F4F3  * B 0457FEEN.070275N02511134443*
0D2E00  40404040  40404040  40404040  40404040  F3F9F2F8  F0F0F0F6  00FD9DC0  F3F0F0F0  *39280006 . . . . . . . .3000*
0D2E20  F0F0F0F0  F0C3C8C1  D9D3C5E2  40404040  40404040  404040C3  40F0F6F5  F8D4C8C9  *00000CHARLES    C 0658MHI*
0D2E40  E2F2F1F0  F9F2F8F6  E8F1F0F0  F5F0F1F3  F5F0F3F3  40F0F4F3  F5F0F4F3  F5F0F6F3  *S2109286Y1005013503350435050350063*
0D2E60  40404040  F2F6F2F3  F0F0F0F6  000D2ECO  00000000  00000000  00000000  00000000  *26230006 . . . . . . . . . .*
0D2E80  00000000  00000000  00000000  00000000  00000000  00000000  00000000  00000000  *                          *
        LINE 0D2EA0 SAME AS ABOVE
```

FIGURE C.12 (Continued)

Solutions to Selected Exercises

CHAPTER 1

True/False

1. False. A statement may contain both keyword and positional parameters.

2. False. /* indicates the end of a data set and consequently may appear several times within a jobstream.

3. True.

4. False. A blank in column 3 indicates that the statement is unnamed. All DD statements, with the exception of concatenated data sets, require a name. Moreover, it is good practice to name EXEC statements when a jobstream has more than one.

5. False. Comments are separated from the last operand by one or more blanks.

6. False. // is the last statement.

7. False. A comma is not required if no other positional parameters follow.

8. True.

9. True.

10. True.

11. False. It is required for *output* data sets on mass storage only.

12. True.

13. False. Cylinders or blocks can be specified also.

14. False. The system will choose its own volume if omitted.

15. False. It is attempted a maximum of 15 times.

16. True.

17. False. They follow the EXEC statement.

18. True.

19. False. The COBOL FD has precedence.

20. False. The data set is kept.

21. True.

22. False. Tighter control is obtained using the EXEC statement.

Problems

1. (a) The jobname, SMITH, begins in column 3. The programmer name, J. SMITH, appears after the accounting information.
   (b) Two (123 and 456).
   (c) Two steps, STEP10 and STEP20.
   (d) UPDATE; its execution is dependent on the results of STEP10.
   (e) UM.EDIT.DATA.
   (f) 10 and 15, respectively. The blocking factor is the number of logical records in a physical record, and it is determined by dividing BLKSIZE by LRECL.
   (g) NEWMAST and UM.EDIT.DATA, respectively.
   (h) 20 tracks (the secondary allocation is attempted a maximum of 15 times).
   (i) As the *first* file on the tape volume, USR001.

2. (a) FIRST is the jobname and must begin in column 3. The space before CLASS and before MSGCLASS should be removed.
   (b) Put parentheses around 1,1; i.e., MSGLEVEL=(1,1).

(c) Put a comma at the end of the first line to indicate continuation. Note well that the comma before SMITH is *required* to indicate that the accounting positional parameter has been omitted.

(d) REGION must specify K; i.e., REGION=120K.

(e) The jobname is too long (limit is eight characters). Note well, $ is a valid character. In addition, a blank is required in column 3 of the continued card.

(f) Valid.

(g) Accounting information should be specified before programmer name. MSGCLASS should specify a single letter.

(h) The JOB operand is missing. In addition, CLASS=F will be treated as comments. The probable intent calls for a comma before CLASS.

(i) Valid.

(j) The programmer name and extension should be enclosed in apostrophes and the continued statement requires a blank in column 3. Note that both TIME and MSGLEVEL omitted their ending positional parameters and hence have neither parentheses nor commas.

3. (a) Valid.

(b) A space is required in column 3.

(c) Valid syntactically, but TIME=3 will be taken as a comment because the comma is missing.

(d) The stepname is too long (maximum length is eight characters).

(e) PGM is missing; i.e., EXEC PGM=IEBGENER.

(f) Valid.

(g) The stepname should begin in column 3. In addition, remove PGM= since COBUCLG is a procedure, not a program.

(h) Valid.

(i) Valid syntactically, but most of the statement will be taken as comments, since a comma is missing after COBUCLG.

(j) The continued statement must begin before column 16. Insert PGM= before IEBGENER. Region should be specified as 120K. Insert an equal sign after TIME. Finally, the COND parameter should logically refer to a previous step.

(k) Change EXECUTE to EXEC; also remove the comma on the last line.

(l) Insert a comma at the end of the first and second statements.

4. (a) Remove the space after FILE, put parentheses around NEW, KEEP, and an ending parenthesis around (1,1).

(b) The stepname is two characters too long. The probable intent was STEP1.FILE1. A comma is missing at the end of the first line to indicate continuation. Finally, SPACE implies disk while UNIT requests tape, a contradiction.

(c) Leave a space between DD and *.

(d) Remove the space before FILE2.

(e) Put parentheses around the DCB parameter and add a SPACE parameter, which is required for new datasets on disk.

(f) Put parentheses around the DISP parameter and add DD after FILE4.

(g) NEWERFILE is nine characters long but only eight are allowed. Put a space after // on the second line. VOL=SER=-----

(h) Change BLOCKSIZE to BLKSIZE, and LREC to LRECL. DISP= OLD requires a DSN parameter and does *not* require a SPACE parameter.

(i) Remove the comma after UNIT=DISK, and add a comma after DISP=SHR. In addition, DISP=SHR implies an existing dataset, while SPACE implies it is being created, a contradiction.

(j) Valid as written.

(k) Valid syntactically, but poor choice of PRINTER for DDname as * indicates a card file.

(l) FILEEIGHT is one character over the limit. The dataset &&TEMP is temporary, but the DISP parameter specifies KEEP. CONTIG is a positional subparameter and should be preceded by two commas. Finally, a blocksize of 540 is not an even multiple of record length.

(m) SPACE is not permitted for existing, i.e., DISP=OLD, datasets. In addition, remove the blank before VOL.

5. (a) True.
   (b) True.
   (c) False. The label is USR456.
   (d) False. The disposition defaults to KEEP.
   (e) True.

6. (a) False. NEWFILE is the COBOL SELECT entry.
   (b) False. The file will be retained until the last day of 1984.
   (c) True.
   (d) True.
   (e) False. CONTIG was not specified in the SPACE parameter.
   (f) False. A specific volume, USR456, was requested.
   (g) False. The message will not be issued if the pack is already mounted.

7. The code in the COND parameter is compared to the system return code. If the relationship is *true*, execution is *bypassed*.

Code in COND parameter	Operation	System return code from last step	Executed or bypassed
5	LT	4	Executed
9	GT	8	Bypassed
5	LT	(C level diagnostic)	Bypassed
5	LT	(W level diagnostic)	Executed
12	EQ	(E level diagnostic)	Bypassed
12	NE	12	Executed

CHAPTER 2

True/False

1. False. It refers to the current generation of a generation data group.

2. False. It refers to the next generation.

3. False. They are used for sequential data sets as well.

4. True.

5. True.

6. True.

7. False. The main program, i.e., the one containing the *first* executable instruction, comes first.

8. False. They invoke COBVC and COBVCLG, respectively. (See Figure 2.11.)

9. False. They follow the COBVCLG procedure.

10. True.

11. True.

12. True.

13. True.

14. False. The exception is a concatenated DD statement.

15. False. OS does not require stepnames, but their use is *strongly* encouraged.

16. False. JOBCAT refers to a VSAM catalog; JOBLIB refers to a program library.

17. False. STEPLIB is associated with a program library; a SORTLIB DD statement may be necessary for sorting.

18. False. It depends on the associated compiler options.

19. True.

20. True.

21. True.

22. False. They can reside on separate volumes (see Figure 2.12).

23. True.

24. False. A VSAM file *must* be catalogued.

25. False. They are not used with VSAM.

26. False. VSAM data sets are catalogued via IDCAMS.

27. True.

Problems

1. *Statement #*   *Explanation*

3	DSN parameter exceeds 44 characters
4	LREC should be coded as LRECL
5	The stepname, STEP2, should begin in column 3
6	DSN should be ABC.DEF, not ABC,DEF
7	Tricky in that the SPACE parameter requires an equal sign; since it was omitted, the erroneous information is associated with the previous keyword
8	A space is required between the DD and *
9	Very tricky; SYS0UT is spelled with a zero rather than the letter O (see "WOES" on next line)
10	A space is required in column 3
11	Remove the ending comma
12	Parentheses are required around the DISP parameters
13	The SPACE parameter requires a closing parenthesis
14	DD is missing
15	A blank precedes the closing parenthesis on the SPACE parameter
16	A nonblank character (the I in DISP) appears in column 72 which indicates continuation
17	Remove the closing right parenthesis
18	The RECFM parameter belongs in the parenthesis associated with the DCB parameter

19	A temporary dataset may not be qualified
20	Tricky; BLKS1ZE is spelled with a 1; not an I
21	An equal sign is required between VOL and SER
22	An equal sign is required after PGM

2. (a) Three.

   (b) ASM, LKED, and GO.

   (c) The LKED step is executed for ASM condition codes of 4 and 8; it will not be executed for a condition code of 12.

   (d) SYSLIB, SYSUT1, SYSUT2, SYSUT3, SYSPRINT, SYSPUNCH, and SYSGO.

   (e) SYSLIB.

   (f) IFOX00.

   (g) The linkage editor; i.e., PGM=IEWL.

   (h) &&OBJSET.

   (i) The SYSLMOD DD statement contains the output of the linkage-editor; i.e., the load module. It is named &&GOSET(GO); the GO step uses a referback parameter to access this program.

   (j) 0000 for the ASM and LKED steps; 1420 for the GO step.

   (k) The JOB, EXEC, ASM.SYSIN, and three DD statements for the GO step.

3. Additional EXEC statements, invoking COBVC, for the subprogram(s) would *precede* the final EXEC statement invoking COBVCLG. This approach requires that *every* program be recompiled even if it doesn't change. A better technique is to invoke the linkage editor explicitly and catalog the individual object modules. The latter is discussed in Chapter 4.

4. Modify Figure 2.9 as follows:

   (a) Include the STATE and FLOW options after PARM.COB; e.g., PARM.COB=(STATE,'FLOW=10').

   (b) Add VOL=SER=USR456, UNIT=TAPE, and LABEL=(,SL) to the GO.OLD DD statement; change the DSN parameter.

   (c) Modify the TRANS DD statement to read DD *.

   (d) Add VOL=SER=USR321 to the GO.NEW DD statement.

5. (a) Include BLOCK CONTAINS 0 RECORDS in the COBOL FD; add the JCL parameter, DCB=(RECFM=FB,LRECL=100,BLKSIZE=1000).

   (b) Specify SPACE=(TRK,(15,2)) and UNIT=3350.

   (c) No change.

    (d) Code DSN, UNIT, and VOL information.

    (e) See the DSN parameters in Figure 2.10.

6. The solution resembles Figure 2.14, with the following changes:

    (a) There is no OUTPUT DD statement per se; i.e., there is no file corresponding to the GIVING clause of the SORT verb; a DD statement should be added, however, to accommodate the generated report.

    (b) The INPUT DD statement has to be altered to reflect a tape data set.

    (c) The COB.SYSIN DD statement must be changed to

```
//COB.SYSIN DD DSN=COBOL.SOURCE.LIB(SORT),DISP=SHR
```

7. (a) Two procedures, COBVC and COBVCLG, in lines 2 and 17, respectively.

    (b) &&OBJ.

    (c) They are the same. A disposition of (MOD,PASS) causes the output data set to be added at the *end* of an *existing* data set, whereas DISP=(NEW,PASS) begins a *new* output file. In this example, the load module consists of both a main and subprogram, with the latter appended at the end of the former.

    (d) &&OBJ. The data set which is input to the linkage editor was produced as output by the previous compile step(s). This data set is not needed when the linkage editor step is complete.

    (e) The SYSLMOD DD statement contains the output produced by the linkage editor; i.e., the executable load module. Its disposition (,PASS) is equivalent to (NEW,PASS). The DSN implies a temporary data set, &&LOD(X).

    (f) EXEC PGM=&&LOD(X) as opposed to use of a referback.

CHAPTER 3

True/False

1. False. A procedure is most commonly tested instream, via PROC and PEND statements.

2. False. Symbolic parameters are denoted by a single ampersand; temporary data sets are indicated by two ampersands.

3. False. The order is *critical*.

4. True.

5. False. A parameter is nullified by an equal sign, followed immediately by a comma.

6. True.

7. True.

8. True.

9. True.

10. False. Life would be simpler if duplicate statements were clearly indicated, but such is not the case.

11. False. The programmer must compare the corresponding submitted and procedure statements to determine the overridden parameters.

12. False. DD DATA implies that data follows immediately, an impossible condition in a procedure.

13. True.

14. False. They appear together only when a procedure is tested instream. PROC appears by itself as the first statement of a catalogued procedure.

15. True.

16. True.

17. False. Surprisingly, it doesn't—the procedure name is actually the *member* name when the proc was added to the procedure library. Good practice is to code a procedure name identical to the member name.

Problems

1. (a) Submitted Jobstream:

```
//JSC$3016 JOB (MAS526),JACKIE
//STEP1    EXEC UTM01X00,N='TEST.DATA'
//UTM01X10.SYSUT1 DD DSN=MEN.PGM.JSC.TEST(TRANS),DISP=SHR
//UTM01X20.SYSUT2 DD SYSOUT=R
//UTM01X20.SYSPRINT DD SYSOUT=R
```

(b) Procedure JCL

```
//UTM01X00 PROC
//UTM01X10 EXEC PGM=IEBGENER
//SYSUT2   DD DSN=&N,UNIT=SYSDA,SPACE=(TRK,(5,1)),
//         DCB=(LRECL=80,BLKSIZE=80,RECFM=FB),DISP=(NEW,CATLG,DELETE)
//SYSUT1   DD DUMMY
//SYSIN    DD DUMMY
//SYSPRINT DD SYSOUT=B
//UTM01X20 EXEC PGM=IEBGENER
//SYSUT1   DD DSN=&N,DISP=(OLD,KEEP,KEEP)
//SYSUT2   DD SYSOUT=1,COPIES=2
//SYSIN    DD DUMMY
//SYSPRINT DD SYSOUT=B
```

(c) Overridden statements are indicated by an X/ in Figure 3.7; i.e., SYSUT1, SYSUT2, and SYSPRINT.

(d) There is a single symbolic parameter, N. No default value has been established as evidenced by the PROC statement which does not have any operands. Its execution-time value, TEST.DATA, is enclosed in apostrophes on the EXEC statement because of the period.

2. Effective Jobstream:

```
1    //JSC$3236 JOB (MAS526),JACKIE,CLASS=W
2    //STEP1    EXEC CSA
3    XXCSA PROC
4    XXSTEP1      EXEC PGM=TEMPNAME
5    XXSTEPLIB    DD  DSN=CSA.TEST.LOADLIB,DISP=SHR
6    XX           DD  DSN=SYS1.COBLIB,DISP=SHR
7    XX           DD  DSN=SYS2.LINKLIB,DISP=SHR
8    XXWORKFL1    DD  UNIT=DISK,SPACE=(CYL,(2,1))
9    XXWORKFL2    DD  UNIT=DISK,SPACE=(CYL,(2,1))
10   XXPRINT      DD  SYSOUT=R
11   XXSORTLIB    DD  DSN=SYS1.SORTLIB,DISP=SHR
12   XXSORTWK01   DD  UNIT=DISK,SPACE=(CYL,(3),,CONTIG)
13   XXSORTWK02   DD  UNIT=DISK,SPACE=(CYL,(3),,CONTIG)
14   XXSORTWK03   DD  UNIT=DISK,SPACE=(CYL,(3),,CONTIG)
15   XXSYSOUT     DD  SYSOUT=R
16   //OLDCOBOL DD DISP=SHR,DSN=MEN.PGM.JSC.RTG(FILEDUMP)
17   //NEWCOBOL DD DISP=(NEW,PASS),DSN=&&TEMP,UNIT=SYSDA,
     //          SPACE=(TRK,(5,5)),DCB=(RECFM=FB,LRECL=80,BLKSIZE=80)
18   //COMMANDS DD DSN=MFN.PGM.JSC.TEST(COMMANDS),DISP=SHR
     //
```

3. (a) A stepname is *not* required for the SYSLIB DD statement, as it is being overridden; i.e., a SYSLIB DD statement already exists in the COB step. A stepname *is* required for the FILEIN DD statement, otherwise, the system would not be able to determine in which step the statement belongs.

(b) SYSUDUMP could certainly have been included in the procedure as its value remains constant. FILEIN and FILEOUT are generally not included because their values change, and because they are dependent on COBOL SELECT statements. In addition, DD * may never appear in a procedure.

(c) Code the following procedure statement:

```
//SYSLIB DD DSN=&COPYLIB,DISP=SHR
```

A default value is established in the PROC statement; that is,

```
//COBVCLG PROC COPYLIB='MY.COBOL.LIB'
```

(d) The DDnames are in *different* steps; COB and LKED, respectively.

4.
```
//TRYIT JOB
// EXEC HOMEWORK,DATASET=OUTPUT
XXHOMEWORK PROC DATASET=YOURS
XXSTEP1 EXEC PGM=MINE
X/DD1 DD DSN=LAST,DISP=SHR,DCB=BLKSIZE=80
XXDD2 DD DSN=SECOND,DISP=(NEW,KEEP),
XX SPACE=(CYL,(10,1)),VOL=SER=USR001,
XX UNIT=SYSDA
X/DD3 DD DSN=OUTPUT,DISP=(NEW,CATLG),UNIT=SYSDA,
X/ SPACE=(TRK,(100,5))
//DD4 DD *
```

Note: //DD2 DD * has no effect; realize that the effective jobstream is shown conceptually, rather than how it would actually appear.

5.
```
//PROBLEM5 JOB
//CTOD PROC DATASET=FIRST,DEVICE=SYSDA
// EXEC PGM=IEBGENER
//SYSPRINT DD SYSOUT=A
//SYSUT2   DD DSN=&DATASET,UNIT=&DEVICE,
//    DISP=(NEW,CATLG),SPACE=(TRK,(10,1)),
//    DCB=(BLKSIZE=800,LRECL=80,RECFM=FB)
//SYSIN    DD DUMMY
//   PEND
//   EXEC CTOD,DEVICE=TAPE
//SYSUT2   DD SPACE=,DCB=BLKSIZE=400
//SYSUT1   DD *
/*
//
```

6. Reversing FILEIN and FILEOUT would have no effect as they are both new DD statements for the same step. The stepname could be removed from the SYSUDUMP DD statement as it was preceded by other statements for that step. The stepname could not be removed from FILE-OUT (i.e., the first new DD statement in a step), as the system would be unable to determine which step FILEOUT belongs to.

Reversing DD statements for DEF and SYSIN would cause both to be treated as *new* DD statements. The intended override of DEF would not take effect, as the system would have duplicate DD statements.

7. (a) They indicate an instream procedure.

(b) There is one symbolic parameter, N, with a default value of TEST. FILE, and an execution value of FILEONE.

(c) SYSUT1, SYSUT2, and SYSPRINT were overriden.

(d) PEND indicates that a procedure is to be tested instream. JCL statements, pulled from an instream procedure rather than from one which is catalogued, are shown with two plus signs.

8. A blank line in a submitted jobstream produces a *generated* SYSIN DD * statement. (See line 16 in Figure 3.11*b*.) The system is confronted with *duplicate* DD statements for the COB.SYSIN file (lines

16 and 17 in Figure 3.11*b*), and *ignores* the second occurrence. The first SYSIN file is empty, i.e., there is no COBOL program and hence the D level diagnostic.

CHAPTER 4

True/False

1. True.

2. True.

3. False. The DDnames are SYSLIN and SYSLMOD, respectively.

4. True.

5. False. OS does not require stepnames, although the practice is highly recommended.

6. False. It indicates an empty data set.

7. False. SYSUT1 and SYSUT2 typically denote input and output for utilities.

8. False. A COPY clause requires a SYSLIB DD statement.

9. True.

10. False. It is constantly used to reference partitioned data sets.

11. False. See Figure 4.16, for example.

12. False. They begin in column 2 or beyond.

13. False. IEHPROGM or IDCAMS are used.

14. True.

15. True.

16. True.

17. False. It generally contains commands for the utility.

18. True.

19. False. SYSPRINT is used in lieu of SYSOUT.

20. True.

21. True.

22. True.

23. True.

24. False. SORTWK01, SORTWK02, etc. indicate the work areas.

Problems

1. (a) Two steps; the STEP1 EXEC statement is considered data.

(b)
```
//STEP1        EXEC  COBVCLG
//COB.SYSIN    DD    DSN=MEN.PGM.JSC.RTG(FILEDUMP),DISP=SHR
//GO.FILEIN    DD    DSN=MEN.PGM.JSC.RTG(DUMPDATA),DISP=SHR
//GO.FILEOUT   DD    SYSOUT=R
//GO.SYSUDUMP  DD    SYSOUT=R
```

2. (a) IEBISAM

(b) IEHPROGM

(c) IEBCOPY

(d) IEHPROGM

(e) IEBPTPCH

(f) IEHPROGM or IEBCOPY

(g) IEBUPDTE

(h) IEBGENER

(i) IEBISAM

(j) IDCAMS or IEHPROGM

(k) IDCAMS

(l) IEBCOPY

3. IEBPTPCH requires control statements in the SYSIN file, i.e., specification of SYSIN DD *. Specific commands are:

```
PRINT   MAXFLDS=1
TITLE   ITEM=('PROBLEM 3 SOLUTION',15)
RECORD  FIELD=(20)
```

CHAPTER 5

True/False

1. True.

2. True.

3. True.

4. False. It is separate and distinct.

5. False. The updating takes place at the end of the job.

6. False. A control area contains one or more control intervals.

7. True.

8. True.

9. False. The index set is the highest level index.

10. False. They pertain to a job and step, respectively.

11. True.

12. True.

13. False. A PDS is the only type of file which cannot be processed by IDCAMS.

14. False. It is required for user catalogs only.

15. False. They begin in or past column 2.

16. True.

17. True.

18. True.

19. True.

20. True.

21. True.

22. False. It is optional as indicated by the brackets in the SELECT statement.

23. True.

24. True.

25. False. One can specify equivalent information via INDATASET and OUTDATASET.

26. True.

27. True.

Problems

1. VSAM imposes a strict "less than" condition; i.e., in order to add a record to a control area and/or control interval, its key must be *less* than the existing entry in the index. Hence, 289 will become the *first* entry in the second interval and 620 will be added to the *third* control area. Note well that adding records in this fashion does not require any changes to existing indexes.

   The addition of record key 900 mandates a new control area as per the "less than" condition. Since this record is added at the end of the existing VSAM data set, it does require additional entries in the highest level index.

2. Key 401 causes a *control interval split* which in turn causes a *control area split* as there are no free control intervals. Keys 723 and 724 are added in place in the last control area, but the addition of 725 causes a *control interval split* with appropriate adjustments in the sequence set.

   Deletion of 502 and 619 causes the space vacated to be immediately reusable; the latter requires an adjustment to the sequence set and the index set.

3. The essence of this problem is to use a *concatenated* key consisting of both the customer and sequence numbers. That is:

```
RECORD KEY IS CUSTOMER-LOAN-NUMBER
   .
    .
     .
05   CUSTOMER-LOAN-NUMBER.
     10   CUSTOMER-NUMBER      PIC 9(6).
     10   SEQUENCE-NUMBER      PIC 9(3).
```

To retrieve all loans for a given customer, e.g., 111111, code:

```
START INDEXED-FILE
     KEY IS NOT LESS THAN 111111000.
READ INDEXED-FILE
     AT END MOVE 'YES' TO EOF-SWITCH.
PERFORM PROCESS-LOAN
     UNTIL CUSTOMER-NUMBER NOT EQUAL 111111
          OR EOF-SWITCH = 'YES'.
     .
      .
       .
PROCESS-LOAN.
     .
      .
       .
READ INDEXED-FILE
     AT END MOVE 'YES' TO EOF-SWITCH.
```

4. Extract the DEFINE, REPRO, and PRINT commands into a single SYSIN file as was done in Figure 5.5. Incorporate the PRINT statement into an IF/THEN condition, testing the value of LASTCC, again following Figure 5.5. Modify the LIMIT and TO parameters of Figure 5.6 to 10 and 86365, respectively.

CHAPTER 6

True/False

1. True.

2. True.

3. False. The op code is the first byte.

4. False. Instructions are 2, 4, or 6 bytes in length.

5. False. Instructions are 2, 4, or 6 bytes in length.

6. True.

7. False. Omission of the usage clause defaults to display.

8. True.

9. False. C1 is the representation for A.

10. True.

11. True.

12. True.

13. True.

14. True.

15. True.

16. False. Binary data are stored in 2, 4, or 8 bytes (a halfword, fullword, or double word).

17. True.

18. True.

19. False. The sign is contained in the low order four bits.

20. True.

21. True.

22. True.

23. False. It takes 3 bytes if USAGE IS COMP-3.

24. False. It is obtained by switching zeros and ones, and adding one to the result.

Problems

2. (a) | F0 | F0 | F2 | F0 |
   |---|---|---|---|

   (b) | F0 | F0 | F2 | F0 |
   |---|---|---|---|

   (c) | 00 | 14 |
   |---|---|

   (d) | 00 | 14 |
   |---|---|

   (e) | 00 | 00 | 00 | 14 |
   |---|---|---|---|

   (f) | 00 | 00 | 00 | 00 | 00 | 00 | 00 | 14 |
   |---|---|---|---|---|---|---|---|

   (g) | 00 | 00 | 00 | 00 | 02 | 0F |
   |---|---|---|---|---|---|

   (h) | 00 | 02 | 0F |
   |---|---|---|

   (i) | 00 | 00 | 00 | 02 | 0F |
   |---|---|---|---|---|

3. (a) 1,490
   (b) −1
   (c) 32,767
   (d) −32,768

4. (a) 12,345
   (b) 12,345
   (c) −54,321

5. Negative numbers are stored in two's complement. (See problem 3 above, parts c and d.)

6. It's not possible.

7. The characteristic (or exponent) determines the magnitude of the number. The largest possible binary exponent is $(01111111)_2$ which equals $(127)_{10}$. The true exponent is $127-64=63$; hence, the magnitude of the largest possible number is 2^{63} which is approximately 10^{20}.

   An exponent of binary zeros would fix the magnitude of the smallest possible number as 2^{-64}.

8. The precision available is determined by the number of bits in the mantissa. Single and double precision have 24 and 56 bits, respectively; this corresponds to approximately 8 and 18 places of decimal accuracy.

9. (a) BE01
    (b) 1A69B
    (c) 9999
    (d) 4F01

10. (a) SI
    (b) RX
    (c) SS
    (d) SS
    (e) RR
    (f) RR
    (g) SS
    (h) SS

11. (a) 5B78
    (b) 1357
    (c) It packs what is in the three bytes beginning at location 5B78 into the two bytes beginning at 1357.

12. (a)   10,485,760
                 720,896
                  49,152
                   3,328
                     224
        +   15
             11,259,375

    (b) F in column 5; remainder = 987654–983040 = 4614
         1 in column 4; remainder = 4614–4096 = 518
         2 in column 3; remainder = 518–512 = 6
         0 in column 2; remainder = 6
         6 in column 1; remainder = 0

13. A decimal number of four digits or less is assigned a *halfword*, if it is stored as a binary number; i.e., USAGE IS COMP. Since two bytes are allocated anyway, one may as well request the largest decimal value; i.e., four digits.

14. (a) 00001110
    (b) 11111110
    (c) 00011110

    Note well that the *high order carry is discarded* when present (parts *a* and *b*). In part *a*, 15 plus –1 yields 14; in part *g*, –1 plus –1 yields –2; and in part *c*, 15 plus 15 yields 30.

15. To subtract 7 from 9, add the two's complement of 7 to 9, yielding a plus 2 *after* the high order carry is discarded, that is:

$$\begin{array}{r} 00001001 \\ + \ 11111001 \\ \hline 00000010 \end{array}$$

To subtract 9 from 7, add the two's complement of 9 to 7, yielding a minus 2:

$$\begin{array}{r} 00000111 \\ + \ 11110111 \\ \hline 11111110 \end{array}$$

CHAPTER 7

True/False

1. False. It refers to the instruction which would have been executed if the ABEND had not occurred.

2. False. The address is contained in the last 3 bytes.

3. False. One subtracts the EPA from the PSW.

4. True.

5. True.

6. True.

7. False. It may be in a subprogram, or an IBM supplied routine.

8. True.

9. False. One must request it via the PMAP parameter in the JCL.

10. False. It ties them to either a BL or BLL cell.

Problems

2. Three potential checks include:

   (a) Modification of the 030-FIND-MAJOR paragraph to ensure that the table is not exceeded; i.e., that WS-SUB is not greater than 10

   (b) Verification that WS-TOTAL-CREDITS is greater than zero (line 51 of the subroutine), and

(c) Verification that ST-COURSE-CREDITS is numeric for every course.

3. A data exception occurs if and only if one tries to do arithmetic on invalid decimal data (e.g., an invalid sign). When a counter is not initialized, the computer uses whatever happens to be in that storage location. Hence, if by chance a valid decimal number were contained in the storage location for WS-TOTAL-STUDENTS, a data exception will not occur. The resulting sum, however, would be *incorrect*.

4. (a) A data exception would *not* occur. Consider, for example, an incoming four-position field with 7 in the low-order byte and preceded by high-order blanks (e.g., | 40 | 40 | 40 | F7 |). After packing, the field would appear as | 00 | 00 | 7F | . The packing operation "strips" the sign portion of each byte (i.e., the 4 from each blank), leaving a valid field.

    (b) Consider an incoming three-byte field, 7.0, as shown:

    | F7 | 4B | F0 | . After packing, the field would appear as

    | 7B | 0F | . (Remember that packing switches the sign and digit of the low-order byte and strips the sign of the high order digits.) B is an invalid decimal digit and would cause a data exception.

5. Since TOTAL-COUNTER was defined as a binary (i.e., COMPUTATIONAL) field, the generated machine instructions will specify binary arithmetic. *Any* combination of bits is *valid* as a binary number and hence a data exception will never occur. The value of TOTAL-COUNTER will be incorrect since it will pick up whatever was there as an initial value.

6. (a) There is no difference.

    (b) There is all the difference in the world. As the subprogram stands now, WS-QUALITY-POINTS and WS-TOTAL-CREDITS are initialized to zero (via MOVE statements) everytime SUBRTN is entered. If a value clause were used instead, they would be initialized only once (i.e., when the program is first loaded). In effect, WS-TOTAL-CREDITS and WS-QUALITY-POINTS would become running counters from student to student.

7. (1) 0CB
    (2) Attempt to divide by zero.
    (3) 1D2AD8
    (4) 1D0CF8

(5) 1DE0

(6) No

(7) 19F0

(8) 3F0

(9) SUBRTN

(10) F8 73 D 200 D 202

(11) 1D2AD8

(12) COMPUTE statement in line 50 of SUBRTN

(13) The instruction at 3EA (i.e., FD 51 D 202 D 1FE)

(14) FD (Divide Packed)

(15) D (register 13)

(16) 202

(17) 1D299A (1D2798 + 202)

(18) 6

(19) 00000000000C; yes

(20) D (register 13)

(21) 1FE

(22) 2

(23) 000F; yes (in locations 1D2996 and 7)

(24) The ABEND occurred because an attempt was made to divide by zero.

(25) WS-STUDENT-RECORD

(26) BL=3

(27) 834

(28) 1D152C

(29) 0020EA08 (the value of BL=1)

(30) 1D0D98 [found in the third word from 1D152C (i.e., beginning at location 1D1534)]

(31) SMITH,J (Beginning at location 1D0DB8, which is the value of BL=3, 1D0D98, plus the displacement of 020)

(32) DATA-PASSED-FROM-MAIN

(33) BLL=4

(34) 2B8

(35) 1D29A0 (1D0CF8 + 19F0 + 2B8)

(36) 00000000 (The value of BLL=1)

(37) 1D0DB8

(38) Both are used to point to the record in question. WS-STUDENT-RECORD is found at BL=3 plus its displacement of 020; DATA-

PASSED-FROM-MAIN is found at BLL=4 plus its displacement of 000.

(39) Register 14 points to the return address in the calling program; register 15 points to the entry point in the called program.

(40) 1D0CF8

(41) 1D185C

(42) B64—the instruction at B64 in the main program is within the COBOL CALL of line 112. It is the place where processing resumes after a return from the subprogram. Note well the instruction immediately above BALR 14,15.

8. Answers for Appendix C appear at the end of this appendix.

CHAPTER 8

True/False

1. True.

2. True.

3. False. They were used extensively in the chapter.

4. False. The chapter contained substantial debugging material, without referring to control blocks.

5. True.

6. True.

7. True.

8. True.

9. True.

10. False. They identify the DD name which is tied to the COBOL file name in the COBOL SELECT statement.

11. True.

12. False. They serve to identify the last record which was read or written.

Problems

2. Subtraction of the EPA from the PSW will yield a relative location not found in the PMAP of the COBOL program. A possible solution is the "so-called register 14 trick." (See Chapter 11, problem 2.)

3. (a) Replace COBOL line 88 by the statement, PERFORM 015-PRO-CESS-DUPLICATES, then add the module:

```
015-PROCESS-DUPLICATES.
    IF WS-REC-ONE-SALARY > WS-REC-TWO-SALARY
        WRITE MERGED-RECORD FROM WS-RECORD-ONE
    ELSE
        IF WS-REC-TWO-SALARY > WS-REC-ONE-SALARY
            WRITE MERGED-RECORD FROM WS-RECORD-TWO
        ELSE
            DISPLAY 'DUPLICATE IDS' WS-REC-ONE-ID.
```

(b) Expand the two paragraphs which read the input records; for example,

```
020-READ-FIRST-FILE.
    READ INPUT-FILE-ONE INTO WS-RECORD-ONE
        AT END MOVE HIGH-VALUES TO WS-REC-ONE-ID.
    IF WS-REC-ONE-ID < PREVIOUS-REC-ONE-ID
        DISPLAY 'FILE ONE OUT OF SEQUENCE'
        MOVE HIGH-VALUES TO WS-REC-ONE-ID, WS-REC-TWO-ID
    ELSE
        IF WS-REC-ONE-ID = PREVIOUS-REC-ONE-ID
            DISPLAY 'FILE ONE HAS DUPLICATE IDS'
            MOVE HIGH-VALUES TO WS-REC-ONE-ID, WS-REC-TWO-ID
        ELSE
            MOVE WS-REC-ONE-ID TO PREVIOUS-REC-ONE-ID.
```

4. (a) D37

(b) Insufficient space to write an output data set (see list of common ABENDs).

(c) MERGED and MERGED-FILE, respectively.

(d) The program is in an infinite loop, the SPACE parameter request was insufficient, or the system did not have sufficient space available.

(e) An infinite loop.

(f) A READ statement is missing after line 81; i.e., the paragraph 015-READ-FIRST-FILE is not performed.

(g) 100000000.

(h) 111111111.

(i) It indicates repeated execution of the paragraph in line 79; i.e., an infinite loop.

(j) The infinite loop is due to the fact that the same records are continually compared.

(k) Condition code is 0000.

(l) &&FILEONE in the JCL; note well, however, that the system creates a qualified DSN value containing the date and time of execution, and the jobname; i.e., SYS83017.T175542.RA000.JSC $3706.FILEONE.

(m) See part l.

(n) It is eventually deleted, which is consistent with a temporary data set; i.e., one that exists only for the duration of a job.

(o) &&FILETWO which is eventually deleted.

(p) The LKED step creates the *load module*, SYS83017.T175542. RA000.JSC$3706.LOD which is executed in the GO step, and eventually deleted.

(q) The LKED step deletes the output of the compile step, SYS83017. T175542.RA000.JSC$3706.OBJ.

(r) They represent the jobname, stepname, DDname, disk drive address, and specific volume associated with the problem file.

CHAPTER 9

True/False

1. True.

2. False. A store instruction takes the contents of a register and puts it into a storage location.

3. True.

4. False. Data may also be in packed format.

5. False. The COBOL programmer is most certainly permitted to mix data types in an instruction. However, this will necessitate that additional machine language instructions be generated by the compiler.

6. False. An add half-word instruction is used with binary data.

7. True.

8. True.

9. False. The pack instruction may operate on two fields of different length.

10. False. It has two length fields.

11. True.

12. False. The convert to binary (CVB) must work on packed data.

13. True.

14. True.

15. False. The COBOL programmer may combine datanames with different decimal alignments; however, this will necessitate that the compiler generate additional machine instructions to force identical alignment.

16. True.

17. False. The sign of the answer depends on which operand retains the answer. If it is the signed operand, then the answer is signed. If the answer is stored in the unsigned operand, it is unsigned.

18. False. The format of the answer depends on which operand contains the answer as in Question 17.

Problems

1. Computational fields are assigned 2, 4, or 8 bytes in storage, as explained in Chapter 6. Thus, BINARY-FIELD-ONE, BINARY-FIELD-UNSIGNED, and BINARY-FIELD-WITH-POINT are all assigned 2 bytes and have entries of DS 2C in the displacement column. Note also that the displacement of a subsequent entry is obtained by taking the displacement of the previous entry and adding the number of bytes in its definition. For example, the displacement of BINARY-FIELD-TWO (002) is equal to the displacement of BINARY-FIELD-ONE (000) plus the number of bytes in BINARY-FIELD-ONE (002). The displacement of BINARY-FIELD-UNSIGNED (006) is the displacement of BINARY-FIELD-TWO (002) plus the number of bytes in BINARY-FIELD-TWO (004), etc.

   Display fields require a number of bytes exactly equal to the number of decimal digits. Thus, ZONED-DECIMAL-FIELD-ONE and ZONED-DECIMAL-FIELD-TWO have definitions of 3C and 5C, respectively.

   Packed fields require a number of bytes equal to (the number of decimal digits plus one)/2. Thus, PACKED-FIELD-ONE and PACKED-FIELD-TWO have definitions of 2P and 3P, respectively.

2. `ADD ZONED-DECIMAL-FIELD-ONE TO ZONED-DECIMAL-FIELD-TWO.`

   where:

   ```
   05   ZONED-DECIMAL-FIELD-ONE      PIC S9(3).
   05   ZONED-DECIMAL-FIELD-TWO      PIC S9(5).
   ```

   generates:

   ```
                     ┌─Length code for field ZONED-DECIMAL-FIELD-ONE
   F2    7│2│  D 208 6 010 PACK
   F2    7│4│  D 210 6 013 PACK
                     └─Length code for field ZONED-DECIMAL-FIELD-TWO
   ```

ZONED-DECIMAL-FIELD-ONE and ZONED-DECIMAL-FIELD-TWO require 3 and 5 bytes, respectively. The machine instructions to pack these fields specify corresponding lengths of 2 and 4 bytes. (Remember the machine instruction has a length of code of *one less* than the actual number of bytes.) Note also that the displacements in Figure 9.2 are 010 and 013, respectively, and that these appear in the machine instructions. Finally, note that both fields are tied to BL=1, which in turn specifies base register 6.

The symbolic assembler format for the two PACK instructions are extracted from Figure 9.4 as:

```
PACK 208(8,13),010(3,6)
PACK 210(8,13),013(5,6)
```

The symbolic form for the PACK instruction, extracted from the appendix is:

```
PACK D1(L1,B1),D2(L2,B2)
```

Note that the length codes in the symbolic assembler format are one more than in the corresponding machine format.

3. (a) Base register 3, displacement 168. It contains 16 bytes, one more than the length code (F) in the machine instruction.

   (b) From the COBOL USAGE clause, COMP3-DATA-NAME is already packed, whereas DISPLAY-DATA-NAME must be packed prior to addition. Hence, A 009 refers to DISPLAY-DATA-NAME and A 021 to COMP3-DATA-NAME.

   A second consistent argument is that the COBOL sum is to be stored in DISPLAY-DATA-NAME. The sum in the assembler instruction is stored in 3 168, which in turn is unpacked into A 009 or DISPLAY-DATA-NAME.

4. (a) COBOL statements 66 and 67 of Figure 9.1 illustrate considerations of signed and unsigned operands. Numerically, FIELD-A plus FIELD-B equals 579 and appears as F5F7C9 after unpacking. Since SUM1 is unsigned, an OI instruction is generated to convert the low order sign (C) to F. SUM2, however, is signed, and in this instance the sign is retained. Hence, SUM2 would print as 57I. (Recall that C9 is EBCDIC for I).

   (b) The compiler strips away the sign with the Or Immediate instruction after putting the results in SUM4. An unsigned field can never contain a negative number.

5. *Any move to a group field is treated as an alphanumeric move.* Hence, the three move statements of parts *a*, *b*, and *c* will cause display zeros

(F0F0... etc.) to be moved. There is no problem in part *a* where the receiving fields are in fact display. However, part *b* requires binary zeros and thus subsequent calculation on counters D, E, and F will be incorrect. Part *c* requires packed zeros; i.e., a C or F as the low order sign. Hence, subsequent calculation on counters G, H, and I will produce a data exception.

CHAPTER 10

True/False

1. False. The first operand is the *odd* register of the *even/odd* register pair; hence, the contents of register 7 are multiplied by the contents of register 6.

2. False. First one is subtracted from the designated register; i.e., register 5. If the contents of register 5 are not zero, the branch is taken.

3. True.

4. False. Most do, but some do not. Store instructions and CVD are exceptions to the rule.

5. True.

6. True.

7. True.

8. True.

9. False. The MVI instruction is in the SI format. Hence, the first operand is always one *byte* in length and a length code may not be specified.

10. False. It is usually the last.

11. False. It moves only a single byte; MVC can move up to 256 bytes.

12. True.

13. False. AH, SH, and MH are valid instructions and operate on a half word and a register. The DH instruction does not exist.

14. False. It has two length codes, each of which can reference a maximum length of 16 bytes.

15. False. It merely sets the condition code.

16. False. It is equivalent to a PICTURE clause *without* a VALUE clause.

17. False. The exclusive or is used to reverse a switch.

18. True.

19. False. Many other instructions set the condition code.

20. False. See examples 11.9*b* and 11.9*c*.

21. False. An or immediate instruction is usually executed to eliminate the sign of a packed field.

22. False. It can be performed on half word, full word, or storage operands.

23. True.

24. True.

25. True.

Problems

1. (a) C has a value of 152C1C.
   (b) A has a value of 01236C.
   (c) This statement will *not* execute, because the first operand does not have a sufficient number of leading zeros (remember the Tricks of the Trade section, and the ZAP instruction).
   (d) D has a value of 0002468D.
   (e) The instruction will not execute as the two leftmost bytes of A do not constitute a valid packed field.
   (f) F has a value of 098C.
   (g) E has a value of 044C.

2. (a) Register 3 has a value of 0000ADD7. (The arithmetic is done in hexadecimal.)
   (b) The contents of register 3 (the odd register in the even/odd pair) are multiplied by the full word X, producing a result of 0000061E. (The multiplication is done in hexadecimal.)
   (c) Register 4 will contain 00000000 after the hexadecimal multiplication. (The MH instruction uses only the first two bytes of X.)
   (d) A *syntactical* error results in that the first register must be even.
   (e) Register 5 will contain 00000002. Note that the algebraic result of minus one (hexadecimal Fs) and plus 3 is plus 2. The high order carry disappears and indicates a positive result.
   (f) The contents of register 3 are divided by the full word X, leaving the quotient in register 3, and the remainder in register 2. Hence, registers 2 and 3 contain 00000000 and 000000AE. (The arithmetic is done in hex; i.e., 20A ÷ 3 = AE.)
   (g) A *syntactical* error results in that there is no DH instruction.

(h)   A *syntactical* error results in that the subtract full word instruction requires that a register be specified as the first operand.

(i)   The contents of register 3 are squared in hexadecimal, with the results placed in registers 2 and 3; hence, the contents of these registers are 00000000 and 00042864, respectively.

3. (a)   01. The logical comparison ignores the algebraic sign.

   (b)   10.

   (c)   10.

   (d)   A syntactical error results as CLC requires a single length code.

   (e)   01.   The arithmetic comparison accounts for the algebraic sign; hence, zero is greater than any negative number.

   (f)   10. Register 4 has a negative number stored in two's complement as indicated by the high order 1.

   (g)   01. CLR is a *logical* comparison.

   (h)   An execution error results as the first byte of A is not a valid packed field.

   (i)   01.

4. (a)   The bits in FIELDA are reversed causing FIELDA to become 0F (see "Techniques of the Trade" in the chapter summary).

   (b)   FIELDB becomes F6 (see "Tricks of the Trade" on eliminating the sign of a packed field).

   (c)   FIELDC becomes 00.

   (d)   FIELDD becomes 000000 (see "Tricks of the Trade" on initializing a storage location to binary zeros).

   (e)   A syntactical error results as the length may not be specified in an SI instruction.

   (f)   A syntactical error results as XC is an SS instruction with a single length code.

5. (a)   A will contain C6C7C8D5. The length of the move defaults to the length of the first operand, and hence the first byte after C is moved to the last byte in A.

   (b)   A will contain D5D6D7D8.

   (c)   Only the leftmost three bytes of A are changed; hence, A contains C6C7C8F3 after the move.

   (d)   A syntactical error results as MVC requires that the length of the move be associated with the *first* operand.

   (e)   B will contain F8F9.

   (f)   C will contain F6D7D8D9.

   (g)   B will contain F440.

(h) A syntactical error results in that literals may *not* be coded in an SI instruction.

(i) A syntactical error in that the MVI instruction may not contain a length code.

6. (a) Register 2 will contain 0000007B.

  (b) Register 3 will contain FFFFFFF8.

  (c) FIELDC will contain F7F8C9.

  (d) ANS2 will contain 012345678F.

  (e) ANS3 will contain 000000000000256D. (Register 2 contains -256, which is stored in twos complement.)

  (f) ANS4 will contain 00000000002748C.

  (g) An execution error will result in that FIELDC is not a double-word.

  (h) An execution error will result in that FIELDD is not a packed field.

7. (a) Register 2 will contain C1C2C3C4.

  (b) Register 2 will contain 0000C1C2.

  (c) Register 3 will contain C5C6C7C8. Note that since B is only a half-word, the remaining two bytes are loaded from C, the next contiguous locations.

  (d) Registers 2, 3, and 4 will contain C1C2C3C4, C5C6C7C8, and D1D2D3D4, respectively.

  (e) The rightmost two bytes of register 5 are stored in the two left-most bytes of W, with the remaining two bytes unaffected. Hence, W contains 45670000.

  (f) W will contain 01234567.

  (g) W will contain 00004567. (The remaining two bytes of register 5 are stored in the first two bytes of X.)

  (h) Y and Z will contain 01234567 and 89ABCDEF, respectively.

8. (a) Subtracts one from register 6.

  (b) Initializes register 5 to binary zeros.

  (c) Puts 15 into register 10.

  (d) Increments register 10 by 2.

  (e) Puts twice the value of register 10 plus 5 into register 10.

  (f) Reverses the contents of fields C and D.

  (g) Transfers control to PARA and simultaneously puts the address of the next sequential instruction into register 6. In all likelihood, the last statement of PARA will be BR R6, thereby effecting the equivalent of a COBOL PERFORM.

  (h) Identical to part *g* but achieved with one less instruction. Note well the difference between the BAL and BALR instructions.

(i)   No-operation.

(j)   An *unconditional* branch to TAG.

(k)   A branch to TAG, if and only if the condition code is set to 00; i.e., the results of the last comparison produced an equality.

(l)   Reverses all bits in BYTE.

(m) Initializes a print line to spaces.

(n)   Converts the zone portion of NUMBER to an F.

9. The binary op codes for AP, AH, A, and AR are FA, 4A, 5A, and 1A, respectively. The low order hex digit is A in all instances. In similar fashion, the lower order digit of the subtract, multiply, and divide operations are B, C, and D, respectively.

The first two bits of an RR instruction are 00. The first two bits of an SS instruction are 11. The leftmost hex digit in the op code of AP, SP, MP, and DP is F in all instances. It is 1 for the RR instructions and 5 for the full-word operations.

In general, the first two bits indicate the instruction type, and consequently the length of the instruction. 00 implies an RR instruction, 01 or 10 an RX, SI, or RS instruction, and 11 an SS instruction.

10. AP, SP, MP, DP, PACK, UNPK, and CP are all SS instructions with two length codes. The others all have a single length code. In general, arithmetic instructions will have *two* length codes because it makes sense; for example, one can add a three byte field to a five byte field. The so-called logical instructions will have only a single length code.

11. BO is equivalent to BC 1.
BZ is equivalent to BC 8.
BM is equivalent to BC 4.
BNO is equivalent to BC 14.

12. (a)   MVC 123(50,R7),456(R8)

(b)   AP 345(4,R2),789(2,R6)

(c)   AH R3,100(R4)

(d)   AR R11,R12

13. In general, literals should be avoided in favor of defining constants elsewhere in the program and assigning *meaningful* datanames. The COBOL analogy is exact; namely, that one should avoid constants in the Procedure Division.

The equal sign is required in BAL if one is defining a literal (a practice that should be avoided). It is not required when the operand is contained in the generated object code of the instruction itself, i.e., with SI instructions.

CHAPTER 11

True/False

1. True.

2. False. It is done automatically for the COBOL programmer, but it must be done explicitly by the Assembler programmer.

3. True.

4. False. The correct instruction is BALR 14,15.

5. True.

6. True.

7. False. A file must be opened before it can be read in any language.

8. False. Registers 0,1,13,14, and 15 should not be used as base registers.

9. False. Register 1 is used for that purpose.

10. True.

11. False. DS merely allocates space; DC allocates space and assigns an initial value.

12. True.

13. False. A VCON refers to an external address; an ADCON references an address within the same program.

14. False. That information is contained in the *second* word of the save area.

15. True.

16. False. It should be preceded by the instruction BALR R12,R0.

17. False. They are instructions to the Assembler, but are not considered macros as they do not generate any object code.

18. False. Unlike COBOL, blank lines are not permitted and will cause error diagnostics.

19. True.

20. False. It is the DCB which ties filenames to DD statements.

21. True.

22. False. The op code begins in column 10; operands usually start in column 16.

23. False. Blanks separate the label, op code, operand, and comment portions.

24. True.

25. True.

Problems

1. (a)   1) 95 D5 C 107

2) 000030

3) SI format; 4 bytes long

4) 000034

5) D5

6) D5; yes in that the second operand, i.e., the letter N, is contained in the instruction

7) 00010D 0010D

8) The BALR instruction of line 3 loads the address of the *next* sequential instruction into register 12. Hence, register 12 contains the relative address 000006.

9) The operand in the CLI instruction is displayed 107 bytes from the address in register 12. This is consistent with the USING instruction of line 4, which designated register 12 as the base register. The relative location of EMPLOC is 10D. This, too, is consistent in that the BALR instruction put 00006 into register 12, as indicated in question 8; hence, 10D – 6 = 107.

(b) 10) D2 03 C 142 C D2A

11) The programmer specified a length code of 4; however, the generated object code is always one byte less.

12) 2E0 in both instances

13) 142; 148; 148

14) A displacement of 142 (i.e., 148-6); the instruction contains C 142.

15) 000D6; 6 bytes; 000DC

(c) 16) 47 in all three instructions

17) All extended mnemonics, BNE, BL, B, etc. have the *same* op code. The difference is the mask.

18) 7, 4, F; yes

19) 000052; the base/displacement indicates 04C bytes from register 12. Given that register 12 is initialized to 6 (part 14), it corresponds exactly; i.e., 04C + 6 = 052. Note well the ADDR1 entry is also 052.

(d) 20) 4C and 0000000C. The lengths are different because different lengths were specified in the Assembler statements.

21) A DS statement defines storage requirements but does *not* generate an initial value.

22) The PRINT NOGEN statement of line 1 suppresses macro expansion.

23) The literals are defined after the END statement of line 220. The ADDR2 entry is 2E0.

2. The standard linkage convention loads *the return address in the calling program into register 14.* When a data management, i.e., I/O routine, is called from a COBOL program, the return point is established in register 14. This, in turn, provides a clue as to where the problem originated. The technique will *not* work when one I/O routine calls another.

3. The single instruction utility branches to the address contained in register 14; i.e., it returns control to the operating system as per the standard linkage conventions. However, before IEFBR14 is executed, OS will do all the data management requests indicated in the associated JCL.

4. BR 14 branches to the address contained in register 14. B 14 indicates an implicit address and branches to *location 014.* This address is within the operating system and hence the ABEND.

5.
```
INPUTREC  DS  0CL42
INNAME    DS  0CL26
LAST      DS  CL15
FIRST     DS  CL10
MIDDLE    DS  CL1
          DS  CL10
DOB       DS  0CL6
MONTH     DS  CL2
DAY       DS  CL2
YEAR      DS  CL2
```

7. (a) 1) 0C7
       2) An attempt to do decimal arithmetic on invalid decimal data
   (b) 3) 0B5D44
        4) 0B5D00
        5) 000044
        6) F900C20AC2E4
        7) FA32C20EC20B
        8) FA
        9) C

10) 20E

11) 0B5F14 (The contents of register 12 plus a displacement of 20E)

12) 4 (one more than the length code)

13) 0075000C; yes

14) C

15) 20B

16) 0B5F11

17) 00211

18) 0B5F11

19) They are always the same; i.e., there are two distinct techniques for finding the second operand.

20) The BALR instruction in line 3 puts the address of the next sequential instruction (i.e., 6) into register 12.

21) 3

22) 000004; no

23) The ABEND occurred because an attempt was made to use an invalid decimal field in an AP instruction.

24) 0000F2

25) 0B5DF2

26) Lavor

27) Blanks (hex 40s)

28) One can never blow up on a PACK instruction; i.e., any field may be packed. The ABEND occurs only when arithmetic is attempted.

8. Compare the invalid listing to Figure 11.1 to determine the correct syntax.

APPENDIX C: DEBUGGING EXERCISE

1. 0C7

2. Data Exception; i.e., an attempt to execute a decimal instruction on invalid decimal data

3. 0B7C24

4. 0B5248

5. 29DC

6. SUBRTN2 (See the Link Edit Map)

7. 24F8

8. 4E4

9. 58 F0 C 024

10. See Figure C.12 (The instruction in part 9 will be found in the 4 bytes beginning at location 0B7C24, the PSW address.)

11. The IF statement of line 65 in SUBRTN2

12. F9 00 D 20F C 030 (The PSW points to the instruction that would have executed if the dump did not occur; hence, the instruction which actually caused the ABEND is the one immediately before.)

13. F9 (compared packed)

14. D

15. 20F

16. 0B7B17 (0B7908 + 20F)

17. 1 (One more than the length code in the instruction.)

18. BF (No)

19. C

20. 030

21. 1

22. 0B7B70 (0B7B40 + 030)

23. 0C (Yes)

24. An invalid decimal field, BF, was present as the first operand in a compare packed instruction.

25. SORT-RECORD (Note well it is *not* WS-STUDENT-RECORD as the ABEND occurred in the Output Procedure.)

26. 3

27. A58

28. 0B5CA0

29. The value of the first BLL cell, in this case 00000000

30. 0D2CC8

31. Baker

32. SRT-SCHOOL-CODE

33. BLL cells indicate passed parameters and normally appear in called programs. We are, however, dealing with sort records, and the sort program is apparently considered a called program.

34. LS-SCHOOL-CODE

35. BLL=3

36. 3D8

37. 0B7B18 (0B5248 + 24F8 + 3D8)

38. The value of the first BLL cell; in this case 00000000

39. 0B5368

40. 0B537A (0B5368 + 012)

41. FB

42. A period

43. 4B

44. Observe that COBOL statement 215 of the main program moves SRT-SCHOOL-CODE to WS–SCHOOL-CODE before calling SUBRTN2. The PMAP for this statement contains an MVC instruction as expected, followed by an OI instruction. The latter instruction was generated to remove a numeric sign since WS-SCHOOL-CODE was defined as unsigned in COBOL line 94. Hence, the incoming period with a hex representation of 4B is converted to an FB prior to being passed to the subprogram.

45. Yes. The RETURN statements of lines 199 and 299 could have been coded RETURN INTO which would have facilitated identification of the erroneous record.

46. The PMAP of the main program contains the assembler statements L 15,=V(SUBRTN2) and BALR 14,15 embedded within the COBOL CALL of line 216. The first instruction loads the address of an *external* routine SUBRTN2 into register 15. The second instruction branches to the address contained in register 15 and simultaneously stores the address of the next sequential instruction into register 14. These are precisely the linkage conventions discussed in Chapter 11, namely register 14 contains the return address in the *calling* program while register 15 holds the entry point of the *called* program.

Index